the WOLVES Who's Who

compiled by tony matthews

a britespot publication

THE WOLVES WHO'S WHO
A Britespot Publication

First Published in Great Britain by
Britespot Publishing Solutions Limited,
Chester Road, Cradley Heath, West Midlands, B64 6AB

December 2001

Dedicated to all Wolves supporters who appreciate the club!

ISBN 1 904103 01 4

Printed and bound in Great Britain by
Cradley Print Limited, Chester Road, Cradley Heath, West Midlands, B64 6AB

Acknowledgments
I would like to thank the following people who, in their own inimitable way, perhaps not in recent years but some time ago, have all helped in the compilation of this book, either by supplying certain facts and figures and/or photographs: Peter Creed, Steve Gordos, John Hendley, Graham Hughes (Molineux historian), Scott Pritchard, Mike Slater, John Smith, Les Smith and Ray Spiller (formerly of the AFS).

I have also referred to many club histories (for clarification of players' records away from Wolves) as well as various other Who's Who publications, far too many to list here.

Also a big thank you to Roger Marshall at Britespot Publishing Solutions Limited for agreeing to publish the book and to his Publishing Manager Paul Burns and all fellow employees of the company. Last but by no means least to my wife, Margaret (will there ever be a day without me tip-tapping away on the keyboard?).

INTRODUCTION

I am positively certain that all supporters of Wolverhampton Wanderers Football Club, young and old, male and female, have, at some time or another, been involved in an argument concerning a player, whether from the past or present!

I know from experience that in numerous pubs and clubs, inside street cafes and bars, at schools and colleges, at home, in office blocks, on the work floor, at various grounds, in cars, trains and buses, even when travelling in an aircraft or walking down the road, discussions have raged - some have got completely out of hand - about certain players (and indeed managers) who have been associated with Wolves.

Some have turned into heated arguments with questions asked but no definite answer given. As a result wagers have been laid as to who is right or wrong!

Some questions revolve round the obvious....when did he join the club and where from?... how many goals did he score?... where did go after leaving Wolves?.... did he play for England (or Wales etc)?..... was he a defender or midfielder, a left or right winger?....did he play in the Cup Final?

This Who's Who can answer most if not all of these questions - and offer you lots more information as well. It will also satisfy that laudible curiosity.

On the following pages you will find multitudinous authentic personal details of every single player who has appeared for Wolves in a competitive League and Cup match from 1883 (when the club first entered the FA Cup). There is also information on certain players who never made it with Wolves but did exceedingly well elsewhere. The men who have managed Wolves down the years are also featured along with trainers, physiotherapists, back-room staff and perhaps for the very first time in a soccer Who's Who, a lady appears in the files!

For easy reference all personnel have been listed in A-Z order with dates and places of birth and deaths given if clarified, although occasionally it has only been possible to ascertain a certain year. In some instances the date of death has not been included at all.
Also included in the pen-picture portraits are details of the junior and non-League clubs that player has served, transfer fees, honours won at club and international level plus the respective senior appearance and goalscoring records (for Wolves) which appears at the end of each individual players' write-up. An asterisk (*) alongside the figures indicates that the player was with Wolves at the time the book was published.

Virtually throughout the book Wolverhampton Wanderers have been referred to as Wolves. Very few abbreviations have been used but among the more common ones are the obvious: FC (Football Club), FAC (FA Cup), FLC (Football League Cup), apps (appearances), sub (substitute).

Where a single year has been used (when talking about an individual player's career), this indicates, in most cases, the second half of a season: i.e. 1975 is 1974-75. However, when the figures (dates) like 1975-80 are given, this means seasons 1975-76 to 1979-80 inclusive.

The text, I believe, is straight forward, easy to read. However, if you do spot any discrepancies, I would appreciate it very much if you could contact me (via the publishers) so that any alterations / amendment / additions can be included in any future publication appertaining to Wolverhampton Wanderers Football Club.

NB - Several supporters have verbally stated that there were errors, omissions, discrepancies etc. in my previous Wolves books - but very few have come forward with a list of what they were!

A

ADDENBROOKE, John Henry

Born in Wolverhampton in 1865, Jack Addenbrooke was Wolves' manager from August 1885 to June 1922 - and for a short while during that time he was also landlord of the Molineux Hotel.

He played football for St. Luke's School, Blakenhall (1875-77) and was appointed secretary of the team aged 10. Four years later he attended Saltley College (Birmingham) and after his educational studies were over he returned to Wolverhampton to pursue a teaching career, commencing with a two-year spell at Bushbury School. During his time here he became associated with Wolves, playing regularly for the second XI. In August 1885 he was appointed the first paid secretary of the club, a position which later took in the managerial duties (as we know them today).

He held office for 37 years - until the summer of 1922 - and during that time Wolves moved into their Molineux home, became founder members of the Football League, won the FA Cup twice (in 1893 & 1908) and were beaten Finalists on three occasions (in 1889, 1896 & 1921).

He was also involved in the recruitment of several quality players including Billy Malpass, George Fleming, England goalkeeper Tom Baddeley, Bill Wooldridge, George Edmonds, Jackery Jones, Billy Harrison, Noel George and the Reverend Kenneth Hunt, the famous Amateur international. He was unfortunately taken ill in June 1922 and was declared unfit for work by Doctor Wolverson. He was allowed six months leave but sadly, on 7 September of that year he passed away at the age of 57.

NB - Addenbrooke was presented with the long-service medal by the Football League in 1908-09 and his record as Wolves manager was 1,124 games played, 454 wins, 220 draws and 450 defeats.

AINSCOW, Alan

A Lancastrian, born in Bolton on 15 July 1953, Alan Ainscow was a hard-working midfielder who spent his first nine years with Blackpool (1969-78) having signed professional forms in July 1971.

After leaving Bloomfield Road he served with Birmingham City (July 1978 to August 1981) His next club was Everton and from Goodison Park he switched to Barnsley on loan in November 1982. A spell with Eastern FC in Hong Kong followed (1983) before moving to Wolves in August 1984. Ainscow remained at Molineux until December 1985 when he was transferred to Blackburn Rovers. He stayed at Ewood Park until June 1989, served Rochdale for a short time and then found his way to Horwich RMI in August 1990. Thereafter the nomadic Ainscow assisted Flint Town Utd for one season (July 1991 to May 1992) before joining the Cheshire club, Ellesmere Port as coach for the 1992-93 campaign.

Capped by England at Youth team level, Ainscow helped Birmingham win promotion from Division Two in 1980 and starred in over 500 senior games as a professional at club level.

Wolves' record: 62+3 sub apps. 6 goals.

AKINBIYI, Adeola (Ade) Peter

Nigerian international striker Ade Akinbiyi was born in Hackney, London on 10 October 1974. Standing 6ft 1in tall and weighing almost 13 stone, he joined Norwich City as a trainee in 1991 and turned professional at Carrow Road in February 1993. He scored five times in 59 first-class appearances for the Canaries before transferring to Gillingham for £250,000 in January 1997, after loan spells with both Hereford United and Brighton & Hove Albion. He did very well at The Priestfield Stadium and netted 29 times in 69 outings for the Kent club, up to May 1998 when a £1.3 million deal was agreed with Bristol City. At Ashton Gate Akinbiyi continued to produce the goods - netting 25 goals in 53 games before his expensive £3.5 million transfer to Molineux in September 1999.

Signed to replace the departed Robbie Keane, he scored 16 goals in 37 League games for Wolves, including a hat-trick against Grimsby Town and winning his first cap for his country against Greece. Unfortunately the lure of Premiership football took Akinbiyi away from Molineux to Leicester City in July 2000, Wolves accepting the Foxes' £5 million bid with no hesitation. In his first season in the top flight Akinbiyi netted 10 goals in 43 League and Cup appearances and he has now played in 10 full internationals.

Wolves record: 36+1 apps. 16 goals.

AL JABER, Sami Abdullah

Born in Riyadh, Saudi Arabia on 11 December 1972 and captain of his country on many occasions, Sami Al Jaber , short, sharp with a neat first touch, was a prolific scorer in Saudi Arabian football. Nicknamed the 'Blue Wolf' he joined Wolves on an extended five-month trial in September 2000 (from the Al Hilal club in his home country) but managed only five outings for the club (four as a substitute) before returning home.

Wolves' record: 1+4 sub apps.

ALDERTON, James Harris

Born in Wingate, County Durham on 6 December 1924, wing-half Jimmy Alderton joined Wolves in December 1941 and made 111 appearances during the hostilities (plus a handful afterwards) and was a guest player with Chester before transferring to Coventry City in October 1947 for a small fee.

He starred in 60 first team matches for the Sky Blues, up to May 1952, when he withdrew from competitive soccer through injury.

Wolves' record: 15 apps.

ALLEN, Harry

Harry Allen was a formidable defender, 'rather rash at times' but nevertheless a great competitor for Wolves, whom he joined in 1886 after spending three years with Walsall Town Swifts. Capped by England on five occasions, he appeared in two FA Cup Finals for Wolves - 1889 & 1893 - skippering the side in the second. He collected a winners' medal in the latter when he scored the only goal against Everton at Fallowfield in Manchester. After retiring through injury in October 1894 he became a publican in Wolverhampton. Allen, who was born in Walsall on 19 January 1866, died suddenly in the same Midlands town on 23 February 1895, aged 29.

Wolves' record: 152 apps. 13 goals.

ALLEN, Ronald

Ronnie Allen was Wolves' manager from September 1965 to November 1968 and during that time he guided the team back into the First Division (1967).

Born in Fenton, Stoke-on-Trent on 15 January 1929, he played junior football for a number of teams in the Potteries and in 1944 signed for Port Vale as a right-winger. He made steady progress with the Valiants and after the hostilities of World War Two he established himself in the first team.

In March 1950, he was transferred to West Bromwich Albion for a record fee of £20,000 and over the next eleven years scored 234 goals in 458 senior appearances.

He was a key member of the Baggies side that finished runners-up to Wolves and won the FA Cup in 1954 (netting twice in the 3-2 Final victory over Preston). He was in the Albion side that reached the Cup semi-finals in 1957 and he gained five full England caps as well as representing his country at 'B' team level, while also playing for the FA XI and the Football League.

Allen left Albion in May 1961 to join Crystal Palace, later taking over as player-coach at Selhurst Park. He retired in March 1965, and six months later, after a brief coaching spell at Molineux and a short period as acting-manager, he took over as Wolves' boss from Andy Beattie.

He did reasonably well with the club for the first two-and-a-half years or so. He signed four excellent players - Derek Dougan, snapped up for a bargain £50,000 fee in March 1967, defender Frank Munro (bought from Aberdeen), wing-half Mike Bailey (from Charlton Athletic) and full-back Derek Parkin (secured from Huddersfield Town).

Among the many others he introduced to league soccer were goalkeeper Phil Parkes, defender John McAlle, strikers John Richards and inside-forward Alun Evans, whom he he later sold to Liverpool for £100,000 (the most money ever paid for a teenager at that time).

Allen's days at Molineux were numbered following a crushing 6-0 home defeat at the hands of Liverpool in late September 1968 and five weeks later he left the club to be replaced by Bill McGarry.

Allen remained in football for the next 18 years, holding the following positions: Athletic Bilbao (manager, 1969-71), Sporting Lisbon (manager, 1972-73), Walsall (manager, 1973), West Bromwich Albion (scouting adviser from January 1977, then team manager from June to December 1977), Football Advisor to the Saudi Arabian FA (1978-80), Panathinaikos, Greece (manager, 1980-81), West Bromwich Albion (manager for a second

time from July 1981 to May 1982, then general manager to 1983).

Thereafter Allen continued his association with the Baggies as a shareholder (just failing to get onto the Board of Directors) and later acted as assistant-coach, a position he held until ill-health set him back in 1996. Indeed, Allen played in an end-of-season friendly v. Cheltenham Town in 1995, aged 66.

NB - Allen scored goals at first team level for 22 years: 1944-65 inclusive, and he held the Albion record for most League goals (208) from 1961-78 until it was bettered by current holder Tony Brown. West Bromwich Albion entertained Aston Villa in a Testimonial match for Allen at The Hawthorns on 3 August 1997. He sadly died in Sutton Coldfield on 9 June 2001.

Allen's record as Wolves manager: 150 games played, 66 won, 35 drawn and 49 lost.

ALLEN, Thomas

Born in Moxley near Bilston on 1 May 1897, goalkeeper Tom Allen played for Wednesbury Old Park, Bilston United and Hickman's Institute before joining Wolves during the First World War, basically as a reserve.

Released by the club in April 1919, without ever playing a competitive first team game, Allen went on to make 515 Football League appearances while serving, in turn, with Sunderland (from May 1919), Southampton (May 1920 to June 1928....for whom he starred in 323 games), Coventry City (until July 1932), Accrington Stanley (for a little over a season to September 1933), Northampton Town (until August 1934) and finally Kidderminster Harriers. He eventually retired in the summer of 1936.

Allen's slender build was frequently the target of friendly banter in the changing room. Players in the bath used to cry a mock alarm: 'Look out the plug's come out - we don't want to lose Tom down the drain.'

ANDERSON, Edward Walton

Born in Newcastle-upon-Tyne on 17 July 1911, Ted Anderson played his early football in the North East with Jarrow. In July 1930, he was recruited by Wolves from Worksop Town, but played only three League games, all in the left-half position in place of Dai Richards before leaving for Torquay United in December 1931.

He later assisted West Ham United (1933-35), Chester (1935-37) and Tranmere Rovers (1937-48) and played for Everton, New Brighton and Wrexham as a wartime guest. On retiring, in the summer of 1948, Anderson returned to Newcastle where he enjoyed tennis and swimming. Anderson died in Birkenhead on 23 March 1979

Wolves' record: 3 apps.

ANDERSON, Nicholas R

Nick Anderson, who was born in Wolverhampton, circa 1865, played for Wolves during the club's first season in the Football League competition of 1888-89. A stocky

centre-forward, he failed to make an impact at Dudley Road and left the club in May 1889.
Wolves' record: 2 apps.

ANDREWS, Keith
Irish Under-18 international midfielder Keith Andrews, who took time to establish himself in the Wolves side, joined the club as an apprentice in 1997 and turned professional on 1 August 1999. He had a loan spell with Oxford United in November/December 2000 and ended that season with a total of 26 first-class appearances under his belt for Wolves. He was born in Dublin's fair city on 13 September 1980.
Wolves' record: 20+4 apps. 2 goals.

ANNIS, Walter
Walter Annis was a hard-tackling defender who, as part of a fine half-back line at Molineux with initially Ted Pheasant and George Fleming, and later with Jack

Walter Annis

Whitehouse, Pheasant and for a time, George Walker, gave Wolves splendid service for seven seasons.
Born in Wolverhampton in 1874, he joined the club from Stafford Road FC in August 1898, having earlier assisted Wolverhampton St. Luke's, and he left Molineux for Cradley Heath in April 1905.
Wolves' record: 147 apps. one goal.

ARKWRIGHT, Ian
Ian Arkwright, an England Schoolboy international, had only a handful of outings for Wolves, all in 1978-79, when he wore the No.10 shirt. Born in Shalton, Yorkshire on 18

September 1959, he represented Yorkshire Boys before joining the club as an apprentice in 1975, turning professional in September 1977. He left Molineux for Wrexham in March 1979 and later had loan spells with Scunthorpe United (November-December 1981) and Torquay United (March-April 1984) before quitting League football at the end of that season.
Wolves' record: 4 apps.

ARROWSMITH, Arthur
Inside-forward Arthur Arrowsmith played once for Wolves, lining up against Birmingham in October 1908 in place of Walter Radford. Born in Finchfield, Wolverhampton in 1880, he started out with Compton FC and joined Coventry City in July 1904. Two years later he gained a Junior International cap when he represented the Birmingham Association v. Scotland Juniors. In August 1906 he left Highfield Road for Stoke and made almost 40 appearances for the Potters before signing for Wolves in July 1908. He left Molineux for Willenhall Swifts in April 1909.
Wolves' record: 1 app.

ASHALL, George Henry
Stocky left-winger Ashall had two fine seasons with Wolves: 1936-38. Born in Killamarsh, Derbyshire on 29 September 1911, he joined the club from Frickley Colliery in February 1936 and made a goalscoring debut in the gold and black against Grimsby Town the following month. On leaving Molineux in July 1938, he signed for Coventry City and remained at Highfield Road until the summer of 1948 when he drifted into non-League football before finally hanging up his boots in 1952. Ashall represented the Football League v. the Scottish League in 1937 and guested for Northampton Town during the Second World War.
Wolves' record: 94 apps. 19 goals.

George Ashall

ASHLEY, Kevin Mark
A quick-recovering full-back who loved to overlap, Kevin Ashley played junior football for Wheelers Lane School before joining Birmingham City on YTS forms in June 1984. He turned professional in December 1986 and after 67 outings for Blues was transferred to Wolves for £500,000 in September 1990. He had a useful first season at Molineux, but after that struggled with his form and finally left the club in August 1994 to join Peterborough United on a free transfer. He later played for Doncaster Rovers, Telford United in the Vauxhall Conference (1996-

97) and then for Bromsgrove Rovers (under the managership of ex-Wolves star Steve Daley) before teaming up with Shifnal Town in 1998-99. Ashley, who was born in Kings Heath, Birmingham on 31 December 1968, is now a postman and lives in Halesowen.
Wolves' record: 97+2 sub apps. one goal.

ASHTON, Derek
Solid full-back or centre-half, Derek Ashton was born in Worksop, Nottinghamshire on 4 July 1922 and represented Worksop Schools before joining Wolves in 1941. He played throughout the hostilities, accumulating 151 games for the Wanderers in Wartime and FA Cup football. But with so many quality defenders at Molineux around that time, Ashton was allowed to leave Wolves for Aston Villa in May 1946. He played in eight games for the Birmingham-based club before moving into non-League soccer with Wellington Town in 1951.
Wolves' record: 4 apps.

ASTILL, Leonard Victor
Len Astill was a reserve outside-left (or left-half) for Wolves in the mid-1930s, breaking into the first XI in April 1935 after playing initially as an amateur in the 'A' side. Born in Wolverhampton on 30 December 1916, he was educated at Hordern Road and Old Hall Schools and played for Wolverhampton Boys in the English Schools Shield Final v. Islington at Highbury in 1931 in front of 13,531 fans. It was his form in this game that led to Major Frank Buckley recruiting him to Wolves. Astill progressed through the 'A' and reserve teams and made his debut for Wolves in a 2-1 win over Stoke.
In May 1935, a month after representing the Birmingham County FA against the Scottish Junior FA at The Hawthorns and playing against the Irish Free State, he was surprisingly transferred to Blackburn Rovers. He later assisted Ipswich Town, linking up with Gilbert Alsop, one of the greatest goalscorers of his time and then had a spell with Colchester United (from March 1938). Astill retired from the game during the early part of the War and started a business as market trader in Walsall, later becoming a newsagent in Telford. He was also a very fine club cricketer and once scored a century in less than an hour.
Wolves' record: 2 apps.

ASTON, Harry
Harry Aston was a speedy, wholehearted utility forward who was born in Bloxwich on 20 October 1855 and attended Spon Lane School, West Bromwich. He played for George Salter's works team before becoming a key member of West Bromwich Albion's first senior squad in 1879-80. He left the Throstles' nest for Wolves in July 1885 and the following summer switched to Burslem Port Vale for whom he made over 40 appearances. He later assisted Preston North End (albeit briefly) and Oldbury Town for two seasons before retiring in 1891.

Wolves' record: 5 apps. 4 goals
NB. Aston scored Albion's first recorded goal versus Black Lake Victoria in a friendly on 20 December 1879.

ASTON, Jack
Centre-half Jack Aston (no relation to Harry, above) was one of the first dominant defenders to pull on a Wolves shirt. Born in Wednesbury in the April quarter of 1863, he spent a couple of seasons at the club, from July 1884 to May 1886, having been recruited from local junior football. After leaving Wolves he served with several minor teams including Willenhall Pickwick, Stafford Road and Oldbury Saints.
Wolves' record: 5 apps. 3 goals.

ATKINS, Mark Nigel
The versatile Mark Atkins has occupied a number of positions in his League career, which began in 1986 with Scunthorpe United whom he joined two years earlier as a teenager.
Born in Doncaster on 14 August 1968, he gained England Schoolboy honours as a teenager and played in 66 games for the 'Iron' before transferring to Blackburn Rovers for £45,000 in June 1988. In the next seven years, he amassed more than 300 appearances for Rovers, helping them win the Premiership title in 1994-95. He was sold to Wolves for £1 million in September 1995 and over the next two campaigns gave the club excellent service, mainly as a central defender although occasionally filling in at right-back and in midfield.
Atkins, on leaving Wolves, joined York City on a free transfer in August 1999. Three months later he moved to Doncaster Rovers and switched to Hull City on transfer deadline day in March 2001 (signed by former Wolves boss Brian Little).
Wolves' record: 140+11 sub apps. 11 goals.

ATKINSON, Hugh Anthony
Hardworking Irish midfielder who could also play at left-back, Hugh Atkinson's early days in football were spent with Cabinteely Youth Club and Dundrum Boys before he joined Wolves as an apprentice in 1976, finally turning professional in the autumn of 1978.
Born in Dublin on 8 November 1960, he spent five years as a 'pro' at Molineux, up to November 1983, when he was sold to Exeter City, later assisting York City (July 1984) and Darlington (on loan, March/April 1985).
Wolves' record: 52 apps. 3 goals.

BADDELEY, Thomas
Born in the town of Bycars, Stoke-on-Trent on 2 November 1874, Tom Baddeley was an excellent goalkeeper, as 'safe as houses' and despite standing only 5ft. 9ins tall and weighing 11 stone (relatively

lightweight for a custodian of that era) he feared no-one and often dived bravely at opponents' feet. The fourth member of the Baddeley clan, he commenced his career with Burslem Swifts in 1890. In September 1893 he signed for Burslem Port Vale and after more than 70 outings for the Valiants he moved to Wolves for £50 in October 1896 after being suspended for signing a second professional form for an another club! He spent the next 11 seasons at Molineux (up to 1907) when he switched his allegiance to Yorkshire to sign for Bradford Park Avenue (being a founder member of that club - and playing in their first League game versus Hull City in September 1908). During March and April 1910 he played eight games for Stoke and finally called it a day in 1911 after briefly assisting Whitfield Colliery FC. Winner of five England caps (1903-04), Baddeley could throw a ball out up to 50 yards (an unusual feature for a 'keeper at this time) and in a fine career accumulated almost 400 appearances at club level, being the first Wolves player to star in 300 matches.

Thomas Baddeley

Wolves' record: 315 apps.

BAILEY, Herbert

Herbert Bailey was a reserve utility forward who played for Wolves during the 1891-92 season. Born in Wolverhampton, circa 1870, he was recruited as cover for Messrs. Devey, Heath and Topham and when released from Molineux he signed for Willenhall Pickwick.

Wolves' record: 1 app.

BAILEY, Michael Alfred

Mike Bailey gave Wolves splendid service, contributing greatly to the club's long-awaited revival in the 1970s and early '80s as a teak-tough wing-half, who oozed confidence and determination. Capped twice by England (v. U.S.A. in 1964 & Wales in 1965), Bailey also won five Under-23 caps, was voted 'Midland Footballer of the Year' in 1967 and in 1974 skippered Wolves to victory in the League Cup Final against Manchester City.

Born in Wisbech on 27 February 1942, Bailey, a pupil at Edward Worlidge & Alderman Leech Schools (Gorleston) was a junior player with Precasters FC and after a short spell with Gorleston signed amateur forms for Charlton Athletic in May 1957, turning professional at The Valley in March 1959.

Mike Bailey

Prior to him joining Wolves, he broke a leg against Middlesbrough, but made a full recovery and arrived at Molineux for £40,000 in March 1966. Then, over the next 11 years, Bailey became a big favourite with the club's fans. His contract with Wolves was cancelled in January 1977 and five months later he signed for Minnesota Kicks (NASL) for £15,000. After seventeen months as player-manager of Hereford United (from June 1978 to October 1979) he became chief coach at his old club Charlton (from October 1979, taking over as manager in March 1980 and holding office until June 1981).

He then managed Brighton & Hove Albion from June 1981 to December 1982; coached briefly in Cyprus in season 1983-84; was player-manager of Bexley FC in 1985-86; acted as co-manager of New Valley FC, while at the same time penning a column in a Sunday Newspaper. He managed non-League Fisher Athletic from December 1989 to January 1991 and then held a coaching position, coupled with that of reserve team manager/coach at Portsmouth in season 1992-93 before becoming General Manager of the Surrey-based club, Leatherhead (members of the ICIS League). Bailey, who was granted a Testimonial (Wolves v. WBA) in 1976, later scouted for Blackburn Rovers, Newcastle United, Everton and Derby County and is currently more involved with the Goodison Park club.
Wolves' record: 436 apps. 25 goals.

BAILLIE, Joseph

Joe Baillie was a powerfully built full-back, who, for eighteen months at Molineux, was first reserve to the likes of Bill Shorthouse and Eddie Stuart. Born in Dumfries on 26 February 1929, Baillie played junior football as a half-back for St Roch's FC before going on to make 177 appearances for Celtic as well as representing Scotland 'B' and also the Scottish League while winning a Scottish Cup winners medal in 1951. He was recruited by Wolves' manager Stan Cullis in December 1954 and left Molineux for Bristol City in June 1956. Twelve months later Baillie switched his allegiance to Leicester City. He played in 80 League and Cup games for the Filbert Street club before rounding off his senior career with a spell at Bradford Park Avenue (1960-61), reverting back to a half-back with the Yorkshire club.
Baillee was killed in a car crash in Glasgow in March 1966.
Wolves' record: one app.

BAKER, Charles

Inside-forward Charlie Baker, who was born in Stafford on 10 February 1870, was described as a 'neat dribbler' in various newspapers. He played for Stafford Rangers, Stoke (from April 1889 to May 1891), Wolves (from August 1891 to February 1893), Stoke, for a second time (from January 1893 to June 1894) and Southampton St. Mary's (from August 1894 to April 1896). When he quit competitive football he returned to his home-town of

Stafford and again assisted Stafford Rangers before finally hanging up his boots in 1900 to pursue a shoemaking trade. Baker was presented with a gold watch on his departure from The Dell.
Wolves' record: 41 apps. 10 goals.

BAKER, James Edward

A Welshman, born in Trethomas, Rhondda Valley on 27 March 1904, Jack Baker was a strong, forceful wing-half, 6ft. tall and weighing over 12 stone, who deputised for Frank Higham during his time at Molineux. He played for Lovell's Athletic before joining Wolves in May 1926. From Molineux he went to Coventry City (May 1929) and after a second spell with the Lovell's Athletic club (1932) he returned to Highfield Road in February 1933. Later he assisted Bristol City (from June 1935) and Colchester United (1937-41) before retiring during the War.
Wolves' record: 17 apps.

BANSFORD, George

An amateur inside-forward, recruited by Wolves soon after World War One, George Bansford was born in Wednesfield in 1894 and played for Dudley Road Methodists, the St Matthews' Church team, West Park Juniors and Bushbury Rovers prior to moving to Molineux in August 1919. He had one season with Wolves, leaving to join Lanesfield Rovers in May 1920. His only League game in the old gold and black was the 1-0 away win at Grimsby in September 1919. There is no record of him playing beyond 1922.
Wolves' record: one app.

BARKER, George

A well built full-back with strong tackle, George Barker partnered George Walker in Wolves' defence during the first season of the twentieth century. Born in Blakenhall in February 1875, he played local football in the Wolverhampton League before going north to Merseyside to join Everton in 1896. From there he went to Bristol City (1898) and then returned to the Black Country to sign for Wolves. His brief spell at Molineux lasted from December 1900 to September 1901, when he was forced to retire through injury.
Wolves' record: 13 apps.

BARKER, Richard

Born in Burton-on-Trent on 23 November 1939, Richie Barker did not play League Football until joining Derby County at the age of 28 in October 1967, having previously assisted Morris Sports FC, Burton Albion (two spells), Loughborough, Matlock Town (1963), and the Canadian side, Primo Hamilton (on loan). He helped the 'Rams' win the Second Division in 1969 and later assisted Notts County, gaining a Fourth Division championship medal with them in 1971. After breaking a leg playing for Peterborough, whom he served from September 1971, he moved into management, first as assistant to Alan Durban at Shrewsbury, and when Durban left for Stoke in February 1978, Barker took the manager's chair at Gay Meadow. Ten months later he moved to Wolves (as assistant to John Barnwell). In June 1981 he became manager of Stoke, staying there until December 1983 before returning to Meadow Lane as boss in November 1984 (to April 1985). He then coached Ethnikos (Greece) and FC Zamalek (Egypt) prior to becoming Ron Atkinson's assistant at Sheffield Wednesday in February 1989 to May 1995. Barker was later chief scout at West Bromwich Albion (1998-2000) and soon afterwards he was appointed assistant-manager of Halifax Town.

BARLOW, Herbert

Bert Barlow spent less than eight months at Molineux and amazingly ten weeks after leaving the club he won a FA Cup winners' medal with Portsmouth who ironically defeated Wolves 4-1 in the 1939 Final at Wembley, Barlow scoring one of Pompey's goals!

An enthusiastic inside-right, Barlow, who was born in Kilnhurst, Yorkshire on 22 July 1916, played for Silverwood Colliery and Barnsley (July 1935) before teaming up with Wolves (on the 'never never') in June 1938. He switched to Fratton Park in February 1939 and played for Pompey for the next 10 years, transferring to Leicester City in December 1949. He ended his playing career with Colchester United (July 1952-May 1954). Barlow, who guested for Barnsley, Brighton & Hove Albion, Chelsea and Rotherham United during the Second World War, appeared in well over 300 games at club level and helped Portsmouth win the First Division championship in 1948-49, netting eight goals.

During the 1960s Barlow was a garage mechanic and he also assisted his wife in the family's grocery business.
Wolves' record: 3 apps. one goal.

BARNES, David

Strong, athletic full-back or midfielder, David Barnes was born in Paddington, London on 16 November 1961. On leaving school, he joined Coventry City as an apprentice (June 1977) and turned 'pro' at Highfield Road in May 1979. Three years later he was transferred to Ipswich Town and in October 1982 was recruited by Wolves, manager Graham Hawkins paying £30,000 for his signature. He did very well at Molineux during his three-year stay before switching to Aldershot in August 1987. From there he went to Sheffield United for £50,000 (July 1989) and helped the Blades win promotion to the First Division in 1990. He made over 100 appearances for United before transferring to Watford for £50,000 in January 1994. Unfortunately he was troubled by an Achiles tendon injury during his time at Vicarage Road and was given a 'free' in the summer of 1996 when he moved to Colchester United, helping them reach the Auto-Windscreen Shield Final at Wembley. His contract was cancelled at Layer

David Barnes (right)

Road in March 1997 by mutual consent.
Wolves' record: 107 apps. 4 goals.

BARNWELL, John

Born in Newcastle-on-Tyne on 24 December 1938, John Barnwell was manager of Wolves for three years - from November 1978 to November 1981. In 1980 he proudly led his team to victory in the League Cup Final at Wembley, having previously seen his side lose to Arsenal in the 1979 FA Cup semi-final.

A true Geordie, Barnwell was an amateur inside-left with Bishop Auckland before turning professional with Arsenal in November 1956. He spent over seven years at Highbury, making more than 160 senior appearances and scoring 24 goals.

In March 1964 he switched to Nottingham Forest and after netting 22 times in 182 League games during his six years at The City Ground, he joined Sheffield United. He retired as a player in 1971 after amassing a League record of 329 appearances and 47 goals as well as gaining Youth and Under-23 caps for England.

In July 1977, Barnwell stepped into management with Peterborough United from where he joined Wolves. He made some excellent signings (and sales) during his time at Molineux, although he did admit that it was 'hard' making the transfer from the Third to the First Division in one swift move.

Indeed, it was Barnwell who arranged the transfer to Wolves of Scottish-born striker Andy Gray for £1.15 million and also the sale of midfielder Steve Daley to

Manchester City for roughly the same amount early in the 1979-80 season. He was responsible too for the recruitment of 'Crazy Horse' himself, Emlyn Hughes, from Liverpool - all this after a serious car crash in March 1979 had left him with a fractured skull.

Thankfully he recovered from that horrific accident which had threatened his career and he duly continued in the game. (Brian Garvey had taken over the reins at Molineux during Barnwell's enforced absence). Soon after his return to management Barnwell was voted the Variety Club's 'Midland Sports Personality of the Year' 1979-80.

After a disappointing run of results soon after the start of the 1981-82 season Barnwell came under intense pressure and it was no surprise when he left the club with Wolves situated at the bottom end of the First Division table. He had, in fact, received legal advice before terminating his contract.

For Barnwell there followed a period out of the game before a brief sojourn in Saudi Arabia got him back into the routine.

He became manager-coach of AEK Athens and was then banned from working in Greece (January 1984) before moving back to England to eventually take over as boss at Notts County (June 1987). He led the Magpies into the Third Division play-offs at the end of his first season at Meadow Lane. His next move was to struggling Walsall in mid-January 1989, but sadly he couldn't save the Saddlers from losing their Second Division status as they were passed on the way down by Wolves!

Barnwell was sacked by Walsall in March 1990 and for a time was out of football, although he still contributed to a soccer magazine as well as summarising at certain matches. In 1992-93 he acted as a scout for several clubs before joining Third Division strugglers Northampton Town as a consultant to player-manager and ex-Wolves star Phil Chard.

In July 1996 Barnwell was given the job as Chairman of the League Managers' Association.

Barnwell's record as Wolves manager was played 167, won 64, drawn 40, lost 63. (exactly 200 goals scored).

BARRACLOUGH, William

Outside-left Bill Barraclough was a small, stocky player with powerful thighs and strong shot. Born in Hull on 3 January 1909, he served Wolves from June 1928 until October 1934 when he was transferred to Chelsea for £1,500. After more than 80 games for the Londoners, he switched to Colchester United and before retiring in the War, he assisted Doncaster Rovers. His career began with Bridlington Town from where he joined Hull City, whom he served prior to his move to Molineux. Barraclough, who won a Second Division championship medal with Wolves in 1932, later worked as a clerk in the Humberside docks and was also a fruit merchant, a keen golfer and respected tennis player.

Wolves' record: 183 apps. 19 goals.

Bill Barraclough

12

BARRETT, Scott

Goalkeeper Scott Barrett was handed his Football League debut by Wolves boss Tommy Docherty in 1984.

Born in Ilkeston, Derbyshire on 2 April 1963, he played for his local club, Ilkeston Town and was a junior with Notts County before signing for Wolves in September 1984.

He moved from Molineux to Stoke City for £10,000 in July 1987 and had 60 first team outings for the Potters, to August 1992, when he signed for Colchester United, this after loan spells at Layer Road (January 1990) and Stockport County (March 1990).

He left Colchester for Gillingham in August 1992 and three years later signed for Cambridge United (August 1995). In 1998 he passed the milestone of 150 appearances for the Abbey Stadium club. A loan spell with non-League Kingstonian (August 1998) preceded Barrett's move to Leyton Orient. He continued to perform well for the 'O's right up until the end of the 2000-01 season when he was appointed goalkeeping coach at Brisbane Road, having appeared 62 first-class games for the London club and almost 400 in senior football.

In 1992 Barrett appeared on BBC's 'Question of Sport'. Wolves' record: 35 apps.

BARRON, James

Goalkeeper Jim Barron had a fine career, accumulating 416 League appearances between 1963 and 1981. Born the son of a former Blackburn Rovers and Darlington 'keeper at Tanobie, County Durham on 19 October 1943, he joined Wolves as an amateur in 1960 from Newcastle West End Boys Club, having previously starred for Raby Street School and Byker & Newcastle Boys, as a goalkeeper and inside-right! It was as a goalkeeper, though, that Barron was to star. He signed 'pro' forms at Molineux in November 1961 and after winning an FA Youth Cup medal in 1962, he made his League bow v. Everton the following year. Unfortunately with Malcolm Finlayson holding the fort, Barron's chances of regular first team football were limited and in April 1965 he was sold to Chelsea. He failed to establish himself at Stamford Bridge and in March 1966 went to Oxford United. At The Manor Ground he did well, making over 150 senior appearances for the 'U's' before trying his luck with Nottingham Forest (July 1970 to August 1974).

He made a further 155 League appearances for Forest and then added 79 to his tally with Swindon Town (to August 1977) before ending his career with 21 League games for Peterborough, retiring in May 1981.

Barron then became assistant-manager of Mansfield Town and returned to Molineux as coach/assistant-manager (1981-83), later having a third spell with Wolves as coach and caretaker-manager (five games) prior to becoming boss at Cheltenham Town in November 1989, at the same time running a Goalkeeping School in the Gloucestershire area. He lost his job at Cheltenham in October 1990, but was then given the position of goalkeeping coach by Howard Kendall at Everton.

He was later appointed assistant-manager to Ron Atkinson at Villa Park (season 1992-93). And then, after serving a short prison sentence following a car crash which killed his wife, he became assistant-boss at Sheffield United (working under Steve Thompson), Barron had a big hand in team tactics as the Blades' chased promotion and reached the FA Cup semi-final in 1997-98.

In November 1998, he left Bramall Lane to become a coach with Birmingham City. He remained at St Andrew's in that capacity until October 2001 when he was appointed joint caretaker-manager of Blues (with Mick Mills) following the departure of Trevor Francis.

NB - Barron's son played in goal for Cheltenham Town when he was manager of the Vauxhall Conference club.
Wolves' record: 8 apps.

BARTLEY, John Patrick

Born in the town of New Washington, County Durham in February 1908 (and now deceased) Jack Bartley was a well-built, proportionate player who spent less two seasons as a reserve at Molineux, occupying the inside-right berth.

He played for Spennymoor United from May 1926 before joining Wolves in December 1928.

Bartley left Molineux for Walsall in June 1930 and after a brief spell with Usworth Colliery FC, he rounded off his career by having a brief spell with Stockport County (1932-33) with no first team outings.
Wolves' record: 2 apps.

BARTRAM, Vincent Lee

Goalkeeper Vince Bartram was an avid West Bromwich Albion supporter right up until he joined Wolves from Oldswinford FC in May 1985 (he even visited The Hawthorns when he could after that). Born in Birmingham on 7 August 1968, he was a pupil at the Hagley Roman Catholic School and represented Halesowen & Stourbridge District Boys before being recruited to Molineux when Wolves had a goalkeeping crisis. He never got a good run in the first XI and when Graham Turner arrived, Mark Kendall became first choice. Loan spells with Blackpool in 1989-90 and his boyhood heroes WBA in 1990-91, plus a stint with Cheltenham Town (under ex-Wolves 'keeper Jim Barron) preceded his transfer to AFC Bournemouth for £165,000 in August 1991. Bartram matured at Dean Court and made 162 appearances for the Cherries before moving to Arsenal for £400,000 in August 1994, signed as reserve to John Lukic and David Seaman. In February 1997 Bartram returned to Molineux on loan for a month as cover for Stowell and he also had a spell with Huddersfield Town (October 1997). In March 1998 he moved to Gillingham and helped the Kent club reach the Second Division 1999 play-off final at Wembley where they lost 3-2 to Manchester City after throwing away a 2-0 lead with the game ready to go into added-time. He went one better the following season when, under manager Peter Taylor, Gillingham - with Bartram in superb form - won promotion to the First Division via their second successive Wembley Play-off Final. Bartram - one of the best shot-stoppers in the country - has now made well over 175 appearances for the Gills and was the club's undisputed 'Player of the Year' in 2000-01.

Wolves' record: 10 apps.

BASFORD, Walter John

Jock Basford was born in Crewe on 24 July 1925. He was a junior footballer with Wolves before World War Two but failed to make the grade at Molineux and after the hostilities played as an inside-forward for Crewe Alexandra (from April 1948), Chester (January 1954), Guildford City and Margate before retiring to become trainer-coach of Charlton Athletic. He left The Valley for Exeter City in November 1965 where he was appointed assistant-manager and trainer prior to taking over as team manager in June 1966, holding office until April 1967.

He then returned to The Valley as Charlton's chief scout for the 1967-68 season, and was coach at Mansfield Town for two years after that (1968-70) before becoming the Stags' manager in July 1970. He retained that position he held until November 1971 when he took over as Youth team coach at Field Mill.

BATE, Walter William

Wolves acquired the services of utility forward Billy Bate from Darlaston in the summer of 1919. Born in West Bromwich circa 1895 and now deceased, he stayed at Molineux for just the one season, signing for West Smethwick in August 1920.

Wolves' record: 11 apps. 5 goals.

BAUGH, Richard

Dickie Baugh was a teak-tough full-back, quick off the mark with a timely tackle who could kick long and true. Born in Wolverhampton on 14 February 1864, he attended St. Luke's School, Blakenhall and played for Rose Villa, Wolverhampton Rangers and Stafford Road before joining Wolves as a professional in May 1886. Capped twice by England (in 1886 & 1890, both against Ireland) he appeared in three FA Cup Finals during his ten years with Wolves, gaining a winners' medal in 1893. He left Molineux for neighbouring Walsall in September 1896, and retired a year later through injury.

Wolves' record: 227 apps. One goal.

BAUGH, Richard Horace

Son of Richard Baugh senior, Dickie Baugh junior was also born in Wolverhampton on 6 March 1902, a week after Wolves had qualified for the FA Cup semi-final. He, too, was a fine full-back, a grafter, keen and resilient who also played for Stafford Road before joining the amateur

ranks at Molineux in August 1918, turning professional a year later. After missing the 1921 FA Cup Final through injury, Baugh was induced by an agent to join Cardiff City (April 1921). However, a joint FA and Welsh FA Commission, investigated the issue and subsequently cancelled the deal, fining Cardiff £50 and Baugh £20, while also severely censuring the player. After another three seasons at Molineux, Baugh was transferred to West Bromwich Albion in June 1924. He made 65 appearances for the Baggies before moving to Exeter City in May 1929, later assisting Kidderminster Harriers, from May 1932 to April 1936 when he retired.

Wolves' record: 120 apps. 4 goals.

BAXTER, Thomas William

Born in Mansfield on 1 February 1903, Tom Baxter - 5ft 4ins tall - was a fast, energetic outside-left who spent two seasons at Molineux - from August 1927. He joined Wolves from Mansfield Town and left the club for Port Vale in August 1929. He helped the Valiants win the Third Division (North) title in 1930 and made almost 60 appearances for the Potteries club before returning to Mansfield in May 1931. Thereafter he had two spells with Margate Town (1932 and 1933), served briefly with Carlisle United and rounded off his career in Ireland with Distillery. Earlier Baxter had played for Warsop Church Lads, Welbeck Colliery, Newark Town and Worksop Town before signing for Mansfield in 1925.

Wolves' record: 53 apps. 15 goals.

BAXTER, William

An efficient wing-half, strong with his tackle and a player who never gave less than 100 per-cent, Bill Baxter was a patient mortal who served in the Royal Navy and had to wait seven years before making his League debut for Wolves v. Everton in December 1948. Born in Methill, Fife, on 21 September 1924, he joined the groundstaff at Molineux on leaving the Vale of Leven School in August 1939 and turned professional in September 1945, having guested for Leicester City, Mansfield Town and Notts County during the War. After battling on, mainly in the second XI, Baxter, who made a record 224 reserve team appearances for Wolves (213 in the Central League) finally left Molineux for Aston Villa in November 1953. He added more than 100 senior outings to his career tally during the next four years at Villa Park before retiring in June 1957 to become Villa's third team coach. He was the club's assistant-manager in the early '60s and was reserve team trainer for two years: 1965-67. He later managed the Scottish club East Fife (1968-70).

Wolves' record: 47 apps. One goal.

BAYLY, Martin Joseph

Republic of Ireland Youth international midfielder Martin Bayly was given his senior debut with Wolves by manager Graham Hawkins in 1983 as a teenager.

Born in Dublin on 14 September 1966, Bayly played Schoolboy football in his home city and after a brief spell with Little Bray FC he joined Wolves as an apprentice in 1982, turning professional in July 1984.

Although voted the club's 'Young Player of the Year' in 1984, he was perhaps too fragile to make a real impact in competitive League football and on leaving Molineux in July 1985 had a brief association with Coventry City before drifting into non-League soccer back in his homeland.

Wolves' record: 11 apps.

BAYNHAM, Albert

Outside-right Albert Baynham was born in the Black Country circa 1880 and joined Wolves from Halesowen at the start of the 1903-04 season.

Positive and reliable, he replaced Arthur Fellows on the wing and did a fine job in the first XI for well over two seasons before damaging his right knee on Boxing Day 1905 when playing against Sheffield Wednesday.

He aggravated the injury six weeks later in an FA Cup-tie away to Bradford City and didn't figure again that season. He left Molineux in the summer of 1906, but played very little football after that, retiring during the Great War.

Wolves' record: 77 apps. 4 goals.

BAYNTON, John M

One of the original founder members of the club in 1877, Jack Baynton served 'Wolves' for 12 years (to 1889) before retiring through injury.

A pupil-teacher at St. Luke's School, he lined up initially for Blakenhall St. Luke's, as a centre-half, appearing in his first-match on 15 March 1877.

He then officially joined Wolves, acting as secretary and treasurer in the early days, and seven years later helped them win their first trophy, the Wrekin Cup (1884). He also starred in the club's first FA Cup-tie v. Long Eaton Rangers (October 1883).

Not the tallest of defenders at just 5ft 9ins, he then surprisingly changed positions to become a goalkeeper, taking over between the posts in the club's first League campaign of 1888-89 when he conceded 32 goals in 18 appearances.

He also helped Wolves reach that season's FA Cup Final when they lost 3-0 to Preston North End (his last game for the club).

A wholehearted outfield player and team captain, who never gave less than 100 percent, Baynton was also a very capable goalkeeper. Indeed, as a 'keeper, he once scored a goal from almost 100 yards, fly-kicking the ball downfield and between the posts when playing in a game at Dudley Road.

On retiring from football he became a teacher at All Saints School, Hockley, Birmingham.

He also took up refereeing (like his pal Jack Brodie) and officiated in several first-class matches.

Born at Rushock Wood, Wolverhampton in March 1859. Wolves' record: 28 apps.

BAZELEY, Darren Shaun

In his first season at Molineux (1999-2000) Darren Bazeley competed in all of Wolves' 51 matches, scoring three goals. He was bang in form again the following year but was then bowled over when he tore a cartilage in the away game with Sheffield Wednesday shortly before Christmas 2000.

He had left promoted Watford to remain in the Nationwide League with Wolves and he certainly proved his worth, giving some excellent displays until suffering that injury blow at Hillsborough.

Born in Northampton on 5 October 1972, Bazeley, who can play as a full-back or right-sided midfielder, joined the apprentice ranks at Vicarage Road in 1988 and turned professional in May 1991.

He made 281 appearances for the Hornets, scored 27 goals and gained one England Under-21 cap while also gaining a Second Division championship medal in 1998 and of course helping the club reach the Premiership under Graham Taylor's management in 1999.

Wolves' record: 79+1 apps. 4 goals.

BEASANT, David John

Goalkeeper Dave Beasant was secured on loan by Wolves in January 1993, following an injury to Mike Stowell. One of the tallest 'keepers in the country at 6ft. 3ins.

Beasant was born in Willesden on 20 March 1959 and played his early football with Edgware Town before turning professional with Wimbledon in June 1979.

He became a very popular figure at Plough Lane and in 1988 became the first keeper to captain an FA Cup winning side, leading the Dons to a 1-0 victory over

Dave Beasant

Liverpool after he himself had also become the first man to save a penalty in such a Final.

He made over 400 appearances for Wimbledon, whom he helped rise from the Third to the old First Division.

A month after his Wembley glory, he left Plough Lane for Newcastle United for £800,000 but seven months later he was back in London, having left St. James' Park for Chelsea in a £725,000 deal.

Capped by England 'B' on seven occasions and twice at senior level, he helped Chelsea win the Z.D.S.C. at Wembley, and all-told played in more than 150 games for the Stamford Bridge club.

He left Chelsea for Southampton for £300,000 in November 1993, following his short spell with Wolves and also a period on loan with Grimsby Town (October 1992). Beasant passed the personal milestone of 100 outings for Saints in 1996-97 and during the early part of the 1997-98 campaign he was loaned out to Nottingham Forest, the club he joined on a permanent basis in November 1997, helping them regain their Premiership status in 1998.

But, alas, Forest duly returned to the Nationwide League after just one season in the top flight and Beasant was released in May 2001, having taken his career appearance-tally at club level to a magnificent 843.

In August 2001 the evergreen Beasant signed for First Division side Portsmouth after turning down an offer from Birmingham City. In November 2001 Beasant joined Tottenham Hotspur on a two-month deal.

Wolves' record: 5 apps.

BEATS, William Edwin

An opportunist goalscorer, totally reliable, determined and clever, Billy Beats arrived at Molineux in June 1895 for just £80 (plus a benefit match guaranteed to raise a further £50).

He had become an established marksman while serving with Porthill Victoria, Port Vale Rovers (1899) and Burslem Port Vale (from 1891 - he scored a hat-trick in Vale's 4-1 Staffordshire Cup win over Wolves in March 1894).

Beats spent eight seasons with Wolves, amassing a fine record, while twice representing England, as well as being in the national team on the day of the Ibrox Park disaster (5 April 1902) when the match was abandoned and re-arranged the following month.

Born at Wolstanton in North Staffordshire on 13 November 1871, Beats was a regular in the Wolves side until 1901 and played in the 1896 FA Cup Final against Sheffield Wednesday. He left Molineux in May 1903 for Bristol Rovers and two years later skippered Rovers to the Southern League championship. In August 1906 he returned to the Potteries, teaming up again with Port Vale. In May 1907, when Vale were faced with a financial crisis and after he had taken his appearance tally with the Valiants up to 130 (47 goals), he joined Reading. In the summer of 1911, he was appointed trainer at Bristol

Rovers and switched back to Elm Park in the same capacity in 1914.

On quitting football, in 1917, Beats became a publican, taking over the Truro Inn in Castle Street, Reading - a position he held until 1936.

Wolves' record: 199 apps. 73 goals.

BEATTIE, Andrew

Andy Beattie was manager at Molineux for a year: September 1964 to September 1965. The former Scottish international took over from Stan Cullis, but after a disastrous season which saw Wolves relegated to the Second Division for the first time since 1932, he was replaced by Ronnie Allen just a few weeks into the 1965-66 campaign.

Born at Kintore, Aberdeenshire on 11 August 1913, Beattie was a junior footballer with Inverurie Loco and then Kilmarnock prior to joining Preston North End for £135 in 1935. He spent 12 years at Deepdale, making over 130 senior appearances before the hostilities and many more during the War, when he also guested for Aldershot, Bradford City, Clapton Orient, Derby County, Leicester City, Manchester City, Northampton Town and Notts County.

He played in two FA Cup Finals, picking up a loser's medal in 1937 and a winners' prize twelve months later. He gained seven full caps for Scotland, as well as starring in five wartime and Victory internationals.

A superb defender, who was capable of outwitting the trickiest opponent, Beattie retired from 'match play' in March 1947 to become secretary-manager of Barrow.

He then held a similar position with Stockport County (March 1949 to April 1952) before being appointed manager of Huddersfield Town, holding office at Leeds Road until November 1956. Whilst at Huddersfield he also took charge of the Scottish national team for four months: February-June 1954.

After a short period out of football, Beattie was given the manager's job at Carlisle United (May 1958 - March 1960) and during his time in office at Brunton Park, he again looked after the Scottish national team: March 1959 to October 1960.

In September 1960 he had become manager of Nottingham Forest, taking over from Billy Walker. He remained at The City Ground until July 1963 and prior to his appointment at Wolves, Beattie was caretaker-manager of Plymouth Argyle (October 1963 to March 1964).

On leaving Wolves, Beattie remained in the game, joining Peter Doherty at Notts County as Professional Advisor (December 1965) later taking the position of General Manager at Meadow Lane.

Two years later he became assistant-manager to ex-Wolves player John Harris at Sheffield United (October 1967) and at various times after this he coached and scouted for a number of clubs including Brentford, Liverpool, Notts County, Walsall and Wolves.

Beattie died at Rushcliffe on 20 September 1983, aged 70. His record as Wolves manager was played 44, won 19, drawn seven, lost 18.

BEATTIE, John Murdoch

WILLS'S CIGARETTES

J. M. BEATTIE (BLACKBURN ROVERS)

Jack Beattie was a quality inside-forward, possessing a fierce right-foot shot who played all his senior football with top-Division clubs.

Born in Newhills, Scotland on 28 May 1912, he played for Hall Russells FC before starting his professional career with Aberdeen in August 31. In September 1933 he was transferred to Wolves for £1,500 and was first choice at Molineux until leaving for Blackburn Rovers in December 1934 for £5,000.

In January 1937, a player-exchange deal plus £2,000 took him to Birmingham and twelve months later he was sold to Huddersfield Town for £2,500. And from February 1938 to May 1946, Beattie was registered with Grimsby Town, who had paid £2,500 for his services. He retired in 1940 after guesting for Walsall.

Wolves' record: 46 apps. 13 goals.

BELL, John

Inside-forward Jackie Bell was recruited to the Molineux playing staff in the summer of 1894 from Bacup. Mainly a reserve, he was not retained for the following season and left Wolves for Grimsby Town in July 1895.

Born in Dundee in June 1877, he played initially for Dundee Wanderers and then Renton before joining Bacup.

He was successfully converted into a centre-half when he joined Grimsby and made 77 League appearances for the Mariners. He then assisted Chesterfield Town (from June 1899 - 54 League outings), Millwall Athletic (August 1900 - over 50 games) and Leicester Fosse (May 1903 to May 1904 - 21 appearances).

An engine fitter by trade, there is no doubt that Bell played his best football with Grimsby where he had steady influence on the team and specialised in feeding the attack. .

Wolves' record: 6 apps. 2 goals.

BELL, Norman

An inside or centre-forward, Norman Bell spent a little over 10 years at Molineux, initially joining Wolves as an apprentice in July 1971 and turning professional in November 1973. Often referred to as 'Super Sub' he was

born in Sunderland on 16 November 1955 and played local junior football prior to signing for Wolves. He unfortunately broke a leg during Wolves' FA Cup-tie with Crystal Palace in 1978-79.

He left Molineux in November 1981 for Blackburn Rovers, but was then forced to give up League soccer in 1983 through injury, although he did make a comeback in non-League football in 1984-86. He is now in business in Blackburn.

Wolves' record: 100 apps. 24 goals.

BELLAMY, Gary

Prior to becoming a Wolves player - signed by manager Graham Turner for £17,000 in September 1987 - full-back or central defender Gary Bellamy appeared in over 200 games for Chesterfield, whom he joined in July 1978, turning professional two years later. He helped the 'Spire-ites' win the Fourth Division championship in 1985.

Brought in to bolster up a flagging Molineux defence, Bellamy went on to give Wolves tremendous service over the next five years. He was certainly a key member of the side that gained promotion from the Fourth to the Second Division in successive seasons, as well as winning the Sherpa Van Trophy at Wembley.

He also skippered the side before a niggling injury began to interrupt his performances. After a loan spell with Cardiff City (March - May 1992) with whom he won a Welsh Cup winners medal, Bellamy signed for Leyton Orient for £30,000 in September 1992.

He went on to play in more than 150 games for the London club before pulling out of League football in June 1996 when he joined Chelmsford City as player-coach

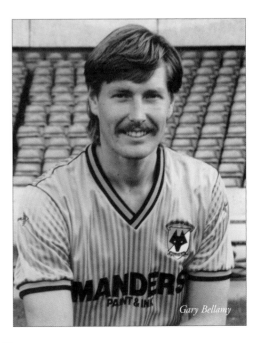

Gary Bellamy

and commercial manager. In May 2001 Bellamy was appointed manager of the Nationwide Conference side, Dover Athletic.

Bellamy was born in Worksop on 4 July 1962.

Wolves' record: 165 apps. 9 goals.

BELLIS, George Alfred

George Bellis was described as being 'a big, powerful fellow' who scarcely knew his own strength. Few could get by him.' Indeed, at 5ft 11ins tall and weighing almost 12 stone Bellis was a solidly built defender, and although a shade lethargic at times, he was as strong as an ox and often came out of a game unscathed.

Born the son of a company Sergeant Major in the Royal Engineers at Kirkee in India on 8 June 1904, Bellis attended St. John's School in Seaforth, Lancashire and started playing football with Waterloo FC in 1921.

He then assisted LMS Railway United (in Formby near Liverpool) and also Seaforth Fellowship FC before signing amateur forms for Southport in August 1923. A year later - after serving his apprenticeship as an electrician - he became a professional and in May 1927 was transferred to Wrexham for £150. From there he joined Wolves for £600 in June 1929, replacing Tom Pritchard.

After making a successful debut against West Bromwich Albion on the opening day of the 1929-30 Second Division campaign, Bellis went on to appear in roughly half of Wolves' games that season.

But following the arrival at Molineux of Jack Nelson in November 1932, his first team outings became limited and the following month he was sold to Burnley.

In June 1935 he moved to Bournemouth, served with Wellington Town from June 1937 to May 1939 and during the War he guested for Tranmere Rovers.

Wolves' record: 43 apps.

BENNETT, Michael

Born in Bolton on 24 December 1962, full-back Mick Bennett was an apprentice at Burnden Park for almost two years before turning professional in January 1980.

A compact player, he moved to Wolves in June 1983, but stayed less than a season at Molineux before transferring to Cambridge United in March 1984. From there he went to Bradford City (August 1986) and then had a good spell with Preston North End (September 1986 - September 1992), helping them to runners-up spot in Division 4 in 1986-87.

Bennett was a non-contract player with Bradford City before joining Carlisle United in July 1990. He dropped out of League soccer to sign for Northwich Victoria two years later.

Wolves' record: 8 apps.

BENNETT, Thomas McNeill

Born in Falkirk on 12 December 1969, Scotsman Tom Bennett signed for Wolves on a free transfer from Aston

Villa in July 1988 having failed to make the breakthrough at Villa Park.

A versatile defender, he spent five years at Molineux, during which time he always gave 100 per-cent effort whether in the first XI or reserves.

He left the club for Stockport County for £75,000 in June 1995 and two years later starred for the Edgeley Park club as they won promotion to Division One for the first time in the club's history.

He sadly broke his leg in a game against Birmingham in January 1998, but thankfully made a full recovery. He had two loan spells with Walsall (in December 1999 and March 2000) before joining the Saddlers on a permanent basis for the 2000-01 season.

Barrett was a key figure in helping Ray Graydon's team regain their Nationwide First Division status when they came from behind to beat Reading 3-2 at the Millennium Stadium in the Play-off Final in May 2001.

Wolves' record: 133 apps. 2 goals.

BENTON, John

Burly wing-half, born in Wolverhampton in 1865, Jack Benton played for Wolves during their first season of League football (1888-89). Previously with St. Phillips FC, Stafford Royal and Willenhall White Star, he later assisted Blakenhall and Wightwick.

Wolves' record: one app.

BERESFORD, Marlon

Goalkeeper Marlon Beresford joined Wolves on a month's loan from Middlesbrough in August 2001 - as cover for Michael Oakes (and following Mike Stowell's departure to Bristol City).

Born in Lincoln on 2 September 1969, he started his career with Sheffield Wednesday in the mid-1980s and after loan spells with Bury, Northampton Town (twice) and Crewe Alexandra he joined Burnley for £95,000 in August 1992. He made almost 300 appearances for the Clarets before transferring to Middlesbrough for £500,000 in March 1998. Unfortunately with Mark Schwarzer in good form for the Riverside club his chances in the Premiership where limited and he made only 12 senior appearances in his first three years on Teesside. He went back on loan to Hillsborough in January 2000 (4 games).

BERRY, George Frederick

A strong-tackling, determined and wholehearted central defender who became a firm favourite with the fans wherever he played, George Berry was born in the town of Rostrop, West Germany on 19 November 1957.

His father was a Jamaican, his mother Welsh (she came from Mountain Ash, Glamorgan) and he had a Scottish grandfather. Berry, who was educated at Holy Trinity and St. Thomas of Canterbury Schools (both in Blackpool), joined Wolves as a youngster in 1973 after playing junior

George Berry

football for Bipsham FC (Blackpool) and in Handsworth (Birmingham) as well as having trials with Ipswich Town. He turned professional in November 1975 (aged 18) and went on to give Wolves sterling service, helping them win the Football League Cup in 1980. He left Molineux for Stoke City in the summer of 1982 and went on to star in 260 competitive matches for the Potters, scoring 30 goals, a third of them from the penalty spot.

He had a loan spell with Doncaster Rovers in 1984 and rounded off his senior career with brief spells at Peterborough United, Preston North End and Aldershot. In 1992 he teamed up with Stafford Rangers, later becoming their Commercial Manager.

Four years later Berry left Stafford to take a full-time job with the P.FA, working alongside Chief Executive Gordon Taylor and Brendan Batson. And in 1998 he took a position with P.FA Enterprizes Ltd. (Manchester branch). Berry won five full caps for Wales - his first ironically against West Germany! He was granted a Testimonial whilst with Stoke City and during his stay at The Victoria Ground he also had his own local radio programme on BBC Radio Stoke.

Wolves' record: 160 apps. 6 goals.

BEST, Robert

Bobby Best was born in the village of Mickley on 12 September 1891. He was an enterprising outside-right, who was signed from Sunderland in June 1922.

He spent less than a season at Molineux before leaving for Durham City in May 1923, later assisting Hartlepools United (1924-27). Prior to joining Sunderland in August 1911, Best had been with Mickley Colliery FC.

His record for the Wearsiders was 25 goals in 94 outings.

Wolves' record: 23 apps.

BETTELEY, Richard Harold

Dick Betteley had five excellent years at Molineux and afterwards he spent a further six seasons with West Bromwich Albion, whom he helped win the Second Division championship in 1911.

A very consistent performer Betteley was born in Bradley, Bilston on 14 July 1880. He played for Bilston Schools, Bradley Athletic, Priestfield Albion, Bilston St. Leonard's and Bilston Utd before signing for Wolves in Aug 1901.

A fee of £100 took him to The Hawthorns in May 1906 and after his service with the Baggies he rounded off his career with a second spell at Bilston United, retiring through injury in May 1914. Betteley later ran the Town Hall Stores in Bilston.

Wolves' record: 123 apps. 1 goal.

BEVIN, Frederick Walter

Tricky inside-forward with good, solid shot, Fred Bevin spent three seasons with Wolves, acting mainly as a reserve.

Born in Walsall circa 1880, he played initially for Walsall

Dynamos and then Darlaston before moving to Molineux in August 1903.

Ironically he made his League debut against the team he supported as a lad - West Bromwich Albion - occupying the left-wing position from where he scored at The Hawthorns in a 2-1 win in a Second Division encounter.

He also netted in the next match, at home to Aston Villa in front of 12,000 fans and played in nine games that season.

The following year - 1904-05 - he had 22 outings (19 in the League, three in the FA Cup) and netted four goals including a hat-trick in a 5-3 home win over Middlesbrough in the League.

He also scored a cracking goal in an FA Cup 2nd round tie against Southampton at Molineux, when almost 30,000 fans saw Wolves beaten 2-1. His last seven games for the club came in 1905-06.

He left Wolves in May 1906 for Stourbridge and later assisted Bilston (from May 1907) and Bloxwich Strollers (1909).

Wolves' record: 38 apps. nine goals.

NB - Some reference books spell his name as Bevan.

BICKNELL, Roy

Centre-half Roy Bicknell graduated through the junior ranks at Molineux, but his career with Wolves was curtailed owing to World War Two and he left the club for Charlton Athletic in May 1947.

Born in Doncaster on 19 February 1926, he came south in 1942 and turned professional with Wolves three years later, having guested for Notts County and Swindon Town in the War. From The Valley he went to Bristol City (June 1949 - June 1952) and rounded off his League career with Colchester United, retiring in May 1955 after a brief spell with Gravesend & Northfleet.

He then ran a cafe and later managed Clacton Town (from April 1958-60). Bicknell became a bookmaker in 1963.

Wolves' record: one app.

BIGGINS, Steven James

A good player in the lower Leagues, centre-forward Steve Biggins was born in Walsall on 26 June 1954, and served with Hednesford Town before breaking into League football with Shrewsbury Town in December 1977, following his £6,000 move from Cross Keys. In July 1982 he switched to Oxford United for £8,000 and then a £20,000 transfer took him to Third Division Derby County in October 1984.

He was still at the Baseball Ground when he served with Wolves, on loan, during March/April 1985. He later assisted Port Vale, also on loan, in March 1986 and after a brief spell in Sweden with FC Trelleborg, he signed as a non-contract player with Exeter City (October 1986), later assisting for Telford United (gaining a runners-up medal in the 1988 FA Trophy Final) and Worcester City.

Wolves' record: 4 apps.

BIRCH, Alan

Brother of Paul Birch (q.v), Alan Birch was an enthusiastic goalscoring midfielder. Born in West Bromwich on 12 August 1956 he had three trial games with West Bromwich Albion in 1971, before joining Walsall as an apprentice in 1972, turning professional at Fellows Park in August 1973. From the Saddlers he went to Chesterfield for £40,000 in July 1979 and two years later Wolves secured his services for the healthy sum of £180,000. Unfortunately Birch never fitted in at Molineux and after barely seven months at the club he moved to Barnsley in February 1982, returning to Chesterfield (August 1983) and thereafter having spells with Rotherham United (March 1984), Scunthorpe United (June 1986) and Stockport County (December 1987 to April 1988).

All told Birch scored more than 100 goals in well over 500 appearances in senior football. He helped Chesterfield beat Glasgow Rangers to win the Anglo-Scottish Cup in season 1980-81.

Wolves' record: 18 apps.

BIRCH, Brian

Brian Birch was a brainy inside-forward with good ball control who gained England Youth caps as a teenager before going on to score over 60 goals in more than 200 appearances in his 12 years at senior club level.

Born in Salford near Manchester, on 18 November 1931, Birch represented Salford Boys and England & Great Britain Schools before joining Manchester United as a junior in 1946, turning professional in May 1949. He moved from Old Trafford to Molineux in March 1952, but spent only nine months with Wolves before transferring to Lincoln City in December of that year.

Afterwards Birch's career took him everywhere ..to Boston United (1955), Barrow (June 1956), Exeter City (for £3,000 in September 1958), Oldham Athletic (January 1960), Rochdale (£750 in March 1961), coach in the Phillipines (from June 1962), Mossley FC (1963), coach to the Australian club, Sydney FC (from February to August 1964), Ellesmere Port as a player (for six months: August 1966 to January 1967) and finally as junior coach with Blackburn Rovers (from November 1967 to May 1968). He was very popular with the press!

Wolves' record: 3 apps. one goal.

BIRCH, Paul

Born in Birmingham on 20 November 1962, Paul Birch, a right-sided midfield player, with flair and stamina, began his career as an apprentice with Aston Villa.

He turned professional in July 1980 and went on to score 29 goals in 219 first-class appearances over the next eleven years with the Villa. He won a European Super Cup medal in 1982 and helped them clinch promotion from Division Two in 1988, as well as gaining an FA Youth Cup winners medal in 1980.

In February 1991, Birch was transferred to Wolves for £400,000 and he certainly gave the Molineux club

Paul Birch

BISHOP, Alfred John

Born in the heart of the Black Country, in Stourbridge, on 8 April 1866, Alf Bishop began his Football League career as a powerful centre-half with Wolves in December 1906 after signing from Halesowen.

He switched to the wing-half position the following season, and went on to give the Molineux club supreme service until 1920.

As well as team skipper, he was also the driving force behind most attacks and despite being only 5ft 8ins tall, he battled it out with the toughest players in the game, never shirking a tackle.

Bishop won a FA Cup winners' medal in 1908 when he lined up in the middle line with Billy Wooldridge and the Reverend Kenneth Hunt. An ever-present in Wolves' ranks on four occasions, he guested for Merthyr Town in 1917 and returned to play in six Victory League games for Wolves in 1919. On leaving Molineux in July 1920, Bishop signed for Wrexham, but spent only a short time with the Welsh club before retiring in 1923.

Wolves' record: 357 apps. 6 goals.

BISSET, George

George Bisset was a useful winger or inside-forward who joined Wolves from Old Trafford in November 1921 and left Molineux for Pontypridd in February 1924.

In his time with the club he worked very well alongside Sammy Brooks and centre-forward George Edmunds, being strong and competent.

Born in Cowdenbeath, Scotland on 25 January 1897, he started off with Glencraig Thistle, played next for Third Lanark (1914-15), and during the Great War served in the Army. In November 1919, he teamed up with Manchester United, making 42 appearances for the Reds, some in place of the great Billy Meredith.

After his spell with Pontypridd (January-May 1924), Bisset spent two years with Southend United, retiring in May 1926.

NB - Bisset's name has sometimes been seen spelt as Bissett.

Wolves' record: 44 apps. 10 goals.

BLACK, David Gibson

When David Black joined Wolves in July 1893, he was already a Scottish international, having gained what was to be his only cap four years earlier against Ireland.

Able to play at inside or outside-left, he was a small but strong runner, good on the ball who was perhaps too greedy at times, but nonetheless was quite a handful for his opponents.

Born in Hurlford, Ayrshire on 22 January 1870, Black

---

excellent service during his five-year stay, which lasted until 1996 when, after a brief loan spell with Preston North End (March 1996), he moved to Doncaster Rovers (July 1996), before joining Exeter City in March 1997.

Birch was granted a Testimonial Match in August 1991 (Aston Villa v. Wolves).

In July 1998, he made his debut for non-League side Halesowen Town.

Wolves' record: 149+17 sub apps. 19 goals.

BIRD, Horace

Outside-right Horace Bird was basically a reserve team player with Wolves during the first two seasons after World War One (1919-21).

Born in Smethwick circa 1895, and now deceased, he played for Handsworth Victoria and Walsall reserves before moving to Wolves and after leaving Molineux he assisted Bloxwich Strollers.

Wolves' record: 3 apps.

played his early football for his home-town club, Hurlford and in 1889 was transferred to Grimsby Town. Two years later he switched to Middlesbrough and moved south to Molineux in 1893. Ten months after scoring for Wolves in the 1896 FA Cup Final defeat by Sheffield Wednesday, Black left the club for Burnley.

He then had a useful spell with Tottenham Hotspur in the Southern and Western Leagues before switching across London to join Woolwich Arsenal in May 1898. He later returned to Scotland to assist Clyde before retiring in the summer of 1900.

Wolves' record: 83 apps. 17 goals.

BLACK, John

A Scotsman from Helensburgh (born on 10 November 1957) left-winger John Black played for Wolves' second and third teams for three seasons before breaking into the senior side during the 1977-78 campaign.

Having turned professional at Molineux in December 1975, he failed to make an impression and left the club for Bradford City in January 1980, later spending the 1983-84 season with Hereford United before dropping into non-League football where he stayed until 1988.

Wolves' record: 6 apps.

BLACKETT, Joseph

Left-back Joe Blackett was recruited by Wolves in readiness for the 1896-97 season, following the departure of George Fleming, Tommy Dunn and Harry Wood.

A strong player, with excellent kick, he fitted in very well alongside Jack Eccles, playing with equal skill and dexterity.

Born in Newcastle-upon-Tyne in June 1875, he played first for Newcastle United's reserve side and after a spell with Gateshead (from May 1895) he joined Loughborough Town in June 1896. From there he switched to Wolves (May 1896) and was an ever-present in his initial campaign at Molineux, missing only one game in 1898-99 and just one the following season.

To everyone's surprise he was then snatched away from Wolves by Derby County in April 1900. But while at The Baseball Ground, Blackett suffered ill-health, and likewise when serving with Sunderland (from April 1901) and Middlesbrough (October 1901 to May 1905).

He later assisted Luton Town (to June 1906) and Leicester Fosse (to May 1909 - signed for £115). A three-year stint as player-manager of Rochdale followed (to May 1912) and he next served with Barrow (June 1912 - July 1913) before rounding off his footballing life as Reading's trainer from August 1913 to May 1915 when he enlisted for WW1 service.

Blackett represented an England XI in the Annual Players' Union international at Ibrox Park in March 1900 and was selected for the Football League against the Irish League in Belfast in October 1904. He helped Middlesbrough win promotion in 1902 and guided Rochdale to the championship of the Lancashire Combination.

Blackett spent four years in the Army during World War One and made over 300 appearances at club level.

Wolves' record: 103 apps. 12 goals.

BLACKHAM, Arthur Thomas

Born in Blakenhall, Wolverhampton in July 1859, Arthur Blackham attended and played for St. Luke's School, and after serving with Stafford Royal, joined Wolves in August 1883.

He managed only a season with the club before he was forced into early retirement in May 1884 after breaking a leg playing wing-half in a Birmingham Cup-tie against Aston Cross the previous December.

After this set back he became Wolves' official linesman (1885) and also worked on the club's Committee, looking after travel arrangements.

Later on he was appointed steward of the Blakenhall Conservative Club, holding office for over four years before taking over as licensee at The British Crown (on Dudley Road). He was steward of the Bilston-based Conservative Club after that and in the meantime also ran a successful general stores in Colway Road, Wolverhampton.

A fine cricketer-footballer, Blackham also enjoyed a round of golf and was keen on horse racing.

Wolves' record: 15 apps. 7 goals.

BLACKWELL, Steven Geoffrey

Born in Wolverhampton on 8 June 1967, Steve Blackwell was a member of the successful Wolverhampton Town Boys side before joining Wolves on the YTS, turning professional in November 1984. He failed to make the grade as a midfielder and was released by the club the following year. In season 1998-99 Blackwell was playing for non-League Wednesfield. A Wolves supporter as a lad, Blackwell was later arrested after allegedly being involved in a criminal offence.

Wolves' record: 1 app.

BLADES, Paul Andrew

Defender Paul Blades began his playing career as a junior with Derby County, turning professional at The Baseball Ground in December 1982.

An England Youth international, he appeared in 200 games for the Rams and gained a Second Division championship medal in 1987 before transferring to Norwich City for £700,000 three years later.

From Carrow Road he joined Wolves, manager Graham Turner paying £325,000 for his services in August 1992. He did very well at Molineux, performing in both full-back berths as well as a central defender.

Blades left Molineux for Rotherham United for £10,000 in July 1995, and the following year helped the Millers win the Auto Windscreen Shield at Wembley.

In June 1997 he moved to non-League Hednesford Town,

teaming up with former Molineux colleague Robbie Dennison.

Blades became player-manager of Gresley Rovers in readiness for the 1999-2000 season.

Wolves' record: 127 apps. 3 goals.

BLAIR, Andrew

Scotsman Andy Blair is one of the few players to score a hat-trick of penalties in a major competition - achieving the feat for Sheffield Wednesday against Luton Town in a Milk Cup-tie at Hillsborough in November 1984.

A stylish midfielder, Blair was born in Kirkcaldy on 18 December 1959 and attended Nicholas Chamberlain School at Bedworth.

He played for Bedworth Juniors and Warwickshire County Boys before joining Coventry City as an apprentice in July 1975, turning professional in Oct 1977. A shade under four years later he was transferred to Aston Villa for £300,000 and it was from there that he switched to Wolves for a three-month loan spell (October-December 1983).

In August 1984 he left Villa Park for Sheffield Wednesday for £60,000, but in March 1986 he returned to Villa Park for a fee of £100,000.

Loan spells with Barnsley (March/April 1988) and Northampton Town (March/April 1989) preceded his move to Kidderminster Harriers in August 1989 and afterwards Blair assisted Nuneaton Town prior to taking a coaching job with Racing Club of Warwick in 1991-92.

Capped five times by Scotland at Under-21 level, Blair made his Villa debut at Wembley in the 1981 Charity Shield draw with Spurs; he was on the bench when Villa won the European Cup in 1982 and helped them lift the European Super Cup in season 1982-83. He made over 200 League appearances all told.

Wolves' record: 10 apps.

BLAKE, Mark Anthony

Midfielder Mark Blake was born in Nottingham on 16 December 1970 and signed professional forms for Aston Villa in July 1989 after two years as an apprentice. Following a loan spell with Darlington (October 1990 when he played alongside ex-Wolves star Steve Mardenborough) Wolves also acquired him on loan in January 1991, and in May 1993 he was transferred by Villa to Portsmouth for £400,000.

Ten months later, in March 1994, Blake became Leicester City's record buy when he moved from Fratton Park to Filbert Street for £360,000. Released by Leicester in May 1996, three months later signed for Walsall, later signing for Kidderminster Harriers (August 2001).

Capped by England at Schoolboy and Youth team levels, he went on to play in nine Under-21 internationals for his country.

Wolves' record: 2 apps.

BLAKE, Nathan Alexander

Welsh international striker Nathan Blake joined Wolves from Blackburn Rovers for £1.5 million in mid-September 2001.

Born in Cardiff on 27 January 1972, he was a trainee with Chelsea before signing professional forms for his home town club, Cardiff City, in August 1990. He scored 40 goals in 164 games for the Bluebirds prior to his transfer to Sheffield United for £300,000 in February 1994.

Once a goalscorer, always a goalscorer and Blake, strong and mobile, continued to bulge the net during his time at Bramall Lane, claiming another 35 goals in only 75 outings for the Blades who then sold him to Bolton Wanderers for £1.5 million in December 1995.

During his time with the Trotters, he passed the milestone of 100 League goals in his career and went on to register a total of 48 for the Lancashire club who then allowed him to leave The Reebok Stadium for neighbouring Blackburn Rovers in a £4.25 million deal in October 1998.

Injuries hadn't helped his game during his latter months with Bolton and he continued to struggle to retain full fitness at Ewood Park, although he did net another 15 goals 62 outings for Rovers as they strove to reclaim their Premiership status. Then, with several newcomers arriving at the club, Blake was sold by manager Graeme Souness to Wolves who have already benefitted from his experience in the goalscoring stakes.

Capped 20 times by his country at senior level, Blake has also wore the red of Wales in youth, Under-21 and 'B' internationals.

He was a Welsh Cup winner with Cardiff in 1992 and 1993, also gaining a Third Division championship medal in the latter year. In 1997 he helped Bolton reach the Premiership as Division One champions.

Wolves' record: 10 apps. 3 goals.*

BLUNT, William

Hard-shooting inside-forward Billy Blunt was signed by Wolves from Stafford Rangers in August 1908 as cover for Jack Shelton, George Hedley and Walter Radford.

He played mainly in the reserves during his first season at Molineux, but then burst into life the following campaign when he top-scored with 27 goals, including four-timers against Leicester Fosse (League) and Reading (FA Cup).

He was then surprisingly transferred to Bristol Rovers in the summer of 1912, following the emergence of the two Needhams.

Blunt, who was born in Bilston in 1886 and educated in Stafford, later assisted Bath City and Taunton Town. He retired in 1916 and died in 1962, aged 76.

Wolves' record: 61 apps. 42 goals

NB - Billy Blunt's younger brother, Sidney, (born in April 1902) was also associated with Wolves (as a reserve), as well as playing for Worcester City, Bilston United, Lichfield City, Port Vale, Shrewsbury Town and Hednesford Town.

BONSON, Joseph

One-time schoolboy sprint champion in Yorkshire, Joe Bonson was a hefty six-footer who played as an inside or centre-forward.

He progressed through the junior ranks at Molineux (with Wath Wanderers) and signed  professionally in July 1953. In season 1953-54 he netted 48 goals for Wolves 'A' team in the Birmingham League, claimed 14 in the FA Youth Cup and four in the Central League. His first team outings, however, were limited owing to the presence of some fine forwards, and in November 1957 Bonson was sold to Cardiff City for £5,000. In June 1960 he moved to Scunthorpe United (in an exchange deal involving Peter Donnelly) and thereafter served with Doncaster Rovers (February 1962), Newport County (June 1962), Brentford (June 1964) and Lincoln City (January - May 1967). In a fine career he hit 132 goals in 313 Football League games.

Wolves' record: 12 apps. 5 goals.

BOON, Reginald

Reggie Boon was an orthodox centre-forward who signed for Wolves in May 1905 from Stafford Rangers.

A local man, born in Wolverhampton circa 1880, he served with a number of Midland-based non-League teams including Tettenhall and Featherstone Rangers after leaving Molineux.

Wolves' record: 3 apps. 1 goal.

BOOTH, Charles

Charlie Booth was born in Gainsborough in 1869 and joined Wolves at the age of 20 from his home-town club Gainsborough Trinity in August 1889.

He spent three seasons at Molineux, occupying in the main, the outside-left position. In May 1892 he left Wolves for Royal Arsenal and later assisted Loughborough Town (1894-95).

Wolves' record: 73 apps. 10 goals.

BOOTH, Colin

Raven-haired Colin Booth was a fine marksman who netted over 150 goals in almost 350 senior appearances at club level.

A Lancastrian, born at Middleton near Manchester on 30 December 1934, he attended and played for Newton Heath Secondary School and starred for Manchester Boys v. Swansea in the English Schools Final of 1950.

An England Schoolboy international trialist, he also skippered the Lancashire Boys County FA Representative side before joining Wolves as a junior in June 1950, turning professional in January 1952. Booth battled hard

to earn a place in Wolves' first XI and when he did play he always gave a good account of himself.

He helped the Wanderers win the League title in successive seasons: 1957-59, and also gained an England Under-23 cap. He left Molineux for Nottingham Forest in October 1959 for £20,000.

In August 1962 he transferred to Doncaster Rovers and signed for Oxford United for a then record fee of £7,500 in July 1964 before retiring through injury in May 1967.

Wolves' record: 82 apps. 27 goals.

BOSWELL, Alan Henry

Alan Boswell was an eccentric goalkeeper, yet still had an excellent career between the posts.

Born in Wednesbury on 8 August 1943, he was educated in Walsall and represented South-east Staffs Schools as a teenager before signing for Walsall as a junior in 1958, turning professional at Fellows Park in August 1960.

He made his League debut for the Saddlers in November 1961 and played over 60 games for the club before moving to Shrewsbury Town in August 1963. Whilst at Gay Meadow, he amassed 222 League appearances, up to September 1968, when he was recruited to Molineux by Wolves boss Ronnie Allen, who signed him as cover for Phil Parkes. Unfortunately, after only a handful of first team outings and being reluctant to play in the reserves, he left Molineux to join Bolton Wanderers in October 1969. In July 1972 he returned to the Midlands to sign for Port Vale, playing in almost 100 games for the Valiants up to May 1974. He then had a brief spell with Blackburn Rovers before teaming up with Oswestry Town (1975-80). After that he chose to play in charity matches up to 1985. In his senior career Boswell made almost 500 appearances, 435 at League level.

As a Vale player, he was sent-off for fighting against Swansea City in April 1973.

Wolves' record: 10 apps.

BOSWELL, William

Billy Boswell began his career as a wing-half, but developed into a direct inside-forward, who spent a long time in the game.

Born in Cradley Heath on 5 August 1902, he played for Tansey Green Rovers, Coombe Wood Colliery and Walsall (from December 1924) before joining Wolves in May 1925. He spent a little over two seasons at Molineux (mostly in the reserves) before transferring to Gillingham in November 1927.

From there he moved to Worcester City (July 1928) and afterwards assisted Burton Town (December 1930), Oldham Athletic (signed for £275 in January 1932), Burton Town again (April 1932) and finally Kidderminster Harriers (June 1934 - May 1936).

He won two Birmingham League championship medals with Worcester (1928-29 and 1929-30) when he scored 90 goals (44 and 46 respectively).

Wolves' record: 9 apps. 5 goals.

BOTTO, Anthony Lewis

Goalkeeper Lewis Botto was born in Jarrow on 12 July 1898, and after 'learning the game' with Hebburn Colliery, Durham City (August 1923 - June 1926), Stockton and then Shildon, he moved to Molineux in May 1927 where he contested the No.1 position with Noel George, Jack Hampton and Alf Canavon.

Botto spent less than two years with Wolves before transferring to Norwich City in February 1929 - and when making his debut for the Canaries, his name on the team-sheet was down as G O Alie - and quite regularly afterwards he was referred to as A L Blotto!

In September 1929, he moved from Norwich to Nelson and two months later was back in the North East with Jarrow FC. He retired in May 1932 and died in Jarrow on 4 June 1953.

Wolves' record: 16 apps.

BOTTRILL, Walter Gibson

Yorkshireman Walter Bottrill was a strong inside-forward - a clever schemer, over elaborate at times - who served with six different League clubs over a period of 15 years: 1922 to 1936 inclusive.

Born in Elston, Yorkshire on 8 January 1903, he started his career with South Bank FC, then assisted Middlesbrough (1922-24), Nelson (1924-28), Rotherham United (1928-29), York City (1929-30), Wolves (from 20 July 1930 to 16 June 1933), Huddersfield Town (signed for £2,000 - 1934-35) and finally Chesterfield.

He retired through injury in 1936 after scoring 105 goals in 314 League appearances at club level.

Bottrill later became a publican in Yorkshire.

Wolves' record: 109 apps. 44 goals.

BOULD, George

Inside-forward George Bould was a Wolves player for just one season: 1907-08.

Born in Tettenhall in 1885, he played for Goldthorn Alexandra, St. Saviour's FC and Penkridge before moving to Molineux. On leaving Wolves Bould assisted Darlaston and then Bilston Town, retiring during the Great War.

Wolves' record: 6 apps. 1 goal.

BOWDLER, John Charles Henry

Born in Shrewsbury on 24 April 1869, Jack Bowdler was an inside or outside-left who won five caps for Wales between 1890 and 1894.

After skippering the Shrewsbury Public School team (a soccer stronghold), he helped found Shrewsbury Town Football Club (in 1886) and spent four excellent years at The Old Racecourse Ground, Copthorne, being regarded as the Shrews best player in 1889-90, when he performed on both wings with dash and enterprise.

So much so that in August 1890 - after he had won three Welsh Cup winners medals in successive seasons from 1887 - Bowdler became the first Shrewsbury Town player to join a Football League club when he moved to Molineux for a fee of £50.

He stayed two years with Wolves (appearing in two FA Cup semi-finals) and after a season with Blackburn Rovers (1892-93) he returned to Shrewsbury where he stayed until May 1897, Rovers having made a fruitless attempt to re-sign him in 1895.

In 1895, Bowdler qualified as a solicitor and later served Shrewsbury Town as secretary and then chairman.

In 1901 he came to Shrewsbury's financial rescue by putting in money from his personal savings to keep the club afloat. Bowdler was a member of the Shropshire FA and served on the town's council from 1901.

During the First World War he was a corporal in the Shropshire Regiment and for some years acted as an agent for the local MP.

Wolves' record: 25 apps. 3 goals.

BOWEN, George

A hard-shooting inside or centre-forward, George Bowen moved to Molineux from the Staffordshire League side Bridgetown Amateurs in July 1899, as cover for Billy Beats. Born in Walsall circa 1875, he was a first team regular during the 1900-01 campaign, but then left the club to sign for Liverpool (with George Fleming) in May 1901.

After struggling to get into the Liverpool side, making only two appearances, he returned to Molineux for a second spell in November 1901 and left for Burslem Port Vale in June 1904.

Bowen retired from League soccer in April 1906 and went to work in a factory in Bilston, but continued to play local football for various non-League clubs.

Wolves' record: 56 apps. 16 goals.

BOWEN, Thomas George

Tommy Bowen was a forceful inside-right, forever involved in the action, who was recruited by Wolves from Walsall in March 1924 (with Ben Timmins) in a combined deal worth £130. Standing only 5ft 5ins tall he spent five seasons at Molineux, up to June 1928, when he was transferred to Coventry City.

He quit League football when he left Highfield Road and moved to Kidderminster Harriers in August 1930.

Bowen was born in West Bromwich on 16 January 1900 and played for Bush Rangers before having a brief spell as an amateur with Birmingham (1920), signing for Walsall in July 1921. As a Coventry player he gained representative honours when appearing for the

Birmingham & District side against the FA XI in September 1925.

Bowen scored 17 goals in 81 games for Walsall.

Wolves' career: 94 apps. 24 goals.

NB. Bowen's son, Tom junior, played for Walsall and Newport County.

BOXLEY, Frank

Goalkeeper Frank Boxley was a Black Country man through and through.

Born in Cradley Heath in August 1887, he joined Wolves from Cradley St. Luke's in April 1909, immediately after winning a Junior international cap for England against Scotland.

Brought to Molineux initially as cover for Tommy Lunn, he was a first team regular from September 1910 until February 1912 and was perhaps unlucky to lose his place in the side to Teddy Peers.

Strong and physical, he left Molineux in April 1912, when he transferred to Shrewsbury Town, later having a brief spell with Wellington Town.

During the First World War, he badly injured his back, which forced him into an early retirement at the age of 30.

Wolves' record: 74 apps.

BRADBURY, Shaun

Shaun Bradbury made his senior debut for Wolves in October 1991, wearing the No. 9 shirt against Shrewsbury Town in a Football League Cup-tie at Gay Meadow.

His Football League baptism followed more than six months later when he scored two cracking goals in a 3-1 win over Millwall.

Unfortunately he failed to maintain this form and in May 1994 he joined Hereford Utd, later assisting Shifnal Town.

Bradbury, who was born in Birmingham on 11 February 1974, joined Wolves as an apprentice in June 1990 and turned professional in June 1992.

Wolves' record: 3 apps. 2 goals.

BRADFORD, John

Jack Bradford was a solid, chunky left-half who was always involved in the action.

A real tough-nut he was born in Pilsey, Derbyshire on 9 April 1895 and played for Hucknall Byron FC and Grimsby Town (from May 1920) before joining Wolves in March 1924. He was an ever-present in the Wanderers side in his first season, lining up across the middle with Mitton and Caddick.

He left Molineux for Bournemouth in October 1927 and later assisted Letchworth Town (as player-coach from May 1931).

Bradford's cousin John William Bradford played for Birmingham and Walsall.

Wolves' record: 80 apps.

BRADLEY, Claude

Claude Bradley was a lithe wing-half, a stern tackler, who spent the 1891-92 season at Molineux.

Born in Walsall in 1868, he played for Birchills FC before signing for Wolves and afterwards assisting Dudley Town.

Wolves' record: 6 apps.

BRADLEY, Patrick J

Pat Bradley was a reserve outside-left, who spent three seasons at Molineux - from July 1924 to May 1927.

Born locally in Wolverhampton in 1901, and now deceased, he left Wolves for Gillingham and later returned to the Midlands to play for Walsall Wood, assisting Brownhills Albion in 1932-34.

Wolves' record: 5 apps.

BRADSHAW, Paul William

Goalkeeper Paul Bradshaw was Wolves' record signing when he joined the club from Blackburn Rovers for £150,000 in September 1977.

Commanding his area well, he was a fine shot-stopper, handled crosses with confidence and remained at Molineux until August 1984, when he signed for Vancouver Whitecaps.

Born in Altrincham on 28 April 1956, Bradshaw represented Altrincham & Cheshire Boys and had trials with Manchester United in 1971 before becoming an apprentice with Blackburn in January 1972, turning professional at Ewood Park in July 1973.

He played for England Youth and made over 80 appearances for Rovers prior to his move to Wolves. He quickly gained a place in the first XI at Molineux and remained there until May 1982, when replaced by John Burridge.

After his spell in the NASL Bradshaw joined West Bromwich Albion (February 1985) being one of Johnny Giles' first recruits after he had taken over as manager at The Hawthorns for a second time. He stayed with Albion until June 1986 and after a coaching spell with Walsall, signed for Bristol Rovers on a non-contract basis, later assisting Newport County (1987-88) before undertaking a second term at The Hawthorns (as understudy to Stuart Naylor). In May 1990 Bradshaw left Albion for Peterborough United, teaming up with former Wolves colleague George Berry.

On retiring from the game in 1992 he returned to live and work in Wolverhampton. Twice voted Wolves 'Player of the Year' in 1981 & 1982, Bradshaw won four England Under-23 caps with Blackburn and in 1980 helped Wolves win the League Cup at Wembley.

Wolves' record: 243 apps.

BRANCH, Paul Michael

Prior to joining Wolves from Goodison Park (initially on loan for two months) before signing for £500,000 (rising, with added clauses to £625,000) on 20 January 2000, pacy and versatile forward Michael Branch had been unable to fulfil his youthful promise owing to a spate of niggling injuries.

Indeed, he had made only 45 first-class appearances for Everton (28 as substitute) and just four on loan for Manchester City. He also went on loan to Birmingham City (October/November 11999) but wasn't called into action by manager Trevor Francis.

He was born in Liverpool on 18 October 1978 and was capped by England at Schoolboy, Youth and Under-21 levels whilst with the Merseysiders.

He linked up very well with Ade Akinbiyi in the Wolves' attack and then assisted George Ndah, Tamuri Ketsbaia and others during the 2000-01 campaign when he was delighted to have played in more than 40 games.

Wolves' record: 71 apps. 9 goals*

BRAZIER, Colin James

Colin Brazier could occupy several positions, mainly in defence and was generally a very steady player, giving nothing away.

Born in Solihull on 6 June 1957, he played for Northfield Town before joining to Wolves as an apprentice in June 1973, turning professional at Molineux in August 1975. He spent the next six seasons vying for a first team place with several quality players and in June 1981 was transferred to the NASL club, Jacksonville Teamen.

He returned to England to sign for Birmingham City in October 1982, but fell out with manager Ron Saunders at St. Andrew's and in March 1983 signed for AP Leamington, quickly re-entering the Football League with Lincoln City the following month. From Sincil Bank he switched to Walsall (August 1983) and then had an excellent spell with Kidderminster Harriers (October 1986 to June 1990).

A League Cup winner with Wolves in 1980 (as sub), Brazier twice represented the England semi-professional team in 1987.

Wolves' record: 91 apps. 2 goals.

BRAZIER, Gilbert

A forceful inside-left, with good speed, Gil Brazier was a regular in the Wolves' side in 1884-85, but then found it difficult to get first team football following the arrival of Harry Wood.

Born in the village of Beckbury near Shifnal in August 1860, he played for Shifnal FC before joining Wolves in April 1884. He left the club in August 1886 to join Lyttleton Rangers.

Wolves' record: 2 apps. One goal.

Paul Bradshaw (centre) in confrontation with Denis Smith (Stoke City)

BREAKWELL, Arthur James

The versatile Archie Breakwell was a strong player with an eye for goal who joined Wolves as a centre-forward from Sedgley in September 1904.

He did very well in the second XI before establishing himself in the senior side the following year, playing superbly well alongside Sid Corfield and Billy Wooldridge. An injury ruined his career at Molineux and in 1907 he was transferred to Brierley Hill, later assisting Bilston. Wolves' record: 24 apps. 3 goals.

BREWSTER, George

Scotsman George 'Dod' Brewster was precisely the right height and build for a centre-half, six feet tall and 13 stones in weight.

He was born in the Aberdonian village of Culsalmond on 7 October 1893 and scored nine goals in 112 appearances for Aberdeen over a period of eight years from August 1912, having earlier gained winners' medals in both League and Cup competitions with the junior club, Aberdeen Mugiemoss.

He guested for Ayr United and Falkirk during the War and in January 1920, left Pittodrie for Everton for £1,200. In November 1922, after almost 70 outings for the Merseysiders, he was transferred to Wolves as manager George Robey sought to bolster up his defence (inside-forward Stan Fazackerley came with him. Sadly Brewster never settled down at Molineux and after spending barely six months in the Midlands he moved to Lovells Athletic (May 1923), quickly switching his loyalties to Wallasey United. From March to August 1924 he coached the Brooklands Wanderers in New York and on his return to Scotland became player-manager of Inverness.

A much-liked and well-respected gentleman, both on and off the field, Brewster was a great sheet-anchor at the heart of the defence, never letting his side down. Wolves' record: 13 apps.

BRICE, Gordon Henry John

When skipper Stan Cullis retired as a player in April 1947, Wolves manager Ted Vizard went out and secured the services (on Cullis' recommendation) of the Luton Town centre-half Gordon Bryce, bringing him to Molineux for just £10,000.

Brice, nicknamed 'Whiz', played in the first quarter of the 1947-48 season but then lost his place in the side to Bill Shorthouse (following a 5-1 defeat at Charlton). He appeared in only one more senior game for the club before being sold to Reading in March 1948. Born in Bedford on 4 May 1924, and educated at Bedford Secondary Modern School, Brice played for Bedford St. Clement's before joining Luton Town as an amateur in June 1939. Owing to World War Two, he had very little time for football, but when peace was restored, he rejoined the Hatters and appeared in over 50 games for the Kenilworth Road club before switching to Wolves.

From Reading, for whom he played in more than 200 games, he went to Fulham (December 1952) and remained at Craven Cottage until May 1956, when he signed for Ayr United. He remained in Scotland where he ran a successful hotel.

A useful cricketer with Northamptonshire and Bedfordshire, Brice scored 412 runs in the County Championship for an average of 13.73. He also took 72 wickets (average 33.69) with a best return of 8-124, and he claimed 14 catches, mainly in the deep. Wolves' record: 12 apps.

BRINDLEY, Christopher Peter

Chris Brindley was a reserve central defender at Molineux from November 1986 to June 1988. He left Wolves to join the Vauxhall Conference side Telford United where he teamed up with another ex-Wanderers star, Paul Grainger. He moved to Kidderminster Harriers for a then record fee for the Aggborough club of £20,000 in August 1992 and helped them win the GM Vauxhall Conference three years later.

Born in Cannock on 5 July 1969, Brindley played for Hednesford Town before embarking on his career with Wolves and in March 1999 he returned to Keys Park for a second spell. Wolves' record: 9 apps.

BROADBENT, Peter Frank

Peter Broadbent was a brilliant inside-forward who spent 14 years with Wolves.

Born in Elvington, near Dover, Kent on 15 May 1933, he played for Dover FC prior to joining Brentford in May 1950 and from Griffin Park he was transferred to Molineux for £10,000 in February 1951.

Playing under manager Stan Cullis, Broadbent was the workhorse in the middle of the field. He helped Wolves win three League championships and the FA Cup as well as gaining seven full England caps plus others at 'B' and Under-23 levels.

He also represented the Football League XI and was the scorer of Wolves' first-ever goal in a major European competition, netting against the German Bundesliga side FC Schalke 04 in the European Cup in November 1958.

Broadbent left Wolves in January 1965 for Shrewsbury Town and later served with Aston Villa, Stockport County and Bromsgrove Rovers. On retiring he opened a baby-wear shop in Halesowen. Jimmy Greaves, who played with Broadbent at

PETER BROADBENT

Peter Broadbent in action in the 1960 FA Cup Final v. Blackburn Rovers

international level, described him thus: "He was the brains of the side, making the team tick with carefully plotted passes. He was an elegant, beautifully balanced player who was a complete master of the ball."

Many supporters who followed the club during the 1950s rate Broadbent the best player ever to don a Wolves shirt! Wolves' record: 497 apps. 145 goals.

BROCKSOPP, Albert Arthur

Archie Brocksopp

Archie Brocksopp played only one season of first team football for Wolves - in 1894-95 - during which time he lined up on the left-wing in three League games.

He was born locally circa 1870 and was signed from Ironbridge. All told he spent three years at Molineux, up to 1896 when he moved to Willenhall.

Wolves' record: 3 apps.

BRODIE, Charles Thomas George

Scotsman 'Chic' Brodie spent seven months with Wolves - from February to September 1961 - during which time he played in one League game, at home against Manchester United on 11 February when he replaced goalkeeper Malcolm Finlayson in a 2-1 win in front of 38,526 fans. In fact, during the year of 1961 Brodie played in three different Divisions of the Football League (4th, 1st and 3rd South) in consecutive League games - for Aldershot on 4 February, then for Wolves and finally for Northampton Town.

Born in Duntocher on 22 February 1937, Brodie began his career in Scotland with Partick Avondale in 1952, gaining schoolboy international honours at the age of 15. In March 1954 he signed as a professional for Manchester City, but failed to break into the first team at Maine Road and left the club for Gillingham in July 1957.

Twelve months later he was transferred to Aldershot and after his spell at Molineux, he played in 87 League games for Northampton Town (up to November 1963) and a further 201 for Brentford (to May 1971).

In a fine career, Brodie amassed a grand total of 466 senior appearances between the posts (403 in the Football League) and, in fact, his League days were brought to an abrupt end by a dog, which ran into him on the field at Griffin Park, causing him injury! On leaving Brentford Brodie assisted Margate and in 1971 was on the receiving end of Ted MacDougall's record-breaking nine-goal bombardment when Bournemouth won a FA Cup-tie against the non-League side by 11-0.

Later on Brodie became a London taxi driver and was involved in a road accident in Westminster - the driver of the other vehicle being no other than Geoff Hurst!

Wolves' record: one app.

BRODIE John Brant

Born in Wightwick village near Wolverhampton on 30 August 1862, Jack Brodie was a splendidly gifted footballer who could, and would, play in any position on the field, having good pace, excellent ball control, a keen eye and powerful shot.

Educated at St. Luke's School, Blakenhall and later a pupil-teacher at Saltley College, Birmingham, Brodie helped form Wolverhampton Wanderers FC in 1877 and he continued to serve the club as a player until retiring in the summer of 1891.

He then took up refereeing which he did outside his teaching duties as assistant headmaster at St. Peter's School, Wolverhampton. In 1913, some thirty-six years after he had initially signed for Wolves, Brodie was opted onto the Board of Directors at Molineux where he was always a very popular person, frequently livening up the proceedings with his witty remarks.

Capped three times by England as an inside-forward between 1889 and 1891, he netted in his first international against Ireland, helping England to a resounding 6-1 victory.

He also claimed Wolves' first competitive goal - scoring against Long Eaton Rangers in the club's initial FA Cup-tie in October 1883.

He was Wolves' top-scorer during the five-year period to 1888 when League football was introduced and at the end of that season he was a bitterly disappointed man as Wolves' skipper when Preston North End beat the Wanderers 3-0 to win the 1889 FA Cup Final.

Brodie guested for neighbours West Bromwich Albion v. Aston Villa in July 1886.

Wolves' record: 65 apps. 44 goals.

BROOKES, Albert Arthur

Signed as cover for full-back Ted Collins, Arthur Brookes (some reference books give the spelling of his surname as Brooks) was a powerfully built player who always put his heart and sole into the game.

A Brummie, born in Small Heath in 1888, he played for Bordesley Rangers and Small Heath Taverners prior to joining Wolves in May 1910. He remained at Molineux until May 1915 when he moved to Newport County.

He made 133 Birmingham League appearances for Wolves in those five seasons.

Brooks did not play competitive football after World War One.

Wolves' record: 14 apps.

BROOKS, Albert Walter

After a brief spell with Rotherham County, rugged right-back or centre-half Albert Brooks (whose surname sometimes appeared with an 'e' ...Brookes) spent three seasons at Molineux, from July 1913 to May 1915.

Playing mostly in the Central League side, he deputised in the first team for Albert Bishop, Bob Young, Albert Groves

and Alf Riley during that time. He played briefly for Newport County after the War, retiring in 1922.
Wolves' record: 18 apps.

BROOKS, Samuel Ernest

Sammy Brooks, a goalscoring left-winger at 5ft. 2ins tall and weighing barely eight stone is one of the smallest and lightest players ever to appear in a first team game for Wolves, doing so between August 1910 and July 1922.

Born in Brierley Hill on 28 March 1890 and educated at Bent Street School, he joined Wolves after service with local teams Brierley Hill Corinthians, Brierley Hill Alliance, Bilston United (September 1906) and Cradley Heath.

Known as the 'Little Giant', he spent 12 seasons at Molineux and after guesting for Birmingham during the War, he moved to London to sign for Tottenham Hotspur. He played only 16 times for Spurs who transferred him to Southend United in December 1923. From there he joined Kidderminster Harriers (June 1925) and finished his career with spells at Cradley Heath and Stourbridge, retiring in 1927.

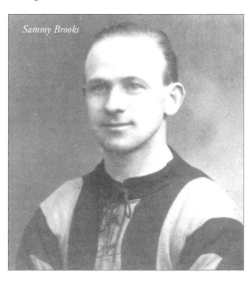
Sammy Brooks

'Capped' by England against Wales in the 1919 Victory international, Brooks also represented the Football League against the Irish League in October 1914 and was a member of the Wolves side which was beaten 1-0 by Spurs in the 1921 FA Cup Final at Chelsea's ground.
NB - Brooks' brother Ernie played for Blackburn Rovers, Wolves (reserves) and Brierley Hill Alliance.
Wolves' record: 246 apps. 53 goals.

BROWN, Henry Stamford

Harry Brown was born Workington on 23 May 1918 and joined Wolves from his home-town club, Workington, in 1938.

Basically a reserve outside-left at Molineux, he played in two away League games for Wolves right at the end of that last pre-war season when Stan Burton moved to Portsmouth.

He was still on the books at Molineux when the War broke out, but after the hostilities made his way to Hull City for whom he appeared in 22 League games in 1946-47 before going back to his native county of Cumbria.
Wolves' record: 2 apps.

BROWN, John

Outside-right Jackie Brown was born in Belfast on 8 November 1914.

He worked and played for William Ewart & Son before joining Belfast Celtic in 1933. From there he joined Wolves (December 1934) and spent two years at Molineux, up to October 1936 when he signed for Coventry City, transferring to Birmingham in Sept 1938. He remained at St. Andrew's throughout the war when he guested for Brighton & Hove Albion, Crystal Palace and Watford. He finally left Blues to sign for Barry Town in January 1948, spending only five months with the Welsh club.

From May 1948 to June 1951 he played for Ipswich Town, before announcing his retirement through injury. Brown - 5ft 8in tall and weighing 11 stones - sprang to fame as a teenager in Ireland whilst serving his apprenticeship in the linen trade. He never really settled at Molineux although he did gain the first three of his ten full caps with Wolves, later adding two Republic of Ireland caps to his collection with Coventry.

He had a direct approach to football and was a fine crosser of the ball.
Wolves' record: 31 apps. 7 goals.

BROWN, William

Scotsman Bill Brown was 6ft 1in tall and weighed just over 12 stones. He was a confident-looking right-half whose cleverness was manifest to everybody.

He served Wolves for one season (1928-29) before losing his place to George Lax.

Born in the town of Burnbank, Hamilton on 17 November 1902, he played for Belshill Athletic and Coventry City (from June 1925 to May 1928).

On leaving Molineux he moved to Norwich City (May 1929) and spent two years with the Canaries before returning to the Midlands to play (as an amateur) for Boulton & Paul Works FC (May 1931 to April 1932).
Wolves' record: 34 apps.

BRYAN, John Thomas

Jack Bryan, a well built, orthodox winger, came into the Wolves side for ten games during the 1899-1900 season, playing mainly on the right.

A native of Wolverhampton he spent three years at Molineux (from July 1898) predominantly as a reserve before leaving the club to join Blakenhall in the summer of 1901. He later played for Willenhall.

Wolves' record: 10 apps. 2 goals.

BRYANT, William
Right-winger Bill Bryant was born in Shildon on 26 November 1913.

A pupil at Timothy Huckworth School in County Durham, he represented Durham Boys and played for Bishop Auckland Training Centre Juniors and Cockfield FC (one game) before joining Wolves in September 1931. He spent two seasons at Molineux, acting as reserve to Mark Crook and Charlie Phillips, leaving Wolves for Wrexham in October 1933. He later served with Manchester United (October 1934), Chester (as a guest in 1941-42), Bradford City (November 1945), Luton Town (1946), Altrincham (1946-47) and Stalybridge Celtic, retiring circa 1950.

He won a Darlington Junior League Championship medal with Bishop Auckland TCJ, gained a Second Division championship medal and Lancashire senior Cup medal with Manchester United in 1935-36 and played in both legs of the Wartime League Cup Final of 1945. He also gained a Hyde Charity Shield medal. On retiring Bryant worked for ICI at Old Trafford in their standardising stores.

Wolves' record: 5 apps.

BRYCE, Frederick
A solidly built Welshman, born in 1905, and now deceased, goalkeeper Fred Bryce conceded 12 goals in his two League outings for Wolves, letting in five at Preston and seven at Fulham in January 1928.

His career collapsed after that and he left Wolves during the following summer to join Nuneaton Borough, later serving with Bedworth and Rugby Town.

He joined Wolves from Flint Town early in 1928.

Wolves' record: 2 apps.

BUCHANAN, Cameron Campbell
Inside-forward Cameron Buchanan was born on 31 July 1928 in Airdrie, Scotland. In September 1942, he created  a footballing record which may never be broken when, at the age of 14 years, 57 days he made his senior debut for Wolves in a Wartime Football League North game against West Bromwich Albion at Molineux in front of 8,382 spectators.

Buchanan went on to play in 18 Wartime games for Wolves, scoring six goals, including a hat-trick against Southampton in 1945. He left Molineux for Bournemouth in August 1949 without ever playing in a major League or FA Cup game for the Wanderers. And after serving the Cherries for over seven years, during which time he scored 19 goals in 83 Third Division (South) matches, he was transferred to Norwich City (October 1956), eventually drifting into non-League football the following year.

In later life Buchanan moved to Devon where he became associated with Tiverton Town. He is now resident in Fife (Scotland) and is a frequent visitor to Molineux.

Wolves' record: No senior appearances.

BUCKLAND, Mark Christopher
Nicknamed 'Buckers', Mark Buckland was a hardworking midfielder, born in Cheltenham on 18 August 1961, who played for AP Leamington for three years before joining Wolves in February 1984.

A scaffold worker by trade, he did well during his time at Molineux and after leaving Wolves (in 1985) he moved to Kidderminster Harriers, later assisting Cheltenham Town and Gloucester City (1992-94).

He won medals with both the Harriers and Cheltenham.

Wolves' record: 56 apps. 5 goals.

BUCKLEY, Major Franklin Charles
Major Frank Buckley was associated with the game of football for 53 years.

One of five brothers, he was born in Urmston, Manchester on 9 November 1882 (three years later his brother Charles who became Aston Villa's chairman, was born on the same day) and after leaving school he enlisted in the Army (1898).

He served in the Boer War and in the summer of 1903, at the age of 22, joined Aston Villa as an attacking defender. Unfortunately he failed to make the grade at Villa Park and in July 1905 was transferred to Brighton & Hove Albion.

In August 1907 he switched to Manchester United and thereafter had spells with Manchester City (to July 1909), Birmingham (to August 1911), Derby County (to July 1914) and Bradford City.

He retired as a player towards the end of the First World War after serving with the 17th Middlesex Regiment (known as the Footballers' battalion) when he became a Commanding Officer, attaining the rank of Major in 1918.

Whilst with Derby, Buckley gained his only England cap (v. Ireland in 1914) having helped County win promotion to the First Division two years earlier.

In March 1919, he was appointed manager of Norwich City, a position he held until May 1920, when he left football briefly to become a Commercial Traveller in London.

In July 1923 he returned to the game as Blackpool's manager and after spending four years at Bloomfield Road, he switched to Molineux, taking over the manager's hot seat in June 1927 from Fred Scotchbrook. Over the next seventeen years Buckley transformed Wolves into a solid and capable First Division side.

They won the Second Division championship in 1932, reached the FA Cup Final in 1939 and clinched the Wartime Football League Cup in 1942. He introduced several quality players to the club, some young, some old, a few already established professionals and a handful of inexperienced ones. Included among his 'finds' were Stan Cullis, Tom Galley, Joe Gardiner, Billy Hartill, Bryn Jones, Wilf Lowton, Jimmy Mullen, Charlie Phillips, Cecil Shaw, Dennis Westcott and Billy Wright. When in charge at Molineux, various headlines in the local and national press referred to Buckley as the 'baby snatcher' and the 'kidnapper' and even the club was called the 'football factory.'

Buckley left Wolves in March 1944, handing over the reins to Ted Vizard.

From May 1946 to May 1948 he was in charge of Hull City and then spent five seasons (to the summer of 1953) as team manager of Leeds United, bringing the great John Charles into the football arena.

After leaving Elland Road, he managed Walsall, announcing his retirement from football in June 1955.

As a player Buckley was a vigorous attack-minded centre-half, who tackled hard but fair. When he took charge at Molineux, he introduced himself to the players and staff without too much superfluous ceremony. Indeed, he immediately handed the players a strict routine, issued each one with a printed rule book and clearly emphasised that these were to be clearly observed at all times, demanding punctuality as well.

He brought in several items of equipment for the gym including a rowing machine. Known as the 'Iron Major' Buckley was unequivocal, progressive, ambitious and voluble. His ideas were freely communicated to the local and national press. He publicly stated that he was totally against the use of the white football (Cowdenbeath had experimented with one in Scotland) and he also revealed that it was he who had initially advocated the numbering of players' jerseys for the benefit of supporters.

Buckley had no illusions whatsoever about coming to Molineux and there was only one test when he moved in....the acid test. Football was like War to him - the team simply had to win matches to succeed! Buckley designed a brand new strip - black and gold vertical striped shirts, black shorts - and his first match in charge saw Wolves draw 2-2 at home with Manchester City.

In his first four seasons in charge Wolves had mixed fortunes in Division Two, before winning promotion in 1932. In 1936-37 Buckley transferred a complete team from Molineux for less than £20,000. In 1938 he sold inside-forward Bryn Jones to Arsenal for a record fee of £14,000 - and immediately bought himself a Welsh terrier and called it 'Bryn Jones.'

It was common knowledge that Major Frank Buckley was a ruthless disciplinarian and the youngsters at Molineux were genuinely afraid of him. But he was a terrific manager, one of the very best, certainly in the Wolves camp.

His record as Wolves manager was played 542, won 225, drawn 114, lost 203 (over 1,000 goals scored).

BUCKLEY, Patrick McCabe

Scottish outside-left Pat Buckley amassed a splendid record in Wolves' reserve team, scoring 55 goals in three complete seasons: 1964-65 to 1966-67, including a haul of 33 in the latter campaign.

Born in Leith on 12 August 1946, he was signed from Third Lanark in February 1964, but his first team outings were restricted owing to the presence of Dick Le Flem and Dave Wagstaffe, and in January 1968 he was transferred to Sheffield United.

He later assisted Rotherham United (from June 1972) and quit first-class soccer the following May (1973).

Wolves' record: 29 apps. 8 goals.

BULL, Stephen George, MBE

Regarded as the greatest goalscorer in Wolves' history, Steve Bull was born in Tipton on 28 March 1965.

On leaving school he worked in a bed-making factory and at weekends played for Tipton Town. In 1984 he joined

Steve Bull

Bully in action

West Bromwich Albion and played in the Baggies' intermediate side before being offered a full professional contract at The Hawthorns in 1985.

After just nine first team appearances for Albion (three goals scored) he was transferred to Wolves by manager Ron Saunders in a deal which also involved Andy Thompson, Bull being valued at £65,000, the transaction going through on 21 November 1986.

He made his Wolves debut the following day (against Wrexham) and scored the first of more than 300 goals for the club against Cardiff City in a Freight Rover Cup-tie at Ninian Park on 2 December. He ended his first 'half season' at Molineux with 19 goals to his name and in 1987-88 netted a staggering 52, collecting a Sherpa Van Trophy winners' medal at Wembley and helping Wolves win the Fourth Division title in the process.

A Third Division championship medal was won the following year and by now he was a cult hero at Molineux. Bull, strong, forceful, determined with a powerful right foot shot, simply couldn't stop scoring. Having earlier represented England at 'B' and Under-21 levels, he won the first of his 13 full caps in May 1989 v. Scotland, scoring to mark the occasion. 'Bully', as he became affectionately known, was also taken by England boss Graham Taylor to the World Cup Finals.

He knows he failed to hit the dizzy heights on the international scene (remember Gary Lineker was around at the same time) but the goals still flowed thick and fast at club level.

He notched another 64 in the League in three seasons (1991 to 1994 inclusive) and in the 1997-98 campaign reached two more personal milestones. He claimed the 300th senior goal of his career (for Albion, Wolves and England) and whipped in his 300th competitive goal for Wolves - the winner in a 2-1 victory over Bradford City at Molineux in February 1998.

Granted a Testimonial in 1996-97 (Wolves v. Santos), Bull agreed to stay at Molineux until the end of his career - despite Wolves twice missing out on the play-offs which may well have brought Premiership football for 'Bully' and of course, for Wolves. And in August 1998 to show he was still goal-hungry he whipped in his 18th hat-trick for the club in a 5-0 League Cup win over Barnet at Molineux. Injuries severely disrupted the 1998-99 season - and how Wolves missed him!

He quit the Football League scene in the summer of 1999 and after a brief coaching spell at Molineux, rejoined his former manager Graham Turner as player-coach of the Conference side, Hereford United. He played in several Conference games for the Bulls before retiring in June 2001 and is now working as a PR officer at Molineux.

Senior football apart, Bully once scored five goals in a friendly for Wolves v. FC Smedly (Sweden) in July 1994 and whilst recovering from injury he rattled in another five against Peterborough United in a third team game!

Bull was awarded the MBE in the Queen's Millennium New Year's honours list.

NB - West Brom boss Ron Saunders allowed Bully to leave The Hawthorns because he thought his first touch wasn't good enough. A year or so after buying him, Wolves manager Graham Turner said: "Okay his first touch still isn't good, but he usually scores with his second."

Wolves' record: 542+17 sub apps. 306 goals.

BUNCH, Walter Wilbert Swanson

Walter Bunch was a reserve defender, capable of occupying several positions, but preferring the full-back berth.

Born in Weston-Super-Mare in 1872, he played for Compton Colts, Willenhall Institute and Blakenhall prior to spending four seasons at Molineux (August 1895 to May 1899). He left Wolves for Walsall and after 72 games for the Saddlers, had a spell with Birmingham (from September 1901 to April 1902, appearing in three games).

He retired through illness and injury in May 1902, although he did turn out occasionally in later years for Stourbridge Swifts and Lye Commadores, playing his last game at the age of 40 in 1905. Bunch then became licensee of the Golden Lion in Chell Street, Dudley before moving to the West Country.

He died in Somerset.

Wolves' record: 7 apps.

BURKE, Mark Stephen

Born in Solihull on 12 February 1969, midfielder Mark Burke joined Aston Villa as an apprentice in June 1985 and turned professional in February 1987.

He won England Schoolboy honours at the age of 15, playing twice at Wembley and scoring a hat-trick against Holland. After becoming a professional he then added Youth caps to his collection, but failed to establish himself at Villa Park, transferring to Middlesbrough for £50,000 in December 1987.

A loan spell with Darlington (October 1990) preceded his move to Wolves for £25,000 in March 1991.

He had some good runs in the first XI at Molineux but after another loan period, this time with Luton Town in March/April 1994, and a trial with Tottenham Hotspur, he moved to Port Vale in August 1994. He remained in the Potteries until May 1995 when he signed for Fortuna Sittard on a free transfer, having had trials with Sporting Lisbon in May-June 1994. He returned to England to play non-League football in the late 1990s.

Wolves' record: 77 apps. 14 goals.

BURLEIGH, James

Utility forward Jim Burleigh spent two seasons at Molineux (from July 1890 to May 1892) playing most of his football in the reserves.

Born locally circa 1869, he remained an amateur throughout his career and after leaving Wolves assisted several non-League teams in and around the Wolverhampton and Willenhall areas.

Wolves' record: 2 apps.

BURNS, William

Irishman Billy Burns had two spells with Wolves - the first from December 1925 to January 1926 and the second during season 1928-29.

A very capable centre-half, born at Newtonards, Belfast in 1904 (and now deceased) he played his early football with Nortonville FC (Belfast) and after unsuccessful trials with Stoke (August-September 1923) he signed for Glentoran. He was transferred to Wolves after gaining County Antrim Shield and Irish League championship medals. After his first spell at Molineux, Burns spent a short time in America before returning to Ireland to assist Dublin Shelbourne and when he left Wolves second time round he signed for Ards.

In June 1929, Burns was recruited by Workington, but he never settled in Cumbria and went back to the Emerald Isle in May 1930 where he rounded off his career by assisting a handful of minor clubs including Belfast St. Peter's.

Once rated the best centre-half in Ireland, Burns was a strong defender, a powerful header of the ball and fearless on the ground.

He represented the Irish League v. The Football League in October 1924 and coached briefly in Washington (USA) in the early 1930s.

Wolves' record: 4 apps.

BURNSIDE, David Gort

Davey Burnside was a ball-playing inside-forward who appeared in more than 450 competitive games in a 20-year career.

Born in Kingswood, Bristol on 10 December 1939, he attended and played for Kingswood Secondary Modern School and represented Bristol & District Boys before signing for Bristol City as an amateur.

In December 1955 he joined the groundstaff at West Bromwich Albion and turned professional at The Hawthorns in February 1957. Over the next five years or so he made 135 appearances for the Baggies, gained England Youth and Under-23 honours and in 1960 entered the European footballers 'Heading' competition which saw him finish runner-up with 495 headers to the Austrian George Kaul's amazing tally of 3,025.

From Albion, Burnside moved to Southampton for £17,000 in September 1962. He played for Crystal Palace from December 1964 to September 1966 when he joined Wolves, linking up again with manager Ronnie Allen, whom he had been with at West Brom and Selhurst Park. After a good spell at Molineux, during which time he helped Wolves regain their First Division status (1967), he left the club in March 1968 and switched south to Plymouth Argyle. He later assisted Bristol City (from December 1971), Colchester United (March 1972), Bath City (as player-manager from April 1972 to March 1973), Walsall (as assistant-manager for half-a-season: August-December 1973), Cadbury Heath (as a player, August

1974 to May 1975), Bridgwater Town (as player-manager, August 1975 to May 1979) and finally Taunton Town (from September 1979 until June 1980).

He then retired to take up coaching, and between July 1983 and December 1996 was associated with the FA, mainly looking after the England Youth side and helping bring through some exceptionally fine players.

Over the last three years or so Burnside has been Director of Youth Football at his former club, Bristol City.

Wolves' record: 43 apps. 5 goals.

BURRIDGE, John

A fitness fanatic all his life, consistent goalkeeper John 'Budgie' Burridge had a superb career between the posts, and when he quit top-class football in 1996-97, he had accumulated an appearance record bettered by only one other keeper in the history of the game - Peter Shilton.

Burridge played in 917 competitive matches at senior club level (over 1,000 if you include friendly matches etc).

He started out with Workington, whom he joined as an apprentice in 1968, turning professional in January 1970. He left the Cumbrian club for Blackpool in a £100,000 deal in April 1971 and over the next 27 years his career went as follows: Aston Villa (signed for £100,000 in September 1975), Southend United (loan, January 1978), Crystal Palace (£65,000, March 1978), Queens Park Rangers (£200,000, December 1980), Wolverhampton Wanderers (£75,000, August 1982), Derby County (loan, September 1984), Sheffield United (£10,000, October 1984), Southampton ((£30,000, August 1987 - to replace Shilton!), Newcastle United (£25,000, October 1989), Hibernian (July 1991), Newcastle United (free transfer, August 1993), Scarborough (free, October 1993), Lincoln City (free, December 1993), Enfield (February 1994), Aberdeen (free, March 1994), Barrow (September 1994), Dumbarton (free, October 1994), Falkirk (November 1994), Manchester City (free, December 1994), Notts County (free, August 1995), Witton Albion (October 1995), Darlington (free, November 1995), Grimsby Town (free, December 1995), Gateshead (January 1996), Northampton Town (January 1996), Queen of the South (March 1996), player-manager of Blyth Spartans (July 1996), Scarborough (on loan, December 1996).

He was part-time goalkeeping coach at both Newcastle United and Leeds United while playing for Blyth Spartans. Burridge won an Anglo-Italian Cup winners medal with Blackpool in 1970, a League Cup winners medal with Villa in 1977, a Second Division championship medal with Crystal Palace in 1979 and a Scottish Premier League Cup winners medal with Hibernian 1991.

'Budgie' helped Wolves win promotion from Division Two in 1983 and the following season was voted the club's 'Player of the Year'.

On 6 November 1993 Burridge became the oldest player ever to line-up in a Football League game for Scarborough - aged 41 years, 338 days v. Doncaster Rovers. And he was

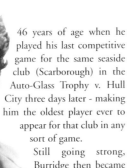

46 years of age when he played his last competitive game for the same seaside club (Scarborough) in the Auto-Glass Trophy v. Hull City three days later - making him the oldest player ever to appear for that club in any sort of game.

Still going strong, Burridge then became the oldest ever Darlington player when he kept goal for the Quakers against Rochdale in an FA Cup-tie in December 1995 at the age of 45.

He had earlier set the record of becoming Lincoln City's oldest-ever footballer, aged 42 years, 57 days, also v. Rochdale, in January 1994. And then, in April 1995, he created yet another record when he became the oldest player to star in the Premiership, keeping goal for Manchester City v. Newcastle United at the age of 43 years, four months and 26 days.

'Budgie' Burridge, who was born in Workington on 13 December 1951, was at loggerheads with Wolves during 1984-85 and at one stage refused to play in goal.

Wolves' record: 81 apps.

BURRILL, Frederick

Fred Burrill could play equally well at left-half or as an inside-forward.

A skilful dribbler, born at Manor Park, East London in 1894, he was recruited by Wolves from Southend United in May 1920, having earlier assisted East London Schools and West Ham United (1911-14).

Two years after appearing in the 1921 FA Cup Final for Wolves against Tottenham Hotspur, he left Molineux to join Charlton Athletic (July 1923). He later assisted Walsall (May 1924 to May 1925) before drifting into non-League soccer (to 1930).

Wolves' record: 69 apps. 17 goals.

BURTON, Stanley

Yorkshireman Stan 'Dizzy' Burton was born at Thurnscoe on 3 December 1912 and died in Sheffield on 10 February 1977.

An out-and-out attacker, driving down the right-wing, he represented Yorkshire Schools at the age of 14 and started his career, in earnest, with Wombwell FC later joining Thurnscoe Victoria (August 1931) from where he switched to Doncaster Rovers (February 1933). Five-and-a-half years later (in September 1938) he was transferred to Wolves for £4,000 - and quickly established himself in the first team.

He left Molineux for West Ham United on 29 April 1939 in a record £6,000 transfer, just five days after having played in the FA Cup Final against Portsmouth.

He then turned out for the Londoners v. Manchester City in the final League game of that season, thus becoming the only footballer in history to appear in the FA Cup Final, and then afterwards in a League match for a different team in the same season. During the War Burton guested for several clubs in Yorkshire inc. Barnsley, Bradford City, Doncaster Rovers, Leeds Utd and Sheffield Wednesday.

Wolves' record: 32 apps. 4 goals.

BUTCHER, Joseph Henry

Joe Butcher's claim to fame was to score all five goals for Wolves in a 5-3 League victory over Accrington in November 1892.

He was also the youngest player on the pitch (at 18) when Wolves defeated Everton 1-0 in the 1893 FA Cup Final.

An out-and-out centre-forward, strong on the ball with a powerful right-foot shot, Butcher was born in Willenhall in February 1875, and joined Wolves from Wolverhampton East End in June 1892.

He spent just over three seasons at Molineux before transferring to West Bromwich Albion for £25 in September 1895. Unfortunately before he could make his

Butcher with ball at his feet in 1893 Wolves team line up

senior debut for the Throstles he suffered a crippling knee injury which forced him into an early retirement aged 21. He chose to go into business in Wolverhampton and certainly had a good life.

Wolves' record: 76 apps. 31 goals.

BUTLER, Paul John

Paul Butler was an eager-beaver wing-forward, who was never really a first team regular at Molineux.

Born in Stockton-on-Tees on 9 June 1964, he joined Wolves as a junior at the age of 16 and turned professional in June 1982. He was on the bench more often than not during the 1982-83 and 1983-84 seasons before becoming surplus to requirements.

At this juncture (January 1984) he went on loan to

C

Hereford United and after Tommy Docherty had taken over as manager, Butler joined the Edgar Street club on a permanent basis in February 1985.

He made almost 120 appearances for the Bulls who then sold him to Hartlepool United in July 1987. He failed to continue his good form at The Victoria Ground and in May 1988 Butler given a free transfer to enter non-League soccer in County Durham.

Wolves' record: 21+14 apps. 2 goals.

BUTLER, Paul John

Born in Manchester on 2 November 1972, centre-half Paul Butler joined Wolves on loan from Sunderland in November 2000, signing on a permanent basis for the Molineux club two months later for £1 million. A strong tackling defender, 6ft 2ins tall and weighing over 13st, he started his career with Rochdale as a trainee, turning professional at Spotland in July 1991 at the age of 18. He made 188 senior appearances for the 'Dale before transferring to Bury for £100,000 in July 1996. Two years and 97 games later, he was secured by Sunderland, boss Peter Reid paying £600,000 for his signature. Unfortunately he lost his place in the Wearsiders' back-line, hence his move to Molineux after he had made almost 100 appearances for the Premiership side.

Capped by the Republic of Ireland at senior and 'B' team levels, Butler helped Bury win the Second Division title in 1997 and Sunderland the First Division championship two years later.

Wolves' record: 15 apps.*

BUTTERY, Arthur John

Regarded as a good schemer, Arthur Buttery was basically a reserve inside-forward during his time at Molineux.

Born in Hednesford on 20 December 1908 (and now deceased) he played for Hednesford Town for four years, while also having unsuccessful trials with Motherwell and Swansea Town, before joining Wolves in November 1929. He spent three years at the club, up to June 1932 when he was transferred to Bury, later assisting Bradford City (January 1937), Walsall (June 1938) and Bristol Rovers (July 1939). He guested for Walsall and Wolves during the World War Two.

Wolves' record: 10 apps. 6 goals.

BYWATER, Stephen Michael

An England Youth and Under-21 international, signed on loan from West Ham United during the early part of the 2001-02 season, 6ft 3in goalkeeper Stephen Bywater was not called into action by Wolves manager David Jones and he duly returned to Upton Park to continue as back-up to Shaka Hislop. Born in Manchester on 7 June 1981, he joined the Hammers for £300,000 in August 1998 after making one league appearance for Rochdale who took him on as a professional at the age of 17. Bywater had also played on loan for Wycombe Wanderers and Hull City

before being engaged by Wolves. He was an FA Youth Cup winner with West Ham in 1999.

CADDICK, William

Centre-half Bill Caddick - whose grandfather William senior had been a reserve team goalkeeper with Wolves between 1880-83 - had seven excellent seasons at Molineux, being a regular in the side in five of those campaigns.

Born at Wolverhampton on 14 March 1898, he attended St. Luke's School until he was 15. He then played for All Saints FC (Wolverhampton) and served with and played for the 3rd Battalion Grenadier Guards (also the Household Battalion) behind the enemy lines between 1916-19.

In 1919-20 he became a professional footballer with Wellington Town (in the highly competitive Birmingham & District League). Both Aston Villa and Wolves then sought his signature and it was the latter who secured his services in December 1920, Wolves signing him as cover for Maurice Woodward and Joe Hodnett. Caddick, who stood 6ft 1in tall and weighed 12 stones, had to wait until 10 March 1921 before making his senior debut (at Stoke) and by the following October he had established himself as a regular member of the first XI, holding his position until Sammy Charnley replaced him in 1925.

Caddick, who helped Wolves win the Third Division (North) championship in 1923-24, returned to Wellington Town in June 1927. After twice helping Stafford Rangers win the Keys Cup (1928 and 1929) he retired in 1931 and later became licensee of the Hop Pole pub on Oxley Moor Road, Wolverhampton.

Wolves' record: 154 apps. 2 goals.

CADDICK, William

Bill Caddick senior was born in Wolverhampton on 20 July 1859.

An ironmonger's clerk, he was a committee member, auditor and goalkeeper for various Wolves teams between 1880 and 1883 but never appeared in a major competitive game.

CALLANAN, William W

Bill Callanan was a solid centre-half, who played mainly reserve team football during his two years with Wolves - June 1907 to May 1909.

Born in Featherstone, Staffs in June 1885, he started his career with Oxley St. Mark's and joined Wolves from Willenhall Pickwick.

He left Molineux to sign for Bilston Town.

Wolves' record: 3 apps.

CAMARA, Mohamed

Born in Conakry, Guinea on 25 June 1975, defender Conny Camara was recruited by Wolves for £50,000 (with another £50,000 to follow after 25 first team appearances) in early September 2000 after serving with Beavais FC and Le Havre (two spells). Standing almost 6ft tall and weighing 11st 9lbs, he was a team-mate of Gus Pollet's at Le Havre. A quarter of his first 20 senior appearances for Wolves came as a substitute.

Wolves' record: 5+16 sub apps.*

CAMERON. Colin

Born in Kirkcaldy, Fife on 23 October 1972, midfielder Colin Cameron joined Wolves for £1.75 million from the Scottish Premier club Heart of Midlothian in September 2001. Previously with Raith Rovers (from 1990) and Sligo Rovers (on loan) he helped Raith lift the Coca-Cola Cup in 1995 as well as starring in two First Division championship triumphs (in 1993 & 1995). Capped by his country at Under-21 level, he joined Hearts in March 1996 for £400,000 (plus John Miller). He did very well at Tynecastle and made over 200 senior appearances for the Edinburgh club.

Wolves' record: 12 apps.*

CANAVON, Alfred

Goalkeeper Alf Canavon joined Wolves from Stafford Rangers in May 1925.

At six feet tall and weighing 12 stones, he certainly looked the part, but found it difficult to get first team football during his three seasons at Molineux owing to the form Noel George. He was, in fact, a regular in the reserves throughout 1925-26 before breaking into League football the following year.

Born in Coventry in 1904, Canavon left Wolves for Shrewsbury Town in July 1928 and later assisted Newtown Albion and Wellington White Star, retiring during the Second World War.

Wolves' record: 15 apps.

CANNON, Alfred Alec

Alec Cannon was a reliable wing-half, who deputised for both Arthur Fletcher and Arthur Lowder during his two seasons with the club.

Born in Cannock circa 1865 (the son of a coal-miner), he played for Cannock Royal and Easington White Rose before joining Wolves in August 1887.

He left Molineux for Kidderminster Harriers in the summer of 1899 and later assisted Springhill Athletic, retiring circa 1901.

Wolves' record: 7 apps.

CARR, William McIanny

Willie Carr was a slightly built but highly effective flame-haired midfielder, who worked tirelessly in the engine-room, feeding his strikers efficiently while grafting hard and long throughout his career.

Born in Glasgow on 6 January 1950, Carr moved south as a youngster and after attending school in Cambridge, he signed as an apprentice for Coventry City (July 1965),

turning professional at Highfield Road two years later. In March 1975 after more than 250 appearances for the Sky Blues he was transferred to Wolves for £80,000 and over the next seven years gave the Molineux faithful some vintage moments.

Carr played six times at full international level for Scotland and also won four Under-23 caps as well as helping Wolves win the Second Division championship in 1977 and the League Cup in 1980. On leaving Molineux in August 1982, he teamed up with Millwall and from The Den he joined Worcester City (August 1983). Later he assisted Willenhall Town and Stourbridge before retiring in 1988.

NB - It was Carr, accompanied by Ernie Hunt (a future Wolves player) who instituted the famous donkey-kick against the reigning League champions Everton in October 1970. When Coventry were awarded a free-kick on the edge of the penalty area, Carr stood over the ball and then casually flicked it up and backwards for Hunt to volley into the net.

Wolves' record: 289 apps. 26 goals.

Willie Carr

CARTER, Edward Thomas

An efficient, well built centre or left-half, Ted Carter stood in for Alf Riley and Albert Kay during his two-year stay at Molineux.

Born in the lakeland town of Harrington, Cumbria in April 1895, he played for Ashington from August 1919 to June 1921 when he joined Wolves.

On leaving Molineux in August 1923 he went back north to sign for Durham Town.

Wolves' record: 17 apps.

CARTWRIGHT, Archibald

A reserve inside-forward for Wolves over a two-year period, from August 1907 to June 1909, Archie Cartwright was born in Wolverhampton in 1885. He played for Bankside Wanderers and Willenhall Pickwick before joining the club and on his departure from Molineux he signed for Bilston Town, later assisting Whitehall Swifts.

Wolves' record: 2 apps.

CARTWRIGHT, Ian James.

A useful player on his day, but one who never really produced consistent form at League level, Ian Cartwright was born at Brierley Hill on 13 November 1964.

He joined Wolves as a youngster on leaving school in the summer of 1980 and turned professional in Sept 1982.

He was released by the club at the end of the 1985-86 season when he moved into local non-League football.

Wolves' record: 61 apps, 2 goals.

CASWELL, Brian Leonard

Brian Caswell had an excellent professional career as a defender or midfielder. He spent 14 years with Walsall - his first club - signing as a junior in June 1971, turning professional in September 1973 and remaining there until August 1985. He played in 458 League and Cup games and scored 19 goals for the Saddlers.

Born in Wednesbury on 14 February 1956, he attended and played for Wood Green School prior to linking up with Walsall and on leaving Fellows Park he joined Doncaster Rovers. He stayed only three months at Belle Vue before transferring to Leeds United. His brief association with Wolves came in January 1987 when he had a month's loan at Molineux.

He retired in May 1987 and later coached at both Birmingham City (1990) and Stoke City.

Caswell still plays in local Charity matches and in 1992 helped the ex-players of West Bromwich Albion win the over 35's Cup Final at Wembley.

Wolves' record: 1 app.

CHADBURN, John

The moustachio'd Jack Chadburn could play as a right-back or right-winger. A plucky footballer, he had good pace and always gave a battling performance.

Born in Mansfield in February 1873, he represented Mansfield & District Schools as a teenager before joining Lincoln City in 1892.

Two years later he moved to Notts County from where he signed for Wolves in October 1897.

He remained at Molineux for a little over two years before transferring to West Bromwich Albion in January 1900. He went on to play in almost 50 first team games for Albion, helping them win the Second Division title in 1902.

In May 1903 Chadburn switched his allegiance to Liverpool, and thereafter had relatively short spells with Barnsley, Mansfield Town (1905), Reading (1906), Plymouth Argyle (1907) and Swindon Town, retiring from competitive football in 1909.

Wolves' record: 12 apps. 1 goal.

CHADWICK, WILFRED

Inside-forward Wilf Chadwick was a soccer 'nomad' and during a lengthy career served with eight different clubs at various levels.

He started out with Bury Juniors in 1917 and then played, in turn, for Nelson (from November 1920), Rossendale United (from August 1921 - he hit 35 goals in 23 games for the Shakers), Everton (signed in February 1922), Leeds United (recruited in November 1925), Wolverhampton Wanderers (from August 1926), Stoke City (transferred for £250 in May 1929) and finally Halifax Town (from October 1930 until May 1932).

He struck 55 goals in 109 League and Cup games for Everton and was top-scorer at Goodison Park in 1923-24 with a total of 30. In his entire League career, the impressive Chadwick netted 104 goals in 251 appearances.

A clever and at times, very creative player, he was born in Bury on 7 September 1900 and died in the same Lancashire town on 14 February 1973.

Wolves' record: 101 apps. 44 goals.

CHAPMAN, Campbell

Born in Sutton-in-Ashfield on 28 June 1963, midfielder Campbell Chapman, son of the former Wolves manager Sammy Chapman and brother of Cavan, began his playing career with Peterborough United whom he joined as an apprentice in 1978, turning professional in July 1981.

He failed to make the grade at London Road and in 1982 joined non-League Bilston Town from where he switched to Wolves in December 1984. He did reasonably well at Molineux before signing as a non-contract player for Preston North End and doing likewise for Crewe Alexandra in November 1986.

He remained at Gresty Road until May 1987 and later took over as player-manager of Willenhall Town (1992-93).

Wolves' record: 58 apps. 4 goals.

CHAPMAN, Cavan

Younger brother of Campbell, Cavan Chapman was also a midfield player, born at Emsworth on 11 September 1967 who came to Wolves on the YTS in June 1983, turning professional in September 1984.

He failed to produce the goods at Molineux and was released by the club in May 1986. He later had an unsuccessful month's trial with neighbours West Bromwich Albion.

His only appearance for Wolves was in the No.9 shirt alongside his brother at Cardiff in a Second Division match in February 1985.

Wolves' record: 1 app.

CHAPMAN, Samuel Edward Campbell

Sammy Chapman had two separate spells in charge of Wolves - the first from August to September 1985 and his second from November 1985 to August 1986.

Former England star Mike Channon was tipped to become the first player-manager in Wolves' history following Tommy Docherty's departure from Molineux in the summer of 1985, but surprisingly Chapman, the club's chief scout at the time, was given the job as caretaker-manager instead.

He was under considerable pressure from the word go, having taken the job as a temporary measure - until Bill McGarry returned to the club. McGarry, in fact, spent just over two months in office (61 days to be precise) and when he left Wolves immediately gave Chapman the opportunity of a second spell in the hot seat.

Born in Belfast on 16 February 1938, he did all he could at Molineux but things never worked out for the Irishman. He gave debuts to 18 players among them Andy Mutch, signed from non-League Southport and defender Floyd Streete.

But out on the park results were a disaster and Wolves slithered into the Fourth Division at the end of the 1985-86 campaign. Chapman struggled on through the summer before handing over the duties to Brian Little. A year after leaving Wolves Chapman was appointed chief scout of Leicester City and had 14 men working for him up and down the country. He is now Youth Development Officer at Filbert Street.

As a player himself, Chapman occupied the wing-half berth and served, in turn, with Shamrock Rovers, Mansfield Town (October 1956), Portsmouth (February 1958) and Mansfield again, from December 1961 to May 1964, when he retired.

He won one 'B' cap for Northern Ireland and appeared in 216 Football League games, scoring 51 goals.

Chapman's record as Wolves manager was played 39, won 9, drawn 10, lost 20.

CHARD, Philip John

During his playing career Phil Chard occupied a number of positions in defence and midfield. Born in Corby,

Northamptonshire on 16 October 1960, he joined Nottingham Forest as an amateur (1975) but failed to make the breakthrough and left to sign for his home team Corby Town (1976) from where he switched to Peterborough United in January 1979. He played well in more than 170 games for Posh before transferring to Northampton Town in August 1985.

After 115 outings for the Cobblers he was signed by Wolves boss Graham Turner in March 1988 and in the next 18 months helped the Wanderers win promotion from the Fourth to the Second Division in successive seasons. Chard left Molineux in October 1989 to rejoin Northampton Town.

He later took over as player-manager (April 1992) and held office until the summer of 1993 when he was replaced by former Wolves boss John Barnwell.

Wolves' record: 38 apps. 5 goals.

CHARNLEY, Samuel

Rather small for a centre-half at 5ft 10ins tall and 11st 9lbs in weight, Scotsman Sammy Charnley was, nevertheless, a sturdy defender, who performed exceedingly well in the Wolves middle line between Jack Mitton and Albert Kay during the mid-1920s.

Born in Craigneuk, near Motherwell in 1902, Charnley (now deceased) moved to Molineux from Burnbank Athletic in January 1925, initially as cover for Billy Caddick.

He remained with Wolves until August 1928 when, following the emergence of Tom Pritchard, he was transferred by Major Buckley to York City, later assisting Dartford and then Kettering Town (September 1929 to May 1931) before moving back to Scotland to round off his career.

Wolves' record: 55 apps. one goal.

CHATHAM, Raymond Harold

Ray Chatham was a real character, the dressing room comedian, who played as a semi-professional throughout his career, being a 'rep' for an engineering firm based in the Midlands.

Born in Wolverhampton on 20 July 1924, Chatham spent most of his childhood in Coventry and as a 16 year-old represented Coventry Schoolboys before joining Wolves the following year from Oxley FC.

Initially a good, honest centre-forward, Chatham was converted into an old fashioned centre-half, hard but fair, who passed the ball shrewdly. During the transitional

Ray Chatham

Wartime season of 1945-46 he scored 16 goals for Wolves, but with Dennis Westcott and Jesse Pye the main attackers, he decided to change positions - for the best. After receiving a benefit in 1950, Chatham was transferred to Notts County (January 1954), but when the Magpies were relegated in 1958, he left Meadow Lane (after more than 130 appearances) and drifted into non-League soccer, ending his career in Kent with Margate.

He retired in 1962 to concentrate on his job as a 'rep' working in London but sadly died a few years ago.

Wolves' record: 86 apps. 2 goals.

CHUNG, Cyril

Sammy Chung managed Wolves for five months - from June to November 1976 - serving between the reigns of Bill McGarry and John Barnwell. Known affectionately as Sammy, Chung was born in Abingdon, Oxford on 16 July 1932 to a Chinese father and English mother, and was a part-time professional with Headington United (now Oxford United) before moving into the Football League as a wing-half with Reading in August 1949. After completing his Army service in November 1951 he signed professional forms at Elm Park and remained there until January 1955 when he switched to Norwich City for £6,000.

A year-and-a-half later he moved to Watford where he

Sammy Chung

stayed for eight years, amassing almost 250 League and Cup appearances for the Hornets, scoring 25 goals. During his time at Vicarage Road, Chung gained his FA coaching badge and graduated to player-coach with Watford. In July 1963 he came in contact with Bill McGarry for the first time when the former England international became manager of the Hornets. McGarry gave Chung three months to prove his worth as a coach. He did just that and when McGarry left to become boss of Ipswich Town in 1964, he took Chung with him, and in double-quick time, between them they guided the Portman Road club to the top of the Second Division. In 1967 Chung became manager of the Swedish side, IFK Vastera before returning to England as McGarry's assistant at Wolves, taking over the mantle himself as team manager at Molineux in 1976.

He left Wolves for the United Arab Emirates, but when Mick Mills was appointed boss of Stoke City in May 1985, he asked Chung to be his No.2 (the pair having worked together at Ipswich). Chung remained at The Victoria Ground for two years, leaving the Potteries to take over as manager of the Beazer Homes League side Tamworth where he stayed until January 1993. After a brief association as scout with Blackburn Rovers, he was named manager of Doncaster Rovers in July 1994, a position he held until 1997.

In January 1999, at the age of 66, Chung was appointed Director of Football in Barbados.

Chung's record as Wolves manager was played 108, won 41, drawn 27, lost 40.

CLAMP, Harold Edwin

Eddie Clamp was a tough, determined wing-half, who was dubbed 'Chopper' by the fans at Molineux.

A great character during the 1950s and early '60s, he was one of the most aggressive players in the game, never shirking a tackle, totally committed and above all, a terrific competitor with a never-say-die attitude.

Born in Coalville, Leicestershire on 14 September 1934, he was a pupil at the village state school and actually joined Wolverhampton Wanderers halfway through his paper round. This was in 1949. Wolves' boss Stan Cullis immediately placed him the club's nursery team, Wath Wanderers, where his game developed rapidly.

Clamp turned professional in April 1952 and made his senior debut in the 'old gold and black' strip in March 1954 against Manchester United at Old Trafford in front of almost 39,000 fans. This was the start of a superb career for 'Chopper' who with Wolves won two First Division championship medals (1958 & 1959) and an FA Cup winners medal in 1960. He also received four England caps, all in 1958 against Russia (twice), Brazil and Austria - three coming in the World Cup Finals in Sweden when he starred alongside his team-mates Billy Wright and Bill Slater to form an all-Wolves half-back line. Clamp left Molineux in November 1961 to sign for Arsenal for

Eddie Clamp

£12,000, but he never settled in London and moved from Highbury after just ten months, switching to Stoke City in September 1952 to be re-united with his former Wolves colleague Eddie Stuart.

He helped the Potters regain their First Division status in 1963 and played in 62 games (two goals scored) during his time at The Victoria Ground before leaving for Peterborough United in October 1964. After a season at London Road (when he took his career tally up to 335 League games) Clamp then had brief spells with Worcester City and Lower Gornal, and finally called it a day in 1970, although he still figured in the occasional charity match for the Wolves Old Stars.

Thereafter he ran his own business and was a regular visitor to both The Victoria Ground and Molineux right up until his death on 10 November 1995.

NB - Eddie Clamp's mother was the laundry lady at Molineux during the 1950s/early '60s.

Wolves' record: 241 apps. 25 goals.

CLARIDGE, Stephen Edward

Since making his Football League debut for Bournemouth in 1984, striker Steve Claridge has created and scored goals wherever he's played!

A real workhorse, no matter what the circumstances, he often has his socks rolled down near his ankles as he grafts tirelessly away, never giving less than 110 per-cent effort out on the park

Born in Portsmouth on 4 October 1966, he began his career at Fratton Park in 1982, but failed to make the breakthrough and in November 1984 moved to nearby Bournemouth. From Dean Court he surprisingly switched to Weymouth in October 1985, but returned to League action with Aldershot a year later - and he's never looked back to this day! From The Recreation Ground Claridge went to Cambridge United for £75,000 in February 1990; he joined Luton Town for £160,000 in July 1992, only to return to The Abbey Stadium four months later, this time for £195,000!

In January 1995, Birmingham City boss Barry Fry took Claridge to St. Andrew's for a fee of £325,000 and in March 1996, almost four times that amount changed hands when a record £1.2 million deal was struck with Leicester City. Some of that money was quickly paid back as Claridge netted the Wembley play-off winner, which shot the Foxes into the Premiership. Then he helped Leicester win the Coca-Cola Cup and get into Europe. His next move on the football merry-go-round took Claridge from Filbert Street to Wolves in March 1998 for £350,000, but he never really settled in at Molineux and was transferred to Portsmouth for £200,000 in August 1998.

Then when Wolves played Pompey in a League game soon after his move, he was involved in a penalty incident that saw Keith Curle sent-off! In season 1998-99 Claridge reached the milestone of 500 appearances at club level and was well on his way to the target of 150 goals.

He continued to find the net after that, acting also as caretaker-manager at Fratton Park from the start of the 2000-01 season (until Graham Rix came along).

He then assisted Millwall, on loan, from March-May 2001, and helped the Lions clinch promotion to the First Division before joining permanently for the London club in June 2001, signed by ex-Wolves boss Mark McGhee.

Wolves' record: 5+1 sub apps.

CLARKE, Derek

A member of the famous footballing family, Derek Clarke, like three of his four brothers, Allan, Frank and Wayne, was also a fine goalscorer.

Born in Willenhall on 19 February 1950, he left school in 1965 and immediately joined Walsall, turning professional at Fellows Park in December 1967. From there he moved to Molineux (May 1968) but owing to the number of established goalscorers in the camp, he was allowed to leave Wolves for Oxford United for £11,500 in October 1970.

He did well at The Manor Ground, scoring 40 goals in less than 200 League and Cup games before switching to Leyton Orient in August 1976.

He played for the Londoners in their 1978 FA Cup semi-final defeat by Arsenal and the following year, after a loan spell with Carlisle United (October 1978) Clarke dropped into non-League soccer in the south east.

Wolves' record: 3 apps.

CLARKE, Nicholas John

Defender Nicky Clarke was born in Willenhall on 20 August 1967 and joined the Molineux apprentice staff on leaving school in June 1983, turning professional in February 1985.

He took time to establish himself in the first team, but then a terrible knee injury sidelined him for two seasons before he left Molineux for Mansfield Town in December 1991 for a fee of £25,000. The following season Clarke helped the Stags win promotion from Division Four.

He later had loan spells with Chesterfield (March/April 1993), Doncaster Rovers (December 1993) and Preston (March 1994) before moving into non-League football with Bromsgrove Rovers, switching to Bilston Town in August 1997.

Wolves' record: 88+9 apps. 1 goal.

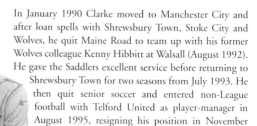

Nicky Clarke

CLARKE, Wayne

A former England Schoolboy and Youth international and West Midlands representative player, Wayne Clarke had two spells with Wolves. The first lasted eight years from June 1976 and the second time was on loan in September 1991.

Born in Willenhall on 28 February 1961, Clarke, a natural goal-poacher, like his three brothers Allan, Derek and Frank, was signed initially by Wolves as an apprentice at the age of 15 and turned professional in March 1978.

He was transferred from Molineux to Birmingham City for £80,000 in August 1984 and then after scoring 43 goals in 105 games for Blues he left St. Andrew's in March 1987 to join Everton for £500,000. Whilst at Goodison Park he quickly gained a League Championship medal, but the arrival on Merseyside of Tony Cottee prompted his departure to Leicester City in July 1989 for £500,000. (Cottee himself later joined the Foxes!)

Wayne Clarke

In January 1990 Clarke moved to Manchester City and after loan spells with Shrewsbury Town, Stoke City and Wolves, he quit Maine Road to team up with his former Wolves colleague Kenny Hibbitt at Walsall (August 1992). He gave the Saddlers excellent service before returning to Shrewsbury Town for two seasons from July 1993. He then quit senior soccer and entered non-League football with Telford United as player-manager in August 1995, resigning his position in November 1996.

In all Clarke netted over 130 goals in more than 500 League appearances during an exceptionally fine career. In 1999 he surprisingly became a postman.

NB - When Wolves were relegated at the end of the 1981-82 season it completed an unhappy sequence for the Clarke family! The Wolves striker became the fifth brother to suffer a similar fate with a different club. Allan was with Fulham when they went down in 1967-68; Frank with Carlisle in 1974-75, Derek with Oxford in 1975-76 and Kevin with Walsall in 1978-79. Allan, as manager of Leeds United in 1981-82, also suffered a similar experience.

Wolves' record: 171 apps. 33 goals.

CLAYTON, James Gordon George

Former policeman Gordon Clayton was a tall, strapping centre-forward who drew up an exceptionally fine scoring record.

Born in Sunderland in July 1910, he joined Wolves from Shotton Colliery in October 1932 and spent five years at Molineux before transferring to Aston Villa in October 1937. Clayton (now deceased) helped Villa win the Second Division title that season, but in October 1938 he was sold to Burnley.

He retired in 1945 after guesting for Swansea Town during the Second World War

Wolves' record: 55 apps. 39 goals.

CLEWS, Malcolm Derek

Born in Tipton on 12 March 1931, inside-forward Malcolm Clews was at Molineux at a time when there was ample strength in all front-line positions - consequently his first team outings were limited to just one!

He signed for Wolves on leaving school in 1946 and turned professional under manager Stan Cullis in February 1948. Amazingly he stayed with the club for the next six years, playing happily in the reserves before deciding to leave Molineux for Lincoln City in February 1954. He played just seven games for the Imps who released him in May 1955 when he entered non-League football back in the West Midlands.

Clews also played a lot of club cricket.

Wolves' record: one app.

CLIFF, Thomas

A hard-nut defender, born in Wolverhampton in December 1860, Tommy Cliff joined the club from Blakenhall St Luke's in August 1883, but spent only two years with Wolves before moving to Excelsior FC in 1885, later assisting Hockley Belmont and Smethwick Centaur.
Wolves' record: 4 FA Cup apps.

COADY, Michael Liam

Mike Coady was brought back to England, from the Australian club Sydney Olympic, in January 1985 by Wolves' manager Tommy Docherty.

A steady full-back, he unfortunately failed to impress at Molineux and after spending two-and-a-half years with the club, he was transferred to Lincoln City. Born in Dipton, County Durham on 1 October 1958, Coady had played for Sunderland (apprentice June 1975, professional from July 1976) and then Carlisle United (from July 1980 to 1982) before trying his luck 'down under'.

He made over 50 League appearances during his time at Brunton Park.
Wolves' record: 14+1 apps. 1 goal.

COCK, Donald James

Don Cock was a strong, bustling utility forward with a fierce shot. He was a regular goalscorer as well as being a fine distributor of the ball throughout his career.

Born at Hayle, Cornwall on 8 July 1896, and brother of the former Chelsea, Everton and England star Jack Cock, and Herbert, once of Brentford, Don played Army football in 1917-18 and was a reserve with Brentford before joining Fulham in June 1919.

He then had a two-and-a-half year association with Notts County (October 1922 to March 1925, signed for £1,750) prior to teaming up with Arsenal for £4,000. He stayed at Highbury only a few months, moving across London to Clapton Orient for £1,500 in October 1925. From there he joined Wolves for £1,000 in July 1927, but spent barely six weeks at Molineux before going to Newport County in a £750,000 deal in September of that same year. Cock broke a leg whilst at Highbury.
Wolves' record: 3 apps. one goal.

COCKER, Leslie James Robert

As a teenager Les Cocker won eleven England Youth caps as a wing-half, skippered Wolves' Staffordshire League side to the championship in 1957-58 and was also a member of the club's successful FA Youth Cup winning side that same season.

He spent five years in the reserves at Molineux, playing in the shadows of Messrs. Clamp, Slater and Flowers among others.

Born in Wolverhampton on 18 September 1939, and educated in the town, Cocker joined Wolves as a junior in 1956, turned professional in June 1958 and was released in 1960. He later became senior trainer with Leeds United (under Don Revie) and spent several memorable years at Elland Road, also acting as spongeman to various England teams over the same period (1960s-early '70s).
Wolves' record: 1 app.

COLEMAN, Simon

Experienced central defender, signed on a month's loan from Bolton Wanderers in September 1997 when injuries disrupted Wolves' back four plans.

Simon Coleman was born in Worksop on 19 October 1966 and began his professional career with Mansfield Town in July 1985. He played almost 120 games for the Stags before a £400,000 transfer took him to Middlesbrough in September 1989. From Ayresome Park he moved to Derby County for £300,000 in August 1991 and in January 1994 Sheffield Wednesday boss Trevor Francis engaged him at Hillsborough for £325,000 after he had made almost 100 appearances for the Rams.

Coleman's next move - in October 1994 - saw him join Bolton Wanderers for £350,000, and he did well with the Lancashire club, helping them win a place in the Premiership in 1997. After returning to The Reebok Stadium, from his loan spell at Molineux Coleman moved to Southend United in February 1998.

In July 2000, Coleman moved on a free transfer from Roots Hall to Rochdale and whilst at Spotland he took his career tally (at competitive level) to past the 450 mark.
Wolves' record: 3+1 sub apps.

COLEY, William Ernest

Bill Coley was a well built, hard-tackling left-half who spent six years at Molineux during which time he played mainly in the reserve and intermediate teams.

Born in Wolverhampton on 17 September 1916, and now deceased, he attended and played for Dudley Road Council School, represented Wolverhampton Town Boys (playing alongside Len Astill) and served with Belle Vue Rovers before joining Wolves as an amateur in May 1931, turning professional in September 1933.

Four years later, in May 1937, he was transferred to Bournemouth. In July 1938 he switched to Torquay United (for £500) and in August 1947 Coley signed for Northampton Town, having guested for the Cobblers as well as Chester, Bristol City & Tranmere Rovers during the war. He later served with Exeter City (from July 1951) before retiring in May 1953.

At that juncture he returned to Northampton as reserve team coach, a position he held until May 1955. He scored seven goals in 112 games for Northampton and was, in fact, the first Cobblers player to be sent-off after the war. He was fined £2 for this misdemeanour.

In later years he became a hotelier on the south coast, playing club cricket until well past his sixtieth birthday.

NB - Coley's father, Albert, played for Wolves' 2nd XI in 1906.
Wolves' record: 2 apps.

COLLEY, Albert J Robert

Bob Colley played two seasons with Wolves - 1899-1901 - and during that time acted as reserve outside-right. He was later with Newtown and Shrewsbury Town (1907-08), Wellington Town, Stafford Rangers (1911-12) and Darlaston. Colley was a local man, born circa 1875 whose father ran an ironmonger's shop in Wolverhampton.
Wolves' record: 8 apps. 2 goals.

COLLINS, Edward

Full-back Ted Collins was a rock-hard performer, born in Wolverhampton on 16 June 1884 who started his career with Bilston United.
He played next for Verity Athletic (Birmingham Works Association) and Brownhills Albion before joining Wolves in August 1907, quickly making his senior debut for the club against rivals West Bromwich Albion. He formed a fine partnership with Jack Jones and remained at Molineux until 1915 when he moved to Sunbeam Motors, later assisting Newport County (from 1917), Notts County (albeit briefly in 1919-20) and Hednesford Town. During the hostilities Collins guested for Port Vale and Walsall, and once scored five goals for the Saddlers as an emergency centre-forward. He helped Wolves win the FA Cup in 1908.
Wolves' record: 307 apps.

COLLYMORE, Stanley Victor

Stan Collymore was the one that got away...from Molineux!
In June 1997 he became the most expensive footballer in Midlands soccer history when he joined Aston Villa from Liverpool for £7 million, having been rejected by Wolves seven years earlier!
Born in Cannock, Staffs on 22 January 1971, and a pupil at Broomhall Primary School (Cannock) and Sherbrook Comprehensive, Collymore played for Longford Boys team (Cannock) before joining Walsall on the Youth Training Scheme.
He quickly left the Saddlers to sign for Wolves (July 1989), but surprisingly tossed aside the prospect of League football by signing for Stafford Rangers the following year. He did well in the Vauxhall Conference, so much so, that in January 1991 Crystal Palace moved in and paid £100,000 for his services.
Collymore scored once in 20 League games for the Eagles who then sold him to Southend United in November 1992 for precisely the same fee. After netting 18 times in only 33 games for the Shrimpers, 'Stan The Man' (as he became known) moved into the bigtime and signed for Nottingham Forest in a City Ground record deal worth £2 million in July 1993.
He immediately became the idol of the fans and registered 50 goals in 78 outings for East Midland club, helping them win promotion to the Premiership and also gain a place in Europe, before a massive £8.5 million record transfer took him to Liverpool in July 1995.

It was generally agreed that Collymore was the right man to replace Ian Rush and play alongside Robbie Fowler at Anfield. He did well, at times, but was also rather inconsistent and in truth, was never happy at Liverpool - hence his move to Aston Villa. He gained two England caps during his two years on Merseyside, while also scoring 35 goals in 81 appearances for the Liverpudlians. He later added a third full cap to his tally before he became a victim of stress in 1998, causing his club, Aston Villa, some concern as they were paying him a very large salary! In July 1999, Collymore chose to join Fulham on a seven-month loan period. On his return from Craven Cottage in February 2000 he signed for Leicester City but stayed at Filbert Street barely eight months before transferring to the struggling Premiership side Bradford City.
He then left the Pulse Stadium in January 2001 for the Spanish club Real Oviedo. However, in March, after just six weeks in the sun, he decided to quit football altogether, hinting that he might take up politics!

CONNELLY, Sean Patrick

Signed from Stockport County on loan from Edgeley Park on 21 March 2001, right-back Sean Connelly had already appeared in 364 senior games for the Hatters and had netted seven goals. He was born in Sheffield on 26 june 1970 and joined County from Hallam FC as a professional in August 1991. He helped the Cheshire club win promotion to the First Division in 1997.
Wolves boss David Jones (who had managed him at Stockport) signed Connelly on a free transfer in July 2001, but he was unable to get into the first XI and during the early part of the season, he had to be content with a place on the bench or a game or two in the reserves!
Wolves' record: 6 apps.*

CONNOLLY, David James

David Connolly, a Republic of Ireland international forward, was signed in August 1998 by Wolves' boss Mark McGhee on a year's loan from the Dutch club Feyenoord - the deal finally going through after four months of negotiations!
Born in London of Irish parents on 8 August 1977, Connolly signed professional forms for Watford - his first club - in November 1994 and he scored eight goals in his first 13 League games for the Hornets, six of which came after going onto the field as a substitute. He went to Holland in the summer of 1997 but never really succeeded over there and was always looking to come back to England.
In November 1998 he was the hero of all travelling Wolves fans when he scored four goals in an emphatic 6-1 League win at Bristol City. He returned to Feyenoord in the summer of 1999 and after two more years in Dutch soccer he re-entered the Football League by signing on a free transfer for First Division Wimbledon in July 2001.
Wolves' record: 20+15 sub apps. 6 goals.

CONWAY, Arthur Albert J

A former Halesowen player (1905-07) right-half Arthur Conway was signed by Wolves in the summer of 1908 after failing to make the grade with Aston Villa. He took time to establish himself at Molineux and, indeed, it wasn't until the following season that he finally gained a permanent position in the side.

Surprisingly, in July 1910 after being replaced by Albert Groves, he left Wolves and joined his old club Halesowen, later assisting Cradley Heath and Netherton. Conway was born in Stourbridge in 1886.

Wolves' record: 30 apps.

COOK, Paul Anthony

Midfielder Paul Cook was born in Liverpool on 22 February 1967 and began his career with Marine FC before becoming a professional with Wigan Athletic in July 1984.

In May 1988, after 100 appearances for Wigan, he was transferred to Norwich City for £73,000 and in November 1989 Cook arrived at Wolves for £250,000 (a record sale for the Canaries).

With an excellent left foot, he did well at Molineux initially, being the club's penalty-taker in 1991-92, but thereafter his form deteriorated and in August 1994 he was sold to Coventry City for £600,000, switching north to sign for Tranmere Rovers in February 1996 for a further £250,000.

In October 1997 Cook moved again, this time from Prenton Park to Stockport County, also for £250,000, replacing former Wolves star Chris Marsden at Edgeley Park, who was sold to Birmingham City. During the 1997-98 season Cook passed the milestone of 400 League appearances at club level but after losing his place in the Hatters' side the following campaign, he was eventually loaned out to Burnley (March 1999).

He quickly signed on a permanent basis for the Clarets and helped them win promotion to the Nationwide First Division in 2000.

Wolves' record: 209+5 sub apps. 21 goals.

Paul Cook

COOPER, Jeremiah

Strong-running inside-forward, always thirsty for the ball, Jerry Cooper was a member of Wolves' first-ever Football League side versus Aston Villa on 8 September 1888. Unfortunately a serious ankle injury forced him out of the side and in May 1891, he left Molineux for Stourbridge Standard.

Born in Heathtown, Wolverhampton in 1865, he played for Milton FC and Amblecote Nomads before signing for Wolves in August 1888.

Wolves' record: 26 apps. 6 goals.

CORBETT, Percy Baxter

Percy Corbett remained an amateur all his life. As keen as mustard and a willing worker, he occupied the inside-left berth in the main, being a valuable member of the Wolves side that started on the road to winning the FA Cup in 1908.

Born in Penn, Wolverhampton in February 1885, Corbett played most his football with the Wulfrunians club and was recruited by Wolves for a six-year period, starting in August 1905 although he was only a first team player for two seasons: August 1907 to April 1909. He continued to play for his former club until 1918.

An England Amateur international, capped seven times between 1905 and 1910, he also represented the Birmingham County Youth team and the Birmingham County Amateur side.

NB - Percy is not related to Walter Samuel Corbett, who won an Olympic soccer Gold medal in 1908.

Wolves' record: 8 apps. 3 goals.

CORFIELD, Sidney

Sid Corfield was a stylish centre-half whose career was disrupted by his parents!

A Black Country man, born at Princes End, Tipton in June 1883, he attended St. Martin's School (Tipton) and played for Toll End Wesley (1900) before joining West Bromwich Albion as a professional in November 1902.

He made just eight first team appearances for the Baggies before his mother and father pulled him out of the game and asked him to go into engineering! Corfield was out of football for at least fifteen months, up to August 1905 when he was enticed back into the game by Wolves who signed him to help bolster up a rather leaky defence.

Sadly Corfield never really commanded a first team place at Molineux although he did remain at the club for four years, his best season coming in 1905-06 when he played in 29 senior games. In 1909 he left Wolves for Wrexham with whom he won two Welsh Cup winners medals (1910 and 1911) before returning to the Midlands to sign for Tipton Victoria, retiring in 1915.

A very useful cricketer with West Bromwich Dartmouth in 1913 and 1914, Corfield once scored 55 runs in two overs.

Wolves' record: 47 apps. 3 goals.

CORICA, Stephen Christopher

Skilful, industrious right-sided midfielder, born in Cairns, Australia on 24 March 1973, Steve Corica joined Wolves for £1.1 million from Leicester City on 16 February 1996. He had been a big success in Australian soccer with Marconi FC of Sydney (winning Youth and intermediate honours for his country) before moving to Filbert Street in August 1995 for £325,000 (the fee decided by a FIFA tribunal).

He played under Mark McGhee at Leicester and had no hesitation in following his boss to Molineux. He did well in his first season with Wolves despite a few injury problems and in 1997 was called into the Australian World Cup squad, coached by former England boss Terry Venables.

In fact, Corica had taken his tally of senior caps to 17 (as well as gaining Under-23 honours) by the time he left Wolves in the summer of 2000 for the Japanese club Sanfrecce Hiroshima.

Wolves' record: 88+22 sub apps. 5 goals.

COUNDON, Cuthbert

Competent utility forward, sturdily built, brimful of enthusiasm, Bert Coundon - nicknamed 'Kid' - was signed from Southampton in July 1928.

Unfortunately he was struck down by diptheria in December 1927 and never really recovered his full health, and as a consequence was transferred to Southend United in May 1929.

Born in Sunderland on 3 April 1905, Coundon represented Sunderland & District Schools, played for Mercantile Dock XI and Jarrow (1923) before moving 400 miles to The Dell in April 1925.

From Southend he switched to Guildford City (July 1930) and in September 1935 was appointed trainer-coach of Sutton United.

Wolves' record: 13 apps. 1 goal.

COWANS, Gordon Sidney

Midfielder Gordon 'Sid' Cowans was born in Cornworth on 27 October 1958.

His career began in earnest when he joined Aston Villa as an apprentice in 1974, turning professional in September 1976. In the next nine years he helped Villa win the League Cup (1977), the First Division title (1981), the European Cup (1982) and the European Super Cup (also in 1982).

He was capped by England, later taking his tally of full caps to 10, as well as representing his country in two 'B' and five Under-21 internationals, having earlier played at Youth team level. From Villa Park he went to the Italian club Bari for £500,000 in July 1985, but returned to Villa for half that amount in July 1988, having had three good years in Serie 'A', making almost 100 appearances.

In November 1991, a fee of £200,000 took Cowans to Blackburn Rovers, but surprisingly in July 1993, he returned for a third spell with Aston Villa. His next move was to Derby County for £80,000 in February 1994 and his association with Wolves commenced in December 1994 when the Rams accepted £20,000 for his departure. Almost a year later - in December 1995 - Cowans was on the road again, this time to Sheffield United on a free transfer.

He switched clubs once more early in the 1996-97 season when he went to Bradford City, and before the campaign had ended he signed for Stockport County, helping the Edgeley Park side win promotion to the First Division. The much-travelled Cowans, who was replaced in the Stockport midfield by former Wolves man Chris Mardsen, was then linked with the manager's job at Hereford United. Cowans passed the personal milestone of 800 appearances at club level during the 1997-98 season (75

Gordon Cowans

goals scored). In August 1997 he joined Burnley as player-coach under his former England colleague Chris Waddle, moving up to reserve team manager at Turf Moor in 1998 when Waddle left.

Cowans returned to his beloved Villa Park as a coach - under manager and former playing colleague, John Gregory - in the summer of 1999.

Wolves' record: 40+6 sub apps. 1 goal.

COY, Robert Anthony

A precise tackler, strong and solid in his play, Bob Coy had a number of central defensive partners during his time at Molineux including Joe Gallagher, George Berry, John Pender and Alan Dodd.

Born in Birmingham on 30 November 1961, he joined Wolves as an apprentice in 1977 and turned professional on his 18th birthday two years later. He made his senior debut in the old gold and black strip v. Tottenham in September 1981 and in 1982-83 helped Wolves win promotion from the Second Division.

As the team went slithering back down, Coy was transferred in March 1984 to Chester City (with colleague Dave Wintersgill). In later years he served with Northampton Town (from August 1986 to May 1987), Aylesbury United (to July 1989) and Moor Green (August 1989 to March 1993), skippering the latter club for three seasons to 1992.

Earlier in his career Coy was a promising goalkeeper and played in an England Schoolboys Under-15 trial match as well as having a brief spell as a junior with Birmingham City (1976).

Wolves' record: 44+3 sub apps. no goals.

CRABTREE, John

Jack Crabtree's career in League football was cut short after he had been wounded during the First World War.

Born in Bournbrook, Birmingham in September 1887. Crabtree played for Bournville FC before joining Wolves in July 1912. He spent two years as a left-half at Molineux and left for Kings Heath prior to serving his country at War (from April 1915).

He retired on returning home (1919) and although he turned out in various charity matches, he never really took up football again and became secretary of a local team in the Birmingham area.

Wolves' record: 11 apps.

CRAINIE, Daniel

Danny Crainie was a fast raiding, slightly built forward, who became the 'forgotten' man of English football when he was discarded by Wolves in 1985 and then abandoned in the Australian outback.

But the likeable Scot bounced back with Airdrieonians in 1988 and during the next few years often caught the headlines of the Scottish newspapers.

Born in Kilsyth on 24 May 1962, Crainie joined Celtic in 1978 and won a League championship medal at the age of 19, later adding an Under-21 cap to his collection. But when manager Billy McNeill left Parkhead to join Manchester City, David Hay took over and Crainie's days

were numbered in the green and white hoops.

In December 1983 he was transferred to Molineux, but in truth he never really settled down in the Midlands despite scoring a couple of marvellous goals, one a real beauty at West Brom. After a loan spell with Blackpool (March/April 1985) he left Wolves for Dundee but quickly opted for a change of scenery in Australia, signing for the South Melbourne club, Hellas, whose fans were mostly Greek immigrants.

From there he switched to Woolongong City - and that's where things really went wrong for Crainie.

Playing alongside Paul Mariner, Trevor Francis and Alan Brazil one week, he suddenly found himself on the scrap heap after the club's millionaire-owner walked out.

He returned to Britain shortly afterwards to play briefly for Airdrieonians (1990-91) and then entered non-League football.

Wolves' record: 71+2 apps. 4 goals.

CRAWFORD, Raymond

Ray Crawford remained a prolific goalscorer throughout his career and when he retired in May 1971 he had netted well over 300 times in more than 600 appearances as a professional, including a League record of 290 goals in 476 outings.

A marvellous opportunist, Crawford no doubt played his best football with Ipswich Town where he partnered deadly Ted Phillips in attack. Crawford was the more artful while Phillips fired in bullet shots There were few better tandem teams in League football when they were playing together,

Born in Portsmouth on 13 July 1936, Crawford's career started off at Portsmouth where he signed as a professional in December 1954. From Fratton Park he switched to Ipswich Town in September 1958 and five years later joined Wolves (September 1963).

From Molineux he was transferred across the Black Country divide to neighbouring West Bromwich Albion in February 1965 and went back to Ipswich in March 1966. His next move took him to Charlton Athletic in March 1969 and after a loan spell with Kettering Town he finally ended his career with Colchester United, staying one season, at Layer Road, commencing June 1970 and early in 1971 helped Colchester cause a major upset by dumping mighty Leeds United and their stars out of the FA Cup!.

He was capped twice by England and also played for the Football League. He helped Ipswich win the League championship in 1962 and the Second Division title in 1968. After leaving Layer Road he had a brief spell with Durban City (South Africa), coached at Brighton, Portsmouth and in New Zealand and then returned to Fratton Park as Youth-team manager, later taking charge of Fareham Town and Winchester City.

Crawford also played for Malaysia while on National Service over there, and he is still Ipswich Town's champion marksman of all-time with 227 League and Cup goals, which included a five-timer in a European cup clash with the Maltese side FC Floriana in September 1962.

Wolves' record: 61 apps. 41 goals.

CREW, E William

Billy Crew was a gritty performer who loved to battle it out in the middle of the park. Born at Little Lever, Bolton in 1898, he played for the Great Lever club before joining Bolton Wanderers in July 1922.

From Burnden Park he switched to Wolves (May 1923) but spent only a season at Molineux before moving to Tranmere Rovers (May 1924). After that he served with Pontypridd (August 1925), Merthyr Town (October 1925), Southend United (May 1929), Wigan Borough (September 1930), Burton Town (1933) and Mossley (June 1936), retiring in May 1938, aged 40.

He helped Wolves win the Third Division (North) title when deputising for skipper George Getgood at right-half.

Wolves' record: 8 apps.

CROOK, Alfred R

Brother of Billy, Alf Crook was a reserve full-back at Molineux.

Born in the Staffordshire village of at Brewood on 13 August 1923, he joined Wolves from Boulton & Paul's FC in readiness for the 1942-43 Wartime season. However he had to wait seven years before making his senior debut in the FA Cup semi-final replay against Manchester United in April 1949, replacing the injured Larry Kelly. Prior to that he had managed only a handful of Regional League and Cup appearances during the wartime period.

Crook was allowed to leave Wolves at the end of the 1948-49 season and is now an avid member of the ex-players' association, living locally.

Wolves' record: 2 apps.

CROOK, Mark Stanley

A diminutive outside-right or outside-left, Mark Crook was born in Morby, Yorkshire on 29 June 1903.

He developed his football with Wombwell before breaking

Mark Crook

into senior competition with Blackpool, making a much bigger impact with Swindon Town prior to joining Wolves on 4 October 1929. Terrier-like in his persistency, Crook was only 5ft 5ins tall and weighed 10st 8lbs but always gave a good account of himself against the much stronger full-backs.

He made his debut for Wolves v. Bristol City just 24 hours after joining the club and his last outing was at Sunderland in January 1935. His best season came in 1932-33 when he made 25 appearances, helping Wolves win the Second Division championship.

He left Molineux for Luton Town in May 1935 and retired during the early part of the war when he took up scouting, recommending several players to both Wolves and Walsall. It was Crook who formed Wolves' nursery side, Wath Wanderers, when he took over the facilities of the Brampton Welfare Football Club in the late 1940s.

Wolves' record: 81 apps. 16 goals.

CROOK, William Charles

Left-back or wing-half Billy Crook was a key member of the Wolves side during the early post war years, winning a FA Cup winners' medal in 1949.

Billy Crook

Born in Wolverhampton on 7 June 1926, and educated at the local Grammar School, he joined the club as a 14 year-old from Boulton & Paul's FC on schoolboy forms in August 1940, became an amateur in July 1941 and turned part-time professional in August 1943.

After establishing himself in the side during the hostilities, when he also guested for Aldershot and Chelsea, Crook found himself a regular in the Wolves side in 1946 after more than 120 wartime appearances. In October 1954, having by now lost his place in the first team, he was transferred to Walsall, where he stayed until 1956, retiring four years later after a period in non-League soccer.

During his playing days Crook trained as a structural draughtsman and later took up employment in this field with Rubery Owen & Co. (Darlaston).

He was also a fan of Dixieland jazz and like his brother he is also a member of the ex-Wolves' players' association and now resides in Lancashire.

Wolves' record: 221 apps. 3 goals.

CROSS, Charles Alon

Charlie Cross was a sturdy full-back, signed from Crystal Palace in August 1928.

Born in Coventry on 15 May 1900, and now deceased, he played initially for Sideley Deasy FC and then made 11 Football League appearances for Coventry City before joining Palace in 1922.

He played over 220 League games for the London club but never really settled in the Midlands and he spent just one season with Wolves, acting as reserve to Harry Shaw before leaving for Merthyr Town in June 1929. Cross later returned to Coventry.

Wolves' record: 3 apps.

CROWE, Christopher

Born in Newcastle-on-Tyne on 11 June 1939 and educated at St John's School (Edinburgh) Chris Crowe played for Edinburgh Boys and gained England Schoolboy and Youth honours as a teenager before adding four Under-23 caps and one senior cap to his tally.

After trials with Hearts, he joined Leeds United, signing as a junior at Elland Road in July 1954 and turning professional in June 1956. Tutored briefly by the great John Charles, Crowe made over 100 appearances for the Yorkshire club who then sold him to Blackburn in March 1960. He had 51 League outings for Rovers before transferring to Wolves in February 1962. He remained at Molineux for two-and-a-half years, up to August 1964, when he moved to Nottingham Forest.

A blonde inside-forward, he had 74 outings for Forest and later added a further 67 to his collection with Bristol City (between January 1967 and September 1969) and 13 with his last English club, Walsall whom he served for a season (1969-70) after a spell in New Zealand with Auburn. Crowe ended his career with Bath City (February-May 1971).

Wolves' record: 85 apps. 24 goals.

CROWE, Glen Michael

A determined left-footed striker, born in Dublin on Christmas Day 1977, Glen Crowe joined Wolves as a trainee on leaving school in 1994 and turned professional in July 1996 after completing his YTS course.

Capped by the Republic of Ireland at both Youth and Under-21 levels, he went on loan to Exeter City in

February and March 1997 before returning to appear in the play-offs for Wolves at the end of that season.

He was booked on his debut v. Reading in April 1996 and scored in his second game v. Charlton Athletic. In October/November 1997 Crowe was again loaned out, this time to Cardiff City and after returning to Molineux he was later transferred to Plymouth Argyle (January 1999 after a month's trial at Home Park).

Crowe is one of the few red-heads to play for Wolves.

Wolves' record 6+4 sub apps. one goal.

CRUMP, Harold William

Born in Smethwick in 1870, half-back Harry Crump played for Smethwick Centaur, West Smethwick and Wednesfield before joining Wolves in September 1894. He remained at Molineux for just nine months, making one League appearance before transferring to Hereford Thistle in May 1895. Twelve months later - after brief spell with Bloxwich - he had a trial with Spurs, did well and was signed full-time.

After one season with the club he switched his allegiance to Luton Town but returned to White Hart Lane in September 1899 and went on to make 105 first team appearances and scoring 13 goals for Spurs. Having guested for Thames Ironworks he moved to Brentford in May 1900 before ending his career with Watford in 1901-02.

NB - Some reference books show that there was also a Winston Howard Crump playing at the same time as Harry Crump (possibly a brother).

Wolves' record: one app.

CULLIS, Stanley

Stan Cullis was one of a rare breed, a footballing person who achieved outstanding success both as a player and as a manager. Furthermore, he achieved both with the same club - Wolverhampton Wanderers.

Born in Ellesmere Port, Cheshire on 25 October 1915, Cullis, who had trials with Bolton Wanderers at the age of 16, joined Wolves in February 1934 from his local Wednesday club, thus beginning a career which saw him make his mark as a supreme centre-half. He was dominant in the air, as hard as nails in the tackle and always tried to use the ball creatively, very rarely hoofing in downfield in hope of finding a colleague.

He made his Football League debut, at home to Huddersfield Town twelve months after arriving at Molineux, and was appointed skipper of the first team before he was 20. Indeed, he was a natural leader and went on to captain England, initially at the age of 22, the youngest ever at that time (in 1937-38).

He went on to gain 12 full caps, plus a further 20 in wartime football when he was part of a quite brilliant international half-back line comprising Joe Mercer, himself and tough guy Cliff Britton. Cullis captained the Wolves side in the last pre-war FA Cup Final, which the

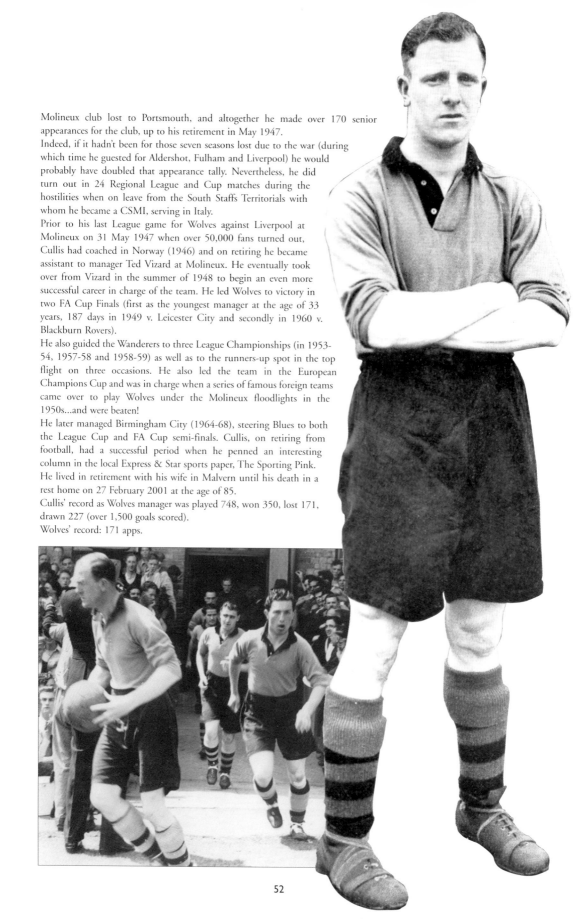

Molineux club lost to Portsmouth, and altogether he made over 170 senior appearances for the club, up to his retirement in May 1947.

Indeed, if it hadn't been for those seven seasons lost due to the war (during which time he guested for Aldershot, Fulham and Liverpool) he would probably have doubled that appearance tally. Nevertheless, he did turn out in 24 Regional League and Cup matches during the hostilities when on leave from the South Staffs Territorials with whom he became a CSMI, serving in Italy.

Prior to his last League game for Wolves against Liverpool at Molineux on 31 May 1947 when over 50,000 fans turned out, Cullis had coached in Norway (1946) and on retiring he became assistant to manager Ted Vizard at Molineux. He eventually took over from Vizard in the summer of 1948 to begin an even more successful career in charge of the team. He led Wolves to victory in two FA Cup Finals (first as the youngest manager at the age of 33 years, 187 days in 1949 v. Leicester City and secondly in 1960 v. Blackburn Rovers).

He also guided the Wanderers to three League Championships (in 1953-54, 1957-58 and 1958-59) as well as to the runners-up spot in the top flight on three occasions. He also led the team in the European Champions Cup and was in charge when a series of famous foreign teams came over to play Wolves under the Molineux floodlights in the 1950s...and were beaten!

He later managed Birmingham City (1964-68), steering Blues to both the League Cup and FA Cup semi-finals. Cullis, on retiring from football, had a successful period when he penned an interesting column in the local Express & Star sports paper, The Sporting Pink.

He lived in retirement with his wife in Malvern until his death in a rest home on 27 February 2001 at the age of 85.

Cullis' record as Wolves manager was played 748, won 350, lost 171, drawn 227 (over 1,500 goals scored).

Wolves' record: 171 apps.

CURLE, Keith

Central defender Keith Curle skippered Manchester City for five years before transferring to Wolves for £650,000 in August 1996.

An excellent footballer, keen in the tackle, decisive, with pace and vision, he began his career with Bristol Rovers as an apprentice in 1979, turning professional at Eastville in November 1981. In November 1983 he was sold to Torquay United for £5,000 and in March of the following year returned to Bristol to sign for City for £10,000.

After gaining an Associated Members Cup winners' medal and playing in almost 150 games for the Ashton Gate club, Curle was transferred to Reading for £150,000 in October 1987.

From Elm Park, where he helped the Royals win the Full Members Cup, he switched to Wimbledon for £500,000 in October 1988, and in his three years with the Dons, appeared in 112 senior matches. He left Wimbledon for Maine Road in a £2.5 million deal in August 1991 and during his time with City won three England caps to go with the four 'B' caps gained earlier.

He made 204 appearances for Manchester City and, ironically, prior to the start of the 1995-96 campaign, he fractured his ankle playing in a friendly against Wolves!

A fine penalty taker, Curle who was born in Bristol on 14 November 1963, was kept out of the Wolves side for almost six months through injury from the time he joined the club, finally making his full debut in January 1997. In December 1998 he was appointed player-coach at Molineux before choosing to leave the club to sign for Sheffield United on a free transfer in July 2000. He was appointed player-coach at Bramall Lane soon after joining the Blades.

Wolves' record: 120+1 sub apps. 8 goals.

CURNOW, John Lester

Jack Curnow, at almost 6ft. 3ins and 13st 6lbs, was one of the tallest and heaviest goalkeepers in the country during the 1930s.

A Yorkshireman, born at Lingdale, Saltburn on 31 January 1910 and now deceased, joined Wolves as a professional from non-League football in 1934 and made his First Division debut at Chelsea four days before Christmas 1935 when he deputised for the injured Jack Weare.

Curnow, a fine judge of crosses, failed to hold down a regular first team place at Molineux and was transferred to Blackpool in December 1936. From Bloomfield Road he switched to Tranmere Rovers (May 1937) and during the war assisted Hull City (1939-45). He retired in 1946 with well over 100 senior appearances under his belt.

Wolves' record: 8 apps.

CURRAN, Hugh Patrick

Hugh Curran amassed a fine scoring record in the Football League, netting 163 goals in 404 games in a career that began with Millwall in 1964 and ended at Oxford United in 1979. For Wolves alone he scored almost 50 times in close-on 100 appearances.

Curran was born in Glasgow on 25 September 1943 and was an apprentice with Manchester United before being released and joining Shamrock Rovers in the League of Ireland. There followed a spell with the Scottish side Third Lanark before he had a trial with Millwall, who - although seemingly impressed - allowed him to drift into the Southern League with Corby Town before finally securing his transfer for £3,000 in March 1964. After 27 goals in 57 League games for Millwall, Curran moved to Norwich City for £10,000 in January 1966 and for the Carrow Road club he netted a further 46 goals in 112 League games.

That induced Wolves to pay £60,000 for his signature in January 1969 and by the time he left for Oxford in September 1972, for £50,000, he had played five times for Scotland. The only other major honour he won was as a

Keith Curle

member of Wolves' team that finished runners-up in the 1972 UEFA Cup Final. Bolton signed him in September 1974 for £40,000, but Curran returned to the Manor Ground in July 1977 and retired through injury in March 1979.
Wolves' record: 91+7 sub apps. 47 goals.

CURTIS, Frank

Born in Llanelli in 1890, and now deceased, inside or centre-forward Frank Curtis served Wolves before, during and after World War One.

He moved to Molineux from his home-town club, Llanelli in June 1914 and after scoring more than a goal every two games, surprisingly left Wolves for Reading in May 1920. Curtis later had useful spells with both Bilston United and Kidderminster Harriers, before returning to South Wales to work in engineering.
Wolves' record: 42 apps. 25 goals.

CUTLER, Eric R

Amateur inside-forward Eric Cutler captained the England Schools team in 1914-15 and was one of the many players recruited by Wolves immediately after the First World War. He stayed at Molineux for just two seasons (1919-21) before drifting back into non-League soccer.

A local man, he became a licensee in Wolverhampton.
Wolves' record: 18 apps. 4 goals.

DALEY, Anthony Mark

Due to injury, fast raiding winger Tony Daley made his full debut for Wolves a year after he had intended, but after just one outing as a substitute under his former manager Graham Taylor he broke down again and then missed all of the 1996-97 campaign.

Born in Birmingham on 18 October 1967, Daley attended and played for The Holte Comprehensive School, Lozells, represented Birmingham Boys and joined Aston Villa as an apprentice in the summer of 1983, turning professional on 31 May 1985.

After playing for his country at Youth team level, he bided his time at Villa Park before gaining a regular place in the first team. Once in, he stayed and did extremely well, going on to win one 'B' and seven full England caps as well as helping Villa lift the League Cup in 1994. After scoring 38 goals in 290 appearances for the Villans, Daley was sold to Wolves for a club record £1.25 million in June 1994 but with injury plaguing him continuously, he managed just 24 outings in his first three seasons at Molineux. Daley was given a free transfer from Wolves in May 1998 and two months later he teamed up with his former boss at Villa Park Graham Taylor at Watford, helping the Hornets reach the 1999 First Division play-off Final.

Soon afterwards Daley joined the Nationwide Conference side Forest Green Rovers where later he was accompanied later by two former Villa colleagues, Nigel Spink and David Norton who became joint-managers. Forest Green lost in the Final of the FA Trophy in 2001 - at Villa Park! Wolves' record: 20+7 sub apps. 4 goals.

DALEY, Stephen

A Yorkshireman, born in Barnsley on 15 April 1953, Steve Daley was rated highly as a youngster and in the mid-1970s he was a key figure in Wolves' midfield, driving forward, looking for openings and always keen to have a shot at goal himself.

He helped Wolves reach the UEFA Cup Final in 1972 and win the Football League Cup Final in 1974. Three years later he was an ever-present when Wolves lifted the Second

Steve Daley

Division championship. After almost 250 appearances for the club, Manchester City boss Malcolm Allison paid a then British transfer record fee of £1.437,500 for Daley's signature on 5 September 1979.

Three days later that money was re-banked when Wolves almost broke that record by signing Andy Gray from Aston Villa for £1.15 million. Whilst at Molineux, Daley won England Youth honours and played six times for the England 'B' team. At Maine Road he appeared in only 53 full games and scored four goals before joining Burnley in November 1983.

He later assisted Walsall, Lye Town, Kettering Town and the Old Wulfrunians whilst in the early 1980s he had two spells in the NASL with Seattle Sounders (1982) and San Diego Sockers (1984). After a short period working for a brewery in the West Midlands, Daley returned to football as manager of Vauxhall Conference side Telford United in June 1997.

In the summer of 1998 he switched clubs, leaving Telford to take charge of Bromsgrove Rovers, replacing Brian Kenning. Towards the end of 2001 Steve took over the reins of Bilston Town.

NB - Steve's father, Alan Daley, was associated with Mansfield Town (two spells), Hull City, Doncaster Rovers, Scunthorpe United, Stockport County, Crewe Alexandra and Coventry City between 1946 and 1961.

Wolves' record: 218+26 sub apps. 43 goals.

DALY, Maurice Celsus

Attacking left-back or orthodox left-winger Maurice Daly spent five seasons at Molineux (July 1973 to May 1978) during which time he struggled to gain a regular place in the side, his best campaign being his last in 1977-78 when he had 28 senior outings under manager Sammy Chung.

Born in Dublin on 28 November 1955, he graduated via the well respected Home Farm club in the Irish Republic before moving to Wolves. He left Molineux for Sweden after gaining two full and four Under-21 caps for his country.

Wolves' record: 31+5 sub apps. one goal.

DANIEL, Peter William

Peter Daniel, who was born in Hull on 12 December 1955, was the driving force in Wolves' midfield for six years (1978-84), making almost 200 senior appearances for the club and scoring 16 goals.

He joined Wolves from Hull City for £82,000 in May 1978 and helped the Molineux club to League Cup glory in 1980 and promotion to the First Division in 1983. He was capped three times by England Under-21s, having earlier played three times for the Under-23s. Daniel broke his right leg in a match against Aston Villa in February 1981 but made a quick recovery.

He had a spell in the NASL with Minnesota Kicks before leaving Wolves for Sunderland in May 1984. He later played for Lincoln City and Burnley and totalled almost 400 League appearances during his career which ended when in retirement in May 1988.

Daniel grew a beard to make him appear more fearsome on the pitch but there was never any doubt that he was one of the most competitive characters in League football.

Wolves' record: 194 apps. 16 goals.

DANKS, Richard

Born in Bilston in March 1865, centre-forward Dicky Danks, a former pupil at Saltley College, joined Wolves as a 22 year-old in the summer of 1887 after scoring over 20 goals for Stafford Road the previous season.

He guested for Burslem Port Vale in 1887, and joined the Potteries' club on a permanent basis in the summer of 1888.

He was appointed secretary of the Vale in October 1889 (whilst still a registered player) but in November 1893 was released and became associated with Wednesbury Town, later assisting Wednesbury Old Athletic.

Wolves' record: 3 apps.

DAVIDSON, Alfred Richmond

Alf Davidson was a short, stocky right-half, fresh-faced, with black wavy hair, who had good footwork and was always totally committed.

Born in Wolverhampton circa 1861, he helped Wolves win their first-ever trophy - the Wrekin Cup in 1884 - having joined the club from Blakenhall a year earlier. He left Wolves to play for Wednesfield St. Luke's in 1886.

Wolves' record: 5 apps.

DAVIES, Frederick

Scouser Fred Davies was born in Liverpool on 22 August 1939 and was spotted by Wolves whilst keeping goal for Borough United in the Welsh League.

He joined the Molineux staff in April 1957 but had to wait almost five years before making his senior debut. This arrived in January 1962 when he stepped out for a 4th round FA Cup-tie against arch rivals West Bromwich Albion (with full-back Bobby Thomson) in front of 46,000 fans at Molineux. The following week he made his League debut, against Spurs, before another 46,000 crowd at Molineux.

That was the first of 369 League appearances Davies made while playing for Wolves, Cardiff City and Bournemouth. In 1966-67 he helped Wolves to win promotion from the

Peter Daniel in action against Cyrille Regis

Fred Davies

Second Division and had made over 170 senior appearances by the time he signed for Cardiff in January 1968.

Davies was transferred to Bournemouth in July 1970 and he served the Cherries until May 1974, starring in their Fourth Division promotion run of 1970-71. After retiring he became trainer-coach at Norwich City (under John Bond) and later worked for Blackpool, Swansea City and Birmingham City.

He had a brief spell as manager of Merthyr Tydfil, then became assistant to Bond at Shrewsbury Town before taking over as manager at Gay Meadow in May 1993 (following a brief spell as caretaker-boss). One of his first signings was the former Wolves player, Wayne Clarke, and he duly led the 'Shrews' to the Third Division championship in 1994.

Davies was sacked as manager of Shrewsbury (after relegation to the Third Division) in May 1997 and he became boss of Weymouth in December 1997.

Wolves' record: 173 apps.

DAVIES, Harry Joseph

Robustic right full-back Harry Davies feared no-one. Physically strong, he was a real hefty player who joined Wolves from Bamford Athletic in March 1898. He remained at Molineux until May 1901, following the emergence of George Walker and the arrival of Jackery Jones.

Born in Wednesbury circa 1873, he deputised initially for George Eccles and then partnered Joe Blackett and later John Matthias and George Fleming before being transferred to Shrewsbury Town.

From August 1902 to July 1904 he assisted Gainsborough Trinity; he was with Doncaster Rovers until March 1905 and ended his League career with Hull City, leaving the Tigers in May 1907.

NB - Davies' son, Harry junior, played for Stoke City.

Wolves' record: 72 apps.

DAVIES, Josiah Joseph

Joe Davies was a stylish footballer who could occupy a number of positions, playing mainly in defence as a right-half.

A Welshman, born in the village of Cefn Mawr near Ruabon in July 1865, he played for Druids (1882-86), Newton Heath (1886-90) and West Bromwich Albion (briefly in August 1890) before joining Wolves in September 1890.

He was replaced in the Wanderers side by Hill Griffiths and after two-and-a-half years at Molineux he left the club to sign for Kidderminster Olympic (May 1893), returning to Druids for a second spell in May 1894. One of five brothers, four of whom were capped by Wales - Lloyd, Thomas, Robert and himself (seven caps won between 1887 and 1894) - Davies was very disappointed not to make Wolves' 1893 FA Cup Final team.

On retiring from football he became a farmer in Wales and in later years ran a butcher's shop in Cefn.

Wolves' record: 39 apps.

DAVIES, Kenneth

Ken Davies was a nippy winger, born in Doncaster on 20 September 1923, who joined Wolves in 1943. He did well during the last three wartime seasons, but even then found it difficult to hold down a first team place. Davies was subsequently transferred to Walsall in June 1946...allowing another winger, Johnny Hancocks, to move to Molineux!

After two seasons at Fellows Park he moved south to Brighton & Hove Albion in May 1948. He remained at Hove until 1950 when he returned to the Midlands to live and work - and play non-League soccer.

He retired as a player in 1957.

Wolves' record: 2 apps. 2 goals.

DAVIES, Richard

Inside-forward Dicky Davies played first team football for Wolves for only one season: 1898-99, when he partnered right-winger John Tonks and centre-forward Billy Beats.

An aggressive footballer, born in Quarrington Hill, Durham in August 1876, he played initially for Admaston FC before joining Manchester City as a reserve in 1894.

From there he moved to Hanley Town and after two seasons with Leicester Fosse (from July 1895) where he flattered to deceive, he switched, albeit briefly, to Altrincham, moving on to Glossop North End in September 1898, then Bristol St. George before signing for Wolves in May 1898.

He never quite reached the level required to become an established Football League player and after leaving Molineux in June 1901 he assisted Reading, later serving with Bristol City, then Shrewsbury Town (June 1902) and finally Wellington St George (1903-05).

Wolves' record: 11 apps. 2 goals.

DAVIES, Royston

An outside-right, Roy Davies spent five months with Wolves during which time he deputised for Mark Crook at the start of the League programme, getting himself sent-off v. Hull City in his seventh outing.

A useful footballer, with good pace, he was born in South Wales circa 1905 and joined the Wanderers from Ebbw Vale in June 1929. On leaving Molineux he signed for West Ham United and later assisted Reading, staying three seasons at Elm Park before returning to the Midlands to play for Walsall Wood, later serving with Lichfield. Wolves' record: 9 apps.

DAVISON, Thomas Reay

Tommy Davison played two seasons with Wolves in the mid-1920s when he stood in for centre-half Bill Caddick, acting as the team's sheet anchor in both constructional and defensive terms.

A stout-hearted footballer, powerful in the tackle, he was recruited from Durham City in June 1923 after making more than 60 appearances for the northern club.

Described in the press as being 'durable, as smart with his head as his feet' Davison was born in County Durham on 3 October 1901 and played initially for Tanfield Lea Juniors before joining his home town club in 1920.

In July 1925, after failing to oust Caddick from the pivotal role, he left Molineux for Derby County and had 85 games for the Rams before switching to Sheffield Wednesday in February 1931. From Hillsborough he moved to Coventry City (July 1932) and after exactly 100 appearances for the Sky Blues he signed for Rhyl Athletic (July 1935) where he became player-coach, retiring from football in 1939 after a brief spell with Bath City. An ex-pit worker, Davison was keen on greyhounds as well as being an accomplished crown green bowler and excellent all-round cricketer.

Wolves' record: 10 apps. one goal.

DE BONT, Andrew Cornelius

Goalkeeper Andy De Bont was third choice at Molineux for five seasons before leaving Wolves to sign for Hereford United in August 1996.

Born in Wolverhampton on 7 February 1974, at 6ft. 2in tall and weighing well over 15 stones he certainly filled the framework of the goal, being strong and confident, and a good shot-stopper. He played on loan with both Hartlepool United (October 1995) and Hereford United (March/April 1996) before leaving Wolves for Edgar Street on a permanent basis after failing to break into the first team at Molineux. In 1998-99 De Bont played for Stourbridge and also had a trial with Charlton Athletic.

DE WOLF, Johannes

Injuries ruined John De Wolf's career at Molineux.

The tall, long haired Dutchman who won eight caps for his country before joining Wolves for £620,000 from Feyenoord on 6 December 1994, made less than a dozen appearances during the second half of the 1994-95 season. He was then restricted to only a fraction above that amount the following campaign when rumours suggested that he could well be in line for the player-manager's job

at Molineux. This never materialised and after eighteen months with Wolves, De Wolf returned to Holland in June 1996, re-signing for Feyenoord, whom he later coached before moving in the same capacity to Sparta Rotterdam.

Born in Schniedam on 10 December 1962, and standing 6ft. 2ins tall and weighing 14 st. 6lbs, he had a varied career in Holland before settling down with Feyenoord for whom he made over 50 senior appearances.

His goal tally for Wolves included a hat-trick in a 4-2 win at Port Vale in February 1995 - becoming the first Wolves defender to achieve this feat for 93 years, since Ted Pheasant netted a treble in a 3-0 victory over Newcastle in March 1902.

John De Wolf

Wolves' record: 32+1 sub apps. 5 goals.

DEACON, James

Born to Irish parents in Glasgow on 4 January 1906 and brought up with his elder brother Richard (q.v.) in Darlington, Jimmy Deacon was a huge favourite with the Wolves fans during the early 1930s.

At 5ft 7ins tall and weighing barely 11 stones, he was not the tallest or heaviest of strikers, but he always gave a good account of himself against the some of the toughest defenders in the game. He had excellent ball skills and was often applauded for his artistry by players and supporters alike.

Deacon never attempted anything flashy and averaged a goal every three games for Wolves whom he joined in the summer of 1929 from Darlington.

After gaining a Second Division championship medal in 1933, he left Molineux in October 1934 for Southend United and retired from competitive football in 1939 after a short association with Hartlepools United.

Wolves' record: 158 apps. 55 goals.

DEACON, Richard

Also born in Glasgow on 26 June 1911, Richard Deacon, brother of Jimmy (q.v) was brought up in Darlington and was an apprentice fitter at a locomotive works before turning to football.

He played for Alliance Juniors, Albert Hill United and Darlington Juniors before having unsuccessful trials with Wolves in September 1928. He then assisted Cockfield FC and returned to Molineux as a professional in January 1930 after a brief trial period with Fulham.

A smart and efficient inside-forward, his first team outings for Wolves were restricted and each time he did get a game he replaced his brother in attack.

On leaving Wolves in June 1931, Deacon signed for West Ham United. Three years later he transferred across London to Chelsea (June 1934); played for Glenavon before the turn of the year and in October 1935 joined Northampton Town.

Deacon junior was with Lincoln City (August 1936 to October 1939) and guested for Northampton during the war. After the hostilities he retired to go and live in the North-east.

Wolves' record: 3 apps. one goal.

DEAKIN, Enoch

Enoch Deakin, born in Wolverhampton circa 1888, was a 1910-11 reserve inside-forward with Wolves. Standing only 5ft. 4ins tall, he made only a handful of senior appearances, replacing one the Needham brothers on four occasions and George Hedley once.

A pupil at Coven Council School, he joined the club from Chillington Rangers in April 1910 and returned to that same club on leaving Molineux in October 1911. He later played for Willenhall Pickwick.

Wolves' record: 5 apps. one goal.

DEAN, John

Jack Dean was a right or left-winger, born in Wolverhampton circa 1880, who played first team football for Wolves during the early part of the 20th century when he acted, in the main, as understudy to Jack Miller.

He played initially for Willenhall White Star and signed for Wolves from Trench Victoria in August 1901. On his release from Molineux in the summer of 1903 he joined Darlaston.

Wolves' record: 4 apps.

DEANS, Harold

Right-winger Harry Deans was a valuable member of Wolves' first team squad in the mid-1880s and was a regular in the side in 1884-85.

Born in Wolverhampton circa 1865, he played for Wednesbury Town and Bilston after leaving Wolves.

Wolves' record: 2 apps.

DEELEY, Norman Victor

The late 1950s were great times for Wolves' versatile winger Norman Deeley, for the Wednesbury-born star gained two League championship medals, was capped twice for England, against Brazil and Peru, and then in 1960 scored two goals as Blackburn Rovers were beaten in the FA Cup Final at Wembley.

Deeley was born on 30 November 1933 and was allegedly the smallest footballer ever to play for England Schoolboys when, in 1948, he stood only 4ft 4in tall. But Deeley's size did not daunt Wolves, who signed him as an amateur before he turned professional in December 1950.

He grew a foot in the meantime and made his League debut at right-half in August of the following year, yet it was not until 1955-56, after a few games at inside-forward, that he switched to the wing. National Service cost him many appearances but in 1957-58, when Wolves lifted the League title, Deeley missed just one game. And when they retained it the following season he was absent only four times.

Deeley eventually left Molineux in February 1962, joining up once more with his former Wolves colleague Bobby Mason at Leyton Orient for whom he netted nine goals in

Norman Deeley

73 outings before going into non-League soccer with Worcester City in July 1964. Later he assisted Bromsgrove Rovers (from August 1967) and Darlaston (from September 1971) before retiring in 1974.

Living in his native Wednesbury, Deeley became manager of the Caldmore Community Agency in Walsall and also took the post of steward with Walsall in the club's guest lounge.

Wolves' record: 237 apps. 73 goals.

DENNISON, Robert

Wolves signed Robbie Dennison from neighbours West Bromwich Albion in March 1987 and some two years later the winger had gained Fourth and Third Division championship medals, a Sherpa Van Trophy winners' medal and been capped at full international level by Northern Ireland.

Robbie Dennison

Born at Banbridge on 30 April 1963, Dennison joined Albion for £40,000 from the Irish League club Glenavon in September 1985. Unable to hold down a place in Albion's first team, he switched to Molineux shortly after Bull and Thompson had made similar journeys.

He cost Graham Turner only £20,000 but established himself as a key performer, playing wide on the left as Wolves rose sweetly from the Fourth to the Second Division in successive seasons. Dennison, who won 18 full caps for Ireland (all with Wolves) as well representing his country at both Youth and 'B' team levels, finally left Molineux in June 1997 after 11 years service, joining the Vauxhall Conference side Hednesford Town where he teamed up with another ex-Wolves star, Paul Blades.

Dennison was rewarded with a testimonial by Wolves in 1997-98, having a match at Molineux against Premier League side Blackburn Rovers. In December 1998 Dennison left the Pitmen to sign for Hereford United where he linked up again with his former manager Graham Turner and playing colleague Keith Downing.

Nowadays Dennison works in the trophy business, selling them, not winning them!

Wolves' record: 316+37 sub apps. 49 goals.

DEVEY, William

Will Devey came from the famous Midlands' footballing family and could play in a variety of positions, including those of wing-half and inside-forward.

Born in Birmingham on 12 April 1865, his career took him to all over the Midlands, from Wellington Road FC (Perry Barr) to Aston Unity (1882), to Small Heath Alliance (now Birmingham City) whom he served from August 1885; on to Wolves (playing at Molineux from August 1891 to December 1892), to Aston Villa (in January 1893), to Walsall Town Swifts (in May 1894), to Burton Wanderers (in 1895), across to Notts County (for almost two seasons: 1896-98), back to Walsall (early in 1898) and finally Small Heath again (from July 1898).

Retiring in 1900, he was a player with skill rather than strength, who did well with every club he served.

Wolves' record: 42 apps. 18 goals

DIAZ, Isidro

Born in Valencia, Spain on 15 May 1972, tricky right-winger 'Izzy' Diaz joined Wolves 'on trial' in September 1997 from Wigan Athletic.

He failed to impress the manager and went back to Springfield Park after just two weeks at Molineux during which time he appeared in one senior game, coming on as a substitute in the away League clash with Oxford United. Diaz was signed by Wigan from SC Balaguer (Spain) in July 1995 and before coming to Molineux he had been on trial with Walsall.

Later he had a spell with West Bromwich Albion and joined Rochdale in August 1998. Four months later, after 18 games for the Lancashire club, he returned home to Spain.

Wolves' record: 0+1 app.

DILLARD, Henry James

In July 1892 Wolves' committee appointed Harry Dillard as the club's reserve team manager, a position he held until shortly after the First World War.

Earlier he had put in a lot of hard work in helping to build up the Wolves first team. Born in Tewkesbury, Gloucestershire, circa 1858, Dillard was taken to Sheffield with his family at the age of two. On returning to the Midlands, he attended Wesley School, Pelsall and later became a founder-member of Walsall Swifts (1874-75). He played for that team for a time until a knee injury halted his progress. He then became the Swifts' official match umpire (a key position in the game at that time). From 1918 to 1940 Dillard represented Wolverhampton Wanderers on the Birmingham County FA and was presented with more than 30 different medals by various clubs and associations for his dedicated service to the game.

A highly respected figure and an avid Wolves supporter all his life.

DINNING, Anthony

Born on 12 April 1975 in Wallsend-on-Tyne, defender/midfielder Tony Dinning joined Wolves for £700,000 from Stockport County on 21 September 2000 and in his first season at Molineux made almost 40 appearances.

He was a trainee with Newcastle United for two years before signing professional forms at St James' Park in October 1993. Unfortunately he failed to make the Geordies' first XI and in June 1994 moved on a free transfer to Edgeley Park. He appeared in more than 200 senior games for the Hatters (30 goals scored).

Strong and positive, he slipped straight into the Wolves side just as if he'd been there all of his career and gave some excellent performances, mainly at the back.

However, things changed for Dinning when, in September 2001 after a loan spell at the Stadium, he joined Wigan Athletic for £750,000.

Wolves' record: 39 app. 7 goals.

DOCHERTY, Thomas Henderson

Tommy Docherty was manager of Wolves for thirteen months - from June 1984 to July 1985.

Born in Pershore, Glasgow on 24 April 1928 and raised in the Gorbals district of the city, he started kicking a ball around the back streets at the age of eight and in 1942 went to work in a bakery. He then started playing junior football for St. Paul's Guild FC and after assisting Shettlestone Juniors and the Highland Light Infantry while in the forces in Palestine, he signed for Glasgow Celtic in July 1948.

In November 1949 Docherty was transferred to Preston North End and made over 350 appearances for the Deepdale club, gaining runners-up medals in the First Division in 1953 and FA Cup Final the following year as well as helping the Deepdale club win the Second Division title in 1951.

In August 1958 he moved to Arsenal for £28,000, and had the misfortune to break an ankle playing against his former club Preston in October 1959. He recovered full fitness and in September 1961 switched to Chelsea as player-coach. He decided to retire as a player in January 1962 with more than 450 senior games under his belt, which included 25 full international appearances for Scotland.

He was immediately appointed team manager at Stamford Bridge and quickly guided Chelsea back into the First Division as well as seeing them lift the League Cup in 1965. In May 1967 he took the London club to Wembley where they lost the FA Cup Final to Spurs but in October of that year he resigned as manager after being banned by the FA following incidents during Chelsea's trip to Bermuda.

For a year from November 1967, the 'Doc' managed Rotherham United and then had 28 days in charge at QPR (November-December 1968). He quit Loftus Road after being refused permission to spend £35,000 on new players!

Twelve days after leaving Rangers he was appointed manager of Aston Villa but with Third Division football threatening Villa Park, he was sacked (January 1970). However, within a matter of weeks the 'Doc' became boss of the Portuguese side, FC Porto, a position he held until April 1971.

His next job was with Hull City, as assistant to manager Terry Neill, also a former Arsenal player, and in September 1971 he took over as caretaker-manager of the Scottish national team, moving up to manager two months later. He retained that post until December 1972 when he left to take over the reins at Manchester United.

Under his control United won the Second Division championship in 1975 and twice reached the FA Cup Final, but soon after winning the trophy in 1977, Docherty was sacked after admitting to having an affair with Laura Brown, wife of the club's physiotherapist.

Down but not out, the 'Doc' returned to football as Derby County boss in September 1977 and he remained at The Baseball Ground for two years before resigning. He then went back to QPR for a second spell in charge, but within a short period of time was sacked by Chairman Jim Gregory, who then re-instated him nine days later!

The axe finally fell on Docherty in October 1980 and two months later he decided to try his luck down under when he was appointed manager of the semi-professional club Sydney Olympic in Australia. In June 1981 he returned to England as manager of his former club Preston North End, but that job lasted for only six months. He returned to Australia to link up as coach with South Melbourne who promptly sacked him after eight months in office.

This brought him to Wolves, but following relegation to the Third Division at the end of his first season in charge, the 'Doc' was ousted yet again and after being out of football for a while he was given the manager's job at Vauxhall Conference side Altrincham.

One of the soccer's most controversial characters, Tommy Docherty who had over 40 years in the game and was associated with 15 clubs in a paid capacity, now earns his money as a popular after dinner speaker.

Docherty's record as Wolves manager was played 48, won 9, drawn 12, lost 27.

Alan Dodd

DODD, ALAN

Born in Stoke-on-Trent on 20 September 1953, 'Doddy' joined the junior ranks of Stoke City on leaving school in 1969 and turned professional in October 1970.

He made his first team debut in November 1972 and after establishing himself in the side, became a class player, with a lot of skill, being strong in both aerial and ground confrontations. But despite his excellent club form (he scored 4 goals in 416 games for the Potters in two spells) he never gained full England honours, collecting just six Under-23 caps for his efforts. Nevertheless, as a club man, Dodd was quite superb and he was eventually sold to Wolverhampton Wanderers for £40,000 in November 1982 after more than 12 years at Stoke.

He helped Wolves win promotion back to the First Division, but then returned to Stoke under manager Bill Asprey in January 1985, initially on a monthly contract. He stayed with the club until the end of the season when he went over to Sweden to assist Elfsborg.

He then played for GAIS Gothenburg and Elfsborg (again) before having two League games for Port Vale in 1986.

Dodd later turned out for Cork City and Landskrona Bols, as well as non-League Rocester and Goldenhill Wanderers before returning to Rocester as player-coach (1992-93). Later he assisted Ball Haye Green Young Men's Club.

Wolves' record: 99 apps. 6 goals.

DORSETT, Richard

Dicky Dorsett was as tough as any player in the game during the 1930s and '40s. He spent 18 years in top-class soccer, serving in the main with just two clubs - Wolves and Aston Villa.

Born in Brownhills, Staffs on 3 December 1919, he represented Walsall & District Boys and the Birmingham County FA before joining Wolves as a junior in April 1935, turning professional on his 17th birthday the following year.

He was still a teenager learning the game when he scored Wolves' goal in their 4-1 FA Cup Final defeat by Portsmouth in 1939. Prior to that Wembley appearance he had netted two four-timers in League games for the Wanderers - against Leicester City in 1938 and Everton a year later, both in the First Division.

Nicknamed the 'Brownhills Bomber' Dorsett was a powerful, hard-shooting, strong-kicking player whose career at Molineux was severely disrupted by the war. Indeed, although serving in the RAF he played for the Wolves in every season during the hostilities (except 1940-41) scoring 42 goals in 61 appearances.

He also guested for Brentford, Grimsby Town, Liverpool, QPR and Southampton during the hostilities. He surprisingly left Molineux for Villa Park in September 1946 and over the next seven years, during which time he was successfully converted into a rugged, no-nonsense defender, Dorsett gave the Claret and Blue faithful plenty to cheer about, scoring 36 goals in 271 appearances.

In January 1950, however, his playing days nearly came to an abrupt end when he was involved in a serious car accident, but he recovered to play another three years with Villa. After retiring Dorsett was given a coaching job at Villa Park and in July 1957 was appointed assistant-trainer at Liverpool. He returned to the Midlands in 1962 to take over the running of a local junior side near Lichfield and resided in Brownhills until his death in 1998.

NB - Dicky Dorsett was the nephew of the former Manchester City and West Bromwich Albion brothers Joe and George Dorsett.

Wolves' record: 52 apps. 35 goals.

DOUGAN, Alexander Derek

An intelligent and skilful attack leader, Derek Dougan was a master of positional play and of using his height to win the ball in the air and playing it off with neat glancing headers. His long, raking stride meant he could outpace most defenders and he often outwitted the opposition with sudden acceleration. Extrovert on and off the pitch, Dougan quietened down late on in his career (especially with Wolves) and became a fine ambassador of the game and an impressive spokesman for the players.

He was certainly one of the most colourful footballers of his day, once shaving his head completely bald.

Always a big favourite with the fans, he played for Distillery, Portsmouth, Blackburn Rovers, Aston Villa, Peterborough United, Leicester City and Wolves. He won 43 caps for Northern Ireland (some as captain) and by the time his playing career was over (in 1975) he had scored 262 goals in 692 senior appearances.

Born in Belfast on 20 January 1938, Dougan had a brief spell in the Irish League before joining Portsmouth in August 1957, by which time he had been capped at

Derek Dougan in action

schoolboy, youth and amateur levels as a wing-half and central defender.

Pompey switched him to centre-forward and after he had scored nine goals in 33 League games (his first against Wolves in November 1957 in a 1-1 draw), Blackburn signed him in March 1959.

The Doog, as he became known, scored 25 goals in 59 First Division games for the Ewood Park club and appeared against Wolves in the 1960 FA Cup Final. In August 1961, Joe Mercer signed him for Villa for £15,000 to replace Gerry Hitchens, who had gone to Inter-Milan, and at Villa Park, Dougan continued to score goals, claiming 26 in 60 League and Cup games.

Then he moved to Peterborough in June 1963, for £21,000 and netted 38 goals in 77 League games for the Posh before yet another move, this time to Leicester for £25,000 in May 1965. With the Filbert Street club he struck 35 goals in 68 League games before what he described as his 'best move' to Wolves for £50,000 in March 1967.

Dougan arrived just in time to help Wolves back to Division One and it was certainly a successful period for both player and club: Dougan gained a League Cup winners' award in 1974 and a UEFA Cup runners-up prize in 1972.

He made a quick impression, scoring a hat-trick on his home debut against Hull City, and altogether he hit five trebles for the club. He was also Wolves' top scorer in 1967-68, 1968-69 and 1971-72.

Altogether for Wolves he scored over 120 goals in more than 320 senior games.

And in fact, the Doog notched more goals in League Football than any other Irishman - 219. And he is one of the few players to score a hat-trick in the Football League, FA Cup, League Cup and in a European competition.

A former PFA chairman, who also managed Kettering Town for a spell, Dougan returned to Molineux in August 1982, as chairman and chief executive, a post he held until the arrival of the Bhatti brothers.

After moving to Codsall, near Wolverhampton, he became involved in raising money for the Duncan Edwards Medical Centre.

In 1998, it was revealed that Dougan, who suffered a heart attack a year earlier, from which he thankfully recovered after treatment, was considering a take-over bid for Stoke City football club - but nothing materialised.

NB - Dougan's brother was married on the same day as Queen Elizabeth and Prince Philip, and another brother was born on the same day as prince Charles, while 'Doog' himself became a father of a boy on the day after the Queen had given birth to her fourth child.

Wolves' record: 307+16 sub apps. 123 goals.

DOUGHERTY, Paul

Nicknamed 'Pee-Wee' midfielder Paul Dougherty, at 5ft. 2ins., became one of the smallest players ever to star in a Football League match for Wolves when he made his debut against neighbours West Bromwich Albion at

Paul Dougherty

Molineux in April 1984.

A terrier-type performer, he always gave 100 per-cent effort out on the park and was certainly a big hit with the fans.

Born in Leamington Spa on 12 May 1964, he joined Wolves as an apprentice in June 1982 and turned professional in May 1984. In February/March 1985 he went on loan to Torquay United before being released by Wolves in May 1987, following relegation to the Forth Division.

At this point he chose to go and play his football in the NASL indoor League with San Diego, but returned to England within two years and actually returned for a trial at Molineux, playing in three reserve games.

In September 1992, having appeared for several non-League sides round the Midlands, Dougherty was given a two-week trial by West Bromwich Albion, playing in two reserve matches without impressing The Hawthorns management team.

Wolves' record: 47 apps. 5 goals.

DOWE, Jens

German midfielder Jens Dowe joined Wolves 'on loan' for £200,000 from the Bundesliga club HSV Hamburg in October 1996, but remained at Molineux for barely seven months before leaving to sign for Sturm Graz for £100,000.

Born in Rostock, Germany (George Berry's birthplace) on 1 June 1968, Dowe never settled in England and he turned out to be a rather expensive player as far as Wolves were concerned!

Wolves' record: 5+3 sub apps.

DOWEN, John Stewart

As a youngster Jack Dowen represented Walsall Boys and played for England v. Scotland and Wales in Schoolboy internationals in 1929. And later on, in 1934, he starred for the Birmingham County FA v. Scotland.

A stocky, but quite robust full-back, Dowen, who never acknowledged defeat, was born in Wolverhampton in November 1914 and joined Wolves from Courtaulds FC as an amateur in March 1931, turning professional in August 1932.

Acting as reserve to Wilf Lowton, Reg Hollingworth, Bill Morris and George Laking, his outings in the first XI were limited and in October 1935 he was transferred to West Ham United, only to return to Molineux in October 1936.

This time he stayed for two years before moving to Hull City (June 1938). During the war he guested for Wolves as well as Hull City, Darlington and Leeds United and later returned to Molineux as first team trainer, a position he held until the early 1970s. In 1968 he was joint caretaker-manager with Gerry Summers for one game!

After this he did some coaching and scouting, was number one kit-man and also acted as the club's all-purpose odd-job man. He had been associated with Wolves for some 50 years when he eventually left Molineux in 1982.

Wolves' record: 12 apps.

DOWNING, Keith Gordon

Nicknamed 'psycho', Keith Downing was a hard-working, impetuous midfielder, often in trouble with referees for his over-robust style of play, but always totally committed to playing football.

Born in Oldbury, West Midlands on 23 July 1965, he had an unsuccessful spell with Chelsea as a teenager and after

Keith Downing

serving with Mile Oak Rovers (Tamworth) he joined Notts County in May 1985. From Meadow Lane he switched to Wolves on a free transfer in August 1987 and had a fine career at Molineux, helping the team win both the Third and Fourth Division championships (in successive seasons) as well as the Sherpa Van Trophy.

He left Wolves for Birmingham City in July 1993 and twelve months later switched to Stoke City for whom he made 24 appearances before joining Cardiff City in August 1995, quickly switching to Hereford United after just a month at Ninian Park.

Under his former manager Graham Turner, he helped the 'Bulls' reach the Third Division play-offs in 1996. Downing retired in 1997 and became a 'rep' for a Dudley Publishing Company, later returning to assist Hereford after they had been relegated to the Vauxhall Conference. He was appointed player-coach (still under Turner) at Edgar Street in 1998 but in March 1999 he made it full circle by going back to Molineux as Youth team coach in place of Chris Turner.

Wolves' record: 200+28 sub apps. 11 goals.

DUDLEY, Robert

Bob Dudley was a strong tackling left-half whose his only first team appearance for the club came in the last game of the inaugural League season.

That was against Notts County at Molineux on 23 February 1889 when he replaced Arthur Lowder who was 'rested' before a vital third round FA Cup-tie v. Sheffield Wednesday.

Born in Audley in 1864, Dudley joined Wolves from Audley Welfare in February 1889 and left for Warwick County seven months later. He then assisted Bradley Primitives (1890), Wallbrook FC and Bilston Royal before retiring in 1900.

Wolves' record: one app.

DUNN, Edwin

Eddie Dunn played for Wolves during the last season prior to World War One.

Born in Coventry circa 1891, he was a short, stocky footballer, occupying the inside-right berth. He joined the Molineux staff from Nuneaton Town in July 1914 and after the hostilities had ended, signed for Rugby Town at the start of the 1919-20 campaign.

Wolves' record: 16 apps. 3 goals.

DUNN, James

Son of the former Everton and Scotland inside-forward and 'Wembley Wizard' of the same name, Jimmy Dunn was born in Edinburgh on 25 November 1923 and was playing for a junior side called St. Theresa's in the Merseyside & District League when Wolves signed him as an amateur in 1941.

He became a professional in November of the following year, but after some success in Wartime football (he played in some 100 games when free from his duties as a railway

Jimmy Dunn

fireman) Dunn found himself in the reserves at Molineux on the resumption of League football in August 1946. Dunn in fact, played only three times for the seniors as Wolves went all the way to the wire in that season's League championship race. But the following season he gained a more regular place in the side and in 1949 collected an FA Cup winners' medal after an outstanding campaign as partner to outside-left Jimmy Mullen. The following year unfortunately he was troubled with a serious back injury, but fought back and was a valuable asset until 1952-53, when he played in the first game, but then lost his place and in November was transferred to struggling Derby County.

The Rams hoped that Dunn might help them retain their First Division status but after only six weeks he suffered a cartilage injury which necessitated an operation. Derby were looking at their first-ever season in the Third Division (North) when they released Dunn to Southern League club Worcester City in the summer of 1955. It had not been a successful time, but Dunn had still managed 21 goals in 58 games for Derby.

From June 1957 to May 1959 he played for Runcorn and then after managing the Roebuck licensed house, Penn, he became a coach at West Bromwich Albion (initially under Jimmy Hagan) and twice went to Wembley with the Baggies. He later worked as a physiotherapist at the Edgbaston Clinic (to 1984) and was then a 'rep' in Dudley while running his own gymnasium in the jewellery quarter in Birmingham.

He retired in 1988 and is now resident in Cradley Heath, and when possible still plays tennis at the Quinton Tennis Club.

Wolves' record: 144 apps. 40 goals.

E

DUNN, Richard R

Dicky Dunn was given just one League outing by Wolves, as a replacement for the injured Bob Young in the away Second Division game at Bradford Park Avenue in April 1913 - and it was a game he quickly wanted to forget as Wolves lost heavily by five goals to one.

Born in Lichfield circa 1890, Dunn played for Cannock before joining Wolves in July 1912. He left Molineux in May 1915 to go to war and on his return signed for Hednesford Thistle with whom he stayed for three years, retiring in May 1922.

Wolves' record: one app.

DUNN, Thomas

Tommy Dunn was a moustachio'd full-back, rather on the small side, both in height and weight, but a player who always gave a good account of himself against a variety of opponents.

A Scotsman, born in 1869, he played for East Stirlingshire prior to teaming up with Wolves in August 1891. He spent six years at Molineux, during which time he appeared in the 1896 FA Cup Final defeat by Sheffield Wednesday.

After being replaced in the first team by Harry Wood (who switched from inside-left), Dunn had a disagreement with the Wolves committee and left the club for Burnley in November 1896, later assisting the Kent club, Chatham (from November 1897) before returning to Scotland where he ended his career.

Wolves' record: 102 apps.

DURANDT, Clifford Michael

A South African left-winger, born in Johannesburg on 16 April 1940, Cliff Durandt attended K.E.S. School in his home town and played for Marist Brothers before joining Wolves as a professional in June 1957.

Over the next six years he was in and out of the Wolves first team and in March 1963, manager Stan Cullis transferred him to Charlton Athletic for a fee of £15,000. Two years later Durandt returned to South Africa to play for Germiston Callies.

'Capped' by his country at the age of 16 (v. Wolves in a friendly - hence his move to Molineux) Durandt also represented Transvaal Province at both rugby and swimming. He now lives in his native Johannesburg.

Wolves' record: 49 apps. 10 goals.

DWYER, Noel Michael

Irishman Noel Dwyer was a 'broth of a boy' who played both Gaelic football and hurling as a teenager.

Born in Dublin on 30 October 1934, he was one of several promising goalkeepers developed at Molineux during the 1950s. He arrived at the club from Ormeau FC in August 1953, signing professional forms two months later.

He spent the next five years at Molineux, acting as understudy to the likes of Bert Williams, Malcolm

Finlayson, Fred Davies and Geoff Sidebottom. He finally made his League debut (in place of Sidebottom) in 1957, but in December of the following year was transferred to West Ham United.

In August 1960, Dwyer moved to Swansea Town and after more than 150 appearances for the Vetch Field club, with whom he won a Welsh Cup winners medal in 1961 (v. Bangor), he switched his allegiance to Plymouth Argyle in January 1965. There he took over between the sticks from Dave MacLaren, who ironically moved to Wolves! Dwyer rounded off his League career with Charlton Athletic (December 1965 to May 1966), finishing with 213 League games under his belt.

Capped 14 times by the Republic of Ireland between 1960-65, he also represented his country's 'B' team and on retiring (sadly through cartilage trouble) he became licensee of the Trafalgar public house in Wimblebury, later moving to Claregate, Tettenhall.

One of Dwyer's three daughters (a former Page 3 pin-up model) married ex-England striker Frank Worthington.

Wolves' record: 5 apps.

EASTOE, Peter Robert

Although he was never really given a chance at Molineux, Peter Eastoe was a fine marksman, who amassed an excellent record in League football, scoring 95 goals in 330 appearances.

Born at Dorden, Tamworth on 2 August 1953, he attended Dorden Junior and Polesworth High Schools, represented Nuneaton & District Boys and played junior football for Glascote Highfield and Warton Hatters before signing as an apprentice for Wolves in June 1970, turning professional twelve months later.

Capped by England Youth eight times, Eastoe found it difficult to break into the Wolves first team and in November 1973 he signed on a temporary transfer for Swindon Town, making the move permanent for £88,000 in March 1974.

He finished up as top-scorer for the Robins in seasons 1973-74 and 1974-75, before becoming a soccer nomad, playing, in turn, for Queens Park Rangers (signed for £80,000 in March 1976), Everton (in a player-exchange involving Mike Walsh, in March 1979), West Bromwich Albion (signed for £250,000, plus future Wolves midfielder Andy King, in July 1982), Leicester City (on loan in October 1983), Walsall (on loan during August and September 1984), Huddersfield Town (on loan in March and April 1984), Wolves (on loan during February 1985), Sporting Farense in Portugal (transferred there in July 1985), Atherstone Town (from August 1988) Bridgnorth Town (during the 1989-90 season), Atherstone Town again (1990-91), Alvechurch (as team manager from August 1991 to April 1992) and finally Nuneaton Borough (as assistant-manager in season 1992-93).

Eastoe top-scored for QPR in season 1977-78 and he

played in two cup semi-finals (in the League Cup for QPR in 1977 and in the FA Cup for Everton in 1979). His best spell was undoubtedly at Goodison Park when he scored 33 goals in 115 games for the Merseysiders.

Wolves' record: 14+3 apps. one goal.

ECCLES, George Samuel

Full-back George Eccles was described as being a 'grand tackler and untiring worker' who played the game 'professionally, never committing a bad foul.'

Born in Newcastle-under-Lyme, Staffs in 1874, Eccles started out with Wolstanton Brotherhood FC and then played, in turn, for Stoke St. Peter's, Titbury Town, Middleport and Burslem Port Vale (June 1893).

He broke his collarbone with Vale, but made a full recovery and was transferred to Wolves in May 1896. He took over from Dickie Baugh at right-back and proved a fine replacement, although he surprisingly left Molineux after just two seasons, switching north to Everton in April 1898.

Four years later he signed for West Ham United (May 1902) and rounded off his career with short spells at Preston North End (from 1904) and Bolton Wanderers. His only goal for Wolves was a cracking 30-yard drive against Nottingham Forest in April 1897 that earned a 2-1 victory. He made over 50 appearances for Vale, 60 for Everton and 64 for West Ham.

Wolves' record: 37 apps. one goal.

EDGE, Robert

Outside-left Bob Edge, brother of Alf Edge, who played for Walsall, had a useful time with Wolves whom he served for almost four years, from August 1893 to May 1897.

He was born in Wolverhampton circa 1871 and played for St. Phillips' Church team before joining Wolves.

On leaving Molineux he played for Loughborough and later returned to the Wolverhampton area to play for Excelsior FC (local League).

Wolves' record: 25 apps. 8 goals.

EDMONDS, George William Neville

George Edmonds, a tough centre-forward, who was born in Holborn on 4 April 1893, played his early football with St. Stephen's, Andre's FC, with whom he gained a Drinking Trades Cup winners' medal, and St Albans City. He joined his local side Watford as a professional in 1912 and helped them win the Southern League championship in 1915. He played for England in a Victory International before moving to Wolves in the 1920 close season.

Edmonds made his Football League debut against the club he was later to join, Fulham, in August of that year, and by the time he left Molineux in September 1923, he had scored over 40 goals in 126 League and Cup games. He was leading scorer in each of his three seasons as a Wanderers player, and played in the 1921 FA Cup Final against Tottenham Hotspur at Stamford Bridge.

George Edmonds

He formed a fine strike force with Stan Fazackerley, but became unsettled when Wolves dropped into the Third Division (North), so the club allowed him to move to Fulham. Alas, he never broke into the Cottagers' League side and eventually returned to Watford in 1926. The following year he entered non-League football before retiring in May 1929.

Wolves' record: 126 apps. 42 goals.

EDWARDS, Dean Stephen

Born in Wolverhampton on 25 February 1962, striker Dean Edwards joined Shrewsbury Town on leaving school and turned professional at Gay Meadow in February 1980.

A spell abroad with Pallosuera (Finland) preceded a move to Telford United in 1983 and from Buck's Head he transferred to Wolves in October 1985.

Unfortunately Edwards failed to make an impact at Molineux, but his game developed considerably after leaving Wolves for Exeter City in March 1987.

From St James' Park he switched to neighbouring Torquay United in July 1988 and after a brief spell as a non-contract player with Northampton Town (from February to April 1992) he entered non-League soccer with Yeovil Town four months later.

After signing for Stafford Rangers in 1993 he then chose to return to South Devon to become manager of Bideford Town. Edwards made over 120 appearances for Torquay, whom he helped reach the Final of the Sherpa Van Trophy at Wembley in 1989 as well as the Fourth Division promotion play-offs.

He quit Bideford in July 1998 to take over Striker's pub near to his old hunting ground at Plainmoor.

Wolves' record: 30+4 apps. 10 goals.

EDWARDS, Evan Jenkin

Welsh Amateur international winger who could also play as an inside-forward or left-half, Evan Edwards was a fine footballer with great vision and telling shot.

Born in Merthyr on 14 December 1898, he served his home-town club Merthyr Town from August 1920 until joining Wolves for £750 in May 1923.

After two years at Molineux he returned to Wales to sign for Mid Rhondda in July 1925, later assisting Swansea Town (October 1925), Northampton Town (July 1926),

Halifax Town (September 1927), Ebbw Vale (early 1928), Darlington (August 1928) and Clapton Orient (September 1929 to May 1930).

He helped Wolves win the Third Division (North) championship in 1924 when he linked up superbly well down the left with Shaw, Kay and Lees.

Wolves' record: 70 apps. 13 goals.

EDWARDS, Neil Anthony

Versatile forward Neil Edwards was born in Rowley Regis, Warley on 14 March 1966 and played for Oldswinford before becoming a professional with Wolves in August 1985. He spent three years at Molineux - breaking his leg in a 5-2 win at Burnley in February 1987 - before pulling out of League football in May 1988 after a recurring knee injury, initially suffered with Wolves.

He signed for Kettering Town at this juncture and remained there for two years.

Wolves' record: 32+4 apps. 7 goals.

EDWARDS, Paul Ronald

Ginger-haired full-back Paul Edwards was a solid performer, who joined Wolves from Coventry City in August 1992 for £100,000.

Always giving a good account of himself, he began his career with Altrincham before entering League football with Crewe Alexandra in January 1988. He made over 100 appearances for the 'Alex' who then sold him to Coventry for £350,000 in March 1990. He was in and out of the side at Highfield Road and jumped at the chance of moving to Wolves.

Unfortunately in his two years at Molineux he struggled from time to time with injury and in January 1994 was transferred to West Bromwich Albion for £80,000. At The Hawthorns Edwards again suffered with a back injury as well as undergoing a hernia operation and after 57 games for the Baggies he was loaned out to Bury (February 1996).

He signed for the Gigg Lane club on a permanent basis a month later, before joining Hednesford Town in September of that same year.

In season 1998-99, after two years recuperating from a serious stomach injury at his Coventry home, Edwards was appointed assistant-manager of Paget Rangers.

Wolves' record: 48+3 apps.

ELI, Roger

A tall, well-built utility player, equally at home in defence or midfield, Roger Eli spent just over 18 months at Molineux, from January 1986 to August 1987.

Born in Bradford on 11 September 1965 he joined Leeds United as an apprentice on leaving school and turned professional at Elland Road in September 1983. Wolves recruited him from the Yorkshire club at a time when things were going badly on the pitch at Molineux.

Unfortunately Eli's presence had little effect on the team's overall performances and on leaving the club he signed for Cambridge United as a non-contract player. A month after moving to The Abbey Stadium, Eli went to Crewe Alexandra and after that he served with Northwich Victoria, York City (November 1988), Bury (on a non contract basis, January 1989), in Hong Kong, Burnley (July 1989), Scunthorpe United and finally Partick Thistle, retiring in 1993.

Wolves' record: 18+3 apps.

ELLIOTT, Edward

Goalkeeper Ted Elliott played second fiddle to Bert Williams during his two-and-a-half years with Wolves.

Born in Carlisle on 24 May 1919, he was registered with his home town club, Carlisle United, for ten years (from 1936) making less than 30 senior appearances for the Cumbrians. In March 1946 he joined Wolves and remained at Molineux until October 1948 when he was transferred to Chester.

He played in a further 59 League games while at Sealand Road before rounding off his career with Halifax Town (November 1950 to May 1952).

Strong-armed with good positional sense, Elliott kicked long, could throw a ball out some fifty yards and was a clean puncher, although at times he was suspect under pressure.

Wolves' record: 7 apps.

ELLIS, John

When Wolves won the Second Division championship in 1932-33 goalkeeper Jack Ellis played in half of his side's 42 matches, doing well in most of them.

Born at Tyldesley, Lancashire on 25 January 1908, and now deceased, Ellis joined Wolves three months into the 1930-31 season having played four years in his native county and briefly as an amateur with West Bromwich Albion (May-October 1930). From Molineux, Ellis switched to Bristol Rovers (July 1934) and following the arrival of Joe Nicholls from Spurs he moved to Hull City (August 1938), rounding off an interesting career with Clapton Orient (July 1939-45).

A fine figure of a man, standing almost six feet tall and weighing around 12 stones, Ellis could deal expertly with high crosses and kicked well out of his hands. Unfortunately he was on the wrong end of Bristol Rovers' 12-0 drubbing by Luton Town in a Third Division (South) match in 1936 when stand-in centre-forward Joe Payne scored ten goals.

Wolves' record: 26 apps.

EMBLEN, Neil Robert

Born in Bromley, Kent on 19 June 1971, the versatile Neil Emblen played for Sittingbourne before becoming a professional with Millwall in November 1993, the Lions paying £175,000 for his signature.

Neil Emblen

After just 13 games for the London club, Wolves stepped in with a £600,000 bid and brought Emblen to Molineux where he did well until suffering a torn hamstring on a summer tour in 1996.

The injury lingered on, yet after regaining full fitness he established himself in the side once more, occupying a number of positions, including those of right-back, centre-half and sweeper, although his best berth was that of an attacking midfielder. However, Emblen was hurt again in March 1997 (at Bradford) and in the August manager Mark McGhee transferred him to Premiership newcomers Crystal Palace for £2 million, only for him to return to Molineux for a second spell in March 1998 for £900,000.

At the end of the 2000-01 season he was placed on the transfer list by new Wolves manager David Jones...and just prior to the start of the next campaign he was recruited by Norwich City for a fee of £500,000 (July 2001), linking up with another former Wolves player, Iwan Roberts.

Wolves' record: 131+18 sub apps. 12 goals

EVANS, Alun William

Born in Stourport-on-Severn on 30 September 1949, the son of the former West Bromwich Albion and Wales wartime international by the same name, striker Alun Evans became Britain's costliest teenager when he was transferred from Wolves to Liverpool for £100,000 in September 1968.

Earlier in his career, after winning England caps at Schoolboy, Youth and Under-23 levels, he was regarded as the 'star of the future' but sadly he never reached the heights expected of him. A pupil at Bewdley State School, he represented mid-Worcester Boys and Birmingham Schools, and after a trial with Aston Villa he signed as an apprentice with Wolves (July 1965), turning professional in October 1966.

A blonde striker, quick off the mark with an eye for goal, Evans did well at Molineux, hence his big-money transfer to Anfield, and for the Merseysiders he scored 21 goals in 79 League games, appearing in the 1971 FA Cup Final.

His stay at Anfield was marred by a much publicised night club incident which resulted in Evans receiving a badly gashed face leaving him scarred him for life, and he also underwent a cartilage operation.

He moved to Aston Villa for £72,000 in June 1972, and three years later gained a League Cup winners' medal. Nine months after that Wembley clash with Norwich City - and a haul of 17 goals in 72 outings - he was transferred to Walsall for £30,000.

While at Fellows Park he played more in midfield than as a striker and amassed 101 appearances (8 goals) up to July 1978 when, after a trial, he joined the Australian club, South Melbourne. From there he went to Hellas FC and returned to Melbourne for £10,000 in August 1979, retiring two years later.

Evans chose to stay in Australia and now resides with his wife and family in Cheltenham, Victoria.

Wolves' record: 20+2 apps. 4 goals.

EVANS, Anthony

A Scouser from Liverpool (born 11 January 1954), striker Tony Evans was an electrician working in Lancashire and playing for Formby FC. From there he became a professional with Blackpool (June 1973) and two years later moved to Cardiff City. At Ninian Park he established himself as a very useful striker and from then until the end of his career scored plenty of goals. From Cardiff he switched to Birmingham City (July 1979) and in August 1983 (after 33 goals in 76 games for Blues) he signed for Crystal Palace (August 1983).

In April 1984 he made his way to Molineux, but found it difficult to fit into a struggling side and after loan spells in 1985 with Bolton Wanderers (February) and Exeter City (March-April) he teamed up with Swindon Town in readiness for the start of the 1985-86 campaign.

After more than a year with the Robins Evans moved back to the Midlands to sign for Walsall on a non contract basis in September 1986 and later that year he was recruited by Stafford Rangers, returning to Molineux as 'Football in the Community Officer' in 1991.

In his senior career Evans scored well over 100 goals in 300 appearances (87 in 254 League games). He netted a four-timer for Cardiff against Bristol Rovers in a League Cup-tie in August 1976.

Wolves' record: 24+3 apps. 6 goals.

EVANS Jasper

Rock-solid left-half, Jasper Evans played for Wolves in the mid-1880s, but his career was cut short by a persistent knee injury.

Born in Wednesbury circa 1861, he played for Wednesbury White Rose, King's Hill FC and Wednesbury Town before joining Wolves in August 1885. He left the Wanderers for West Bromwich Standard in May 1887 and retired a year later.

Wolves' record: 3 apps.

EVES, Melvyn John

Born at Wednesbury on 10 September 1956, striker Mel Eves scored 53 goals in 214 senior games during his 11 years on the Molineux staff, helping Wolves to the Second

Mel Eves

Division championship in 1977 and League Cup glory in 1980.

He joined the club as an apprentice in July 1973 and became a full-time professional in July 1975. Eves, who was Wolves' leading scorer with 19 goals in 1982-83, also won three England 'B' caps, against Singapore (twice) and New Zealand. During the early 1980s, there was a feeling that Eves had not been treated fairly and after suffering a series of injuries he left Wolves for Sheffield United in December 1984, after a loan spell with Huddersfield Town.

In August 1986, the Blades let him go to Gillingham and he later spent short loan spells with Mansfield Town, Manchester City and West Bromwich Albion. He retired in the 1989 close season after an impressive record of 67 League goals in 243 appearances with his seven League clubs.

Eves later played for Telford United and Cheltenham Town in the GM Vauxhall Conference League, for Old Wulfrunians and took part in charity matches. Nowadays Eves in a football agent.

Wolves' record: 202+12 apps. 53 goals.

FARLEY, John Denis

Versatile winger John Farley served with six different League clubs in 12 years between 1969 and 1981.

Born in Middlesbrough on 21 September 1951, he played initially for Stockton (1967) and after that assisted Watford (July 1969), Halifax Town (on loan September 1971), Wolves (May 1974), Blackpool (on loan October 1976), Hull City (May 1978) and Bury (August 1980 to May 1981).

He appeared in more than 250 senior games as a professional and netted over 20 goals, laying on plenty more for his colleagues. He helped Watford establish themselves in the Second Division during his five-year stay at Vicarage Road. Unfortunately he never really established himself at Molineux.

Wolves' record: 38+5 apps.

FARMER, James Edward

Although centre-forward Ted Farmer played only four seasons of League football for Wolves before his career came to a cruel and premature end at the age of 24, he made his mark with a splendid scoring record of 44 goals in only 62 games. And even in his fleeting international career, he wrote his name large with two Under-23 caps, against Israel and Holland in 1961, netting a smart hat-trick against the Dutch.

In the 1960-61 season he scored 28 goals in only 27 League games, including four goals against Birmingham City at Molineux in March.

He was born in Rowley Regis on 21 January 1940 and played for Wednesbury High School, Rowley Regis Boys and Dudley & District Schools. Outside school he turned out at weekends for Wednesbury Commercial and also for

Ted Farmer

Wednesbury Youth Club, and in November 1955 he scored 21 goals in one day, with 13 in the morning and eight in the afternoon.

Those sort of goalscoring exploits soon came to the attention of local League clubs and Wolves won the race to sign him in the 1956 close season. In his first season with Wolves juniors, Farmer netted a remarkable total of 86 goals.

Wolves made him a full-time professional in August 1960 and on his League debut, at Old Trafford of all places, he scored twice in a 3-1 victory over Manchester United. Between his debut day and 21 January 1961 he scored 21 goals in only 17 League games including a hat-trick against Arsenal!

Farmer followed up with a fourtimer against Birmingham City in March 1961 and weighed in another four-goal salvo against Manchester City when Wolves raced to an emphatic 8-1 home victory on the opening day of the 1962-63 season. He seemed set to become the goalscoring sensation of the decade when injury struck when least expected. Sadly he played only six more games in 1963-64 before retiring.

No-one really knew at the time (except perhaps those close to him, especially his trainer and manager at Molineux) but Farmer had been continually plagued by injuries, suffering a damaged bladder, a broken leg (versus Fulham in December 1961 which in effect wasn't diagnosed until five weeks later), numerous dislocations, a couple of bad twists, a handful of cracked or chipped bones, a few

sprains and strains and a bout of concussion. Even boxers don't suffer that much!

Farmer later published a book about his career and he was also the licensee of the Lamp Tavern in Dudley.

Wolves' record: 62 apps. 44 goals.

FARRINGTON, John Robert

John Farrington was an out-and-out winger, rather on the slim side, but fast and clever nonetheless.

Born at Lynemouth on 19 June 1947, he joined Wolves as a junior in 1963 and turned professional in June 1965. In the next four years he drifted in and out of the first team before leaving Molineux for Leicester City in a £30,000 deal in October 1969.

He did very well at Filbert Street and after scoring 18 goals in 118 League appearances he moved to Cardiff City (November 1973).

From Ninian Park he switched to Northampton Town in October 1974. He hit over 30 goals in more than 250 outings for the Cobblers up to 1981 when he dropped into non-League soccer, serving first with AP Leamington (whom he managed for a short time), then Shepshed Charterhouse before taking charge of Barlestone FC in the Influence Combination (1991-92).

He helped keep Cardiff out of the Third Division, made a Welsh Cup Final appearance and also played in a European game during his time at Ninian Park.

Wolves' record: 35+3 apps. 5 goals.

FARROW, George Henry

One of the few players who served Blackpool before and after the Second World War, George Farrow was born in Whitburn on 4 October 1913 and played for Whitburn Boys before becoming a professional with Stockport County in October 1930.

In January 1932 he left Edgeley Park for Molineux, signed by Major Buckley as cover for right-half Dicky Rhodes. A reliable performer, he played in a quarter of Wolves' games on their return to the First Division, but was then sold to Bournemouth in July 1933, later playing for Blackpool (June 1936).

After the hostilities he signed for Sheffield United (January 1948) and retired in May 1950.

Wolves' record: 12 apps.

FAZACKERLEY, Stanley Nicholas

Stan Fazackerley was another forward who spent only a short time with Wolves, barely three seasons, yet he became a big favourite with the fans, helping the club to the Third Division (North) championship in 1923-24.

A Lancastrian, born in Preston on 3 October 1891, Fazackerley, a tall and skilful inside-forward, played with local club Lands End United and had an unsuccessful trial with Preston North End before going over to North America, where he spent a season with Charleston in the Boston League in 1910, helping them win the title.

Stan Fazackerley

He returned to England to sign for Accrington Stanley, then in the Lancashire Combination, before Hull City recruited him in April 1912.

Sheffield United were impressed enough to pay £1,000 for his signature in March 1913, and Fazackerley scored one of the Blades' goals in their 3-0 win over Chelsea in the 1915 FA Cup Final (this was in fact, called the 'Khaki Final' because so many soldiers home on leave from the Western Front were present in the crowd).

After the war Everton paid a then British record fee of £4,000 for him in November 1920 and he arrived at Molineux, with team-mate George Brewster, in November 1922. Former Wolves boss George Jobey, then manager of Derby, signed Fazackerley for the Rams in March 1925, after the player had been loaned out to Kidderminster Harriers whilst on Wolves' transfer list.

Derby had a centre-forward problem and Fazackerley was one of three men tried in the first six games of 1925-26 before Harry Bedford was brought in to solve the problem. For Fazackerley it was the end of the road anyway and he retired on medical advice in April 1926.

As a Sheffield United player he toured South Africa with the FA in 1920 and once scored 11 goals for Hull City in a 16-1 friendly match win over the amateurs Trondheim & District XI in Norway in May 1912.
Wolves' record: 77 apps. 32 goals.

FEATHERBY, Walter Leonard

Len Featherby was one of soccer's globetrotters. An effective inside-forward, he had a wide and varied career which spanned almost 20 years.

Born in King's Lynn on 28 July 1905, he began his playing days with Whitefriars FC in 1921. After that he went on to assist, in turn, Lynn Town, Norfolk County, Glasgow Rangers (as a trialist in January 1924), Norwich City (signed as an amateur in May 1924 and taken on the professional staff in June 1924), Northfleet (secured in early October 1927), Millwall (signed in late October 1927), Peterborough & Fletton United (from March 1928), Merthyr Town (for six months from August 1928), Wolves (signed in January 1929), Reading (from June 1930), Queens Park Rangers (from May 1931 - no first team games), Mansfield Town (bought in December 1931), Crewe Alexandra (for a season from July 1932), Merthyr Town again (this time for nine months from July 1933), Plymouth Argyle (secured in March 1934), Notts County (from June 1935) and finally King's Lynn (from August 1938 to October 1939).

An avid pigeon fancier, Featherby retired during the War and later became a cricket groundsman in Norfolk. He represented Norfolk County and gained a Senior Cup winners medal with King's Lynn in April 1939. During his time in football he turned down lucrative jobs with senior clubs in the north of England and in Switzerland.
Wolves' record: 21 apps. 6 goals.

FELLOWS, Arthur

Wolves signed inside or centre-forward Archie Fellows in August 1901 from Willenhall Pickwick. He stayed at Molineux for just two seasons before a spate of injuries forced him to drop out of League Football.

He was given a free transfer in May 1903 and signed for Darlaston, later assisting Halesowen and Netherton. He was born in Wednesfield circa 1880.
Wolves' record: 55 apps. 8 goals.

FERGUSON, Darren

Son of the Manchester United manager Alex Ferguson, midfielder Darren Ferguson joined Wolves from Old Trafford for £250,000 in January 1994 after appearing in 30 first-class games for United.

Born in Glasgow on 9 February 1972, he joined the Reds as a junior in 1988 and turned professional in July 1990. After representing Scotland at Youth team level, and having had a trial with Nottingham Forest, Ferguson went on to gain five Under-21 caps. A very competitive individual who occasionally let his enthusiasm boil over - he was sent-off playing for Wolves against Bolton Wanderers in October 1996.

In November 1998 Ferguson had a trial with the Italian Serie 'B' side Cosenza, but quickly returned to Britain

Darren Ferguson

after a near riot broke out at the club's training ground following the sacking of boss Juliano Sonzongni. In January 1999, Ferguson was on his travels again, this time to the Dutch side Sparta Rotterdam, on a month's loan. Eight months later he returned to the UK to sign on a free transfer for Wrexham.

He was voted the Welsh club's 'Player of the Year' before taking his career appearance-tally to well past the 250 mark in 2001.

Wolves' record: 122+27 sub apps. 10 goals.

FERGUSON, John James

Outside-right Jack Ferguson joined Wolves in December 1928 from the Spen Black & White club, having earlier played for Grimsby Town and Workington. He spent virtually a season at Molineux, transferring to Watford in October 1929. He later assisted Burton Town, Manchester United (May 1931), Derry City and Gateshead United (1934-35) Born in Rowland's Gill in 1904, he played for Grimsby Town in season 1926-27 (3 League games).

Wolves' record: 20 apps. 4 goals.

FERRES, Walter F Joseph

Goalkeeper Walter Ferres was born in Bloxwich in 1886 and joined Wolves from Willenhall Swifts in August 1907. Reserve to Tommy Lunn and Jim Stringer, he conceded five goals on his League debut at Barnsley and stayed at Molineux until May 1908 when he moved to Wednesfield, later assisting Darlaston, Greets Green Primitives and Cradley Town.

Wolves' record: 2 apps.

FINLAYSON, Malcolm John

Although he had already played in 229 League games for Millwall, goalkeeper Malcolm Finlayson was a relatively unknown Third Division (South) player when Wolves paid £4,000 for him in August 1956 - to eventually replace the great Bert Williams, who was nearing he end of his illustrious career.

Finlayson appeared only 13 times in his first season at Molineux but in the summer of 1957, Williams retired and Finlayson went on to make over 200 appearances for Wolves, winning two League championship medals and an FA Cup winners' medal during his time at Molineux.

He was virtually an ever-present for a number of seasons before making his last appearance at Anfield in September 1963, when he suffered a broken finger. He retired at the end of that campaign with Fred Davies taking over the job.

Finlayson became managing director of R & F Steel Stockholders of Kingswinford, near Dudley. In June 1982 he was appointed vice-chairman of Wolves, although the appointment was short-lived when a new regime took over.

He was born in Dumbarton on 14 June 1930 and played for Renfrew Juniors before Millwall signed him during the

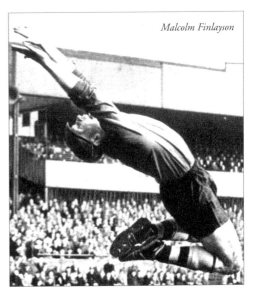

Malcolm Finlayson

1947-48 season. In November 1948, Finlayson was injured in the 20th minute of a League game at Walsall and was taken to hospital. When he returned the second half was 18 minutes old and Millwall were losing 3-1, so Finlayson scaled a wall, resumed his place in goal and inspired the Lions to a 6-5 victory.

Wolves' record: 203 apps.

FLEMING, George

Hard-tackling left-half George Fleming was born at Bannockburn, Stirlingshire, on 20 May 1869 and joined Wolves from East Stirlingshire in July 1894 to become one of six Scottish players on the Molineux club's books at that time. Fleming enjoyed his time with Wolves, making 187 senior appearances and scoring seven goals.

He did not appear in the 1896 FA Cup Final defeat by Sheffield Wednesday, but played 30 times when Wolves finished third in Division One in 1897-98. In May 1901, with the emergence of Jack Whitehouse, Fleming was transferred to Liverpool, thus leaving Wolves without any Scots on their books!

He was a firm favourite at Anfield, making 83 appearances for the Merseysiders and gaining a Second Division championship medal in 1905 before retiring to become assistant trainer at the club.

Wolves' record: 187 apps. 7 goals.

FLETCHER, Albert Thomas

Wing-half Albert Fletcher, who was born in Wolverhampton on 4 June 1867, was a man who was huge in both body and spirit, a real 'man mountain' who nevertheless possessed a great deal of skill.

He joined Wolves in 1886, when secretary Jack Addenbrooke paid a golden sovereign for his signature from Willenhall Pickwick, and went on to make 120 first

Albert Fletcher

team appearances for the club, 58 of them in the Football League, of which competition Wolves became founder-members two years after he joined them.

Fletcher played in the 1889 FA Cup Final against Preston North End and gained two England caps, both against Wales, in 1889 and 1890. His career came to a sad end when he suffered a broken leg during a game against Aston Villa at Perry Barr and in July 1891 he finally gave up his plans for a comeback.

His Molineux days were really just beginning, though, for he spent the next 29 years with Wolves, first as assistant trainer from 1891 to 1896 and then as successor to chief trainer Jack Lewis.

Albert Fletcher left Wolves in August 1920, aged 53.
Wolves' record: 76 apps. 2 goals.

FLO, Haavard

The first Norwegian to sign for Wolves, Haavard Flo was a £750,000 buy from the German Bundesliga side Werder Bremen in January 1999.

A strong, forceful striker, who could also play in midfield, Flo had already won 15 full caps for Norway when he moved to Molineux. A member of his country's 1998 France '98 World Cup squad, he was born on 4 April 1970 and had been with Bremen for three seasons, having earlier assisted FC Aarhus and FC Sogndal.

He made his debut for Wolves in the home League game with Watford four days after signing and admitted: "English football is quicker than what it is in Germany, much quicker!"

In May 2001, Flo was handed a 'Bosman' free transfer by his manager David Jones and at that point he returned to Norway to sign for one his previous clubs, FC Sogndal.
Wolves' record: 19+1 sub apps. 6 goals.

FLOWERS, Ronald

In the 1950s, Wolves were famed for their half-back line and Ron Flowers, of the striking blonde hair, immense stamina and powerful shot was one of its stars.

Born in Edlington, near Doncaster, on 28 July 1934, Flowers starred with his local Grammar School team, Doncaster Rovers juniors and Doncaster & Yorkshire Boys before he joined the Wolves nursery side, Wath Wanderers, in July 1950, turning professional in 1952.

Flowers made his League debut at home to Blackpool in September of that year and celebrated with a headed goal before a crowd of 49,000. He gained three League championship medals with Wolves, plus an FA Cup winners' medal as well as winning 49 full England caps, two for the Under-23s and playing for the Football League.

He spent 15 years as a professional at Molineux, appearing in more than 500 senior games (467 in the League alone) and scoring almost 40 goals. His international career began in 1955 and he was still in contention 11 years later as a member of England's original pool of 40 for the 1966 World Cup finals.

He helped Wolves regain their First Division place before, in September 1967, he switched to Northampton Town. He later became player-coach of the Cobblers prior to becoming player-manager of Wellington Town.

The Shropshire club had been renamed Telford United by the time Flowers guided them to the FA Trophy Final at Wembley, but in 1971 he resigned to concentrate on running his Wolverhampton sports outfitters shop.

NB - Flowers' father and brother both played for Doncaster Rovers.
Wolves' record: 512 apps. 37 goals.

Ron Flowers

FLOWERS, Timothy David

Tim Flowers, born at Kenilworth on 3 February 1967, replaced John Burridge in the Wolves goal at the start of the 1984-85 season after joining the staff at Molineux as an apprentice in June 1983 and turning professional in August 1984. Wolves' manager Tommy Docherty gave him his League debut at home to Sheffield United on the opening day of the campaign and he made 38 appearances that season and 72 in all before he signed for Southampton after a loan period at The Dell. The Saints wanted to groom Flowers to take over from Peter Shilton and paid Wolves £70,000 for him in June 1986.

Tim Flowers

Eventually, after two loan spells at Swindon Town, Flowers eventually replaced Shilton who had gone to Derby County. He gained the first of his eleven full England caps against Brazil in the summer of 1993 (during the USA Cup competition) having earlier won Youth and Under-21 honours with Wolves. In November 1993 - after 242 appearances for Saints - he joined Blackburn Rovers for £2.4 million - a world record fee for a goalkeeper. Liverpool had been prepared to pay precisely that amount of money but Flowers chose Ewood Park instead of Anfield after refusing to speak with the Merseyside club's management.

He helped Rovers into European football for the first time as Premiership champions and in 1998 became the first goalkeeper to appear in 200 Premiership matches, although soon afterwards he asked for a transfer from Ewood Park!

Leicester City manager Martin O'Neill (now with Celtic) signed Flowers for £1.1 million in July 1999 and in his first season at Filbert Street he helped the Foxes win the Worthington Cup Final (v. Tranmere Rovers).

NB - In February 1995 Flowers was sent-off after just 72 seconds play when keeping goal for Blackburn against Leeds United - another Premiership record for a goalkeeper (and possibly outfield player as well).

Wolves' record: 72 apps.

FOLEY, Dominic Joseph

Striker Dominic Foley was born in Cork on 7 July 1976 and was educated at The Christian Brothers School in Charleville.

He played Gaelic football before taking up soccer and in due course signed for Wolves direct from the St. James' Gate club in Ireland for £35,000 in August 1995. But with Steve Bull, Don Goodman and Iwan Roberts ahead of him, his first team appearances were limited.

A Republic of Ireland international at both senior and Under-21 levels (six and eight caps gained respectively at those two categories) he managed only 26 senior outings for Wolves before having loan spells with Watford (February-April 1998), Notts County (December 1998), Lincoln City (January 1999) and the Greek club, Ethnikos (from January to May 1999).

He then signed for Graham Taylor's Watford on a permanent basis in June 1999, but after suffering a stress fracture of the fibula in December 2000, he struggled to reclaim his place in the Hornets' first XI and in October 2001 - having agreed a new three-year contract at Vicarage Road - was loaned out Queen's Park Rangers.

NB - He scored a hat-trick on his debut for Ethnikos whose manager was Howard Kendall.

Wolves' record: 4+22 sub apps. 3 goals.

FORBES, William

Signed by manager Ted Vizard from Dunfermline Athletic in September 1946, ever-reliable wing-half or inside-forward Willie Forbes had a terrific engine and a strong tackle.

Born in Glasgow on 25 May 1922, he played for Glasgow United prior to joining Dunfermline. And after leaving Wolves in December 1949 he joined Preston North End whom he helped win the Second Division title in 1951, finish runners-up in the First Division in 1953 and reach the FA Cup Final the following year (beaten by West Brom).

Willie Forbes

All told, Forbes played in well over 200 games for the Deepdale club before signing for Carlisle United in July 1956.

When he retired in May 1958 he had well over 300 senior appearances in his locker.

Wolves' record: 75 apps. 23 goals.

FORD, Clive

A promising youngster, who supported West Bromwich Albion during his school days, utility forward Clive Ford failed to reach the heights expected of him at Molineux and he was mainly a reserve during his time with Wolves.

Born in West Bromwich on 10 April 1945, he represented West Bromwich Town and joined Wolves as a junior in July 1960, turning professional in October 1962. He left Molineux for Walsall in December 1964 and after 14 League outings for the Saddlers he switched to Lincoln City, making over 50 first team appearances for the Imps before ending his senior career in the summer of 1968 (on his release from Sincil Bank).

Wolves' record: 2 apps.

FORMAN, Matthew Charles

Born in Evesham on 8 September 1967, central midfielder Matt Forman was an apprentice at Villa Park for two years before turning professional in September 1985.

He failed to make the grade with the First Division club and in August 1986 was transferred to Wolves.

After leaving Molineux in September 1988 Forman played for Burton Albion, Oldbury United, Evesham United and Transatlantic FC (in America) before returning to Evesham for the 1992-93 season.

Wolves' record: 28+1 apps. 5 goals.

FORSHAW, Richard

The versatile Dick Forshaw could play at inside-right or centre-forward, even on the wing.

Born in Preston on 20 August 1895, he attended school in Gateshead and played local football in the North-east with St. George's Church Lads' Brigade (Gateshead) and Gateshead St. Vincent's before entering the Army in 1914. He guested for both Middlesbrough and Nottingham Forest during the hostilities and after being demobbed he signed for Liverpool in June 1919.

He became a star player at Anfield and scored 119 goals in a total of 291 League and Cup appearances for the Merseysiders, helping them twice win the First Division championship in 1922 and 1923. In March 1927 he surprisingly moved across Stanley Park to sign for Everton, transferring to Molineux in August 1929 after helping the Toffeemen win the League title in 1928.

He never really settled down with Wolves (he was well into his thirties at the time) and after just a handful of outings he moved to Hednesford Town in August 1930, later assisting Rhyl Athletic from October 1930 to May 1931 when he retired.

Wolves' record: 6 apps. 4 goals.

FOWNES, Walter Jeremiah

Wally Fownes spent five seasons a reserve full-back with Wolves.

Born in Coseley circa 1885, he played for Wednesbury St. Paul's and Wood Green Rovers before joining the staff at Molineux in August 1906.

He left the club to join Willenhall in 1911.

Wolves' record: 12 apps.

FOX, William Victor

Vic Fox was a hefty defender, who loved a challenge! He was a reserve for biggest part of his time at Molineux, appearing in less than 50 first team matches in a six-year spell, his best season coming in 1927-28 when he had 24 outings, mainly as partner to full-back Ted Watson.

Born in Middlesbrough on 8 January 1898, Fox attended Council School in Middlesbrough, represented Teeside Juniors and South Bank Schools before joining South Bank East End from where he was transferred to Bradford Park Avenue, moving to Middlesbrough in 1918 and turning professional in May 1919.

In October 1924 he was signed by Wolves and in August 1930 left Molineux for Newport County, later playing for Exeter City (September 1931), Manchester Central (November 1931), Bradford Park Avenue again (March 1932) and Nantwich Town (August 1932-34).

Fox, who made well over 100 appearances for Middlesbrough, was also a very useful cricketer with Worcestershire (1923-32).

A middle order right-hand batsman and occasional bowler he scored 6,654 runs in 281 innings spread over 163 county matches for an average of 26.61. His highest score was 198. He also took 87 catches and managed two wickets for 137 runs. He topped the 1,000 run mark in a season three times with a best aggregate total of 1,457 (average of over 31) in 1929. Fox also played for Abertillery C.C.

NB - His father, Billy Fox, was a Middlesbrough player in the 1880s and a Northern-based cricket professional, who was instrumental in seeing his son make the grade with both the small and large balls!

Wolves' record: 49 apps.

FRANCIS, Ernest

Wolves recruited inside or centre-forward Ernest Francis from Worcester City in July 1912.

A strong player, born circa 1891, he stayed at Molineux until football was abandoned owing to the Great War, playing mostly in the reserves.

He did not re-sign for Wolves after the hostilities.

Wolves' record: 10 apps. 3 goals.

FREEDMAN. Douglas Alan

Born in Glasgow on 21 January 1974, striker Dougie Freedman made a terrific start to his Wolves career! He scored on his debut against Swindon Town at Molineux on 18 October 1997, just two days after joining the club from Crystal Palace on a month's loan (later signing permanently in a deal that took Jamie Smith to Palace).

A trainee with Queens Park Rangers, Freedman signed professional forms at Loftus Road in May 1992 but never got a first team outing and moved to Barnet on a free transfer in July 1994.

He scored 32 goals in 57 appearances for the Underhill club, four coming in one game v. Rochdale in September 1995. After that salvo he switched to Palace for £800,000, and did very well at Selhurst Park, netting 34 times 103 games for the Eagles.

A hat-trick hero for Palace against Wolves in the 1995-96 League game at Selhurst Park, he then scored another two vital goals past the Wanderers in the 1st leg of the 1997 Play-off semi-final clash in London which ultimately led to the Eagles going on to win a place in the Premiership after they had beaten Sheffield United in the Final at Wembley.

Freedman was sold by Wolves to Premiership newcomers

G

Nottingham Forest for £850,000 in August 1998 and in the summer of 2001, after David Platt had left Forest to become England Under-21 coach, he was transferred by new manager Paul Hart back to his former club Crystal Palace.

Capped by Scotland as a schoolboy, Freedman went on to represent his country eight times at Under-21 level and he also gained a 'B' cap before finally gained a senior cap during the qualifying stages for the 2002 World Cup Finals.

Wolves' record: 30+5 sub apps. 12 goals.

FROGGATT, Stephen Junior

Steve Froggatt completed his transition from outside-left to wing-back during the 1996-97 season when he regained his form and fitness after serious injury and illness problems following his transfer to Molineux from Aston Villa for £1 million in July 1994.

Froggatt was capped twice by England at Under-21 level during his time at Villa Park, which lasted from June 1989 when he became a junior, turning professional in January 1991.

In all he made 44 appearances for Villa and scored three goals. Fast and clever, he enjoyed taking on his opponent when playing as an out-and-out winger with Villa, but then, under Mark McGhee at Wolves, his style changed and he developed into a fine attacking wing-back, winning selection to the PFA's First Division side in 1997.

In September 1998, Froggatt was - perhaps surprisingly in supporters' minds - transferred from Molineux to Coventry City for a club record fee of £1.9 million.

In the Premiership he did very well, playing as a wide midfielder under Gordon Strachan's managership.

Unfortunately injuries forced Froggatt to quit competitive football in 2001.

Wolves' record: 112+8 sub apps. 11 goals.

GALLAGHER, John Christopher

A totally committed midfielder or emergency striker, Jackie Gallagher was born in Wisbech on 6 April 1958 and played for March Town before turning professional with Lincoln City in February 1976.

Over the next decade he served, in turn, with Kings Lynn, Peterborough United (two spells between April 1980 and August 1985), Torquay United (August 1982) and Wisbech Town (1983-84) before joining Wolves in June 1987.

He spent two years at Molineux, gaining a Sherpa Van Trophy winners medal (coming on as substitute) as well as helping Wolves win both the Fourth and Third Division championships in successive seasons.

Gallagher left Molineux for non-League Kettering Town in May 1989.

Wolves' record: 13+23 apps. 5 goals.

GALLAGHER, Joseph Anthony

Joe Gallagher began his career as a right-back, but the lack of manoeuvrability resulted in him converting to the centre-half position where he became a commanding figure, especially in the air, although at times looked a little awkward on the ground.

Joe Gallagher

Born in Liverpool on 11 January 1955, he represented Lancashire & Merseyside Schools and in 1970 joined Birmingham City as a junior, turning professional at St Andrew's on his 17th birthday. He quickly established himself in the first team and went on to score 23 goals in 335 appearances for Blues, gaining an England 'B' cap in 1980. In August 1981 he was perhaps surprisingly sold to Wolves for £350,000 but his stay at Molineux was a relatively short one. It lasted until December 1982 when he switched his allegiance to West Ham United following a newspaper article in which he admitted that he couldn't give full effort out on the field of play when in dispute with the club.

In August 1983 he moved north to Burnley; he played for Padiham (on loan) in 1984 and then five years later became manager of Coleshill Town.

Gallagher returned to St Andrew's as Blues' Community Liaison Officer in November 1990, staying in office for a year before taking over as boss of Atherstone United.

Wolves' record: 34 apps. one goal.

GALLEY, John Edward

John Galley was a useful centre-forward, who started his League career with Wolves and ended it with Hereford United.

Born in Clowne on 7 May 1944, he joined the Molineux groundstaff as a junior in 1959 and turned professional in May 1961.

With so many good strikers at the club, Galley found it hard to get first team football and consequently, in December 1964, he was transferred to Rotherham United. Three years later (after scoring 48 goals in 112 League appearances for the Millers) he switched to Bristol City where he averaged a goal every two games for the Robins (netting 84 in 172 League outings).

In December 1972 he moved to Nottingham Forest and after a loan spell with Peterborough United (October 1974) he rounded off an eventful career by scoring 10 goals in 80 League matches for Hereford United (December 1974 to May 1977).

All told at League level, Galley, the nephew of Tom who also played for Wolves (q.v.), netted 151 goals in 413 matches - a fine return.

Wolves' record: 6 apps. 2 goals.

GALLEY, Thomas

Tom Galley was one of those great club men, a loyal servant, who was on Wolves' books for well over 13 years, playing in almost 280 first team matches (including 75 in wartime) and appearing without complaint in whatever position suited his manager best.

Galley was born in Hednesford on 4 August 1915 and played as an amateur for Notts County and Cannock Town before signing as a part-time professional for the latter club in August 1933.

Wolves secured him on full professional forms in April 1934 and with them he played in seven different positions. He scored 11 goals in the 1938-39 season when he was an ever-present, appeared in the FA Cup Final, skippered the 1942 Wartime League

Tom Galley

(North) Cup winning team which beat Sunderland, won two England caps (against Sweden and Norway in 1937) and also played for the Football League.

During the war he served in France and Germany with the Royal Artillery and guested for Aldershot, Clapton Orient, Leeds United and Watford. After scoring almost 50 goals in more than 200 senior games, he left Molineux in November 1947 and moved to Grimsby Town, who were also in the First Division albeit in relegation trouble.

He skippered the Mariners but after only 33 League games (two goals scored), he was forced to retire from League soccer because of injury. Galley - who also played club cricket for 30 years - returned to the Midlands to sign for Kidderminster Harriers in August 1949, and in May 1950 was appointed player-coach of Clacton Town before retiring in June 1960.

Wolves' record: 204 apps. 49 goals.

GALVIN, David

Born in Denaby on 5 October 1946, defender Dave Galvin joined Wolves as a junior and turned professional at Molineux in May 1965.

He understudied Dave Woodfield for a number of years but only managed a handful of senior appearances before transferring to Gillingham in October 1969, ending his League career with Wimbledon (August 1977 to May 1979).

He scored 17 goals in 245 League games for the Gills, helping them win promotion from the Fourth Division in 1973.

Galvin also assisted the 'Crazy Gang' in their rise from the Fourth Division.

Wolves' record: 5 apps.

GARDINER, John G

A persistent and niggling knee injury, suffered during the opening months of his Wolves career, ended left-half Jack Gardiner's career at Molineux.

Born in Hamilton, Scotland in July 1904, he played Blantyre Victoria and Motherwell before joining Coventry City in May 1926. Two years later he signed for Wolves, but injury resulted in him leaving Molineux for Norwich City in November 1928.

He later assisted Kettering Town (from July 1929), Walsall (June 1930), Workington Town (1931), Barrow (August-September 1932) and Lancaster Town (October 1932-May 1933).

Wolves' record: 3 apps.

GARDINER, Joseph B

Born at Bearpark, County Durham on 23 August 1916, Joe Gardiner was one of Major Buckley's 'Babes', a player who came through the ranks after joining Wolves as an amateur in December 1932.

Buckley signed Gardiner on professional forms as soon as the player was 17 and he went on to make almost 140 League and Cup appearances for Wolves after developing

Joe Gardiner

into an effective defender after Buckley had chosen to switch him following an unsuccessful start as a centre-forward.

Born in the same Durham mining village as the great Derby and England winger Sammy Crooks, Gardiner played for Durham County Boys, and the Wolves scouting net quickly picked him up. He soon gained representative honours with Wolves, representing the Football League against the Scottish League at Molineux when he was 22.

The following year he made a Wembley appearance as a member of the Wolves' team beaten by Portsmouth in the 1939 FA Cup Final.

He first became a regular in the Wolves' first team during the 1936-37 season and continued to play during the war (49 outings) until retiring in 1944.

He stayed on at Molineux on the training staff, then followed manager Stan Cullis to Birmingham City, where he remained until 1969. He later returned to his beloved Wolves where he did some scouting for club (up to the early 1980s) and, in fact, Gardiner was associated with the Molineux side for some 50 years (as player, trainer and scout). Gardiner, who retired to live at Sedgley, near Dudley, was also trainer to the full England team on two occasions.

Wolves' record: 139 apps. 2 goals.

GARDNER, Donald Charles

After acting as reserve to key midfielders Kenny Hibbitt and Willie Carr, Don Gardner was released by Wolves in May 1975 having been at Molineux since July 1972 when he joined the club as an apprentice, turning professional in August 1973.

Born in Jamaica on 30 August 1955, he had an unsuccessful trial with Coventry City immediately prior to him joining Wolves.

Wolves' record: 1+2 sub apps.

GARRATLY, George

George Garratly, born at Walsall in October 1888, began his career with Walsall Constitutionals in 1904 and then played for Bloxwich Strollers, where Walsall spotted him in February 1908.

A solid defender, Garratly appeared in the Birmingham League for the Saddlers and in the summer of 1909, Wolves signed him. He remained at Molineux until 1920, making over 230 senior appearances for the club.

He played alongside Ted Collins from 1910-11 to 1914-15 and their full-back pairing was considered to be one of the best outside the First Division.

Although his career was interrupted by World War One, Garratly was still playing for Wolves in 1919-20 before handing over to George Marshall.

He ended his career with Hednesford Town, retiring to take over as manager at Cross Keys. In 1923 he recommended Jack Harrington to Wolves.

Wolves' record: 232 apps. 6 goals.

GEORGE, Noel

Noel George was serving with the RASC in Salonika during World War One when he discovered his talent for goalkeeping during recreational periods, and in April 1919 he won high praise for his performance for a Salonika XI against an Italian XI.

He was born at Lichfield on 26 December 1897 and had played in Hednesford Town's forward line before the war. Wolves signed him in the summer of 1919 and he made his League debut in February 1921 at Nottingham Forest. His first senior appearance had come two days earlier, in a Thursday afternoon FA Cup replay victory over Derby County at Molineux and he appeared in that season's Final when Wolves lost 1-0 to Spurs at neutral Stamford Bridge. George - 6ft 1in tall - went on to play in almost 250 senior games for Wolves (222 in the Football League), his last

Noel George

appearance coming in a 4-0 defeat at Ashton Gate in November 1927. By then he was in the early stages of a terminal illness.

He battled bravely against it before dying peacefully in his sleep at Lichfield on 16 October 1929.

Wolves had originally signed him as an eventual successor to Welsh international Teddy Peers, and George replaced Peers permanently at the start of the 1921-22 season.

Altogether, George missed only 18 out of the next 190 League games and was an ever-present in 1921-22, 1923-24 and 1924-25. In 1925-26 and 1926-27 he missed many games through injury before his fatal illness.

When Wolves won the Third Division (North) championship in 1923-24, George conceded only 31 goals in 42 games.

Wolves' record: 242 apps.

GETGOOD, George

Known affectionately as 'Goodman', Scotsman George Getgood was a real tough character, a half-back who possessed a crunching tackle and a player who gave 100 per-cent effort every time he took the field.

Born in Coylton, Ayrshire on 15 November 1892, he played for Ayr United, Reading (July 1914 to August 1921), Birmingham (to March 1922) and Southampton before transferring to Wolves in January 1923.

He skippered Wolves and made almost 60 appearances for

George Getgood

the first XI before leaving for Kidderminster Harriers in March 1925. He later assisted Aberdare Athletic (from July 1926), Shrewsbury Town (November 1926), Bathgate, Bo'ness and Nuneaton Town (February-May 1929). He helped Wolves win the Third Division (North) championship in 1923-24.

Getgood died in Kidderminster on 22 July 1970.

Wolves' record: 59 apps. one goal.

GIBBONS, Leonard

Len Gibbons was an efficient junior footballer but after turning professional he never quite reached the heights to make his mark in the Football League.

Born in the Wirrall on 22 November 1930, he signed for Wolves as an amateur in 1946, joined the full-time staff in February 1948, but with so many good class full-backs at the club, he was then released in the summer of 1953 and entered non-League soccer.

Wolves' record: 29 apps.

GILKES, Michael Earl

Left-sided Barbadian international midfielder Michael Gilkes joined Wolves from Reading in March 1997 for a fee reported to be £155,000 - signed by his former manager Mark McGhee.

A Londoner, born near Hackney Marshes on 20 July 1965, he played for Waltham Borough Boys (London) before joining Leicester City as a junior. He failed to make an impression at Filbert Street, quickly moving south to join Reading as a professional in July 1984.

He made his senior debut for the Royals soon after arriving at Elm Park, and went on to accumulate 486 appearances, scoring 52 goals before moving to Wolves, having earlier had loan spells with both Chelsea (January/February 1992) and Southampton (March 1992).

He helped Reading win the Third Division title in 1986, the Full Members' Cup Final of 1988 (when he scored) and the Second Division championship in 1994. He was awarded a Testimonial at Elm Park in 1996-97.

Unfortunately he was injured shortly after joining Wolves and took time to regain full fitness.

In July 1999 Gilkes moved on a free transfer to Millwall where he remained until June 2001.

Wolves' record: 34+6 sub apps. one goal.

GILL, James Archibald

Jimmy Gill played for Wolves' first team during the 1921-22 season when he replaced the injured Dick Richards on the left-wing.

Born in Bury in 1901, and now deceased, he assisted St. Barnard's and Victoria Swifts, Bury and Exeter City (1920) before joining Wolves in June 1921 and on leaving Molineux he signed for Stourbridge in July 1922.

Wolves' record: 7 apps.

GODDARD, George

Centre-forward George Goddard was 30 years old when Major Frank Buckley signed him as cover for Billy Hartill in December 1933.

Although he appeared in less than 20 games for Wolves, he more than earned his wages with a dozen goals in that brief spell, all of them coming in the 1933-34 season. In October 1934 he was on his way again, to Sunderland where he scored six goals in 14 games.

From Roker Park he moved to Southend United in mid-March 1936 and after his playing days were over he took over a butcher's shop near the centre of London and later ran a successful cafe.

Goddard, who was born at Gomshall, Surrey, on 20 December 1903, first played for Redhill FC and represented Surrey as an amateur before QPR signed him as a professional in 1926, taking him from his job in a local bus garage.

He was Rangers' leading scorer in each of his six full seasons with them, netting 36 goals in 1928-29, 37 in 1929-30 (when he was top marksman in Division 3 South) and a club record 189 overall in League and FA Cup matches.

In December 1933, Rangers let him go to Brentford, but he did not appear in the Bees' first team prior to joining Wolves.

Goddard died in Kingston-on-Thames on 24 March 1987.

Wolves' record: 18 apps. 12 goals.

GODDARD, Raymond

Left-half Ray Goddard was born in Ecclesfield, Sheffield on 17 October 1920 and joined Wolves in September 1928 from Red Rovers FC.

The Second World War seriously disrupted his career at Molineux and after his military service, which took him to Burma and Ceylon with the Army soccer team, and a few games as a guest for Cardiff City, he left the club to sign for Chelsea in September 1946. In July 1948 he moved from Stamford Bridge to Plymouth Argyle, played over 150 League and Cup games for Exeter City between December 1949 and May 1954 and rounded off his footballing career as player-manager of Bideford Town (June 1954 to April 1956).

He skippered both Argyle and Exeter and returned to the West Midlands and lived in Dudley until his death (in Gornal) on 1 February 1974.

Wolves' record: 4 apps.

GOLD, James William

Goalkeeper Billy Gold deputised for Alex Scott during the 1936-37 season.

Secured by Wolves from Bournemouth in December 1936, Gold was a tall, well built 'keeper whose appearances were restricted owing to the form of Scott and he left Molineux for Chelsea in May 1937 where he became reserve to Vic Woodley.

Born in the village of Birkenshaw, Strathclyde in 1914, Gold (now deceased) played initially for Ballieston Juniors, moving to Bournemouth in January 1931.

He failed to make Chelsea's first team and in February 1938, left Stamford Bridge to sign for Doncaster Rovers, retiring in 1946 after guesting for Rotherham United during the war.

Wolves' record: 16 apps.

GOMEZ, Fernando

Spanish-born midfielder Fernando Gomez made his senior debut for Wolves in a 5-0 Worthington League Cup win over Barnet in August 1998, scoring his first goal in English football soon afterwards in a 2-2 draw with Stockport County.

He was 33 when he joined Wolves from his native city club Valencia where he had been since 1985 during which time he had scored 117 goals in 457 Spanish League games and netted 17 times in 117 Cup matches.

He also captained Valencia for eight years and became the first Spanish midfielder to score a century of goals at senior level. Capped eight times by his country at senior level, he also played in five Under-21 internationals and in 24 Under-18 games.

A fine passer of the ball, Gomez quickly added confidence and composure to the Wolves midfield and his presence on the field was significant as Wolves made an exceptional start to the 1998-99 season. He left the club in the summer of 1999.

Gomez was born on 11 September 1965.

Wolves' record: 20+2 sub apps. 2 goals.

GOODALL, Archibald Lee

Inside-right-cum-centre-half Archie Goodall was well past his 42nd birthday when he joined Wolves in October 1905. And when he played his last game for the club (versus Everton on 2 December 1905) he was aged 42 years, five months and two days - the oldest player ever to don a Wolves shirt.

An Irishman, born in Belfast on 18 June 1864, he was raised in Scotland and moved down to England as a youngster. After playing for Liverpool Stanley, he signed for Preston North End in the summer of 1887, served briefly with Aston Villa (from October 1888), then scored 52 goals in 423 games for Derby County between May 1889 and May 1903, helping the Rams twice reach the FA Cup Final and finish runners-up in the League championship.

One of the great characters ever to play for Derby, he caused some alarm when, in 1898, he tried to unload his Cup Final tickets on which he had speculated. He also refused to play extra-time in a United Counties League Cup Final (v. West Bromwich Albion) because he said his contract ended after 90 minutes!

On leaving the Baseball Ground, Goodall, who was capped eight times by Northern Ireland between 1898 and 1902, played for Plymouth Argyle from where he switched to Glossop North End (in January 1904), finally linking up with Wolves in October 1905 and staying until January 1906, when he retired.

After this Goodall toured Europe and America with a strongman act, walking around with a massive metal hoop. He was a keen sportsman and followed his country avidly at football, cricket and tennis.

In later life he worked and lived in North London and died in the capital on 29 November 1929, aged 75.

NB - His brother John also played for Preston North End, Glossop and Derby County as well as Kilmarnock and Watford.

Wolves' record: 7 apps.

GOODING, Michael Charles

As a younger player Mick Gooding was a studious, hardworking midfielder, preferring to occupy a position on the left side of the field. Later on in his career he developed into an efficient player-manager, always putting unlimited effort and enthusiasm into his game.

Born in Newcastle-upon-Tyne on 12 April 1959, he played for Bishop Auckland before entering the Football League with Rotherham United in July 1979. After three

Mick Gooding

years at Millmoor during which time United won the Third Division crown, he switched to Chesterfield (December 1982) and in September 1983 returned to Rotherham for a second spell, which lasted until August 1987 when he signed for Peterborough United.

From London Road he was transferred to Wolves for £85,000 in September 1988 but stayed only fifteen months at Molineux before moving to Reading for £65,000 in December 1989, having helped the Wanderers win the Third Division title.

At Elm Park he teamed up with Jimmy Quinn and between them they helped Reading clinch the Second Division championship in 1994 and in 1995-96 Gooding, himself, was elected the Royals 'Player of the Year' for the third time in five seasons.

He was released by Reading in the summer of 1997 along with his co-manager Quinn. In July 1998 - after a brief coaching appointment with Plymouth Argyle - Gooding was appointed player/assistant-manager of Southend United.

Wolves' record: 52+2 sub apps. 5 goals.

GOODMAN, Donald Ralph

Striker Don Goodman's playing career almost came to an abrupt end when he suffered a depressed fracture of the skull in Wolves' penultimate League game of the 1995-96 season against Huddersfield Town.

Thankfully after some nervous moments and several hours of medical care and attention, he recovered full fitness and went on to serve the club until May 1998 when he was given a free transfer to join the Japanese J-League club, Hiroshima Antlers (July 1998).

In December 1998 Goodman returned to England to play on loan for Nationwide League club Barnsley, and in March 1999 he switched his allegiance to Scotland to sign for Motherwell, moving back into the Football League in March 2001 when he joined promotion-chasing Walsall.

Born in Leeds on 9 May 1966, he played junior football for Collingham before signing professional forms for Bradford City in July 1984.

He went on to score 22 goals in 86 outings for the Yorkshire club and was with the Bantams at the time of the Bradford fire disaster. In March 1987, Goodman was sold to West Bromwich Albion for £50,000 and he did supremely well at The Hawthorns, amassing a fine record of 63 goals in 181 senior appearances.

Then, in December 1991, Sunderland came in with a

Don Goodman

£900,000 bid and took Goodman away from West Brom - much to the annoyance of the Baggies' fans. At Roker Park he continued to find the net and claimed 44 more goals in 132 outings for the Wearsiders before his £1.1 million transfer to Wolves in December 1994.

Teaming up with Steve Bull and David Kelly, who subsequently moved to Sunderland, Goodman was also asked to play wide as well as behind the front two, and he had some excellent games, his pace and determination proving decisive. During 1999 he reached two personal milestones, those of 600 appearances and 175 goals at senior level.

NB - With his Afro-Caribbean haircut, Goodman helped the Saddlers win the Second Division Play-off Final in May 2001 at Cardiff's Millennium Stadium, scoring one of the goals in a 3-2 victory over the favourites at the time, Reading.

Wolves' record: 142+12 sub apps. 39 goals.

GOODWIN, Frederick James

Born in Stockport on 4 January 1944, Freddie Goodwin was a useful midfielder, who represented Stockport & Cheshire Schools before joining Wolves as a junior in June 1959, turning professional in January 1961.

He had a lot of excellent players challenging him for a position in the first team at Molineux, but he battled on and made almost 50 appearances for the club before transferring to his native Stockport County in January 1966.

He later served with Blackburn Rovers (March 1970), Southport (October 1971), Port Vale (July 1972), Macclesfield Town (1973-74), Stockport County again (August 1974), New Mills FC, Stalybridge Celtic and Ashton United, before taking up a coaching position in New Zealand with FC Stopout.

Goodwin then became assistant-coach to the New Zealand national side and thereafter coached Papatoetoe FC and Hutt Valley United. He remained in New Zealand for more than 15 years.

Wolves' record: 46+1 sub apps.

GORMAN, James

Jim Gorman had a fine goalscoring record as an inside-forward in non-League football, but failed to make the grade in a higher level.

Born in Stourbridge circa 1883, he played (and scored well) for Woodside Albion and Halesowen before joining Wolves in April 1906. From Molineux he moved to Stoke (April 1907) and from July 1909 to May 1910 assisted Croydon Common.

He then returned to the Black Country to round off his career with Dudley Town (August 1910) and Stourbridge (1912), retiring in 1914.

Gorman also served in the Police Force (based in Halesowen).

Wolves' record: 9 apps. 4 goals.

GOULD, Robert Alfred

Centre-forward Bobby Gould was another much-travelled footballer, serving eight clubs between 1964 and 1980, scoring 160 goals in 439 League games.

A whole-hearted, never-say-die striker, whose iron determination and non-stop endeavour made him a handful for both defenders and goalkeepers. He would not claim to have been the most skilful players ever to have lived, but he always gave the clubs he served and the spectators who watched him, value for money.

Born in Coventry on 12 June 1946, he became an apprentice at Highfield Road in July 1962 and signed full-time professional forms in June 1964.

He hit 40 goals in 78 games for the Sky Blues and after that his playing career flourished (to a certain extent). Transferred to Arsenal for £90,000 in February 1968, he netted 16 goals in 65 games for the Gunners who then sold him to Wolves for £55,000 in June 1970. He helped the Wanderers finish fourth in the First Division (1970-71) and remained at Molineux until September 1971 when he switched across to neighbouring West Bromwich Albion. He hit 18 goals in 52 games for the Baggies up to December 1972 when he ventured south to sign for Bristol City (December 1972. He notched another 15 goals (in 35 outings for the Robins) and followed up by grabbing another 15 in 51 games for West Ham United (from November 1973). A second stint at Molineux followed - from December 1975 - and although he couldn't prevent Wolves from being relegated, he did play in the club's Second Division championship-winning side the very next season (1976-77).

In October 1977 Gould joined Bristol Rovers and hit 12 goals in 36 appearances for the Pirates. He then had a decent spell with Hereford United (from September 1978 to May 1980, firing 13 goals in 45 matches) and after that was also a non-contract player with both Aldershot and Wimbledon.

After ending his playing days (in 1982) Gould worked as a coach and/or assistant manager at Aldershot, Chelsea, Charlton Athletic and QPR. He managed Bristol Rovers (twice), took charge of Wimbledon, whom he guided to FA Cup glory in 1987, West Bromwich Albion (1991-92) and Coventry City (twice). In 1996 was named team manager of Wales, a position he held for eighteen months.

Wolves' record: 81+12 sub apps. 39 goals.

GRAY, Andrew Mullen

Andy Gray was not the most skilful of strikers, but his aggression, determination and courage made him a constant danger to the tightest defences in the land.

He was a real 90-minute battler, the penalty-area menace and when playing alongside John Richards, as the spearhead of the Wolves attack, he produced great excitement and scored plenty of goals.

Gray became the second most expensive footballer in Britain (behind Steve Daley) when Wolves paid Aston

Andy Gray

Villa the princely sum of £1,150,000 for his services in September 1979.

Gray, who was born in Glasgow on 30 November 1955, had always been a colourful figure wherever he played and it was appropriate that the transfer forms should be signed on the pitch in front of 24,580 fans, before the home game against Crystal Palace.

He scored over 40 goals for Wolves, the most vital being the winner against Nottingham Forest in the 1980 League Cup Final at Wembley. A centre-forward, who was never afraid to go in where it hurt,

Gray first played for Clydebank Strollers before joining Dundee United in 1970. He became a full-time professional in May 1973 and made over 75 appearances for the Tayside club, playing in the 1974 Scottish Cup Final when he gained a runners-up medal. Villa signed him for £110,000 in September 1975 and in 114 senior appearances for them he scored 69 goals.

In 1977 he played in the two drawn games of the League Cup Final and was voted both the 'Player of the Year' and 'Young Player of the Year' by the P.F.A.

In July 1985, Gray left Wolves for Everton in a £250,000 deal and in his two seasons at Goodison he collected winners' medals in the FA Cup, League championship and European Cup-winners' Cup.

Against Watford in the 1985 FA Cup Final he scored a somewhat controversial goal - heading the ball out of Steve Sherwood's hands!

Villa signed Gray for a second time in July 1985 for £150,000 and then followed a loan spell with Notts County before his old Villa boss Ron Saunders signed him for West Bromwich Albion for £25,000 in September 1987.

Still his career was not over and early in 1988-89, Gray was signed by Glasgow Rangers, a club he helped win the Skol Cup almost immediately, followed by the Premier League title. At the end of the season, his job done, he was released and went to play for Cheltenham Town before rejoining Villa in he summer of 1991, this time as assistant manager to Ron Atkinson.

Gray was capped 20 times by Scotland as well as winning Under-23, youth and schoolboy honours, and his overall career tally shows well over 200 goals in more than 600 senior club matches. He left Villa to pursue a career in television and became a familiar face as an analyst with BSkyB television. In June 1997 he was linked with the vacant manager's job at his former club Everton, but declined the offer, choosing to stay with BSkyB television instead.

Wolves' record: 159+3 sub apps. 45 goals.

GREATWICH, Frank Edwin

A reserve outside-right, Frank Greatwich played in Wolves' League side during the 1897-98 season.

Born locally circa 1874, he joined the club from Wednesbury Excelsior and spent just two seasons at Molineux, leaving for Stourbridge in May 1899.

Wolves' record: 2 apps.

GREAVES, Ian Denzil

Ian Greaves was manager at Molineux for barely six months - from February to August 1982. In that time Wolves won only five League games and they suffered relegation to the Second Division.

A Lancastrian, born in Oldham on 26 May 1932, Greaves started his career in non-League football with Buxton United and went on to become a sturdy full-back with Manchester United whom he served from May 1953 until December 1960 when he joined Lincoln City.

He made 75 senior appearances whilst at Old Trafford, playing in the 1958 FA Cup Final defeat by Bolton Wanderers - the team he supported as a lad! He also gained a League championship medal in 1955-56. From Sincil Bank he moved to Oldham Athletic (May 1961), announcing his retirement in May 1963.

Five years later he stepped into management with Huddersfield Town where he remained until 1974. He then took charge of Bolton Wanderers with whom he stayed for six seasons.

At the start of the 1980-81 campaign Greaves was appointed assistant-manager of Hereford United (under Frank Lord) and later he took over from Ron Barry as team boss of Oxford United, a position he held until moving to Molineux for his six-month reign!

In January 1983, after an enforced 'long holiday' Greaves returned to football management with Mansfield Town. He held his job at Field Mill until 1989 when he was sacked.

As a manager Greaves guided both Huddersfield (1970) and Bolton (1978) to the Second Division championship triumphs; in 1985 he lifted Mansfield into the Third Division and two years later led the Stags to victory in the Freight Rover Trophy Final at Wembley. On four occasions Greaves was voted 'Manager of the Month' - once at Huddersfield and three times with Bolton.

Greaves' record as Wolves manager was played 20, won 5, drawn 6 and lost 9.

GREEN, Alfred Thomas

Reserve centre-forward Tommy Green appeared in Wolves' League side during the 1895-96 season when he replaced Billy Beats.

Born in Wolverhampton circa 1873, he was signed from Hartshill Unity in August 1894, and on leaving Molineux in the summer of 1896, he teamed up with Hereford Thistle, later assisting Tettenhall Sentinels and Bushbury.

He scored 61 goals in two seasons of Birmingham & District League soccer for Wolves: 1894-96.

Wolves' record: 2 apps.

GREEN, Francis

Frank Green was a big, burly inside-forward, 6ft 2ins tall, 13 stones in weight, who had a good spell at Molineux, finishing second top-scorer in 1928-29 with 16 goals. Born in Ashington, County Durham in 1905 and now

deceased, Green played for his home-town club Ashington before joining Wolves from Frickley Colliery in November 1927, as cover for Messrs. Cock, Phillipson and Chadwick.

He left the club in October 1929 for Crewe Alexandra, later playing for Peterborough & Fletton United, Crewe again (January 1931), Barnsley (June 1931), Racing Club de Paris (1933-34), Northwich Victoria (June 1935), Rhyl Athletic and briefly with Nantwich Town before retiring in 1939.

Green netted 10 goals in 45 games for the 'Alex'.

Wolves' record: 38 apps. 17 goals.

GREEN, John Asher

Sprightly, well proportioned reserve inside-forward, born in St Helens in September 1894, Jack Green joined Wolves from Prescot Cables in August 1919 and left Molineux for Formby FC the following year.

Later he assisted Liverpool RM Services FC.

Wolves' record: 6 apps. one goal.

GREEN, Ryan

Ryan Green became the youngest-ever player to appear in a full international match for Wales when he lined up for his country against Malta in June 1998, aged 17 years, 226 days. He has since added a second full cap to his collection while also playing in 16 Under-21 internationals as well as turning out for his country's youth team..

A composed right full-back, born in Cardiff on 20 February 1980, Green joined Wolves as a trainee on leaving school and, in fact, had not made a senior first team appearance before receiving his initial cap.

Before he had actually signed professional forms for Wolves, Green turned down offers from four other clubs: Blackburn Rovers, Norwich City, Swansea City and his home town club Cardiff City. In April 1999 Green agreed a new contract with Wolves that will keep him at Molineux until the year 2002...although he did have a loan spell with Third Division strugglers Torquay United from March-May 2001. Early in the 2001-02 season Green teamed up again with his former boss, Mark McGhee at Millwall.

NB - Unfortunately Green wasn't very happy when he got himself sent-off in the 1-0 local derby defeat by West Bromwich Albion at The Hawthorns in October 2000.

Wolves' record: 12 apps.

GREENE, Christopher

Irish inside-forward or wing-half Chris Greene never really settled at Molineux.

Born in Dublin in 1908, he played in Leinster League football as a youngster and developed his skills with Brideville FC and then Shelbourne (from 1926) before joining Southport in August 1933. Wolves paid £500 for his services in November 1933, with another £500 available if he made his mark at Molineux.

Unfortunately he didn't, and in May 1936 he was sold to Swansea Town. He later assisted Bury (from December 1937) and retired during the war.
Wolves' record: 7 apps. 2 goals.

GREGORY, John Theodore

Reserve outside-right Jack Gregory spent most almost a year in Wolves' second team before making his senior debut late in the 1908-09 campaign against Leeds City at Molineux.

Born in Wolverhampton circa 1887, he joined Wolves from Victoria Road Swifts and left Molineux (in 1910) for Dudley Town, later playing for St. Phillips FC.
Wolves' record: one app.

GREGORY, Valentine Francis

Val Gregory

Val Gregory was born at Hendon, Middlesex on 14 February 1888 - St Valentine's Day - hence his first name.

An aggressive wing-half with a powerful kick and a biting tackle, he played for Reading, Watford (1910) and Arsenal (from September 1914, although he played only wartime games for the Gunners) before joining Wolves for £3,500 in May 1920.

Gregory had three excellent seasons at Molineux, making over 100 senior appearances and gaining a FA Cup runners-up medal in 1921 when he skippered the side against Tottenham Hotspur.

After retiring in May 1925 he became coach and then trainer at Molineux before leaving the club through ill health in 1938. Gregory died at Heathtown, Wolverhampton on 10 March 1940.
Wolves' record: 106 apps. 2 goals.

GRIFFIN, Alfred

Outside-left Alf Griffin joined Wolves in August 1892 from Walsall, having previously assisted Brierley Hill Alliance.

Born in Walsall on 3 June 1871 and educated in his native town, he became a firm favourite with the Molineux fans and was on the wing when Wolves won the FA Cup in 1893. He was transferred back to Walsall in the summer of 1896 and retired five years later following a serious ankle injury.

A player with an exciting temperament, he hit 34 goals in 88 games for the Saddlers in his two spells at the club.
Wolves' record: 76 apps. 14 goals

GRIFFITHS, Bernard

Eager-beaver outside-left Bernie Griffiths was one of the early stars in Wolves' pre-League days, being a regular in the first team for two years.

Born in Pendeford in 1868, he played for Wolverhampton Rangers before joining Wolves in the summer of 1886.

He scored seven FA Cup goals in season 1886-87, and when Crosswell's were beaten 14-0, he claimed two of those goals and helped set up eight more for his colleagues. He left Wolves in August 1888 to sign for Lanesfield, later assisting Sedgley.
Wolves' record: 8 apps. 8 goals.

GRIFFITHS, Hillary

Powerful, hard-kicking wing-half, Hill Griffiths gave Wolves splendid service for 12 years during which time he made over 200 first team appearances and skippered the side for three seasons.

Born in Wednesfield in August 1871, he joined Wolves from Wednesfield Rovers in April 1889 and left Molineux for Burton Swifts in 1901. He later played for Reading, Nottingham Forest, Bristol Rovers (May 1904), Millwall (October 1905) and Kidderminster Harriers (from December 1905), retiring in 1907.

He starred for Wolves in the 1896 FA Cup Final and was unlucky not to have gained international honours, injuries ruining his chances.

NB - Two of Griffiths' elder brothers, James and Jabez (q.v), were also useful footballers.
Wolves' record: 201 apps. one goal.

GRIFFITHS, Isaac

Competent goalkeeper Ike Griffiths was first choice between the posts for Wolves for four seasons: 1883 to 1887. Indeed, he was the first recognised 'custodian' at the club. Born in Willenhall in the first quarter of 1862, he played in all of Wolves' first 14 FA Cup-ties and made his League debut against Burnley at Molineux in October 1890 - seven years after joining the club from Wolverhampton Rangers, having earlier played for Wednesbury St. Peter's. Griffiths was a confident 'keeper who loved to 'fly-kick' the ball to safety rather than collect it with his hands.

A knee injury restricted his performances from 1888 onwards and in 1891 he retired to go into business in Wolverhampton.
Wolves' record: 15 apps.

GRIFFITHS, Jabez

Signed from Wednesfield Rovers in 1882, Jabez Griffiths played regularly for Wolves in the 1883-84 season.

An outside-left - born in Wednesfield circa 1862 - he netted in the Final of the Wrekin Cup in 1884 when

Wolves beat the Shropshire club, Hadley 11-0 to record their first trophy success.
Wolves' record: 2 apps. 2 goals.

GRIFFITHS, John

Jack Griffiths was a strong, rugged full-back, who acted as reserve to first Harry Shaw and then Cecil Shaw during his time at Molineux.

Born in Fenton, Stoke-on-Trent on 15 September 1909, he worked as a potter and played football for the local Boys Brigade team and for Shirebrook FC, before joining Wolves in May 1929. After three years at Molineux he was transferred to Bolton Wanderers (June 1932), moving to Manchester United in March 1934, before becoming player-coach with non-League Hyde United in May 1939. He played in more than 175 games whilst at Old Trafford, helping United win promotion from the Second Division in 1938, the same year he figured in an England international trial match. During the war, Griffiths (now deceased) guested for Derby County, Notts County, Port Vale, Stoke City and West Bromwich Albion, returning to Hyde in 1945. He also qualified as a masseur during the hostilities.
Wolves' record: 6 apps.

GRIFFITHS, Joseph Bertram

Born in New Tredegar in 1910, Joe Griffiths made one appearance for Wolves in February 1931 (at Reading) when he replaced Billy Hartill.

He left Molineux in May 1931 and spent the next two years with Stockport County (scoring 33 goals in 48 League appearances). Griffiths was forced to quit top line soccer through injury.
Wolves' record: one app.

GRIFFITHS, John Charles Ruskin

John Griffiths was a useful centre-forward, who served Wolves during the last two League seasons prior to the Great War (1913-15).

Born in Wednesfield in 1888, he played his early football with Bushbury White Star, Goldthorn Park, Willenhall and Hednesford Town from where he switched to Molineux in April 1913. He did not figure after the war.
Wolves' record: 13 apps. 2 goals.

GROSVENOR, Sidney Victor

Full-back Sid Grosvenor was signed as cover for Jack Jones and Dick Betteley - but with these two fine players holding their form he failed to establish himself in the Wolves first team and left after three years at Molineux.

Born in Wolverhampton circa 1882, Grosvenor played for Willenhall Swifts prior to joining Wolves in August 1903 and on leaving Molineux in 1906 he had a brief spell with Walsall before signing off with Stafford Royal (1908-10).
Wolves' record: 2 apps.

GROVES, Albert

Albert Groves, born in Newport, Monmouthshire in January 1886, was one of the smallest centre-halves ever to play for Wolves at 5ft 7in, although in those days, of course, the position was more a true midfield link player rather than a defensive 'stopper'.

Groves joined Wolves from Aberdare Athletic in August 1909 and remained at Molineux until May 1920 when he was appointed player-manager of the Birmingham League side, Walsall.

By then he had scored 20 goals in more than 200 League and Cup games for the Wanderers. Groves made his debut at home to Manchester City on the last day of the 1909-10 season and he appeared in several positions thereafter, including inside-right in 1912-13, when he hit ten goals in Division Two.

During World War One he served in the Army and guested for Port Vale, Bury and Sunbeam Motors (Coventry). In 1919 he re-signed for Wolves, but soon afterwards, with other players coming through the ranks, he decided to try his luck in management, taking over at Fellows Park for one season before handing over to Jack Burchell when the Saddlers became founder-members of the Third Division (North). Continuing as secretary at Fellows Park until 1924, he still played competitively, however, scoring eight goals in 36 appearances during Walsall's first season back in the Football League.

In all he made 79 Football League appearances for the Saddlers, netting 15 goals. He also played in 12 FA Cup ties and in 33 other senior games. Later he turned out for Willenhall before becoming licensee of the Hope & Anchor pub, Bloxwich Road, Willenhall.
Wolves' record: 217 apps. 20 goals.

GUELLIAM, Richmond Cedric

Amateur trialist at Molineux, inside-left Rich Guelliam celebrated his debut for Wolves by scoring at Anfield.

Born in Wolverhampton circa 1880, he played for Wolverhampton White Star and Birch Coppice before linking up with Wolves in September 1901. He left the club to sign for Wrens Nest FC in June 1902 and later assisted Dudley.
Wolves' record: 2 apps. one goal.

GUMMERY, Walter Harry

Walter Gummery was a smart outside-left, who played for Wolves during the mid twenties, having his best season in 1924-25.

Born in Worcester on 1 May 1900, he played for St. Thomas' Boys' Club, Hammerford Lads' and Army football (he served with the 3rd Battalion of the Worcester Regiment and spent four years in India). On demob he joined Worcester City and moved to Molineux in May 1924.

He left Wolves for Accrington Stanley in June 1925, staying there until June 1926. Gummery, who helped

Worcester win the Birmingham & District League title, died in Sutton Coldfield on 18 October 1974.
Wolves' record: 10 apps. one goal.

GUTTRIDGE, William Henry

Nicknamed 'Chopper', full-back Bill Guttridge was a fearless tackler, as strong as an ox, powerful in his approach to the game and a defender who always gave 100 per-cent effort at whatever level he played - a really fine competitor.

Bill Guttridge

Born in Darlaston on 4 March 1931, he played for Metroshaft Works FC before joining Wolves as an amateur in 1947, turning professional in March 1948.

He spent the next six years at Molineux playing mainly in the reserves, but in November 1954 he left for Walsall where he immediately gained a first team place. He went on to appear in well over 200 games for the Saddlers, helping them win promotion from the Fourth to the Second Division in quick succession.

He retired in May 1962 and later coached the youngsters at Fellows Park.
Wolves' record: 7 apps.

HADLEY, Edmund

Relatively unknown inside-forward, born in Tettenhall circa 1865, Edmund Hadley played for Wolves from September 1883 to May 1885.
He joined the club from Wednesfield Rovers, having earlier played for Stafford Road, and left for Bilston Saints.
Wolves' record: 3 apps.

HALES, Frederick F

Keen and inventive, utility forward Fred Hales was perhaps too lightweight to make his mark in senior football.
Born in Oldbury in 1898 and a pupil at Matthew Boulton School, he joined Wolves from the Hardy Spicer Works FC in June 1920 and left Molineux for Darlaston in 1922, later assisting Bloxwich Strollers.
Wolves' record: 2 apps. one goal.

HALLIGAN, William

Irish international forward Billy Halligan, born at Athlone in August 1890, had a fine career that spanned 20 years and took in nine Football League clubs (fourteen in total). He netted over 100 competitive goals in more than 220 senior appearances...an excellent return.

He played for Belfast Distillery, Belfast Celtic and Cliftonville in the Irish League before joining Leeds City in 1909. Derby County signed him in February 1910 and he became a Wolverhampton Wanderers player in June 1911, for £450.

His two seasons with Wolves were spent in the Second Division before he was transferred to Hull City in May 1913, for what was then City's record fee of £600.

For the Tigers he scored 28 goals in 64 games. He then played for Manchester United and Rochdale as a guest in World War One before joining Preston North End in July 1919. Oldham Athletic signed him in January 1920 and in July 1921 he signed for Nelson, ending his career in non-League football with Boston Town and Wisbech Town, finally retiring in 1924 at the age of 39.

Although on the small side, Halligan could play in any of the three central forward positions and proved a more than useful marksman. He was capped twice at senior level v. Wales in January 1911 and v. England in February 1912.

He also played for an All-Ireland XI v. England in Dublin in 1912, in two Victory Internationals against Scotland in 1919-20 and for the Irish League against the Scottish League in 1909.
Wolves' record: 73 apps. 41 goals.

HAMILTON, A John

Moustachio'd Scotsman Jack Hamilton was a useful left-half, who had pluck and endurance, and was a champion tackler with excellent judgement.

Born in Ayrshire in 1872 he played for Glasgow United (1890) and Ayr United (1891) before moving down to the Midlands to sign for Wolves in June 1894 (It is reported that he left Scottish football 'in consequence of the dullness of trade').

Unfortunately a serious injury interrupted his performances at Molineux and he was quickly released, moving to Derby County in November of that same year. He then switched to Ilkeston Town before having useful spells with Gainsborough Trinity, Loughborough Town (he was an ever-present in Boro's first League season), Bristol City (making 142 appearances for the Robins between 1897-1900), Leicester Fosse (from September 1900), Watford (April 1901), Wellingborough (July 1902) and finally Fulham.

He joined the Cottagers initially as a player in August 1903, then became the club's assistant-manager (1904-08) and latterly acted as head trainer (1908-10).

Hamilton returned to Ashton Gate as reserve team manager and then managed City's League side during the First World War (May 1915 to August 1919). He actually came out of retirement to play in two matches when City were short of players before returning north of the border to assist Heart of Midlothian and then Airdrieonians, both in a coaching capacity.
Wolves' record: 4 apps.

HAMPTON, John William

Jack Hampton was a capable goalkeeper, who was a member of the first team squad at Molineux for five years from 1922, although for most of the time he had to play second fiddle to Noel George.

Born in Wolverhampton in 1899, he played for Wellington Town (seasons 1917-19) and joined Wolves from Oakengates Town in May 1920.

He left Molineux for Derby County in June 1927 (teaming up with manager George Jobey) and after gaining a First Division runners-up medal with the Rams he was transferred to Preston North End in May 1930, later assisting Dundalk (from June 1931 to May 1933).

Wolves' record: 51 apps.

HANCOCKS, John

Midget outside-right Johnny Hancocks, who was only 5ft 4in tall and wore size-two boots, had a magnificent record with the great Wolves team of the post-war period. In all, he played well over 370 senior games and scored more than 160 goals, 158 of which came in 343 League outings, all of them in the old First Division.

He made a big impact on the game and had a venomous right-foot shot, especially from dead-ball situations. He also had tremendous pace and could cross accurately to the far post, often delivering the ball when in full flight down the wing.

Born at Oakengates, Salop, on 30 April 1919, he played for Oakengates Town before Walsall signed him on professional forms. He scored on his League debut for the Saddlers in a 2-2 draw with Aldershot at Fellows Park in the Third Division (South) in October 1938, and by the end of the season had netted 10 goals in 37 competitive matches.

During the war he scored 32 times in almost 100 games for Walsall. He also guested for Chester, Crewe Alexandra and Wrexham, represented the Army and Western Command and became a fully qualified PT instructor.

Wolves signed him on 11 May 1946, for a bargain fee of £4,000, and the hard-shooting winger went on to collect an FA Cup winners' medal in 1949 and a League championship medal in 1954. He won three full England caps, scoring twice on his international debut in a 6-0 win against Switzerland at Highbury, and also represented the Football League.

Johnny Hancocks

Even after Harry Hooper had replaced him on Wolves' right wing in 1956-57, Hancocks, who actually refused to re-sign for Wolves in 1950-51 after failing to agree terms, continued to delight the Molineux crowd with some sparkling performances in the Central League side.

In June 1958, he eventually moved to Wellington Town (later Telford United) and after a spell as their player-manager he ended his career with Cambridge United (then in the Southern League), Oswestry and GKN Sankey.

Hancocks who once attempted to buy into the Wolverhampton race course (he was a very keen and competitive gambler) later worked at Maddock & Sons, ironfounders, in his hometown of Oakengates before retiring in 1979, on his 60th birthday.

Alas, he later suffered a stroke but still followed the fortunes of his former clubs through newspapers and TV. One of Wolves' greatest players died on 19 February 1994.

Wolves' record: 378 apps. 168 goals.

Johnny Hancocks scoring against Blackpool in 1953-54

HANDYSIDES, Ian Robert

As a youngster Ian Handysides was hailed as the new Trevor Francis when began his professional career at St. Andrew's, but the high expectations proved to be a millstone round his neck and despite him winning England Youth team honours, he never really hit the heights with Birmingham City.

Born in Jarrow on 14 December 1962, Handysides represented Durham Boys before joining Blues as an apprentice in June 1978, turning professional in January 1980. Four years later he was transferred to Walsall for £17,000 and after rejoining Blues in March 1986, he had a loan spell at Molineux during September/October 1986. He was then forced to retire through ill-health in October 1988 after developing a brain tumour.

He underwent surgery and seemed to be on the road to recovery, but further tumours appeared on his spinal chord and sadly he died in Solihull on 17 August 1990, aged 27.
Wolves' record: 11 apps. 2 goals.

HANKIN, Raymond

Striker Ray Hankin had a useful career as a goalscorer during the 1970s/80s.

Born in Wallsend on 2 February 1956, he started his professional duties with Burnley in February 1973 having been at Turf Moor for almost two years as an apprentice. In September 1976 he transferred to Leeds United for £180,000.

In March 1980 he switched to Vancouver Whitecaps, had a trial with Arsenal in January 1982, played for Shamrock Rovers after that and returned to England with Middlesbrough in September 1982 for a fee of £80,000. He served Peterborough United from September 1983 and was sacked after being sent-off five times.

He arrived at Molineux in March 1985 at a time when Wolves were on the slide! Capped by England at both Youth and Under-23 levels, Hankin scored almost 100 goals in close on 300 appearances in League and Cup football before dropping into non-League circles with Whitby Town in March 1986.

He later assisted Blue Star FC, Guisborough Town (July 1987), Northallerton (as player-manager 1989) and then managed Darlington from March to July 1992.
Wolves' record: 9+1 sub apps. one goal.

HANN, Charles William

Charlie Hann

Charlie Hann was a reserve outside left who spent three years at Molineux.

Determined, with a good shot, he was born in Wolverhampton circa 1903, he played for several local clubs including Bilston White Star and Wesley Methodists before joining Wolves in August 1924.

He left Molineux in May 1927 and signed for Darlaston, later assisting Penkridge.
Wolves' record: 14 apps. 2 goals.

HANSBURY, Roger

Goalkeeper Roger Hansbury had a long career in the game.

Born in Barnsley on 26 January 1955, he represented Yorkshire Youths before joining Norwich City as an amateur in 1971, turning professional on his eighteenth birthday. Loan spells with Bolton Wanderers (March 1977), Cambridge United (November 1977) and Leyton Orient (December 1978) preceded his transfer to Eastern Athletic in Hong Kong in December 1981.

He then returned to England to sign for Burnley in August 1983. Afterwards Hansbury assisted Cambridge United for a second time from July 1985 and Birmingham City (from March 1986) before having further loan spells with Sheffield United (October to November 1987), Wolves (from March to April 1989), Colchester United (in August 1989) and Cardiff City (for two months from October 1989). He signed permanently for the Welsh club for £20,000 in December 1989.

He retired from Football League action the following year and entered the non-League scene. Hansbury's career was disrupted early on by a broken leg (at Norwich) but he recovered full fitness and did well generally with every club he served, making over 300 senior appearances in total.
Wolves' record: 6 apps.

HARDWARE, James

Jimmy Hardware was a handy player to have in reserve. Keen and enthusiastic, he acted as understudy to half-backs Alf Bishop and the Reverend Kenneth Hunt during his two-year stay at Molineux.

Born in Finchfield, Wolverhampton in September 1886, he played for Tettenhall Institute and Hurst Lane Social before joining Wolves in August 1907. In May 1910 he was allowed to leave for Bilston United and later assisted Willenhall Pickwick and Wighwick White Star.
Wolves' record: 9 apps.

HARGREAVES, Henry Harold

Inside-left Harold Hargreaves was sent-off for the only time in his career playing for Wolves against Leeds United in December 1922.

He was suspended for a month (January 1923) and left Molineux at the end of that season! A thrustful inside-forward with deadly shot, he was born at Higham, Lancashire on 3 February 1899 and played for Great Harwood and Nelson before joining Wolves in November 1921.

He spent almost two years at Molineux, leaving for Pontypridd in June 1923. He later assisted Tottenham Hotspur (December 1923), Burnley (March 1926), Rotherham (May 1928), Mansfield Town (May 1930), Rossendale United (October 1930) and Baroldswick Town

(March 1931 to April 1932). He scored 13 goals in 39 games for Spurs. Hargreaves died in Nelson on 18 September 1975.
Wolves' record: 55 apps. 8 goals.

HARPER, George

Inside-forward George Harper spent four seasons with Wolves, his best two coming in 1899-1900 and 1900-01 when he was a regular in the first team, top scoring in the former campaign with 10 goals.

Smart on the ball, fast with a strong shot, he was born in Aston, Birmingham in May 1877 and worked and played for the Saltley Gas Company before joining Burton United. From there he went to Aston Villa, then to Hereford Thistle, linking up with Wolves in August 1897. In May 1901 he was transferred to Grimsby Town and from November 1902 to 1904 he assisted Sunderland. Harper died on the 14 July 1914.
Wolves' record: 66 apps. 21 goals.

HARRINGTON, John A

There were few more exciting wingers in the 1920s than Jack Harrington, who made his Football League debut for Wolves on the opening day of the 1923-24 season at Chesterfield.

It was also Wolves first-ever game in the Third Division (North) and they drew 0-0. Harrington held his place in the side for five seasons, injuries permitting, and in all he made almost 120 senior appearances, scoring ten goals and laying on many more for his colleagues. He helped Wolves win the Northern Section title in his first season and then helped them re-establish themselves in the higher division. Although an outside-right with Wolves - recommended to the club by a former player at Molineux, George Garratly - he had previously played on either flank for Hednesford Town and was a big favourite at the Cross Keys.

Harrington, who was born at Bloxwich in 1901, had earlier made his name as a fine local sprinter who could reportedly break the 11-second barrier for the 100 yards. After leaving Molineux in June 1928 he was on Northampton Town's books until June 1929, making six League appearances before going back to non-League football with Brierley Hill Alliance and retiring in 1933.
Wolves' record: 117 apps. 10 goals.

HARRIS, George

Goalkeeper George Harris played for Wolves during the late 1890s.

Reserve to first Billy Tennant and then Tom Baddeley, he was a steady performer who conceded a total of ten goals in his seven senior outings.

Born in Redditch in 1875, he played for Headless Cross FC, Redditch Excelsior and briefly for Aston Villa (1895 as reserve to Tom Wilkes) before joining Wolves in July 1896. In May 1900 he left Molineux for Grimsby Town and later assisted Portsmouth (from November 1901),

Redditch and Kidderminster Harriers.
Harper died in Alcester on 27 June 1910.
Wolves' record: 7 apps.

HARRIS, Gerald William

Left-back Gerry Harris made more 235 League appearances for Wolves, yet he might have been a West Bromwich Albion player had he accepted the offer of a trial with the Baggies, albeit as an outside-left.

Harris was born at Claverley, near Bridgnorth, on 8 October 1935 and was playing for Bobbington FC in the Wolverhampton Amateur League when Wolves scout George Norris took him to Molineux during the 1953-54 season.

Harris signed professional forms in January 1954 and after gaining a first-team place in 1956-57 he won League championship medals in consecutive seasons, 1957-58-59, and a FA Cup winners' medal in 1960. A hard-tackling defender, he also came to the notice of the England selectors and gained four Under-23 caps.

Harris remained at Molineux until April 1966 when he was transferred to neighbours Walsall. He played in only 15 League games for the Saddlers, two of them as a substitute, before retiring in May 1967 through injury, although he still managed to turn out in charity matches for a while.

A keen bowls player, he captained the Bridgnorth club, Bylet, and today he lives in a converted farm-house/barn in his native Claverley.
Wolves' record: 270 apps. 2 goals.

HARRIS, John

John Harris was the first Wolves player to wear the international 'blue shirt' of Scotland, doing so in a wartime international in 1944-45.

Born in Glasgow on 30 June 1917, he was an amateur with Swindon Town before joining Swansea Town as a professional in August 1934 at the age of 17. From the County Ground he went to Tottenham Hotspur (February 1935) and signed for Wolves in May 1939. Unfortunately the hostilities in Europe completely ruined his playing career for six years and, in fact, when peace arrived he surprisingly left Molineux for Chelsea in August 1945 for a fee of £8,000, having guested for Grimsby Town and Southampton.

He remained at Stamford Bridge for 11 years, up to July 1956 when he became player-manager of Chester, holding office there until July 1959, when he was appointed manager of Sheffield United. He sat in the 'hot seat' at Bramall Lane until July 1963 when he was moved upstairs to the position of General Manager for the season 1968-69. He was then given a second stint as United boss from August 1969 to December 1973 and after that was made Chief Scout at Bramall Lane before coaching United's arch rivals Sheffield Wednesday (1972-75).

As a full-back Harris won a two Regional League Wartime

runners-up medal; with Wolves (in 1944 and 1945) and a First Division championship medal with Chelsea in 1955 at the age of 37. And as a manager he saw Sheffield United twice finish runners-up in the Second Division (1961 and 1971).

Harris died on 24 July 1988, aged 71.

HARRIS, David John

Full-back John Harris graduated through the ranks at Molineux and for seven years (injuries apart) he was understudy to the likes of his namesake Gerry, Eddie Stuart, George Showell and Bobby Thomson, among others, before leaving Wolves for neighbouring Walsall.

Born at Upper Gornal, Dudley on 3 April 1939, he joined Wolves as a junior in June 1955 and turned professional in May 1958. His transfer to Fellows Park was finalised in January 1965 and after four years as a player with the Saddlers, he had a spell as reserve team manager-coach at Fellows Park before ending his career with Rushall Olympic (May 1970 to June 1974).

Unfortunately Harris broke his leg in only his second game for Wolves v. Aston Villa early in the 1961-62 season, and after recovering full fitness he then broke his other leg in 1963-64. As Walsall's skipper he did an excellent job as partner to Frank Gregg, making over 80 appearances for the Saddlers.

Wolves' career: 3 apps.

HARRIS, John W

Reserve centre-forward Jack Harris played for Wolves during the mid-1920s. Born locally on 18 March 1896, he served with Bilston Commodores and Bilston Central before moving to Molineux in August 1924.

On leaving Wolves in May 1926 he signed for Watford, and later assisted Darlington, Hartlepools United, Wolves (again as a reserve in 1928), Barrow and Spennymoor United, retiring in 1931.

Wolves' record: 6 apps. 2 goals.

HARRIS, Walter T

Wally Harris had one season of first team football with Wolves, that of 1908-09 when he acted, in the main, as reserve to George Hedley and Jack Shelton.

A strong, mobile player he was born in Wolverhampton in 1887 and played locally for Queen's Park Athletic and Willenhall before joining Wolves from Redditch.

When he left the club in April 1909 he signed for Dudley Town and later served with Blakenhall.

Wolves' record: 5 apps. 1 goal.

HARRISON, William Ewart

Dashing winger Billy Harrison joined Wolves from Crewe Alexandra in the summer of 1907 for a reported fee of just £400. By the end of his first season at Molineux club he had gained an FA Cup winners' medal after scoring a brilliant individual goal in the Final against Newcastle United.

Harrison soon found himself a huge favourite with the Wolves supporters.

He was described as a 'master of the game' and he could either use great pace to get past a full-back, or tease the same defender with some mazy dribbling skills.

Harrison was only a small man, at 5ft 4in tall, but he was never afraid to go in with the burliest defenders and took plenty of knocks. His Wolves career saw him make almost 350 senior appearances and score close on 50 goals before his transfer to Manchester United in October 1920.

He scored five times in 46 games for United before his next move, to Port Vale in September 1922. He joined Wrexham in June 1923 and retired in May the following year. Harrison was almost 37 when he left big-time football but he carried on playing in charity games until he was well past his 40th birthday.

He was another former Wolves player who excelled on the bowling green and he was also landlord of the Rose and Crown public house in Tettenhall for many years.

Billy Harrison was born at Wypunbury on 27 December 1886 and played his early football with Hough United, Crewe South End and Willaston White Star. He died in Wolverhampton in August 1948.

Wolves' record: 345 apps. 49 goals.

HARTILL, William John

They called him 'Artillery Billy' and it was certainly an appropriate name for a striker who amassed a terrific goalscoring record with Wolves. He was their leading marksman in five seasons - 1929-30, 1930-31, 1931-32, 1932-33 and 1934-35 - and finished second to Tom Phillipson in 1933-34.

Hartill was born in Wolverhampton on 18 July 1905, in the same street as his best pal and later Wolves colleague Dicky Rhodes. Indeed, Hartill followed Rhodes into the same Wolverhampton School's side. Leaving his educational studies behind him, Hartill joined the Royal Horse Artillery and served as a bombardier. He scored over 70 goals in two seasons for the RHA XI and the Army team before obtaining his demob to join Wolves in August 1928.

After starting in the Central League team, he made his League debut in November 1928, at Bradford, and scored his first two League

Billy Hartill

goals at Stamford Bridge the following March.

His style pleased the fans. He used to swing a diagonal pass out to the wing before darting into position for the return cross that brought him so many goals. He was good with his head and possessed a powerful kick in either foot, specialising in the hook shot! With Hartill in their side, Wolves regained their First Division status in 1931-32 (when he scored four of his 16 hat-tricks) but three years later - after representing the Football League (Midland) XI - he was transferred to Everton.

He made only five appearances for the Merseysiders, scoring one goal, and his last appearance for them was in a 4-0 drubbing at Molineux. The same year he moved across Stanley Park to Liverpool, where he made another five appearances, this time without managing a goal. He ended his career at Bristol Rovers (1935-38 - scoring 19 goals in 36 League games).

Billy Hartill died in Walsall on 12 August 1980.

Wolves' record: 234 apps. 170 goals.

HARTLAND, Frederick

Goalkeeper Fred Hartland made his only first team appearance for Wolves at Blackpool in a Second Division League game in April 1921 when he replaced Teddy Peers in a 3-0 defeat.

Born in West Bromwich in 1902, he was an amateur with West Bromwich Albion for a season before joining Wolves in 1920. He left Molineux for Smethwick Highfield in the summer of 1922.

Wolves' record: one app.

HARVEY, Joseph

Wing-half Joe Harvey was released by Wolves in 1936 after he had spent one season at Molineux. He then had a year with Bournemouth before joining Bradford City in July 1938. From Valley Parade he transferred north to Newcastle United in October 1945 for £4250 and went on to serve the St. James' Park club until 1953 when he retired to become United's trainer.

Harvey appeared 245 League and Cup games during his eight years with Newcastle, helping them win promotion from Division Two in 1948 and lift the FA Cup in 1951 and 1952 when he was skipper.

He represented the Football League on three occasions. In 1955 he was appointed trainer of Crook Town; soon afterwards he took over as manager of Barrow (1955-57) and was then in charge of Workington (1957-62) before returning to Newcastle as their manager in June 1962, holding office for 13 years, when he resigned in 1975.

Thereafter he was chief scout at St. James' Park. As manager of United Harvey guided them to the Second Division championship in 1965 and victory in the Fairs Cup Final in 1969, while also finishing runners-up in the FA Cup in 1974.

Born in Edlington, Doncaster on 11 June 1918 he was another 'miss' by Wolves!

HARWOOD, Irvine

Irvine Harwood was a strong, willing inside-forward, who was basically a reserve during his one season at Molineux. Born in Bradford on 5 December 1905, he played for Manningham Mills FC, Bradford Park Avenue (May 1929) and Bradford City (May 1931) before joining Wolves in June 1933. On leaving Molineux he signed for Bristol Rovers (May 1934) and later assisted Walsall (from May 1936) before retiring in 1940.

Harwood was an exceptionally fine cricketer who played in the highly respected Bradford League for 15 seasons.

Wolves' record: 6 apps.

HASSALL, Josuah

Joe Hassall, a very competent goalkeeper, became first choice between the posts for Wolves in season 1894-95 after Billy Rose had left for Loughborough Town. Hassall, who had been reserve at Molineux for two years prior to that, stood six feet tall and weighed over 12 stones.

He was born in Wednesfield in November 1871 and played his early football with St. George's FC, Stafford Rangers (1888-91) and Heath Moor. He made his debut early in the 1892-93 season (replacing Rose briefly) but in 1894-95 he was an ever-present.

Then, out of the blue, he was taken ill, leaving Rose free to return to Molineux and claim back his place.

Wolves' record: 52 apps.

HATFIELD, Ernest

Another forceful full-back who possessed a strong tackle, Ernie Hatfield unfortunately failed to make an impact at Molineux and after only a handful of first team appearances was sold to Southend United in May 1931.

Born in Mansfield on 16 January 1905, he played his early football with Frickley Colliery and Wombwell Athletic before joining Sheffield Wednesday in November 1927. Three years later (having made just one appearances for the Owls) he was transferred to Wolves (April 1930), but spent only a season at Molineux.

After two years at Southend he went to Dartford (August 1933), retiring in 1939-40 after a spell in non-League football in the Essex area.

Wolves' record: 4 apps.

HATTON, Robert John

Bob Hatton was a fine marksman, an unselfish player, who did lots of hard work both on and off the ball. A master at snapping up the half-chance, he had smart reflexes, was quick over short distances and packed a strong shot in both feet. He netted 217 goals in 620 League games during his 20-year career.

Born in Hull on 10 April 1947, Hatton played for Wath Wanderers from June 1962 before joining Wolves' apprentice staff in June 1963, turning professional in November 1964. In March 1967 he was transferred to Bolton Wanderers after failing to establish himself in the first team at Molineux.

From Burnden Park he moved to Northampton Town (October 1968) and after a spell with Carlisle United (from July 1969 to October 1971) he signed for Birmingham City where he linked up with Bob Latchford and Trevor Francis. After hitting 73 goals in 218 outings for Blues, Hatton switched to Blackpool (July 1976); two years later he signed for Luton Town and in July 1980 became a Sheffield United player.

After helping the Blades win the Fourth Division title he left Bramall Lane and served with Cardiff City from December 1982, helping the Bluebirds rise from the Third to the Second Division, before quitting League soccer the in May 1983.

He later played for Lodge Cotterill FC (Birmingham Sunday League side) and also worked on local radio, while employed by a Birmingham-based insurance company.
Wolves' record: 13 apps. 8 goals.

HAWKINS, Arthur
Bustling centre-forward Archie Hawkins had one excellent season with Wolves, that of 1906-07 when he averaged almost a goal every two games.

Powerful, with pace and excellent right-foot shot, he was sadly plagued by injuries, suffering a broken arm, dislocated shoulder, cracked ankle and damaged knee all within the space of twelve months.

Born in Wolverhampton circa 1884 he joined Wolves in August 1905 from Heathtown Conservatives and with his career in doubt after those injury problems, he was released by the club in April 1907 and signed for Kidderminster Harriers.
Wolves' record: 20 apps. 9 goals.

HAWKINS, George
Durable full-back who had a useful kick, George Hawkins was born in West Bromwich circa 1862 and played for West Bromwich Standard and Wednesbury Old Athletic before joining Wolves in the summer of 1885.

He left the club to sign for Walsall Victoria in August 1886 after failing to hold down a regular first team place.
Wolves' record: 3 apps.

HAWKINS, Graham Norman
Born in Darlaston on 5 March 1946, Graham Hawkins was a central defender who joined Wolves as an apprentice in June 1961 and turned professional two years later.

He made his League debut in the local derby against West Bromwich Albion in October 1964, but failed to hold down a regular position in the first team.

In December 1967 he was transferred to Preston North End and after a spell with Blackburn Rovers (August 1974 to January 1978) he became Port Vale's player-youth coach, signed for £6,000. In May 1978 he was upgraded to first team coach at Vale Park and became assistant-manager there seven months later.

Unfortunately he was dismissed by the Valiants in September 1979 and immediately took out an unfair dismissal claim, but this was dropped when he received an acceptable compensation offer in April 1980.

Graham Hawkins

After a spell as assistant-manager at Shrewsbury Town, Hawkins returned to Molineux as Wolves boss on 1 August 1982, stepping into the hot-seat vacated by Ian Greaves.

He guided Wolves back into the First Division in his first season, but was then sacked after the team had attained its worst seasonal record in living memory, winning only six League games and suffering 25 defeats as relegation was suffered once more. Hawkins, who was replaced by Tommy Docherty, became disillusioned with English football and elected to coach in Saudi Arabia.

Hawkins' record as Wolves manager was played 88, won 26, drawn 27, lost 356 (exactly 100 goals scored).
Wolves' record: 29+6 sub apps.

HAYES, Jack Walter
Welsh international goalkeeper Teddy Peers missed two games in the 1913-14 season, and in his place stood Walter Hayes.

A native of Oldbury (born in 1894) Hayes joined the staff at Molineux from Hednesford Town in November 1912, having earlier assisted Brownhills Albion. He actually played as an emergency left-half for Wolves reserves v. Birmingham Trams in a Birmingham Cup-tie at Molineux a month after joining the club.

Efficient enough, the chance of regular first team football with Wolves was limited and in July 1914 he was allowed to leave the club to sign for Preston North End. He later returned to the Black Country to play for Cradley Heath and Lye Town.
Wolves' record: 2 apps.

HAYNES, Harold
Wolves recruited centre-half Harry Haynes from non-League soccer.

Basically a reserve, he had one splendid season at Molineux, that of 1894-95, when he played at the heart of the defence between Hill Griffiths and Billy Malpass.

Born on 21 April 1873 in Walsall. Haynes played briefly for his home-town club (Walsall) before joining Walsall Unity in 1891. He found his way to Molineux in February 1893 and spent two-and-a-half years with Wolves before transferring to Birmingham in July 1895.

A year later he moved to Southampton St. Mary's, but was

forced to retire through injury in 1900 after helping Saints win the Southern League championship three seasons running: 1896-99 and reach the 1898 FA Cup semi-final. He was later the landlord of the Turk's Head and Edinburgh Castle pubs in Southampton. Haynes died suddenly in Southampton on 29 March 1902.

Wolves' record: 24 apps. 2 goals

HAYWARD, Sir Jack

Multi-millionaire businessman Sir Jack Hayward, an avid supporter since he was a young lad, bought Wolverhampton Wanderers Football Club in May 1990 and immediately placed his son, Jonathan, and ex-player Billy Wright, on the Board of Directors. Straight away he set about developing the Molineux Stadium and over the next seven years put £19 million into the club as Wolves strove to get into the Premiership.

Born at Dunstall (near the racecourse) on 14 June 1923 and a pupil at Stowe Public School, he used to crawl under the turnstiles as a youngster to get inside Molineux to watch his favourites in action.

In 1941, at the age of 18, he entered the RAF, obtaining his wings after training in Canada and the USA. Posted to India, Hayward volunteered as a glider pilot for war service against the Japanese on the India/Burma border.

Demobbed in 1946, after attaining the rank of Flight Lieutenant, he then worked in South Africa for many years and took charge of his father's business in the USA.

The business was moved to the Bahamas, then part of the British Empire. And over a period of 42 years or so, this one-time desolate island was converted into one of property and thriving economy. It now has a well-developed airport, a substantial seaport, a major tanker terminal and finely established electrical and water companies - all owned by Sir Jack who also purchased Lundy Island off the Devon coast (for the National Trust in 1969).

Hayward also brought the first iron ship - Brunel's SS Great Britain - back from the Falkland Islands... so that it could be restored in this country. He paid £1 million for a hospital in Port Stanley (after the Falklands War) and made a healthy donation towards the building of MCC's Indoor Cricket School.

For all his wonderful achievements Jack Hayward became a Sir - knighted by HM the Queen in 1986.

Married to Jean Mary (nee Foder) in 1948, the Haywards have a daughter and two sons (Jonathan and Rick), who were both associated with Wolves.

When he bought the Molineux club in May 1991 from Gallagher Estates for £2.1 million, Sir Jack immediately put around £20 million of his vast fortune towards rebuilding the Molineux ground, making it into a 28,500 all-seater stadium.

In March 1994 he was the man who sacked Wolves boss Graham Turner and employed Graham Taylor in his place. In November 1995 he dismissed Taylor 'after lack of

Sir Jack Hayward

95

success' (he gave him £7.5 million to spend on players) and replaced him with Mark McGhee.

In May 1997 Sir Jack vowed he would not continue to bail out the club, claiming that it was being run sloppily. Four month later, in September 1997, Sir Jack took over as chairman at Molineux, relegating his son (Jonathan, who had held the chair previously) to vice-chairman, while at the same time appointing ex-player John Richards as the club's Marketing Director.

Just four weeks after assuming the 'chair' Sir Jack paid off an £8 million bank overdraft, this taking his total investment into the club to more than £40 million, and immediately said: "I want to make a fresh start - this is now a new era."

In March 1998, he underwent a triple heart by-pass in Los Angeles and recovered sufficiently well to attend Wolves' FA Cup semi-final with Arsenal at Villa Park.

Then four months into another new season - in November 1998 - he sacked manager Mark McGhee, and within a matter of days appointed Colin Lee as caretaker-boss, soon afterwards giving him the job full-time until the end of the season.

Lee departed halfway through the 2000-01 season and into the hot seat this time stepped David Jones, backed all the way by Sir Jack, who had earlier been behind the appointment of Jez Moxey as the club's Chief Executive (in place of John Richards!)

NB - In January 1999, Sir Jack publicly stated that he had filed papers at the High Court sueing his son Jonathan Hayward, solicitor James Nicholas Stones and his firm, Wiggin and Company, of which he is the senior tax partner, over alleged financial irregularities totalling £237,400.

The action surrounded the movement of money within the club while Jonathan was chairman and related to board approval concerning three major sums of money, without legal authority, of £100,000 in August 1995, a further £37,400 in May 1996 and another £100,000 in May 1997.

Sir Jack Hayward is now Chairman, President and owner of Wolverhampton Wanderers Football Club, and he also said to be the 125th richest person in the world.

HAYWARD, Jonathan

Jonathan Hayward, Sir Jack's son, was born in Nassau, Bahamas on 10 June 1957.

After being educated at Durlston Court School in Hampshire, he followed in his father's footsteps and moved to Stowe Public School.

There he became a useful sportsman, captaining the rugby, hockey and cricket teams. He played rugger for Buckinghamshire County and represented Sussex's Under-19s at cricket. For two years after leaving school he played regularly for Sussex's second XI prior to going to the Royal Agricultural College in Cirencester.

Married in 1979 (to Fiona) the Haywards have resided on a 1,200-acre farm in Northumberland. In 1990 Jonathan was appointed vice-Chairman at Molineux, taking over as Chairman in 1992, a position he held until September 1997 when his father took over the post.

A Football League Director from 1992 to 1994, Jonathan was also a governor at Wolverhampton Grammar School before leaving Molineux.

NB - In January 1999 he was sued by his father (Sir Jack) over money irregularities at club level.

HAYWOOD, Adam S

Utility forward Adam Haywood was a veritable trojan for work, quick and decisive, who joined Wolves from New Brompton (later Gillingham) in 1901.

Born at Horninglow, Burton-on-Trent on 17 May 1875, he stood only 5ft 5in tall and weighed barely 10 stones and had appeared in a North v South England international trial match before taking over from George Harper in the Wolves side.

In May 1905 Haywood left Molineux for West Bromwich Albion; he was transferred from The Hawthorns to Blackpool in December 1907 and for season 1910-11 was player-coach at Crystal Palace. Before joining Southern League club New Brompton he played for Burton Ivanhoe, Burton Wanderers, Swadlincote, Woolwich Arsenal and Queen's Park Rangers.

Wolves' record: 113 apps. 28 goals.

HAZELL, Robert Joseph

Born in Kingston, Jamaica on 14 June 1959, tough-tackling centre-back Bob Hazell signed as an apprentice for Wolves June 1975 and turned professional in May 1977.

He was the first black player to represent the Molineux club in a senior game, he made his League debut at Newcastle United in December 1977. And was also the first black player to score for Wolves (v. Manchester City in March 1978).

As strong as an ox, sturdy, well built and competitive, he won England Youth, Under-21 and 'B' caps during his first spell at Molineux, which lasted until September 1979 when he joined Queens Park Rangers. Four years later, after 106 League outings for the London club, he moved to Leicester City and in September 1985 played one more game on loan with Wolves before joining Luton Town in August 1986.

A spell with Reading preceded his transfer to Port Vale in December 1986. Unfortunately a back injury ruined his career and in June 1989 he was released by the Valiants after appearing in exactly 100 senior games for the Potteries club.

Hazell is now resident in Walsall and has been working for the Birmingham Social Services since 1999.

Wolves' record: 36+1 apps. 1 goal.

HEATH, John Frederick Joseph

Joe Heath (some reference books state John Heath) had the distinction of scoring the first ever penalty goal in the Football League - for Wolves against Accrington on 14 September 1891.

Born in Bristol circa 1869, he moved to the Black Country as a young lad (with his family) and played for Bushbury Principals and Lye Cross before joining Walsall Town Swifts. He transferred to Wolves in August 1891 from Wednesbury Old Athletic.

A centre-forward or half-back, slimly built, Heath spent two years at Molineux (the second of which saw him on the club's injured list) before joining Arsenal in June 1893. He served the Gunners for two years during which time he scored seven times in 12 senior games and also acted as reserve team coach during the 1894-95 season.

In September 1895 he moved to Gravesend United before rejoining Arsenal (as a reserve) in September 1896, returning to the Midlands to play for Pendeford between 1899 and 1901.

Whilst with Arsenal second time round, he won a Kent League championship medal and then added a Sevenoaks Charity Cup medal to his collection with Gravesend in 1897-98. Heath also had the pleasure of netting Arsenal's first ever hat-trick in the Football League - in a 4-0 win over his former club Walsall Town Swifts in September 1893.

Wolves' record: 12 apps. 4 goals.

HEDLEY, George Albert

Born at Southbank, Northumberland on 3 May 1876, centre-forward George Hedley scored a goal every three games for Wolves after joining them from Southampton in May 1906.

He began his career as an amateur in the Northern League before turning professional with Sheffield United in May 1898. In 1899 he gained his first FA Cup winners' medal when the Blades beat Derby County in the Final, and in 1902 he scored the first goal when United beat Southampton in another Final.

George Hedley

In 1901 he had won his only England cap and also collected a FA Cup runners-up medal. Torn heart muscles threatened his career, but he defied medical advice to sign for Southampton in May 1903. Hedley soon became a star at The Dell, scoring 30 goals in 70 games, helping the Saints win the Southern League title before moving to Wolves where he collected his third FA Cup winners' medal, scoring a priceless goal in the 1908 victory over Newcastle United.

After seven fine years at Molineux he managed Bristol City

from April 1913 until April 1915. They were a Second Division club at the time and he guided them to eighth and 13th places.

For his three League clubs he scored 125 goals in 385 League games.

Besides his England cap, which came against Ireland, he also played once for the Football League.

It is said that Hedley wore the same pair of boots for 10 years and when he played in the 1908 FA Cup Final there were no fewer than 17 patches on them!

He was a publican in Bristol from 1918 to 1941 before returning to Wolverhampton to run a boarding house. He died in the town on 16 August 1942.

Wolves' record: 214 apps. 74 goals.

HEELBECK, Leslie Walter

Les Heelbeck was a tremendously hardworking reserve half-back, who always gave a sound performance when called into action.

A Yorkshireman, born in Scarborough in July 1909, and now deceased, he played for Thorne Amateurs, Newark Town and Carlisle United (from July 1931) prior to joining Wolves in March 1932.

He left Molineux for Rotherham United in June 1934, skippering the Millers in his first season, and after a spell with his home town club, Scarborough (from June 1937) he retired in 1941.

Heelbeck died in Scarborough on 25 March 1998.

Wolves' record: 8 apps.

HEGAN, Daniel

Danny Hegan had loads of ability, a midfielder with style, great vision and excellent passing skills, he unfortunately allowed his social life to ruin his football career.

Born of Irish parentage in Coatbridge, Scotland on 14 June 1943, he attended Coatbridge and Ballieston Schools, represented Glasgow Boys and Rutherglen Youths and had trials with Sunderland (August 1958) prior to joining Albion Rovers in August 1959.

In September 1961, Sunderland paid £6,000 for his signature and he spent two years at Roker Park before moving south to Ipswich Town for £20,000 in July 1963. Six years later

Danny Hegan

Hegan was transferred to West Bromwich Albion in a player-exchange deal involving Ian Collard, and from The Hawthorns he switched to Molineux for £50,000 in May 1970.

After more than three years with Wolves, Hegan was sacked for 'persistent infringement of club rules' and duly returned to Sunderland (November 1973).

After that he went to South Africa to play for Highlands Park FC and Johannesburg Spurs before having trials with Partick Thistle (April 1975). He returned to Highlands Park for four months (until August 1975) and his last club was Coleshill (Warwickshire).

He retired in 1978 to become soccer coach at Butlins Holiday Camp, Clacton. Capped by Northern Ireland on seven occasions, Hegan helped Ipswich win the Second Division title in 1968, played for Wolves in the 1972 UEFA Cup Final and in his career he amassed a total 280 League appearances, scoring 42 goals.

Hegan was sued for libel by Billy Bremner, the former Leeds United midfielder in January 1982. Bremner won the case and was subsequently awarded £100,000 in damages.

Hegan also blotted his copybook by becoming the first Wolves player to be sent-off in a European competition v. Academica Coimbra in the UEFA Cup in Sept 1971.
Wolves' record: 65+5 sub apps. 8 goals.

HELLIN, Matthew Karl

Matt Hellin never acquitted himself to English football and during his time at Molineux he played in just one first team game - lining up at left-half against Cambridge United (at home) on the opening Saturday of Wolves' first-ever Fourth Division campaign (23 August 1986).

A Welshman, born in Merthyr on 12 September 1966, Hellin was a junior and then professional with Aston Villa before transferring to Molineux in August 1986. On leaving Wolves in the summer of 1987 he returned to South Wales.
Wolves' record: 1 app.

HEMINGWAY, Cyril Francis

Cyril Hemingway was a creative inside-forward whose career was spent mainly in the Devon area.

A Yorkshireman, born in Rotherham in February 1904, and educated in that town, he represented the County Schools and played for Rotherham United from January 1926, top scoring for the Yorkshire club in 1926-27.

He moved to Torquay United (June 1928) and onto Exeter City in June 1929. He was the Grecians leading marksman in his only season at St James' Park before joining Wolves in May 1930. On leaving Molineux in September 1931, he returned to Torquay and later assisted Dartmouth United (July 1932) and Brixham United.

On his retirement in 1934, he became a publican in the famous harbour town of Dartmouth.
Wolves' record: 4 apps.

HENDERSON, Charles John

Fair-haired, moustacio'd, all-purpose and courageous inside-forward of stocky build with strong right-foot shot, Charlie Henderson had a fine career which spanned 16 years.

Born in Durham in April 1870, he played for South Bank (1885), Darlington as a trialist (1886), Leith Athletic (March 1893), Bolton Wanderers (August 1893), Wolves (signed for £20 in April 1895), Sheffield United (season 1896-97), Dundee Harp (1898), Edinburgh Thistle (1899-1901) and Grimsby Town (April 1902 to February 1933).

He was in the Wolves side for the 1896 FA Cup Final v. Sheffield Wednesday and top-scored for Bolton in his first season at Burnden Park.
Wolves' record: 36 apps. 11 goals.

HENDERSON, John Gillespie

Jackie Henderson was an energetic, fast-raiding Scottish international forward who could play on the wing or through the middle.

Born in Montrose on 17 January 1932, he joined Portsmouth as a teenager and turned professional at Fratton Park on his seventeenth birthday, four months before Pompey won the First Division championship, which they retained the following season. Henderson went on to score 70 goals in 217 League games for Portsmouth before transferring to Wolves in March 1958.

Unfortunately he failed to settle in the Midlands and after just five months moved to London to join Arsenal (October 1958). He notched 29 goals in just over 100 First Division games for the Gunners prior to rounding off his career with Fulham (January 1962 to May 1964).

Henderson won seven full caps for his country and also starred in two 'B' internationals.
Wolves' record: 9 apps. 3 goals.

HENSHALL, Albert Victor

Albert Henshall replaced Harry Hampton in the Wellington Town attack when the dashing centre-forward joined Aston Villa in 1904.

A resolute performer with good pace, he did well in non-League soccer but failed to make the grade with Wolves.

Born in Wellington in 1882, he joined Wellington Town in 1900 and after a spell with Whitchurch (August 1905) he moved to Molineux as a trialist in September 1905, returning for a further spell with Wellington in 1907.

Henshall died in Whitchurch in 1944.
Wolves' record: 2 apps.

HENSON, George Horace

Centre-forward George Henson spent just two seasons at Molineux, making all his first team appearances in 1935-36.

Signed from Northampton Town in August 1935, Henson was born in Stoney Stratford, Buckinghamshire on 25

December 1911 (and now deceased) and played his early football with Stoney Stratford FC and Wolverton before signing for the Cobblers as an amateur in 1932, turning professional a year later.

He scored 18 goals in 52 games before leaving to join Mexborough, signing for Wolves in 1935. He left Molineux in May 1936 for Swansea Town and then played for Bradford Park Avenue in 1937-38, finishing up as top scorer in the Second Division that season with 27 goals.

Henson moved to Sheffield United six months before the outbreak of World War Two but didn't figure again in League football after the hostilities.

Wolves' record: 6 apps. 1 goal.

HERBERT, Rikki Lloyd

Rikki Herbert played for Wolves during two very poor seasons: from October 1984 to May 1986.

A hard tackling defender, who preferred the left-hand side, he could also occupy the full-back position but was always under pressure with the rest of his colleagues during his time at Molineux.

Born on 10 April 1961 in New Zealand, he joined Wolves from Sydney Olympic (Australia) and won his first full cap for his country against the Aussies in 1985-86. He returned to Australian football when leaving Wolves.

Wolves' record: 47+2 apps.

HETHERINGTON, John Arthur

Yorkshireman Jack Hetherington was a useful inside or outside-left, fleet-footed with a positive approach.

Born in Rotherham on 7 August 1908, he played initially for Dalton United before joining Wolves in the summer of 1928 as cover for Tom Baxter.

When Baxter was transferred, Hetherington became first choice on the left wing and did very well for three seasons before losing his place to Billy Barraclough.

He eventually left Molineux for Preston North End in January 1935 after almost 100 appearances for the Wolves. He moved from Deepdale to Swindon Town in 1936 and then spent two seasons with Watford before the war ruined his career!

Wolves' record: 95 apps. 24 goals.

HEWITT, Ronald

An inside-forward, born in Flint on 21 June 1928, Ron Hewitt was transferred from Molineux to Walsall in October 1949 without ever breaking into Wolves' first team, having joined the club as a professional in July 1948.

Over the next 14 years he went on to win five full caps for Wales, three coming in the World Cup Finals of 1958.

During his career he appeared in a total of 427 League games, scoring 155 goals while serving, in turn, with the Saddlers, Darlington (from June 1950), Wrexham (from July 1951), Cardiff City (signed for £4,500 in June 1957), Wrexham again (recruited for £2,000 in July 1959), Coventry City (bought for £4,500 in March 1960) and Wrexham, acquired for a third time in March 1962.

He then moved to Chester and later assisted Hereford United, Northwich Victoria, Witton Albion and Carenarfon before settling in Wrexham where he lives today. Hewitt helped Wrexham win the Welsh Cup in 1957 and represented the Third Division North v. the South in the annual challenge match.

He netted 111 goals in 267 senior games during his three spells with Wrexham.

Certainly another 'one that got away' as far as Wolves were concerned!

HEYHOE-FLINT, Rachael, MBE

Rachael Heyhoe-Flint - the first lady Board Member (a female Director) of Wolverhampton Football Club - is best known as the champion of the cause of women's cricket. She first played for England in 1960, captained the side from 1966-77 and ended her international career in 1983 after making a record 51 appearances for her country.

Born in Wolverhampton, she established herself as a media figure and businesswoman specialising in public relations, sports marketing and promotions. A former journalist and humorous public speaker, in 1973 she was named 'Best After Dinner Speaker' by the Guild of Professional Toastmasters.

Rachael trained as a teacher of Physical Education, became a journalist in 1968 and within four years was Sports Editor of the Wolverhampton Chronicle. Soon afterwards she took up a position as a freelance journalist, working mainly for the Daily and Sunday Telegraph and in 1973 was appointed TV's first woman sports presenter/reporter with ITV's World of Sport. She has also appeared in a variety of radio and TV quiz shows and panel games.

On the cricket field and as captain of the England women's team she proudly led her country in the first ladies match at Lords in 1978. In a fascinating cricketing career she ran up 30 centuries and her top score (for England) was 179 v. Australia at The Oval in 1976 - still a world record score for an English player in Test Matches in England.

In 1972 Rachael was awarded the MBE for services to cricket - the first women to gain this award in this sport, having been Public Relations Officer of the Women's Cricket Association for seven years and Chairman for two, but she resigned from the latter post over a matter of principal in 1968.

Rachael has also played hockey for England (in 1964) as a goalkeeper and represented Staffordshire in this sport for a record 25 years. She also played squash and golf for Staffordshire.

She is also an author, having written books entitled 'Fair Play' (the story of women's cricket) and 'Heyhoe' (her own autobiography) plus two hockey instruction booklets.

Rachael is now a Public Relations, Promotions and Sports

Rachael Heyhoe-Flint

Marketing Consultant, operating from her own office in Wolverhampton.

She is also the PR and Promotions Executive to Hyatt's La Manga Club Resort in Spain, Patshull Park Golf and County Club and Wolverhampton Wanderers Football Club and also an honorary member of the first two named organisations. She is also on the Board of the Family Assurance Friendly Society and the Council of Malvern College, Worcestershire. She organises golf days for national celebrities and corporate clients.

In 1997 Rachael was appointed a Deputy Lieutenant of the West Midlands. She is also Vice-President of the Cricketer' Club of London, an avid member of the Advisory Panel of the Faldo Junior Series and was taken on as a main Board member at Wolverhampton Wanderers Football Club in September 1997. A friend of Sir Jack Hayward since 1970 - she wrote a pleading letter asking him to sponsor the England Women's Cricket team on a tour to the West Indies! He did just that and soon after created the first Women's World Cup in 1973, beating the men by two years!

Now residing in Tettenhall, Rachael has three children and one step son and in 1999 she had the pleasure, and satisfaction, of becoming a founder member of the women's section at Lords...Now she can proudly walk into the famous old cricket ground - and through the historic long room - whenever she chooses!

A Wolves fan since 1949, Rachael has actually worked at Molineux in one capacity or another since 1990 and said that "...becoming a Director never entered my brain. When I was appointed I was speechless and I will admit that a little tear or two appeared.

HEYWOOD, David Ian

As a youth team player David Heywood looked set for a bright future in the game, but he never developed into a League footballer and consequently drifted out of the spotlight in the mid 1980s.

Born in Wolverhampton on 25 July 1967, full-back Heywood joined the Molineux camp on a YTS in 1983. He turned professional in November 1984, but was released into non-League soccer two years later when he joined Burton Albion, later assisting Kettering Town, Halesowen Town and Worcester City (August 1991) and Halesowen again (from February 1993).

Wolves' record: 8 apps.

HIBBITT, Kenneth

Yorkshireman Kenny Hibbitt was born in Bradford on 3 January 1951, and for 16 years starred in Wolves midfield, making more than 570 first-team appearances and thus the £5,000 that Wolves boss Ronnie Allen paid Bradford Park Avenue for his services was by far, the bargain of the decade.

Ironically, Allen left his job within 48 hours of completing Hibbitt's transfer, but the youngster stayed at Molineux and prospered.

A vastly underrated player - in some quarters - he certainly deserved to win international recognition for his efforts but all he had to show for his efforts was one England Under-23 cap, gained as a substitute against Wales in 1970-71.

An accomplished footballer, whether as a playmaker or goalscorer, he loved to drive forward to assist his front men.

Hibbitt, a real top-quality professional, joined Wolves in November 1968 after making only 15 League appearances for Bradford, and remained at Molineux until August 1984. He was an industrious, creative midfielder who also found time to score over 100 goals for Wolves, including a precious effort in the 1974 League Cup Final victory over Manchester City at Wembley and a club record nine penalties the following season. Six years later he collected a second League Cup winners' trophy when Wolves beat Nottingham Forest in the Final.

Two years after receiving a testimonial in 1981-82, Hibbitt was allowed to move to Coventry City and in August 1986 the Sky Blues transferred him to Bristol Rovers.

When he returned to Molineux in 1989, as Rovers coach, the South Bank saluted him in recognition of the magnificent service he had given their club.

Alas, his illustrious playing career had finally come to an end when he suffered a broken leg playing for Rovers against Sunderland in February 1988.

As assistant to Gerry Francis he helped steer Bristol Rovers to the Third Division title and the Leyland DAF Trophy Final in 1989. In May 1990 he was appointed team manager of Walsall and three years later led the Saddlers into the Third Division Play-offs, signing a new two-year contract at the Bescot Stadium soon afterwards.

But in 1995 he quit to become manager of Cardiff City, later assuming the role of Director of Football and Coaching at Ninian Park (initially under manager Russell Osman).

NB - His brother Terry, also a midfield player, assisted Leeds United, Newcastle United and Birmingham City. Terry sadly died in 1994 at the age of 46.

Wolves' record: 522+22 sub apps. 114 goals.

HIGGS, Harold

Born in Stourbridge in 1900, goalkeeper Harry Higgs joined Wolves from Halesowen at the start of the first season after the Great War (1919).

He was reserve to Teddy Peers and therefore got very little opportunity to try his luck in the League side. He eventually left the club for Darlaston in July 1920.

Wolves' record: 3 apps.

HIGHAM, Frank

Hefty wing-half, six foot one inch tall and 12st 6lbs in weight, Frank Higham spent three years at Molineux

Kenny Hibbitt holds aloft the League Cup (with Willie Carr, right) after Wolves' victory in 1980

Frank Higham

during which time he acted as reserve to Mitton, Kay and Bradford.

Born in Daventry in September 1905, he played for Walsall (March 1925) before joining Wolves in May 1925. In June 1928 he was transferred to Coventry City and two years later signed for Lincoln City.

Higham then entered non-League soccer and played, in turn, for Worcester City, Nuneaton, Evesham Town and Hereford United before retiring in 1939.

Wolves' record: 42 apps. 2 goals.

HILL, James

Utility forward Jimmy Hill was born in Wolverhampton in April 1862 and joined Wolves in 1877 as a founder member from Spittal Strollers.

He broke into the first team within six months and remained at the club until 1884 before his career was cut short with a serious knee injury at the age of only 22. He was heart broken at the time and although he tried to make a comeback at a lower level, he was a cripple before he had turned 40.

He later worked in a factory in Surrey and in 1953 was a guest at the Charlton v. Wolves game at The Valley. Hill died in London two years later, aged 93.

Wolves' record: one app.

HILL, J Albert

Albert Hill was Wolves' reserve centre-forward for two seasons: 1928-30.

He was never a serious threat to the likes of regular forwards Deacon, Hartill and Marshall but nevertheless he was a dedicated footballer who never accepted defeat. Born in Rotherham circa 1907 (and now deceased) he played for several clubs locally before joining Wolves in July 1928.

On leaving Molineux in May 1930, he signed for Wrexham.

Wolves' record: 2 apps.

HILL, James Thomas W

Goalkeeper Jimmy Hill spent two seasons as a reserve with Wolves.

Born in Aldridge in 1888, he left Blakenhall for Molineux in July 1909 and moved to Darlaston in May 1911 after just a handful of senior appearances for the Wanderers replacing first Billy Lunn and then Frank Boxley.

A shade on the small side at 5ft 9ins tall yet weighing a healthy 11st. 10lbs, Hill was unfortunate to suffer with arm and back injuries during the early part of his career.

Wolves' record: 3 apps.

HINDMARCH, Robert

Hard-tackling defender Rob Hindmarch was born in Stannington near Morpeth on 27 April 1961.

He joined Sunderland as a youngster and turned professional at Roker Park in April 1978 after representing England at Youth team level. He went on to make well over 100 League appearances for the Wearsiders and after a loan spell with Portsmouth (in December 1983) he moved to Derby County in July 1984.

He spent the next six years at The Baseball Ground, amassing almost 200 outings for the Rams and helping them win the Second Division title in 1987 before he joined Wolves in June 1990 for £325,000.

Hindmarch stayed at Molineux until May 1993 when he was given a free transfer, moving quickly into non-League football with Telford United.

Wolves' record: 43+1 sub apps. 2 goals.

HINTON, Alan Thomas

Winger Alan Hinton's real career highlights came at Derby County, after Brian Clough had rescued him from relative obscurity as he drifted along with Nottingham Forest.

But it was with Wolves that Hinton, who was born in Wednesbury on 6 October 1942, began his career and where he won his first three full England caps.

An outside-left who could cross the ball with remarkable accuracy (Jimmy Greaves thought he was brilliant - vouching for the brilliance of his deliveries) Hinton also possessed a tremendous shot in his left foot, whether cutting in for goal or from dead-ball situations. He played for South-east Staffordshire and Birmingham County Schools before turning professional with Wolves in October 1959.

Hinton's League debut came in January 1961 and altogether he made almost 80 first-team appearances for Wolves and besides his full caps, he appeared for England's Youth and Under-23 teams. Hinton moved to Nottingham Forest in January 1964 where he won another two full caps and hit 24 goals in 123 first-team appearances before Clough signed him for Derby in September 1967 for £30,000.

On his transfer, a Forest committee member reportedly said that the Rams would soon want their money back, but he reckoned without Clough's and Peter Taylor's motivational skills!

Hinton appeared in well over 300 senior games for Derby, scoring 83 goals. He helped the Rams win the Second Division title and was a key member in two League championship-winning sides.

Unfortunately he played very little football in 1975-76 following the tragic death of his young son, Matthew. He eventually went to work in the North American Soccer League with Dallas Tornado (March 1977), switching to Vancouver Whitecaps in October 1977, onto Tulsa Roughnecks in October 1978 and over to Seattle Sounders in November 1979, staying there until January 1983. His last appointment was with Tacoma Stars.

With Vancouver in 1978 he set a new record for 'assists', his 30 beating the old one set jointly by Pele and George Best. In 1980 Hinton was voted the NASL Coach of the Year, but when the NASL eventually folded, he moved to the Major Indoor Soccer League with Tacoma.

Hinton later quit soccer altogether and now helps his wife run a real estate business in the United States.

Wolves' record: 78 apps. 29 goals.

HODNETT, Joseph Edward

Centre-half Joe Hodnett played for Wolves during the first four seasons after World War One.

Born in Wolverhampton on 18 July 1896, he was a real tough character who began his career with Willenhall in 1914 and moved to Molineux in August 1919 when the team was being rebuilt after the hostilities.

At first he found himself in reserve - at one stage he appears to have been Wolves' fourth-choice pivot - but he managed a few games each season and appeared in the 1921 FA Cup Final against Spurs at Stamford Bridge. That was his best season with 34 League and Cup appearances and he was one of the stars of that Cup run, but in 1923 Wolves, with several options at centre-half, transferred him to Pontypridd.

He later played for Chesterfield (from June 1924), Merthyr Town (May 1925), Brentford (August 1926) and Gillingham (June 1927) before returning to the Midlands to join Stafford Rangers in August 1928. Before he retired during the 1935-36 season, he had also played for Stourbridge, Halesowen, Dudley Town and Brierley Hill Alliance.

Hodnett died at Willenhall on 12 November 1943.

Wolves' record: 85 apps. 5 goals.

HOLLEY, George H

Born at Seaham Harbour, Wearside on 25 November 1885, George Holley was a superb inside-forward who made almost 350 senior appearances for Sunderland (299 in the Football League) between 1904 and 1915. He scored 160 goals (150 in the League) and formed a great partnership up front with Charlie Buchan (among others).

He helped the Wearsiders win the First Division title and reach the FA Cup Final (beaten by Aston Villa) in 1912-13, and scored a hat-trick in Sunderland's epic 9-1 win at Newcastle in 1908.

After the Great War he moved to Brighton & Hove Albion and played one season of Southern League football before being appointed as Wolves trainer in 1922 (under the managership of George Robey). He retained that position for a decade, leaving the club after seeing the Second Division championship come to Molineux in 1931-32, although at this juncture he had handed over the first team bucket to Jack Davies. Earlier with Holley as spongeman, Wolves had won the Third Division (North) title in 1923-24.

Holley, who worked as a silver-plater after leaving football, died in the North-east of England on 27 August 1942.

HOLLIFIELD, Michael

A player who showed a lot of ability as a teenager, full-back Mike Hollifield was never a first choice player at Molineux.

Born in Middlesbrough on 2 May 1961, he had trials at Ayresome Park before joining Wolves as an apprentice in June 1977. He turned professional in April 1979 and left the club for Hull City in August 1983.

He made 45 League appearances for the Tigers before moving to Tranmere Rovers in July 1985, remaining at Prenton Park until May 1986.

Wolves' record: 25 apps.

HOLLINGWORTH, Reginald

Centre-half Reg Hollingworth was one of the more unfortunate footballers to have played for Wolverhampton Wanderers.

Reg Hollingworth

True, he made over 180 senior appearances for Wolves, but just before he was due to play in an England international trial at Huddersfield, he was injured playing at Barnsley in March 1932, just when a cap was considered a near-certainty. Then in 1936, another injury forced him to retire.

Hollingworth, who was born at Rainworth, near Mansfield, on 17 October 1909, was a fine centre-half, tall and strong with attacking instincts. He first played for Nuffield Colliery and as an amateur for Mansfield Town before Wolves signed him from Sutton Junction FC in November 1928.

Apparently Mansfield wanted to sign him as a professional but couldn't afford another paid player. Hollingworth helped Wolves to the Second Division title in 1931-32, when he was a regular until the injury at Oakwell, which kept him out for the rest of that season and half of the next. After leaving Molineux he joined the Staffordshire police force.

He then worked at the Goodyear tyre company (Wolverhampton) before being employed as a manager by Batchelor Robinson & Company in Balsall Heath for 22 years. Hollingworth's death was tragic - he died after suffering a heart attack whilst driving a car along Sandy Lane, Sparkbrook, on 8 July 1969.

Wolves' record: 180 apps. 8 goals.

HOLMES, Michael Anthony

Micky Holmes, who was born in Blackpool on 9 September 1965, was a hard-working midfielder who served Wolves from November 1985 to July 1988 and did well in difficult circumstances, making over 100 appearances and winning a Fourth Division championship medal and a Sherpa Van Trophy winners medal at Wembley in 1988.

A former Bradford and West Yorkshire Schools player, Holmes joined Bradford City from Yeadon Colliery in July 1983, but after only five substitute appearances they released him to Hamileff FC and he was on Burnley's book as a non-contract player (without making a senior appearance) before Wolves signed him.

After leaving Molineux, he played for Huddersfield Town, Cambridge United, Rochdale and Torquay United prior to a £15,000 transfer to Carlisle United in February 1992. During 1993-94 he passed the 250 mark in career appearances.

In 1991 Holmes helped Torquay to victory in the Fourth Division Play-off Final against Blackpool at Wembley.

Wolves' record: 89+15 sub apps. 13 goals.

HOLSGROVE, John William

Powerful defender John Holsgrove cost Wolves £18,000 when they signed him from Crystal Palace in May 1965. He was recommended to Wolves by Palace's player-coach Ronnie Allen, who later became his manager at Molineux. Holsgrove, who was born at Southwark on 27 September

1945 and had been on the books of both Arsenal and Spurs as an amateur, spent only one season in Palace's first team, making 22 appearances after joining them as a junior. But the former England Youth international was at Molineux considerably longer, making over 200 senior appearances before he was transferred to Sheffield Wednesday in June 1971.

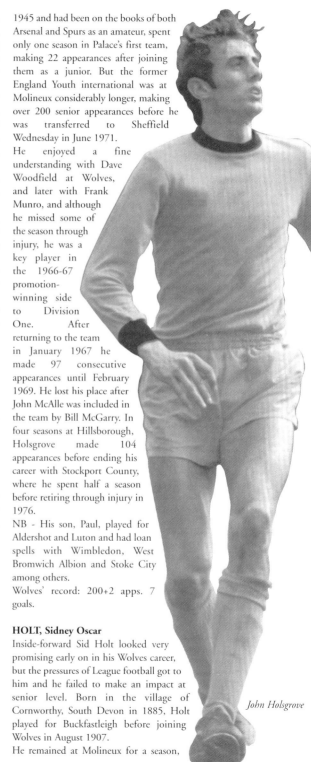

He enjoyed a fine understanding with Dave Woodfield at Wolves, and later with Frank Munro, and although he missed some of the season through injury, he was a key player in the 1966-67 promotion-winning side to Division One. After returning to the team in January 1967 he made 97 consecutive appearances until February 1969. He lost his place after John McAlle was included in the team by Bill McGarry. In four seasons at Hillsborough, Holsgrove made 104 appearances before ending his career with Stockport County, where he spent half a season before retiring through injury in 1976.

NB - His son, Paul, played for Aldershot and Luton and had loan spells with Wimbledon, West Bromwich Albion and Stoke City among others.

Wolves' record: 200+2 apps. 7 goals.

HOLT, Sidney Oscar

Inside-forward Sid Holt looked very promising early on in his Wolves career, but the pressures of League football got to him and he failed to make an impact at senior level. Born in the village of Cornworthy, South Devon in 1885, Holt played for Buckfastleigh before joining Wolves in August 1907.

He remained at Molineux for a season,

John Holsgrove

leaving for Torquay United in May 1908, and later assisting Exeter City and Newton Abbot. Holt died in Totnes in 1958.

Wolves' record: 8 apps.

HOLYHEAD, Joseph Jacob

Born in Wolverhampton in August 1880, Joe Holyhead played for Willenhall Swifts and Wednesbury Old Athletic before joining Wolves in August 1902.

He spent a season at Molineux, leaving for Port Vale in September 1903 (initially on trial) and later serving with Swindon Town (May 1907), Wellington Town (July 1908) and Walsall White Star (August 1910).

Holyhead, who made over 140 first team appearances for the Vale, retired towards the end of World War One.

Wolves' record: 6 apps.

HOMER, Sidney

Outside-right Sid Homer - born in Bloxwich on 14 January 1903 - was highly-rated when playing on the wing for Bloxwich Strollers and in the summer of 1925 he was taken on as a full-time professional at Molineux.

He had an excellent first season with Wolves, appearing in 18 League games in place of Jack Harrington. The following campaign wasn't so good and in May 1927 he was transferred to Bristol Rovers. He spent three years at Eastville (making 38 appearances) before switching to neighbouring Bristol City in November 1929.

At Ashton Gate he became a real star and over the next five-and-a-half years scored 18 goals in 179 appearances for the Robins before quitting League soccer to play for Worcester City, retiring through injury at the age of 31.

Wolves' record: 29 apps. 2 goals.

HOOPER, Harry

Harry Hooper enjoyed a fine career that spanned 13 years, took in over 320 senior appearances and saw him play for four League clubs.

Born in the village of Pittington, County Durham on 14 June 1933, Hooper, the son of a former Hartlepools United, Nelson and Sheffield United defender, also named Harry who skippered the Blades in the 1936 FA Cup Final against Arsenal, joined West Ham United as a full-time professional in December 1950 - after the Upton Park club had appointed his father to their training staff. Earlier, young Harry had played for Hylton Colliery and as an amateur with Sunderland.

A former Durham youth sprint champion he scored 44 goals in 119 Second Division games for the Hammers, winning six England 'B' caps and two at Under-23 level as well as playing for the Football League. When Wolves paid £25,000

Harry Hooper

for him to succeed Johnny Hancocks it was the most any club had paid for a winger at that time.

Hooper, happiest on the right flank, netted 19 goals in 39 League games, all in 1956-57 when he was top scorer. In December 1957, with Norman Deeley now established on the right wing at Molineux, Hooper moved to Birmingham City, thus taking no part in Wolves' championship season. The Blues paid £19,500 for him and he scored 42 goals in 105 games for them, appearing in the 1960 Fairs Cup Final against Barcelona.

In September 1960 he was transferred to Sunderland, a local boy going home, and made 65 League appearances for the Wearsiders before joining Kettering Town in May 1963. He left football in 1967 and went into business in Kettering.

Wolves' record: 41 apps. 19 goals.

HOPKINS, John

Wolves signed winger Jack Hopkins from Liverpool reserves in March 1904. And over the next two seasons he gave some excellent performances on the left flank when deputising for Jack Miller.

Unfortunately he could never hold down a regular first team place and in 1906 was transferred to New Brighton. Born on Merseyside circa 1882, Hopkins later worked near the Mersey shipyard.

Wolves' record: 47 apps. 14 goals.

HORNE, Desmond Tolton

Several players from South Africa found their way to Britain in the 1950s, amongst them outside-left Des Horne, who was born in Johannesburg on 12 December 1939 and signed for Wolves in December 1956.

Horne was an out-and-out winger, fast and direct, but Jimmy Mullen was in possession of the number-11 shirt at Molineux and Horne had to wait until the first day of the 1958-59 season to make his debut, at home to Nottingham Forest.

He made only eight appearances that season as Wolves retained the League championship, but began to establish himself the following season and gained an FA Cup winners' medal in 1960, when Wolves beat Blackburn in the Final. Altogether he made over 50 appearances for Wolves, scoring 18 goals, before being transferred to Blackpool in March 1961.

For the Seasiders, Horne made 188 League appearances, scoring another 18 goals. His time at Bloomfield Road saw Blackpool struggling in Division One, but he helped them to a League Cup semi-final in 1962. In 1966 he returned to South Africa where he now runs his own air-conditioning business, although his daughter works in Wolverhampton. Horne incidentally was the second South-African born winger to play in a FA Cup Final, following Blackpool's Bill Perry in 1953.

Wolves' record: 52 apps. 18 goals.

HORTON, Thomas Ezekial Bruce

Teak-tough inside-forward, very unorthodox in his play, Tom Horton was born in Birmingham in 1863 and played for Crosswells Brewery before joining Wolves in August 1885.

He spent a season with the club and in August 1886 signed for West Bromwich Standard, later assisting Stafford Rangers.

Wolves' record: 2 apps. one goal.

HOSKINS, Albert Herbert

Bert Hoskins was born in Southampton in 1885 and played for St Mary's Guild and Freemantle FC (Hampshire) before joining Southampton in 1904.

A useful forward with good pace, he scored three goals in 21 games for Saints before transferring to Shrewsbury Town. In May 1908 he was recruited by Wolves but failed to make the grade at Molineux and left after a short while to sign for Dudley Town, later assisting St. Peters FC, Darlaston and Wellington Town where he became club secretary. In August 1919 he returned to Molineux as assistant to then manager/secretary Jack Addenbrooke.

He progressed well and became Wolves secretary himself in 1922. Two years later, in June 1924, he was handed the manager's job at Molineux - and was indeed, a proud man. Hoskins looked after team affairs for two years, seeing the team finish 6th in the Second Division in 1924-25, but his appointment was short-lived and in March 1926 he left Wolves to take over a similar position at Gillingham, holding office there for four years.

Thereafter he remained in the game as a trainer, coach and scout, working for several non-League clubs until 1940.

Hoskins who died on 19 February 1968, achieved these statistics as Wolves manager: played 78, won 34, drawn 13, lost 31.

Wolves' playing record: 14 apps. 2 goals.

HOWELL, Henry

Henry Howell was born in Smethwick on 28 June 1895 and besides being a useful centre or inside-forward, he also played Test cricket for England and County cricket for Warwickshire.

As a footballer he starred for St. Michael's Youth Club and Burslem Swifts before joining Wolves in July 1913. During the war he guested for Stoke and Port Vale and soon after re-signing for Wolves (August 1919) he had a trial with Southampton (1920) and later assisted

Northfleet FC (1921), Accrington Stanley (October 1922-23) and Mansfield Town.

As a cricketer, Howell spent 15 years with Warwickshire (1913-28), appearing in 198 first-class matches.

He twice toured Australia with the MCC (in 1920-21 and 1924-25), playing in five Tests against the Aussies.

In his career Howell played in 227 competitive matches and scored 1,679 runs in 326 innings (111 not-outs) for an average of 7.80. His bowling figures were much better - 20,700 runs conceded, 975 wickets taken for an average of 21.23.

His best return was 10-51 v. Yorkshire at Edgbaston in 1923. He also took 5-15 v. Hampshire and claimed five wickets in an innings 75 times and 10 in a match on 18 separate occasions. He took over 100 wickets in a season six times with a best tally of 161 in 1920 (average 17.91). Howell died in Selly Oak on 9 July 1932.

NB - His brother, AL Howell, also represented Warwickshire CCC.

Wolves' record: 41 apps. 8 goals.

HOWELL, William Thomas Richard

Signed as full-back cover by secretary-manager Jack Addenbrook from Wellington Town in August 1900, Bill Howells (sometimes his name was seen without the 's') stayed at Molineux for one season before transferring to Willenhall Pickwick in August 1901.

Wolves' record: one app.

HOWELLS, Ronald

Tall, slim wing-half, Ron Howells, besides being an efficient footballer, was also a very accomplished cricketer, playing for the Warwickshire Club and Ground.

Born the son of a Rugby Union international in the Rhondda Valley on 3 August 1935, he was educated in Coventry and represented Warwickshire County Schools before joining Nuneaton Borough. From there he switched to Molineux, becoming a professional in July 1953.

He stayed with Wolves for six years (as a reserve) before transferring to Portsmouth in March 1959, later assisting Scunthorpe United (June 1961) and Walsall (July 1963 to May 1964). He amassed well over 150 senior appearances at club level.

Wolves' record: 9 apps.

HOWLEY, John T

Jack Howley - who only played football at school - arrived at Molineux as a junior office boy in the summer of 1923. He stayed with Wolves for the rest of his working life, until the arrival of manager Bill McGarry. He was the club secretary for 20 years - from June 1948 until June 1968 - the last five being combined with the duties of General Manager. A dedicated Wolves man, Howley sadly died on 23 March 1971.

Jack Howley (left) with manager Stan Cullis in 1954

HUGHES, Emyln Walter, OBE

When Wolves manager John Barnwell signed Emlyn Hughes in August 1979, he was already a vastly experienced defender, having amassed over 750 senior appearances while playing for Blackpool (34 games), Liverpool (657) and England (59 full and eight Under-23 caps).

He had gained a rich haul of honours with the Merseysiders, helping the Reds win four League championships, two European Cup Finals, two UEFA Cup Finals and the FA Cup. He also appeared in several other Finals and after captaining the Anfield side to European Cup success in 1977, he was duly voted PFA 'Footballer of the Year.'

Barnwell saw him as the man to help solve the problem of a leaky defence that had just conceded 150 goals in two seasons - and it worked.

With Hughes at the centre of their rearguard, Wolves opened the season with two clean sheets and by the end of it Hughes was lifting the League Cup after victory over Nottingham

Emlyn Hughes

Forest at Wembley. Wolves also climbed from 18th to sixth in Division One. Hughes also added three more England caps to his collection as a Wolves defender but his was only ever going to be a short-term signing.

In September 1981 he became player-manager of Rotherham United, after appearing in more than 70 first-team games for Wolves. Hughes ended his career with spells at Hull City, Swansea City and Mansfield Town, although he never appeared for the Stags.

He was born in Barrow on 28 August 1947, the son of a Great Britain Rugby League international and first played for Roose FC and Blackpool (from September 1964) before Liverpool signed him in March 1967 for £65,000. He was on the board at Hull City for a season and worked in television, most notably as one of the captains in 'A Question of Sport' on BBC. He was awarded the OBE for his services to football.

Wolves' record: 75+2 apps. 2 goals.

HUGHES, Harold

Born near Nantwich, Cheshire in 1881, Harry Hughes was reserve to Jack Whitehouse and Ernie Jones during his time at Molineux. He joined Wolves from Crewe Alexandra in July 1905 and left for Leamington Town in May 1906. He later played for Stafford Rangers (1907-08) and then Hanley Swifts (1909) before retiring in 1910.

Wolves' record: 9 apps.

HUGHES, William H

Billy Hughes was a forceful centre-forward, who scored 51 goals in 102 games for Bolton Wanderers before moving to Molineux in September 1913. Born in Stourbridge in 1890, Hughes played for Norton Hall FC, Stourbridge Standard and Connahs Quay before moving into the professional ranks at Burnden Park in April 1908. Unfortunately his association with Wolves was cut short through a knee injury, forcing him to retire in May 1914. After helping Bolton win promotion to the First Division in 1911, the Trotters were fined £28 by the Football League for misleading Hughes into assuming he would receive £200 in lieu of a benefit match if he left Burnden Park.

Wolves' record: 24 apps. 10 goals.

HUMPHREY, John

Londoner John Humphrey was born at Paddington on 31 January 1961. Educated at Aylestone High School, Kersal Rise (QPR territory), he was playing in midfield for Bourne Hall Youth Club in Bushey, Herts when spotted by Wolves manager Sammy Chung who quickly signed him as an apprentice in June 1977.

After being upgraded to the professional ranks in January 1979, Humphrey established himself in the senior side at right-back in season 1981-82, but found himself in a side fighting an unsuccessful battle against relegation to Division Two.

The very next season, though, they bounced straight back as runners-up, Humphrey being an ever-present.

Of course, those were topsy-turvy days at Molineux and twelve months later Humphrey found himself back in the Second Division with Wolves. Another year on and he was facing Third Division football as Wolves hurtled straight down the League.

In July 1985, before he could sample the questionable delights of Third Division football Humphrey was rescued by Charlton Athletic. He spent five years with the London club, appearing in 231 games, helping the Addicks into Division One in his first season at Selhurst Park (to where Charlton had just moved) and to the 1987 Full Members' Cup Final, when they lost to Blackburn.

In July 1990 he was transferred to Crystal Palace for £400,000 and helped Palace win the Zenith Data Systems Cup in 1991. In December 1993 he joined Reading on loan as Palace went on to win the First Division title and so claim Premiership status.

In July 1995 Humphrey had a second spell with Charlton and in August 1996 he joined Gillingham, moving to struggling Brighton & Hove Albion in January 1997. In November 1997 Humphrey signed for non-League Chesham United having made a total of 681 first-class appearances.

Wolves' record: 164 apps. 3 goals.

HUNT, Reverend Kenneth Reginald Gunnery

A top-class footballer in the mould of Reverend Kenneth Hunt could not exist today, of course. But back in the early 1900s there was still room for the gifted amateur to make his mark alongside full-time professionals. Hunt, who was born at Oxford on 24 February 1884, but who attended Wolverhampton Grammar School, remained an amateur throughout his playing days as a creative wing-half.

His career began at Trent College in Derbyshire before he gained a soccer Blue at Oxford University three years in succession. Naturally, he played for the great amateur side, Corinthians, and he also assisted several other clubs including Leyton, Crystal Palace, Tottenham Hotspur, Wolves and Oxford City. He gained 20 England Amateur caps but also played twice for the full international side in 1911, against Scotland and Wales, when he was officially listed as a Leyton player but was

Reverend Kenneth Hunt

also helping Wolves.

Indeed, he appeared for Wolves off and on over a period of 14 years - 1906 to 1920 - in between his studies and other work - and all told he played in more than 60 senior games for the club, scoring two goals, one of them coming in the 1908 FA Cup Final when Newcastle United were beaten 3-1 at the Crystal Palace in front of almost 75,000 fans.

That was his best season for Wolves with 21 League appearances and seven outings in the FA Cup. And in that very same year (1908) he also won an Olympic Gold Medal with the Great Britain soccer team.

Five years later, in 1913, Hunt played for Oxford City in the FA Amateur Cup Final and after World War One, he turned out regularly for Eccleshall Comrades and Stafford Rangers. Hunt was ordained in 1909 and as a house-master at Highgate School, North London, between 1909 and 1945 he did much for Public Schools soccer. Hunt was an FA Council member for many years before retiring through ill health in January 1949. He died three months later, on 28 April, at Heathfield in Sussex.

Wolves' record: 61 apps. 2 goals.

HUNT Roger Patrick

Midfielder 'Ernie' Hunt had a memorable start to his Wolves career. Signed from Swindon Town by manager Andy Beattie on the morning of 17 September 1965, he had every expectation of making his debut at Southampton the following day.

But four hours after the signing was completed, Beattie resigned. Hunt, not surprisingly, decided that he wasn't quite ready, and the following day sat in the stand at The Dell

Ernie Hunt

and watched his new club go down 9-3. Things got better for both player and club, however, and Hunt soon settled down in the Wolves midfield and in 1966-67 helped them win promotion back to the First Division.

He had an excellent striking record for a midfielder with 35 goals in only 82 appearances for Wolves before he was transferred to Everton for £80,000 in September 1967. Six months later Coventry bought him for £70,000 and at Highfield Road he teamed up with future Wolves men Willie Carr and Bobby Gould.

In fact, it was Hunt and Carr who between them perfected the infamous 'donkey-kick' that resulted in a spectacular goal being scored (by Hunt) against the League champions Everton at Highfield Road in October 1970, shown later on BBC TV's 'Match of the Day'. The innovative manoeuvre was later outlawed!

After a loan spell with Doncaster Rovers, Hunt ended his career with Bristol City before he retired in May 1974

I - J

with an overall tally of 165 goals to his name in 467 League appearances. He became landlord of the Full Pitcher public house in Ledbury and later worked as a window cleaner. Hunt, who was born in Swindon on 17 March 1943, played for Wiltshire Boys but was working for British Rail when Bert Head signed him for Swindon as an Amateur in 1957.

He became a full-time professional in March 1960 and with Swindon he won three England under-23 caps and appeared in 214 League games for the Wiltshire club, scoring 82 goals. His real first name is Roger.

Wolves' record: 82 apps. 35 goals.

HUNTER, Thomas

Wolves signed strong-running utility forward Tommy Hunter from nearby Walsall Swifts in August 1886.

Born in Walsall in 1863, he had failed to establish himself with the Swifts, but made a fine start to his career with the Wanderers, scoring plenty of goals in the various friendly matches played by the club. He also claimed five goals in the FA Cup in his first season, including a fourtimer in a 14-0 win against Crosswell's Brewery on 13 November.

When League football arrived in September 1888, Hunter was included in Wolves' line-up for their opening game against Aston Villa at Dudley Road (it finished level at 1-1). And, in fact, he was also in the side that registered its first-ever League win, 4-1 over Burnley, when he scored a fine goal.

Subsequently released by Wolves in the summer of 1889 (after picking up a knee injury), he joined Kidderminster Olympic as player-manager and later served with Pelsall (albeit only briefly) before retiring in April 1895.

In 1901 Hunter was appointed Chairman of Kidderminster Harriers, a position he held for a number of years. During his time on the Board he was also licensee of both The Dolphin (first) and then the Cape of Good Hope. Afterwards Hunter - a businessman to the last - ran a successful tobacconist shop in Kidderminster. He sadly died at the age of 55 in 1918 when the great flu epidemic hit the town.

Wolves' record: 35 apps. 13 goals.

IVERSON, Robert Thomas James

Bob Iverson was a honest competitor, big and strong, with receding hairline (he was almost bald when he retired).

Able to play as a wing-half or inside-forward, he wasn't given much of a chance at Molineux to show off his skills, but after joining Aston Villa he became a firm favourite with the home fans and made over 330 appearances in the claret and blue strip, 181 coming during the war.

Born in Folkestone on 17 October 1910, his career went as follows: Folkestone Council School, Folkestone FC (August 1926), Tottenham Hotspur (August 1932), Northfleet (Spurs nursery side: 1932-33), Ramsgate, Ramsgate Press Wanderers (June 1933), Lincoln City (September 1933), Wolves (February 1935) and Aston

Villa (December 1936).

He retired in May 1948 to become reserve team coach at Villa Park. Iverson guested for Birmingham, Bournemouth, Leicester City, Northampton Town, Notts County and Nottingham Forest during the war. He helped Villa win the Second Division championship in 1938 and the Wartime League (North) Cup in 1944. He also found the net for Villa in just 9.3 seconds after the start of a League game against Charlton in December 1938.

A keen angler and self-taught pianist, Iverson revelled in jazz. He died in Birmingham on 20 April 1953.

Wolves' record: 37 apps. 7 goals.

IVILL, Edward

Ted Ivill spent only three months with Wolves (November 1932 to January 1933). Born (Ivil) in Little Hulton, Lancashire on 7 December 1898, he was an amateur with Bolton Wanderers and after a year with Atherton Athletic he signed professional forms for Oldham Athletic (July 1924). He had given the Latics great service, appearing in 277 games and it was thought that he was the right man to take over the left-back berth owing to an injury to Jack Smith.

Alas Ivill never settled in the Midlands and after twelve weeks Wolves accepted an offer of £1,700 from Charlton Athletic and he left Molineux for the London club in January 1933 where he stayed until switching to Accrington Stanley in August 1935. Ivill took over as reserve team player-coach at Peel Park and in August 1937 he left for Clitheroe where he ended his footballing career during the war.

He made 331 League appearances all told (a fine record). Ivill died in the Blackburn Royal Infirmary on 24 November 1979.

Wolves' record: 4 apps.

NB - Ivill's father was a champion bowls player who won several cups in Lancashire handicaps.

JACKSON, Alan

Born in Swadlincote, Derbyshire (home town of British heavyweight boxing champion Jack Bodell) on 22 August 1938, centre-forward Alan Jackson joined Wolves as a junior in 1953 and turned professional at Molineux on his seventeenth birthday two years later. Initially acting as understudy to Roy Swinbourne and Dennis Wilshaw, he was given only a handful of first team outings by manager Stan Cullis, and owing to the form of Jimmy Murray and indeed, Barry Stobart and Bobby Mason, he subsequently left Molineux to sign for Bury in June 1959.

After scoring 43 goals in 150 League outings for the Shakers he moved to Brighton & Hove Albion in November 1962 and pulled out of League action in the summer of 1964.

Wolves' record: 6 apps. 2 goals.

JACKSON, John

Born in Aston, Birmingham in 1861, John Jackson was Wolves' assistant-trainer (under Albert Fletcher) for six seasons: 1887-93. As a player he served with Singers FC (Coventry) and managed Loughborough for two years after leaving Wolves. He then had a brief spell as trainer at West Bromwich Albion, did a similar job with Liverpool (1895-96) and likewise Leicester Fosse (to 1898).

In September 1898, Jackson was appointed manager of Brighton United, a position he retained until April 1900. He took charge of Brighton (by now renamed Hove Albion) for a second time in August 1901, holding office until March 1905) and then Blackpool (1907-08). Jackson was also a licensee of a Brighton pub from 1900 to 1915.

JACKSON, Joseph George

Born in Wolverhampton on 22 April 1966, utility forward Joe Jackson signed for Wolves as a trainee in June 1981 and became a full-time professional in August 1983.

Despite doing well at reserve and youth team levels, unfortunately he failed to make the grade in the senior side and was released into non-League soccer in the summer of 1984. He served in turn, with Bilston Town, Hednesford Town, Willenhall Town, Gresley Rovers, Worcester City, Yeovil Town, Dover Athletic and Worcester City (again) before taking over as player-manager of Stourbridge and then Bilston Town (from season 1997-98).

Wolves' record: one app.

JAMES, Ernest Josiah

Left-half Ernie James spent two seasons at Molineux where he was a diligent reserve. Born in Wolverhampton in 1885, he played for Wolverhampton Baptists, Stafford Road Juniors and Darlaston before joining Wolves in July 1904.

On leaving Molineux he went to Langley Green (August 1906) and later assisted Brandhall Villa. Wolves' record: 17 apps.

JEAVONS, William

Strongly built player, six feet tall and weighing 11st. 5lbs, Billy Jeavons had to bide his time in the reserves during his two years at Molineux.

Born in Wolverhampton in 1886, he moved from the Hurst Hill club to Wolves in August 1907 and left Molineux for Dudley Town in October 1909, later assisting Halesowen.

Wolves' record: 8 apps.

JEFFERSON, Derek

Centre or left-half Derek Jefferson was born in the North-east of England in the mining village of Morpeth on 5 September 1948. He came south to East Anglia as a youngster and on leaving school joined the groundstaff at Portman Road, turning professional with Ipswich Town in

January 1966. He went on to appear in 166 League and Cup games for the Suffolk club, helping them win promotion to the First Division in 1968.

He left Ipswich for Wolves in October 1972 and did well during his four years at Molineux during which time he had over fifty senior outings.

But soon after the team had suffered relegation (at the end of the 1975-76 campaign) he moved on, joining Hereford United in October 1976 after a month on loan to Sheffield Wednesday and a spell in the NASL.

He later became at coach with Birmingham City. Hard man Jefferson quit competitive football in 1978 with over 250 League appearances under his belt.

Wolves' record: 51+1 sub apps.

JOBEY, George

George Jobey's two-year reign as manager at Molineux was spent in two different Divisions!

At the end of his first campaign in charge - that of 1922-23 - Wolves slipped into the Third Division (North) for the first time in the club's history. However, the following year - with the former Sunderland and England international George Holley as his assistant - promotion was gained at the first attempt...Yet he still left Molineux for pastures new in May 1924!

Born in Heddon, near Newcastle in July 1885, Jobey played for Morpeth Harriers, Newcastle United (1906), Woolwich Arsenal (1913), Bradford Park Avenue (1914-15), Hamilton Academical (1915-19), Leicester City (1919) and Northampton Town (as player-coach from 1920) prior to joining Wolves in September 1922.

He appeared in the 1911 FA Cup Final for Newcastle and scored the first-ever goal at Highbury - for Arsenal against Leicester Fosse in 1913. After leaving Molineux Jobey had a year out of the game before returning as manager of Derby County in 1925.

He spent 16 years at The Baseball Ground. In 1941 a joint FA/Football League Commission, meeting at The Midland Hotel, Derby, found that between 1925 and 1938 Derby County Football Club had paid out illegal bonuses and inducements, balancing their books with some inventive entries.

Jobey was banned from participating in football permanently and County's Directors received sine die suspensions while the club itself was fined £500. Jobey's ban was lifted in 1945, yet it was not until 1952 that he re-entered football, taking over as manager of Mansfield Town, a position he held only briefly.

He died at Chaddesden, Derby in March 1962, aged 76. Jobey's record as Wolves manager was played 91, won 36, drawn 26, lost 29.

JOHNSON, Martin

Martin Johnson was an enterprising footballer, but had far too many quality forwards to contest a place with during his short stay with Wolves.

Born in Windy Nook, County Durham on 9 October 1904, Johnson played for Felling Colliery FC, Durham City (1925), Bradford Park Avenue (1925-27), Sheffield United (from June 1927) and Durham City again (July 1928) before moving to Molineux in October 1928. He left Wolves for North Shields in October 1930. Wolves' record: 8 apps. 2 goals.

JOHNSON, Thomson

Full-back Tom Johnson was a relatively unknown player from the late 1880s. Born locally circa 1867, he joined Wolves in July 1888 from a Wolverhampton junior club, and stayed two years with the club before moving into non-League football.
Wolves' record: one app.

JOHNSTON, James

Outside-left Jim Johnston, despite spending three years at Molineux, made less than 20 senior appearances, fifteen coming in season 1892-93 when he toyed with Griffin for the left-wing position, the latter eventually playing in the FA Cup Final.
Born in Edinburgh circa 1869, Johnston played for St. Bernard's before joining Wolves in the summer of 1890. He left Molineux in May 1893 and went home to Scotland to play for East Stirlingshire.
Wolves' record: 19 apps. 6 goals.

JONES, Brynmor

Inside-forward Bryn Jones was the costliest footballer in Britain when Wolverhampton Wanderers sold him to Arsenal for £14,000 in August 1938. Yet he came into League football by a most convoluted route.
He was born at Penyard, Merthyr Tydfil, on 14 February 1912 and after leaving Queen's Road School, Merthyr, he worked down the pit whilst playing for Merthyr Amateurs and Plymouth United in the South Wales District League. In 1931, Southend United offered him a trial but then rejected him! Obviously disappointed Jones went off to play for Glenavon in the Irish League, before returning to Wales with Aberaman in August 1933.
Less than eight weeks later he was a Wolves player, signed for a fee of £1,500, and soon made his League debut. In five years at Molineux, Jones made 177 senior appearances and scored 57 goals.
He was a superb ball player who could cause havoc amongst opposing defenders. He played with panache and style, was a maker rather than taker of goals and had all-round ability that made him as valuable as two men to any team.
After his record transfer to Arsenal Jones took a while to settle down at Highbury but with war on the horizon, as a consequence the Football League programme was abandoned ...just after he had started to show his true form whilst on the Gunners' 1939 summer tour to Scandinavia.

Bryn Jones

During the war, Jones served in the Royal Artillery in Italy and North Africa and guested for Cardiff City. He found time to play some games for Arsenal and also added eight wartime caps to the 17 he had gained for Wales in peacetime, ten of those coming as a Wolves player. He played his last League game for Arsenal in April 1949 and altogether made 74 League and FA Cup appearances for the Gunners, scoring seven goals.
He became player-coach at Norwich City but retired on medical advice in 1950 and subsequently ran a newsagent's and tobacconist's shop in Stoke Newington, not far from Highbury. He died on 18 October 1985 at Wood Green, North London.
Wolves' record: 177 apps. 57 goals.

JONES, David Ronald

David Jones was appointed Wolves manager in January 2001 in succession to Colin Lee.
Born in Liverpool on 17 August 1956, he won England Youth and Under-21 honours whilst at Everton whom he served as a central defender from May 1974 to May 1979, making 86 League appearances.

Dave Jones

From Goodison Park he was transferred to Coventry City for £275,000 and after a spell in Japan with FC Seiko he ran down his League career with Preston North End, playing in 50 League matches between August 1983 and May 1985. Jones then stepped onto the lower rungs of football management, taking charge of non-League Southport, Mossley and Morecambe between 1986 and 1990.

He then joined Stockport County as chief scout and finally got his chance at senior League management five years later, taking over at Edgeley Park after Danny Begara's departure.

He was recruited into the hot-seat at Southampton in the summer of 1997 and guided Saints to 12th place in the Premiership in his first season at The Dell.

An unfortunate court case then lingered on and on and as a result Jones was immediately replaced as Southampton manager by Glenn Hoddle.

Jones himself was subsequently cleared of all charges made against him and returned to football eager for success, aiming to raise the proverbial phoenix from the flames and bring success to the long-suffering but ardent Molineux supporters.

JONES, Eric Norman

A Brummie, born near Villa Park on 5 February 1915, outside-right Eric Jones played his early football with Kidderminster Harriers before joining Wolves in 1936. He remained at Molineux for less than a season, quickly switching to Portsmouth and then Stoke City before teaming up with West Bromwich Albion, with whom he remained until the mid-1940s. Jones actually scored a hat-trick for the Baggies in a 4-3 home defeat by Tottenham Hotspur on the eve of the Second World War in September 1939.

Soon afterwards the League programme was abandoned and subsequently declared null and void! During the hostilities he guested for his former club, Portsmouth as well as Chelsea, Watford, Southend United, Tottenham Hotspur, Arsenal, Queens Park Rangers, Nottingham Forest, Crystal Palace, Northampton Town, Fulham and Exeter City.

He then signed for Brentford (1945) and in July 1946 was recruited by Crewe Alexandra, retiring out of competitive football in June 1948. He became team manager of De Graafschap (Holland) and also acted as an FA staff Coach, based at Lilleshall before becoming trainer-coach of Port Vale (June 1962).

Jones introduced an intensive training schedule at Vale Park and kept a strict disciplinary record. Unfortunately his methods weren't to the liking of the Port Vale board and in October 1962 he resigned from his position for domestic reasons.

In his first match for the Vale (a Football League fixture away to Wrexham on 18 August 1962) Jones was hit in the face by a bottle thrown from the crowd and was treated by first-aid officials. After leaving the Potteries he went literally around the world, coaching in several countries, including the Belgian Congo, Belgium, Denmark, Egypt, Finland, Nigeria, Switzerland, Turkey and the West Indies
Wolves' record: 3 apps.

JONES, Gwynfor

Gwyn Jones was another player who found it difficult to hold down a first team place at Molineux owing to the depth of full-back talent at the club during the time he was there. Nevertheless he stuck to his guns and always gave a good account of himself.

Born in Llandwrog, mid-Wales on 20 March 1935, Jones joined Wolves from Caernarvon Town in September 1955 and left for Bristol Rovers in August 1962. He played for the Eastville club until May 1962, making 160 senior appearances.
Wolves' record: 22 apps.

JONES, Harold

Outside-left Harry Jones made all his first team appearances for Wolves in season 1910-11 when he deputised for Alf Walker.

Born in Codsall in 1889, he joined the staff at Molineux in May 1909 and left the club in the summer of 1912 for Darlaston, later playing for Walsall Comrades.
Wolves' record: 4 apps.

JONES, Jackery

Jack Jones was born at Wellington, Salop on 16 March

Jack Jones

1877, the same year that Wolverhampton Wanderers were founded, and he joined the club in 1900 from local side Lanesfield FC after first playing for Wrockwardine Wood. Jones was a fine right-back and made most of his senior appearances for the club in that position, being an ever-present for three consecutive seasons from 1901 to 1904 and again in 1905-06 and 1906-07. He gained an FA Cup winners' medal in 1908 and teamed up first with Dick Betteley and later Ted Collins in the Wolves rearguard. Jones, who played once for the Football League (against the Irish League in 1904-05), was a Wolves regular for ten years and became trainer at Molineux after he retired from playing just after the outbreak of World War One.

He was a well-known figure around the ground, always smoking his pipe and with his Cup winners' medal proudly hung from his watch chain. He was a marvellous servant to Wolverhampton Wanderers Football Club and when he died in the town in 1945, a part of the club's history went with him.

Wolves' record: 336 apps. 16 goals.

JONES, James Horace

No relation to Jackery or any of the other Joneses associated with Wolves, full-back Jimmy Jones was born at Cheslyn Hay circa 1892 and joined the Molineux staff in July 1911 from Walsall Wood junior football.

He played regularly in the first team for a season, but was then, perhaps surprisingly, transferred to Shirebrook FC in September 1912 after falling out with the management at Molineux.

Wolves' record: 36 apps. one goal.

JONES, John Joseph Alfred

Born in Wolverhampton circa 1889, amateur full-back Jack Jones joined Wolves in August 1918 from Bristol City, having earlier been rejected at Molineux (during 1913). A confident full-back, he remained with Wolves until June 1921, acting mainly as cover for George Garratly.

He never wanted to turn 'pro' and on leaving Wolves in May 1921 he became a fully qualified teacher, occasionally assisting Bilston Town before retiring in 1927. Jones, who attended Bristol University, died in Wolverhampton on 3 March 1940.

Wolves' record: 42 apps.

JONES, Joseph William

Joe Jones (brother to Jackery q.v) was a Wolves player for five years: from July 1898 to May 1903. A reserve inside or outside-left, he was a very useful performer who had first Tom Worton and Billy Wooldridge and then Jack Miller ahead of him in seniority at Molineux, hence his low number of first team outings.

He did, however, make over 50 Birmingham League appearances for the club, the second highest behind Tommy Green. Born in Wellington in 1880, he too played

for Lanesfield.

Wolves' record: 15 apps. one goal.

JONES, Mark Andrew

Born in Willenhalll on 7 September 1979, and a pupil at Idsall School, Shifnal, striker Mark Jones made his first team debut for Wolves in the Worthington Cup first round, first leg clash against Barnet in August 1998.

Capped by England at Under-17 level, he was a schoolboy footballer with Aston Villa, playing for their Under-14, 15 and 16 sides, having graduated through the Lilleshall School of Excellence. And Villa claimed that Wolves 'poached' from them and as a result the FA ordered that Wolves paid out £75,000 in compensation.

Jones went into hospital in December 1998 to have a piece of floating bone removed from his left ankle but he recovered quickly only to turn down a loan move to Swindon and then rejected an extended contract offer with Wolves! In October 1999 Jones was loaned out for a month to Cheltenham Town before joining Chesterfield in August 2000.

He helped the Spire-ites gain promotion from the Third Division in his first season at Saltergate and also assisted the Scottish club Raith Rovers for two months: February and March 2001.

Wolves' record: 0+5 sub apps.

JONES, Paul Anthony

Paul Jones was a tall, strong midfielder player who made over 180 appearances for Walsall before joining Wolves for £15,000 in November 1989.

Paul Jones

Born in Walsall on 9 September 1965, Jones turned professional with the Saddlers in September 1983 after two years as an apprentice. He also had a loan spell with Wrexham in March/April 1989 prior to his move to Wolves.

He was released in May 1989 and entered non-League football with Kettering Town, later assisting Stafford Rangers (from March 1992).

Wolves' record: 7+8 sub apps. no goals.

JONES, Paul Steven

A very capable and adept goalkeeper, signed as cover for Mike Stowell in July 1991 from Kidderminster Harriers for £40,000, Paul Jones was born in Chirk in mid-Wales on 18 April 1967. He played for Oswestry Boys and Shrewsbury Town as a youngster and then Bridgnorth Town prior to joining the Harriers.

He made his senior debut for Wolves during the course of the 1992-93 season, but with Stowell in pretty good form

K

Paul Jones

he was transferred to Stockport County in July 1996 for £60,000, helping the Edgeley Park club win promotion from the Second Division in his first season. In the summer of 1997 Jones, after 65 games for Stockport, entered the Premiership when his former manager at Edgeley Park, Dave Jones made him his first signing for Southampton at £900,000.

Jones has now gained well over 20 full international caps for Wales and reached the milestone of 150 appearances for Saints during the year 2001.

Wolves' record: 44 apps.

JORDAN, David

Irishman David Jordan made his debut for Wolves against arch rivals West Bromwich Albion at The Hawthorns in October 1936 when he replaced Tom 'Pongo' Waring at centre-forward. He failed to make an impression during his brief stay at Molineux and left the club in May 1937 to join Crystal Palace.

Born in Belfast circa 1912, and now deceased, he played for Ards initially, and joined Wolves from Hull City in June 1936. He returned to Ireland from Palace in October 1939, and did not play competitive football after the hostilities of World War Two.

Wolves' record: 3 apps.

JORDAN, The Reverend William Charles

Centre-forward Billy Jordan, full of dash and vigour, was one of the many outstanding amateur footballers of his era.

A six-footer, born in Langley on 9 December 1885, he won two England Amateur international caps, scoring six goals against France on his debut in 1907. He played for a number of teams including Oxford University, where he was a student, Liverpool reserves, West Bromwich Albion, for whom he starred in their 1907 FA Cup run to the semi-finals, Everton and Wolves, who acquired his services during the 1912-13 season.

In 1911 he had been appointed curate at St Clement's Church in Nechells Green, Birmingham and thereafter devoted most of his time to the cloth, conducting several Sportsman's Services all over the country. He later worked in churches in Widnes, on the Isle of Wight, at Saltburn (West Riding), Darlington and Belbroughton.

In 1936 he became a Director of Darlington Football Club. Jordan graduated in Natural Science at St. John's College, Oxford and was ordained in 1907.

Wolves' record: 3 apps. 2 goals.

JUGGINS, Eleander

Wolves had Eli Juggins on their senior staff for three seasons. A stern, hard tackling moustachio'd full-back, he was reserve to Jack Jones and therefore had limited first team football.

Born in Bilston in 1879, he joined Wolves from Darlaston in July 1904, having earlier starred for Willenhall Swifts. He left Molineux for Coventry City in June 1907 and continued to play on until 1914, making over 70 appearances for the Highfield Road club.

Wolves' record: 22 apps.

KAY, Albert Edward

Albert Kay was a versatile defender who was born in Sheffield on 22 November 1895. He began his footballing career with Tinsley FC and was with Birmingham from June 1919 to November 1920.

He joined Wolves from Willenhall in the close season of 1921 to begin a Molineux career that lasted a decade and saw him make almost 300 senior appearances for the club. Kay was a member of the team that won the Third Division (North) title in 1923-24 and also helped Wolves lift the Second Division championship in 1931-32.

Kay was normally used as a defensive wing-half, but he also appeared at full-back and once in one Central League game he even kept goal in an emergency, saving a penalty in the process. Injury forced his retirement in May 1932, just after he had played his part in helping Wolves regain their First Division status. He later lived in the Tettenhall and Codsall districts of Wolverhampton.

Wolves' record: 295 apps. 2 goals.

KEANE, Robert David

Robbie Keane made a terrific start to his Football League career - scoring twice on his Wolves debut as a 17 year-old at Norwich on 9 August 1997. A two-footed, determined, stylish and aggressive midfielder footballer - like his namesake Roy at Manchester United - Keane was born in Dublin on 8 July 1980.

He played junior football in the Republic of Ireland as a right-back with Crumlin United and Fettercairn FC (on trial) before signing YTS forms with Wolves in June 1996. He turned professional twelve months later on his 17th birthday, agreeing a three-year contract that was later made into a five-year deal.

After being capped by his country at Schoolboy, Under-

Robbie Keane

18, Youth, Under-21 and 'B' team levels, he then gained his first full cap and has since been a regular in the national team, setting a record by becoming Eire's youngest-ever goalscorer at the age of 18. In August 1999 Keane left Molineux to join Coventry City for £6 million - a club record transfer fee.

He was on the move again in August 2000, switching to the Italian giants Inter Milan for £13 million. He failed to settle in Serie 'A' and after a six-month loan spell with Leeds United from December 2000, he signed permanently for the Elland Road club in a £12 million deal in May 2001....having helped the Yorkshire club reach the semi-finals of the European Champions Cup.
Wolves' record: 74+9 sub apps. 27 goals.

KEARNS, Michael

Born in Banbury on 25 November 1950 goalkeeper Mick Kearns, six feet tall and 14 stones in weight, was a commanding figure between the posts. He joined Oxford United as a youngster and turned professional at The Manor Ground in July 1968.

He made 67 League appearances for the 'U's before transferring to Walsall in July 1973 after loan spells with both Plymouth Argyle and Charlton Athletic during the 1972-73 season. He performed supremely well for the

Mick Kearns

Saddlers and made almost 300 appearances for the Fellows Park club (having one spell when he missed only five matches out of a possible 293) before signing for Wolves in July 1979 as cover for Paul Bradshaw.

He made his First Division debut in the local derby against neighbours West Bromwich Albion, saving a penalty in the 0-0 draw at The Hawthorns in April 1980.

Two-and-a-half years later (in August 1982) Kearns returned to Fellows Park for a second spell and later on he came back for the third time as a non-contract player while working as a steward at a Working Mens' Club in nearby Aldridge.

In 1990 Kearns was appointed Walsall's Community Officer and he did a terrific job within the schools and youth clubs around the area. He kept himself supremely fit by playing in various charity matches and was in goal when the West Bromwich Albion All Stars won the over 35's Cup Final at Wembley in August 1992.

During his Football League career Kearns, who won 18 caps for the Republic of Ireland (a record 15 with Walsall) and whose brother, Ollie, was also a professional footballer, playing with him at Walsall, amassed a total of 356 League appearances.

He was also a very fine handicap golfer who won the Midland Professional Footballers' Golf Championship in

1977, while in May 1992 he established an international record for a soccer player by holing-in-one at a course in Scotland, having previously done likewise in both England and Ireland.
Wolves' record: 10 apps.

KEEN, Kevin Ian

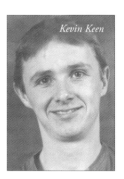
Kevin Keen

Hardworking right-sided midfield player with good pace and excellent vision, Kevin Keen was born in Amersham on 25 February 1967. He played for West Ham United from 1982 (first as an apprentice and then as a professional, March 1984) until moving to Molineux in July 1993 for £600,000 after more than 275 appearances for the Hammers (30 goals scored).

A former England schoolboy and youth international, he was sold to Stoke City for £300,000 in October 1994 at a time when the Potters' engine-room needed stoking up! He did a useful job before losing his place in the side in 1996. He was eventually released by Stoke at the end of the 1999-2000 season, having made over 200 League and Cup appearances for the Potteries club. He signed for Macclesfield Town prior to the start of the 2000-01 campaign and has now amassed an impressive career record of almost 600 appearances at senior level (with over 50 goals scored).

NB - Keen's father, Mike, led Queens Park Rangers to victory in the League Cup Final at Wembley and to the Third Division title in the 1966-67 season.
Wolves' record: 48+6 sub apps. 9 goals.

KEELEY, Arthur

Outside-right Arthur Keeley had one season at Molineux. Born in Cheshire in 1915, he joined Wolves from Ellesmere Port in the summer of 1935 and although he spent three years at Molineux he never really established himself and in May 1937 was transferred to Bournemouth.

From Dean Court he moved to Chester (1938) and was on Portsmouth's books when he was sadly killed in action during World War Two.
Wolves' record: 2 apps.

KEETLEY, Joseph Frederick S

Joe Keetley was one of eleven brothers, the others being Bill, Albert, John, Arthur, Frank, Tom, Harold and Charlie, Lawrence and Sidney. All of them except Lawrence and Sidney played League football at various levels.

Joe himself was a fine goalscoring inside-forward who was

with Wolves at the same time as some other exceptionally quality marksmen and this limited his senior outings. Wanting regular first team football, he left the club after just six months.

Born in Derby on 28 June 1897, Keetley played for Victoria Ironworks, Bolton Wanderers (August 1920), Accrington Stanley (June 1923) and Liverpool (November 1923) before joining Wolves in May 1925. He left Molineux for Wrexham in November 1925 and later assisted Doncaster Rovers (March 1926) and Horwich R.M.I. (1928) before retiring in 1933. He died at Allerton, Derbyshire on 30 March 1958.

Wolves' record: 10 apps. 5 goals

NB. Three of the Keetley brothers were in Doncaster's team in February 1926 - Joe joined them the following month but all four never played together.

KELLOCK, William

Billy Kellock was a powerful midfielder, born in Glasgow on 7 February 1954, who won schoolboy caps for Scottish and represented Glasgow Boys before joining Aston Villa as an apprentice in 1970.

From Villa Park he became something of a soccer nomad, serving with Cardiff City (February 1972), Norwich City (June 1973), Millwall (£25,000, July 1974), Chelmsford City (1975), Kettering Town (1977), Peterborough United (£30,000, August 1979) and Luton Town (£30,000, July 1982) before arriving at Molineux in March 1983 for £20,000.

He spent just six months with Wolves, transferring to Southend United in September 1983 and later assisting Port Vale (December 1984), Halifax Town (July 1985) and Kettering Town (again).

In his senior career, Kellock scored well over 80 goals in more than 350 senior appearances (78 in 298 outings in the Football League).

Billy Kellock

Wolves' record: 12 apps. 3 goals.

KELLY, David Thomas

When Republic of Ireland striker David Kelly joined Wolves from Newcastle United in July 1993, for £750,000 he had just helped the Magpies gain promotion to the Premiership.

Yet Kelly was really coming home to the West Midlands, for he was born in Birmingham on 25 November 1965 and played for Alvechurch and Walsall before becoming the Saddlers' record outgoing transfer when he moved to West Ham United for £600,000 in August 1988. It was his goalscoring prowess that had persuaded the Hammers to pay out that kind of money: top-scorer for Walsall in 1986-87 (26 goals) and 1987-88 (30 goals, including a superb hat-trick in the Play-off Final against Bristol City which clinched promotion from the Third Division).

David Kelly

Kelly netted 80 goals in 190 League and Cup games for Walsall and for West Ham he scored 14 in 64 outings before being transferred to Leicester City in March 1990 for £300,000. For Leicester he netted 25 goals in 75 appearances before Newcastle bought him for £250,000 in December 1991.

After helping the Magpies stave off relegation that season, his League tally of 35 goals in 70 League games proved crucial when promotion was gained from Division One in 1992-93 - and in all matches for Newcastle, Kelly claimed 39 goals in 83 appearances.

At Wolves he did well alongside Steve Bull, notching 14 goals in 1993-94 to be second-highest scorer and then he top-scored in 1994-95 with a total of 22 including a second-half hat-trick in a 5-1 win at Bristol City in November. However, after two years at Molineux, Kelly was transferred to Sunderland for a record fee of £995,000.

Unfortunately he suffered injury problems at Roker Park and at the end of the 1996-97 season left to join Tranmere Rovers for £350,000. He switched to Sheffield United on a free transfer in July 2000 and then ventured north to Scotland to sign for Motherwell, also on a free, in July 2001.

Kelly, who scored for Tranmere in the Worthington Cup Final defeat by Leicester City at Wembley in 2000, has now accumulated an excellent career record at club level - well over 720 League and Cup appearances and more than 240 goals.

He has also won 26 full caps for the Republic of Ireland, played in three 'B' internationals, in one Under-21 game and in three Under-23 matches.

NB - In November 1987 Kelly declined an invitation to play for the England Under-21 side; a week later he made his debut for the Republic of Ireland!

Wolves' record: 96+7 sub apps. 36 goals.

KELLY, James

Born in Aldergrove, Northern Ireland on 6 February 1954, winger Jimmy Kelly played for Cliftonville before joining Wolves in December 1971.

He spent seven years at Molineux, but never really established himself in the first team and actually had a loan spell with Wrexham in 1975 before moving to Walsall in August 1978 after a spell in the NASL (with team-mates Phil Parkes and Derek Jefferson).

He later returned to Ireland.

One interesting point is that Kelly made his debut for Wolves against Sheffield United in February 1974 and did not play another game until March 1976, ironically against the Blades!

Wolves' record: 21+ 2 sub apps. no goals.

KELLY, James

A Liverpudlian, born on 14 February 1973, midfielder Jimmy Kelly - no relation to the Kelly above - was signed by Wolves from Wrexham in part-exchange deal involving John Paskin in February 1992.

Joining the Welsh club as an apprentice, he turned professional on his 18th birthday and played 22 League games during his time at the Racecourse Ground before switching his allegiance to Molineux. In February 1996 Kelly, who was on loan to Walsall in March/April 1993, was sentenced to five years in jail (spending some time in Sudbury Open Prison, Derbyshire) for his part in the manslaughter, in September 1994, of doorman Peter Dunphy outside the Bradford Hotel in Liverpool.

In October 1997, Kelly was allowed out of prison on licence and he went straight back into football - joining the groundstaff of Vauxhall Conference side Hednesford Town, although he was not allowed to play for the non-League club whilst a serving prisoner. Kelly was released in October 1998 and he quickly established himself in the Pitmens' first XI.

He had trials with both Wrexham and Huddersfield Town in July and August 1998.

Wolves' record: 5+3 sub Apps. no goals.

KELLY, James Philip Vincent

During his career Phil Kelly won five caps for the Republic of Ireland and as well as amassing almost 150 senior appearances for Wolves and Norwich City - his two major clubs. A neat footballer with good passing ability, he was a steady rather than a quality full-back.

Born in Dublin on 10 July 1939, he played for Sheldon Town (Birmingham) and Brockhill FC before joining Wolves as a professional in September 1957, signed by manager Stan Cullis as cover for Eddie Stuart, Gerry Harris and George Showell. He spent five years at Molineux before transferring to Carrow Road in August 1962.

After 115 League games for the Canaries he went to Lowestoft Town in May 1967 before becoming player-coach of the non-League club twelve months later. Kelly now lives in East Anglia.

Wolves' record: 18 apps.

KELLY, Lawrence

Local lad Larry Kelly gave Wolves good service at left-back after making his League debut in December 1947, but he made a much greater impact after moving to Huddersfield Town. Kelly, who was born in Wolverhampton on 28 April 1925, joined Wolves as an amateur in 1940 and became a full-time professional in April 1945 - having skippered the side in season 1942-43 as a 17 year-old - possibly Wolves' youngest-ever skipper, and guested for Halifax Town.

In his first season in the League side he helped Wolves reach fifth in the First Division, but the following season was injured in the first match of the FA Cup semi-final against Manchester United at Hillsborough and missed the Cup Final when Wolves beat Leicester City 3-1.

In October 1950, Huddersfield Town, looking to rebuild their side, paid £10,500 for his services and he went on to make 239 League and Cup appearances for the Terriers. Of course, there was not the wealth of competition that had held him back at Molineux and Kelly was first-choice at Leeds Road for six seasons, being a key figure in their 1952-53 Second Division championship winning side.

At the end of 1955-56 Huddersfield were back in Division Two and Kelly, now 30, was thinking about his future. He became player-manager of Nuneaton in May 1957, although he spent only a few months in the job. Wolves awarded him a £750 benefit cheque when he left Molineux.

Wolves' record: 70 apps.

KELLY, Robert Anthony

Born in Birmingham on 21 December 1964, midfielder Robert Kelly joined Leicester City as a junior at the age of 16 and became a full-time professional at Filbert Street in December 1982.

A competitive performer, who loved to drive forward, he was registered with the Foxes for five years but made only 24 League appearances before transferring to Wolves in March 1987, having earlier had a loan spell with Tranmere  Rovers (December 1984). He struggled with his form and fitness at Molineux and in August 1990 moved to Burton Albion.

He was forced to give the game up two years later when he returned to Molineux to join the club's backroom staff. He then moved to Watford with his coaching partner at Wolves Bobby Downes, and when Downes switched north to Blackburn Rovers in

Robert Kelly

May 1997 he was quickly joined by Kelly, both men working under Rovers' new boss, Roy Hodgson.

Wolves' record: 16+4 sub apps. 3 goals.

KEMP, Frederick George

Fred Kemp was an eager-beaver, all-action midfielder, who failed to make the grade in the top flight, but afterwards certainly did the business in the lower Divisions.

Born in Salerno, Italy on 27 February 1946 (his parents stayed over there following the Second World War), Kemp joined Wolves as a teenager in the summer of 1961 on leaving his school in Exeter. He turned professional at Molineux in June 1963 and two years later was transferred to Southampton.

In November 1970 he went north to Blackpool for £35,000 and in December 1971 switched his allegiance to Halifax Town, staying at The Shay until signing for his last League club, Hereford United, in July 1974. He dropped out of the big time in August 1976 and went to South Africa before returning to England to join non-League Telford United with whom he stayed until May 1978. After that Kemp often played in local charity matches.

He accumulated more than 220 senior appearances of which 111 came in the League with Halifax Town.

Wolves' record: 3 apps.

KENDALL, Mark

Goalkeeper Mark Kendall joined Wolves from Newport County in December 1986 and at the end of the season was playing in the Fourth Division Play-off Final against Aldershot, which the Shots won on aggregate.

The following season, of course, Wolves went up as champions and were champions again 12 months later to complete a meteoric rise from the old Fourth to the Second Division. Kendall shared in all these glories. He appeared in 177 senior matches for Wolves, set a club record of 28 clean sheets in 1987-88, kept another 15 blanks in 1988-89,

Mark Kendall

gained those two championship medals, and a Sherpa Van Trophy winners' medal in 1988.

Kendall, who was born in Blackwood, Wales, on 20 September 1958, won Welsh schoolboy caps and then signed as an apprentice for Spurs in 1974, turning professional at White Hart Lane in July 1976. He made 36 senior appearances for Spurs, also winning a Welsh Under-21 cap, before Newport signed him for £25,000 in September 1980 (after a loan spell at Chesterfield). At Somerton Park he made 319 League and Cup appearances before Graham Turner signed him for Wolves.

Kendall left Wolves for Swansea City in May 1990 and in 1991-92 he had a loan spell with Barnsley and played for Newport AFC but quit football at the end of the following season to join the police force (now serving in Ebbw Vale). He made more than 600 first-team appearances during his footballing career.

NB - Kendall's son was once a promising goalkeeper on the books of Crystal Palace.

Wolves' record: 177 apps.

KENNEDY, Mark

Mark Kennedy, the Republic of Ireland international left-sided midfielder/winger, joined Wolves in the summer of 2001 from Manchester City.

A native of Dublin (born on 15 May 1976) he began his playing career in London with Millwall, joining the Lions initially in June 1992, turning professional a year later. In fact, he was a goalkeeper first up, then tried his luck as a forward before settling down into a midfield position.

In March 1995 he was transferred to Liverpool for £1.5 million but appeared in only 21 first-class games for the Merseysiders before switching to Wimbledon for £1.75 million in March 1998 (following a loan spell with Queen's Park Rangers). Surprisingly, he again failed to fit in with his new club, making just 28 senior appearances (11 as a substitute) up to July 1999 when he moved to Maine Road, this time for £1 million (rising £1.5 million after an agreed number of appearances).

City manager Joe Royle was impressed with Kennedy in his first season as he scored ten goals in 47 outings, producing some excellent wing play. But the second was not so good - indeed it was a troublesome one as Royle sacrificed his wing talents early on by using an ultra-defensive system, to the annoyance of the home supporters!

Kennedy came on strong at the end at took his appearance tally with City past the 70 mark before his £2 million move to Molineux.

Capped 31 times by Eire (three goals scored) Kennedy has also represented his country at Schoolboy, Youth and Under-21 levels and will be looking to add to his tally in the years ahead.

Wolves' record: 12 apps.*

KENNING, Michael John

Born in Erdington, Birmingham on 18 August 1940, Mike Kenning played on the wing for Brockhill FC before taking amateur status with Aston Villa in 1957. He signed part-time professional forms in 1958 and became full-time in October 1959. In May 1961, after failing to make an impact at Villa Park, he was transferred to Shrewsbury Town; Charlton Athletic secured his services for £10,500 in November 1982 and in December 1966 he went to Norwich City for £27,000.

Wolves attained Kenning's services for £35,000 in January 1968, but he spent just over a year at Molineux before switching back to Charlton for £20,000 in March 1969. After one game for Queens Park Rangers (May 1971) he assisted Watford from January 1972 to May 1973 before trying his luck in South Africa.

He returned to England to sign for Atherstone Town in 1974, but four years later he went back to South Africa to become player-manager of Germiston Callies, later taking charge of Durban United and then Wilts University. In 1986, after quitting football, Kenning was employed as a representative for a South African safety equipment company. He played in some 450 League and Cup games and scored almost 100 goals during his senior footballing career.

Wolves' record: 40+6 sub apps. 6 goals.

KENT, Michael John

Born in North Anston, near Dinnington on 12 January 1951, central defender Mick Kent played for Wolves' Yorkshire-based nursery side, Wath Wanderers, before signing professional forms at Molineux in August 1968.

He hardly figured in the club's first team plans and after a couple of substitute appearances was transferred to Sheffield Wednesday in September 1973, following a loan spell with Gillingham (March/April 1971). He was not retained at Hillsborough for the 1973-74 season and moved into non-League football.

Wolves' record: 0+2 sub apps.

KERNAN, Anthony Patrick

Tony Kernan was born in Letterkenny, Ireland on 31 August 1963 and played at youth team level for the Republic of Ireland during his early years at Molineux.

He signed for Wolves as a junior, turned professional at the age of 17 (January 1981) but was not retained for the 1982-83 season.

Wolves' record: one app.

KERR, Robert C

Centre-forward Bobby Kerr had a fine scoring record with Wolves, averaging almost a goal every two games. Born in Leicester in 1904, he was recruited from Oadby Town in the summer of 1925 and stayed at Molineux for two years before transferring to Clapton Orient in July 1927.

He later played for Kettering and Grantham.

Wolves' record: 18 apps. 7 goals.

KETSBAIA, Temuri

Born in Gale, Georgia on 18 March 1968, the unpredictable but exciting Temuri Ketsbaia played for Dynamo Sukhumi (1986), Dynamo Tbilisi (August 1987-May 1992), Anorthosis Famagusta (to May 1994), and AEK Athens (for three years) before moving into the English Premiership with Newcastle United in July 1997. He netted 14 goals in 109 first-class games for the St James' Park club during his three seasons in the North-east. He was signed by Wolves for £900,000 in August 2000 and scored four times in his 26 outings for the Wanderers in his first season.

Capped 48 times by Georgia (15 goals) Ketsbaia was a member of two Greek Cup-winning teams (1997 & 1998) whilst a player with AEK Athens.

He was put on the transfer list by manager David Jones in May 2001 and five months later had his contract cancelled by the club.

Wolves' record: 17+9 apps. 4 goals.

KINDON, Stephen Michael

Bustling forward Steve Kindon always let opposing defenders know he was there with his all-action displays of brave attacking football, but he was also a skilful performer and when used as an orthodox outside-left, he left many a full-back in his wake.

Born in Warrington on 17 December 1950 he joined Burnley as an apprentice after leaving school in July 1965. He became a full-time professional on his 17th birthday and made his League debut for Burnley during 1968-69. The following season he was part of a Burnley team whose average age was only 22, the youngest ever to represent the club, and whilst at Turf Moor, Kindon was also capped for England Youth. After more than 120 senior games for Burnley, he was transferred to Wolves for £100,000 in July 1972 and scored on his debut against Newcastle United in the opening game of the 1972-73 season.

But it was not until 1974-75 that Kindon could be sure of his place. Thereafter he was in and out of the side again, and in November 1977 returned to Burnley for £80,000. He spent two more seasons at Turf Moor and had three terms with Huddersfield Town before retiring as a player. Kindon's overall League record was a good one - 109 goals in 396 League games and in 1976 he won a 75 metres sprint race for professional footballers.

After hanging up his boots he stayed in football, having a successful five-year association as Promotions Manager with Huddersfield Town.

He then quit soccer to become an 'After Dinner Speaker', a job he is still enjoying today.

Wolves' record: 131+36 sub apps. 31 goals.

KING, Andrew Edward

Midfielder Andy King had an excellent career in football. Born in Luton on 14 August 1956, he represented Luton & Dunstable Schools, Bedfordshire Boys and Stopsley

Youths and had unsuccessful trials with Spurs before signing apprentice forms for the Hatters as a 16 year-old, turning professional at Kenilworth Road in July 1974.

He went on to appear in 33 League games for Luton before transferring to Everton for £35,000 in March 1976. During his four years at Goodison Park he amassed 151 First Division appearances and scored 38 goals, helping Everton get into the UEFA Cup for the 1978-79 season.

In September 1980, King moved to Queens Park Rangers for £425,000. Twelve months later he joined West Bromwich Albion for £400,000 and was a member of the Baggies' FA Cup semi-final side (v. QPR) in 1982 before returning to Goodison Park three months later in a player-exchange deal involving former Wolves striker Peter Eastoe, plus £250,000.

In August 1984 King went over to Holland to sign for SC Cambuur, returning to England to join Wolves in January 1985. He spent 11 months at Molineux (finishing up as top scorer in 1985-86 under Bill McGarry) having a loan spell with Orebo FC (Sweden) during April & May 1985. He rejoined his first 'love' Luton Town in December 1985 and later assisted Aldershot (Aug 1986), Aylesbury (1988), Waterford (as player-manager from Aug 1988), Cobh Ramblers (Jan 1989) and Southport (Aug 1989).

He then chose to return to Kenilworth Road as Commercial Manager and moved back into football management with Mansfield Town in November 1993, holding that position at Field Mill until September 1996 when he was replaced by another ex-West Brom player, Steve Parkin. He edged himself back into League management with Swindon Town in October 2000 - after Colin Todd had left the struggling Wiltshire club. Unfortunately after a poor start to the 2001-02 season, he was sacked by the Robins.

In his League career King-a joker to the extreme-amassed exactly 350 appearances and scored almost 100 goals. He was also capped twice by England at Under-21 level.

Wolves' record: 30 apps. 10 goals.

KING, Frederick A Robert

Winger Bob King was the first official transfer during the Second World War, joining Wolves from Northampton Town for £2,000 in November 1939.

He never played competitive League football for Wolves (owing to the war) but nevertheless he still had a useful career. Born in Northampton on 19 September 1919, he played for his home-town club, Northampton Town from 1937 and returned there after the war (1947-50) having guested for Leicester City and Manchester City. He scored over 20 goals in more than 100 first-class games for the Cobblers. King assisted Rushden from 1951-53.

KINSEY, George

Wing-half George Kinsey spent the best part of his playing career with Wolves, gaining an FA Cup winners' medal and playing twice for England.

Born at Burton-on-Trent on 20 June 1866, he played for Burton Crusaders, Burton Swifts and Mitchell St George's before joining Wolves in August 1891.

He was a dominating figure at left-half and had a magnificent game for Wolves in the 1893 FA Cup Final against Everton before being transferred to Aston Villa in June 1894. The move to Villa Park did not work out for Kinsey and less than a year later he was on the move again, this time to Derby County.

He was an ever-present in his first season with Derby, in what was their first campaign at the Baseball Ground, and at the end of 1895-96 the Rams were League championship runners-up and had reached another FA Cup semi-final, where Kinsey had a good game against his old club, Wolves.

He played twice more for England and after a short spell with Notts County, helped establish Bristol Rovers (who were then Eastville Rovers) in the Southern League after joining them when they were in the Birmingham & District League.

In 1900, Kinsey rejoined Burton Swifts and in 1902 was playing for Burton Early Closing FC, being reinstated as an amateur in 1904. He died on 10 January 1911.

Wolves' record: 83 apps. 3 goals.

KIRKHAM, John Kenneth

Johnny Kirkham was born at Wednesbury on 13 May 1941 and signed for Wolves as a 15-year-old (June 1956). He did so well that Wanderers took him on as a full-time professional two years later. He received his Football League debut in 1959, and made a good impression during the 1961-62 season when he appeared in 29 senior matches, most in the right-half position in place of the injured Eddie Clamp.

That term he scored in consecutive games, two goals against Forest at Molineux and then a goal at Old Trafford against Manchester United.

Eventually, Freddie Goodwin was installed in the team and in May 1965, after appearing in the last 12 League games of the relegation season, Kirkham signed for Peterborough United. After leaving Posh he went to Exeter City in July 1968 before dropping into non-League football with Horwich RMI in May 1969.

With Wolves, he won England Youth and Under-23 caps.

Wolves' record: 112 apps. 15 goals.

KIRKHAM, Reginald John

Reg Kirkham was a Wolves player during the last two League seasons leading up to the Second World War.

An outside-left with good pace, he was born in Ormskirk, Cheshire on 8 May 1919, and joined the Wanderers in early August 1937 from Ellesmere Port Town.

He left Molineux for Bournemouth in October 1938 and stayed at Dean Court throughout the war when he also guested for Clapton Orient and Notts County. In March 1947 he joined Burnley and retired in 1951.

Wolves' record: 15 apps. 5 goals.

KNIGHT, Thomas

One of the early stars of the Wolves side, Tommy Knight could play in any forward position, but preferred the inside-right berth.

Strong and powerful, he loved to dribble, head down with the ball and occasionally upset his colleagues by doing this far too much!

Born in Wolverhampton in the summer of 1864, Knight joined Wolves at the age of 22 in August 1886 from Pickwick.

He stayed with the Wanderers until May 1890, although his career came to an abrupt end in September 1889 when he was injured playing against Stoke while occupying the right back position (in an emergency).

He had the pleasure of scoring in Wolves' first home League win - a 4-1 victory over Burnley in September 1888.

Wolves' record: 33 apps. 17 goals.

KNIGHTON, Kenneth

Wing-half Ken Knighton was born in Mexborough on 20 February 1944. The tall, blond-haired Yorkshireman, who excelled in both attack and defence, joined Wolves as a junior in July 1960 and turned professional at Molineux in February 1961, having had a few games for the club's junior side, Wath Wanderers.

He failed to establish himself in the Wolves' first XI and was subsequently transferred to Oldham Athletic for £12,000 in November 1966. He later assisted Preston North End (signed for £35,000 in November 1967), Blackburn Rovers (secured for a fee of £45,000 in June 1969), Hull City (transferred for £60,000 in March 1971) and finally Sheffield Wednesday (bought for £50,000 from August 1973 to January 1976).

He then took over as coach at Sunderland before becoming manager at Roker Park in June 1979, a position he held until April 1981. Six months later Knighton was appointed boss of Leyton Orient and remained at Brisbane Road until May 1983. He later managed Dagenham (1984-85) before drifting out of football for awhile only to return to manage Trowbridge Town until January 1998. Knighton made almost 400 appearances at senior level and in the summer of 1969 went to New Zealand with the FA touring party.

Knighton, who some fans thought resembled Ron Flowers on the field, is now living near Bristol.

Wolves' record: 13+3 sub apps.

KNOWLES, Peter

A huge favourite with the girls, Peter Knowles was born at Fitzwilliam near Frickley, Yorkshire, on 30 September 1945 and came through the Wolves ranks via their nursery side Wath Wanderers before signing professional forms at Molineux, under manager Stan Cullis in October 1962.

After accompanying the club on their USA & Canadian tour in May and June 1963, he made his League debut against Leicester City twelve months after signing as a full-

Peter Knowles

time 'pro', and then became an established member of the first team in 1964-65. The previous Easter he had scored in England's 4-0 victory over Spain in the Final of an international Youth tournament in Amsterdam.

When Wolves won promotion back to the old First Division in 1966-67, Knowles contributed eight goals in 21 matches as they finished runners-up to Coventry City. Capped four times at Under-23 level, Knowles looked destined for even more success, but in 1970 he dropped a bombshell on Molineux by announcing that he was turning his back on professional football to become a Jehovah's Witness.

He was only 24 years of age at the time and his sudden

Peter Knowles

departure from the game was a shock to Wolves fans young and old - and indeed to the club itself. Wolves retained Knowles' registration for several years after his departure - in anticipation that he might change his mind and return to the club.

Unfortunately he never did. In 1991, a song entitled God's Footballer by Billy Bragg featured Knowles and ended with commentary describing one of his many goals he scored for Wolves.

NB - His brother Cyril was a full-back with Tottenham Hotspur and managed Hartlepools United before dying prematurely after suffering a brain tumor.

Wolves' record: 188+3 sub apps. 64 goals.

KUBICKI, Daruisz

Polish international full-back Dariusz Kubicki (47 caps won) was born in Warsaw on 6 June 1963. He made his senior debut for Wolves in a 2-0 Nationwide League win at Norwich City on the opening day of the 1997-98 season (9 August) following his free transfer from Sunderland four days earlier.

A fine player, who enjoyed getting forward, he played his early football with the Mielec and Zastra clubs. He moved entered English League soccer with Aston Villa in August 1991 when signed for £200,000 from Legia Warsaw. He played in 34 games for the West Midlands club before transferring to Sunderland for £100,000 in July 1994, after a three-month loan spell at Roker Park.

During his time at Roker Park, Kubicki made over 150 senior appearances and helped the Wearsiders reach the Premiership, but he was then surprisingly released after they suffered relegation in 1997.

Two months after returning to Molineux from a loan spell with Tranmere Rovers (March 1998) Kubicki signed for Carlisle United on a free transfer.

He switched across country to Darlington in October of that year and when the season ended he decided to quit English League football, electing to return home to Poland after eight years in England during which time he made well over 200 first-class appearances.

Wolves' record: 16 apps.

LAKING, George Edward

Full-back George Laking was born at Harthill, near Sheffield on 17 March 1913 and played initially for Kiveton Park and Dinnington FC before joining Wolves in May 1934. A solid player, strong and robust, his best season at Molineux was in 1935-36 when he made 20 appearances as partner to Cecil Shaw.

Unable to hold down a regular place in the team, he was transferred to Middlesbrough in October 1936. During the hostilities he guested for Doncaster Rovers, Leeds United, Sheffield United and Sheffield Wednesday and played just once more for 'Boro in 1946-47 before rounding off his career with Shrewsbury Town, although he made only the odd appearance for the 'Shrews' at non-League level. In fact, he played more cricket than football and was a key member of the Minor Counties side, Shropshire.

Laking, who had almost 100 outings for Middlesbrough, was a property repairer by trade. He died in Codsall on 5 June 1997, aged 84.

Wolves' record: 29 apps.

LANGE, Anthony Stephen

Goalkeeper Tony Lange was born in West Ham on 10 December 1964, and started his League career with Charlton Athletic in December 1982.

After two spells with Aldershot (one on loan) he joined Wolves for £150,000 in July 1989. In 1990 he returned to

Aldershot, again on loan, and also assisted Torquay United, Portsmouth and Cheltenham Town (each in the same category) before transferring to West Bromwich Albion in August 1992.

A good shot-stopper, he helped the Baggies win the Second Division play-off Final at Wembley the following year and in August 1995 switched to Fulham, who went on to gain promotion from Division Three in his second season at Craven Cottage. Lange, released by Fulham in May 1994, later played for St. Leonard's (Sussex)

Wolves' record: 10 apps.

LANGFORD, Thomas Sidney

Born in Wolverhampton in November 1892, Tom Langford attended Stafford Road School, but he went to Wales following his employment and became a prolific marksman with Bargoed FC, topping their scoring charts when they won the South Wales League in 1913-14.

This sort of form prompted Wolves to secure his services in July 1914, but unfortunately the Great War interrupted his progress at Molineux and sadly his footballing career ended abruptly after the hostilities when he failed to re-sign for Wolves. He died in April 1960.

Wolves' record: 7 apps. 3 goals.

LANGLEY, Thomas William

Londoner Tommy Langley was born in Lambeth on 8 February 1958 and was first associated with Chelsea at the age of 10.

He played for the colts side when he was 12 and after winning England Schoolboy honours, he joined the Stamford Bridge club as an apprentice, turning professional in April 1975.

An out-and-out striker, he was subsequently capped by his country at Youth, Under-21 and 'B' team levels, and then went on to score 40 goals in 142 League games for the Blues before transferring to QPR in August 1980.

The following March he moved to neighbouring Crystal Palace and after a brief spell in Greece with AEK Athens he teamed up with Coventry City (March 1984). From Highfield Road he switched his allegiance to Wolves (in July 1984), but his stay at Molineux was short-lived, and after a loan spell with Aldershot (March 1985) and a sojourn in Hong Kong, he signed for Aldershot in August 1986.

A season with Exeter City followed (1988-89) and thereafter Langley played for Billericay Town and Slough Town. He scored 86 goals in 348 League games at top-class level.

Wolves' record: 26+2 apps. apps. 4 goals.

LANGLEY, William B

Wolves recruited reserve centre-forward Billy Langley from Tunbridge Wells Rangers in the summer of 1936. He played intermediate football during his first season at Molineux and then had a handful of senior outings in

1937-38, but was released in May 1938 when he joined Bournemouth, later assisting Poole Town. Langley was born in Wolverhampton circa 1918.

Wolves' record: 7 apps. 3 goals

LARKIN, Colin

Irish midfielder/forward Colin Larkin - who has lightning pace - was born in Dundalk on 27 April 1982. He joined Wolves as an apprentice in June 1998 and turned professional at Molineux in August 1999.

Larkin, capped by his country at Youth team level (Under-18), made his senior debut against Wycombe Wanderers in the League Cup shortly after becoming a full-time player. Loaned to Kidderminster Harriers in October 2001.

Wolves' record: 1+3 sub apps. one goal.*

LAW, Brian John

Central defender, born in Merthyr on New Year's Day 1970, Brian Law signed as a trainee with QPR in June 1986 and turned professional at Loftus Road in August 1987. Capped by Wales at senior, Under-21, Youth and Schoolboy levels, he actually decided to quit soccer at one stage, but in December 1994 was persuaded to change his mind when, after an unsuccessful trial with Millwall, Wolves boss Graham Taylor bought him to Molineux for £134,000.

After a brief loan spell with Oldham Athletic (February 1997) he was released by new boss Mark McGhee three months later and surprisingly joined Millwall in July 1997 on a free transfer. He quit League football in May 1999 after 53 outings for the Lions.

Wolves' record: 34+6 sub apps. one goal.

LAWRENCE, Joseph

Moustachio'd right-winger Joe Lawrence was a reserve at Molineux for two seasons: 1891-93.

Born in Willenhall circa 1871, he joined Wolves from Wolverhampton Rangers, but was given little opportunity in the first team and he left the club for Darlaston in the summer of 1893.

Wolves' record: 2 apps.

LAX, George

Yorkshireman George Lax was a short, stocky half-back, hard-working who spent just over two seasons at Molineux, from June 1929 to October 1931.

A broad-speaking Yorkshireman, born in South Emsall, near Pontefract in 1905, he played initially for Frickley Colliery and after leaving Molineux returned to his native Yorkshire to sign for Barnsley. In 1933 he surprisingly left Oakwell and moved due south to play for Bournemouth, from where he entered non-League football with Worcester City in 1934, later going to Ireland to assist Bohemians. He retired in 1938 to continue his work as a coal-miner back 'home'.

Wolves' record: 66 apps. one goal.

LAYTON, George William

Outside-right Billy Layton was at Molineux for two years. He joined Wolves from Shrewsbury Town in August 1904 and left the club in the summer of 1906.

Born in Newtown circa 1881, he also assisted Wolverhampton Swifts and Willenhall Pickwick.

Wolves' record: 34 apps. 4 goals.

LAZARUS, Mark

Mark Lazarus was a powerfully built outside-right, a former boxer who was unbeaten in ten fights.

He was born in Stepney, London on 5 December 1938 and on leaving school joined Barking, entering the Football League as a professional with Leyton Orient in November 1957. Over the next 15 years he amassed more than 400 senior appearances while playing for Orient, Queens Park Rangers (in three separate spells), Wolves (from September 1961 to February 1962) Brentford, Crystal Palace and Orient (again), finally pulling out of top-line soccer in 1972.

He won a League Cup winners' tankard with QPR in 1967, scoring a dramatic winner against West Bromwich Albion in that competition's first Wembley Final. Lazarus was with a promoted London club in four successions seasons - QPR in 1966-67 and again in 1967-68, Crystal Palace in 1968-69 and Leyton Orient in 1969-70.

Whenever Lazarus moved from one club to another it was always during the season, never in the summer period! Lazarus's departure from Molineux followed a heated discussion with manager Stan Cullis after he had been dropped for a game at West Ham. Lazarus now runs a removal firm in Romford, Essex.

NB - His two brothers Harry and Lew were the famous Lazar boxers and his son, Nicky, is a former snooker professional.

A total of 34 members of Lazarus's family came to Molineux to see him make his debut in the old gold and black strip v. Cardiff City in September 1961 (1-1 draw). Wolves' record: 9 apps. 3 goals.

LEA, Thomas (Tansey)

Tansey Lea

Outside-right Tansey Lea was a member of Wolves' 1921 FA Cup Final team against Tottenham Hotspur. A willing player, he signed for the club in July 1913 from Oswestry and spent nine years at Molineux, playing either side the Great War but getting limited opportunities until 1919.

He left the club in May 1922, signing for Bristol Rovers, where he played for two seasons, making over 50 appearances. He then had a brief spell with Shrewsbury. Born in Oswestry in 1893, Lea returned to Shropshire on retiring in 1924.

Wolves' record: 58 apps. 4 goals.

LEADBEATER, Richard Paul

Born in Gornal, Dudley on 21 October 1977, Richard Leadbeater, a 6ft 1in forward, joined the Molineux playing staff on a YTS in June 1994 and turned professional in October 1996.

He had a loan spell with Hereford United in December 1997, during which time he scored a hat-trick against Kidderminster Harriers. But after returning to Molineux he failed to make an impression and was given a free transfer in May 1998, when he signed for Hereford on a permanent basis.

In February 1999, Leadbetter moved from Edgar Street to Stevenage Borough for a fee of £20,000.

Wolves' record: 0+1 sub app.

LEE, Colin

As a player, Colin Lee was a very useful striker, who later became a confident defender. Born in Torquay, Devon on 12 June 1956, he was educated in Torbay and joined Bristol City as an apprentice in 1972, turning professional at Ashton Gate in July 1974.

A loan spell with Hereford United four months later was followed by a similar spell with his native Torquay in February 1975 before he transferred to Tottenham Hotspur in October 1977, quickly scoring four goals on his debut for the London club v. Bristol Rovers in a Second Division match.

He went on to notch a total of 31 goals in 94 appearances for Spurs and helped them win promotion back to the top flight before switching his allegiance to Chelsea for £200,000 in June 1980. In July 1987 - after winning another Second Division championship medal and a Full Members Cup medal at Wembley - he became a player and Youth Development Officer at Brentford (linking up with his former Spurs colleague Steve Perryman).

Colin Lee

His next job saw him appointed as Watford's Youth team manager in July 1989 and between March and November 1990 he was team manager at Vicarage Road, having taken over from Steve Harrison who was later to become his assistant at Wolves! Lee, himself, was replaced at Watford by Perryman!

In July 1991 he was on the march again, this time to Reading as their Youth Development Officer. And it was at Elm Park where he teamed up with Mark McGhee whom he followed to Filbert Street and then on to Wolves, eventually taking over as boss at Molineux himself in November 1998, when McGhee was dismissed.

Lee then lost his job (to Dave Jones) in January 2001 and soon afterwards joined Torquay United as caretaker-manager at a critical stage in the season. His experience certainly helped the Plainmoor club escape relegation from the Football League and as a result was offered the job full-time - a position he declined after long negotiations with the Gulls' chairman.

Lee's record as manager: played 32, won 14, drawn 12, lost 6.

LEES, Harold B

Between February 1923 and September 1927 Harry Lees scored 43 goals in 129 appearances for Wolverhampton Wanderers after joining them from Ebbw Vale for £50.

Lees was born at West Bridgford, Nottingham on 11 May 1895 and after winning a Midland Alliance championship medal with Woodthorpe FC in 1920 he had a spell as an amateur with Notts County before moving into Welsh football. Lees helped Wolves win the Third Division (North) championship in 1923-24 when he scored 21 goals, including two hat-tricks.

Lees was a clever inside-left but his powers were waning and Wolves let him go to Darlington in October 1927. He scored five times in 26 games in the Third Division (North) for the Feethams club before joining non-League Shrewsbury Town in August 1929. He ended his playing days with Stourbridge and Leamington Town, retiring in 1933 to concentrate on his work as a chartered accountant in Wolverhampton.

Wolves' record: 129 apps. 43 goals.

LE FLEM, Richard Peter

Orthodox outside-left, born in the village of Bradford-upon-Avon on 12 July 1942, Dick Le Flem went to the Channel Island of Guernsey as a youngster and played his early football over there before joining Nottingham Forest as a professional in May 1960. Capped by England at Under-23 level whilst at The City Ground, he scored 18 goals in 132 League outings for Forest before transferring to Wolves in January 1964 to replace Alan Hinton in the No.11 shirt. Le Flem never really settled down in the West Midlands and spent just over a year at Molineux, switching to Middlesbrough in February 1965.

He ended his senior career with Leyton Orient (March-May 1966).

Wolves' record: 19 apps. 5 goals.

LEGGE, Albert E

Albert Legge was an efficient, hard working outside-right or centre-forward, who spent six seasons at Molineux, joining the club in the summer of 1922 and departing in 1928. Born in Wolverhampton in 1902, Legge attended Prestwood Road School and played for Lewisham Athletic

before joining Wolves as a professional, manager George Jobey offering him a contract after watching him score five goals in three games for the junior team. He spent the first season at Molineux in the reserves but then broke into the first XI, helping them win the Third Division (North) championship in 1923-24.

He left Wolves for Gillingham and later assisted Charlton Athletic and Queens Park Rangers before choosing to play non-League football for Wellington Town, Hednesford and Cradley Heath, announcing his retirement in 1939-40. After the war Legge ran a pub in Heathtown, Wolverhampton and was employed as a scout by several Midlands clubs. He then worked for the Goodyear Tyre Company until he attained the age of 65.

He was resident in Wednesfield at the time of his death, in New Cross Hospital in July 1998.

Wolves' record: 56 apps. 5 goals.

LESCOTT, Joleon

Born in Birmingham on 16 August 1982 and a former trainee at Molineux, defender Joleon Lescott signed professional forms in August 1999 and made his Football League debut against Sheffield Wednesday twelve months later.

He made great progress during that season and is now one of the club's hottest pieces of property!

NB - Lescott's brother, Aaaron, played for Aston Villa and is now registered with Sheffield Wednesday.

Wolves' record: 44 apps. 2 goals.

LESTER, Franklyn Leslie

Secured by Wolves for just one season - as cover for Dickie Baugh and Tommy Dunn - full-back Frank Lester was a well-built defender with a telling tackle.

Born in Wolverhampton circa 1871, he played for Fallings Heath Rangers before spending the 1894-95 campaign at Molineux.

He returned to Fallings Heath from Wolves and later made over 70 appearances at left-back for Walsall.

Wolves' record: one app.

LEWIS, Arthur Norman

A very safe and sound goalkeeper, Norman Lewis was born in Wolverhampton on 13 June 1908. He played for his school team and after a useful spell with the Sunbeam Works side (his day job was that of an assembler on the shop floor) he joined Wolves as a professional in July 1928.

After spending just one season at Molineux, Lewis went to Stoke City for £250 on 24 May 1929, signed by Potters' boss Tom Mather as cover for Dick Williams. At 5ft. 10ins tall and weighing over 12 stones Lewis gained a regular place at The Victoria Ground in 1930 and was eventually replaced in the team by the former Huddersfield Town 'keeper Norman Wilkinson after 170 senior appearances for the Potters.

Lewis then moved to Bradford Park Avenue (May 1936) for

£300 and later served with Tranmere Rovers (November 1936 to May 1939). He helped Rovers win the Third Division (North) title in 1938. Lewis retired in 1942.

Wolves' record: 30 apps.

LILL, Michael James

Micky Lill was a useful goalscoring right-winger who, after winning England Youth honours, deputised for Norman Deeley at Molineux.

Born in Romford, Essex on 3 August 1936, he played for

Micky Lill

Stoney Athletic prior to becoming a professional with Wolves in June 1954. He remained at the club until February 1960 when he was transferred to Everton, after failing to establish himself as a first team regular at Molineux despite an excellent goalscoring record.

He moved from Goodison Park to Plymouth Argyle in June 1962 and ended his Football League career with Portsmouth (March 1963 to May 1964).

Afterwards he assisted Guildford, Germiston Callies in South Africa, for whom he scored 13 goals in 13 games which helped them avoid relegation.

On retiring Lill took to coaching, having gained his FA badge whilst at Everton, and nowadays he is still based in South Africa, taking Physical Education at a state school just outside Johannesburg.

In total Lill scored 38 goals in 121 League appearances in England.

Wolves' record: 34 apps. 17 goals.

LITTLE, Brian

Brian Little acted as caretaker-manager at Molineux for a period of three months, August to October 1986, having been Wolves' coach since the previous January. Born in Durham City on 25 November 1953, he played for East Durham Boys and Durham County Youths before becoming an apprentice with Aston Villa.

He turned professional with the West Midlands club in June 1971, made his League debut four months later and went on to amass more than 300 senior appearances, scoring 82 goals, before injury forced him into an early retirement in 1981 at the age of 28.

Capped once by England as a late substitute against Wales in May 1975, Little won an FA Youth Cup medal and two League Cup winners tankards with Villa and after reluctantly hanging up his boots, he worked briefly in the club's Promotions Department while occasionally assisting as a match summarizer on a local radio station. After leaving Wolves he served as coach to another ex-Villa star, Bruce Rioch, at Middlesbrough. In the summer of 1988 he was appointed team manager of Darlington, whom he

quickly led to the GM Vauxhall Conference title - and then back into the Football League - before taking over as boss of Leicester City in March 1990.

He guided the Foxes to three successive Wembley First Division Play-off Finals. The first in 1992 when they lost to Blackburn Rovers; then in 1993 when they were defeated by Swindon Town and finally in 1994 when Crystal Palace were beaten by a Steve Claridge goal to shoot them into the Premiership.

Barely six months after that tremendous Wembley triumph (in the November) Little surprisingly quit Filbert Street to take over from Ron Atkinson as manager of Aston Villa. Two years later he guided Villa to victory in the Coca-Cola Cup Final over Leeds United, taking them into the UEFA Cup competition as a result. Then soon after the halfway stage in the 1997-98 season, Little again hit the headlines by leaving Villa Park. A short break from soccer followed before he returned as manager of relegated Stoke City....And for only the second time in League soccer history, he sat in the dug-out opposite his kid brother Alan who was manager of York City when the Minstermen played Stoke at The Britannia Stadium in November 1998.

Little left the Potters to take over the reins at West Bromwich Albion in July 1999. He failed with his efforts at The Hawthorns and was subsequently sacked in March 2000.

Little bided his time after that before re-entering League management with Hull City whom he guided to the Third Division Play-offs in his first season at Boothferry Park.

Little's record as Wolves manager was played 11, won 5, drawn one, lost 5.

LIVINGSTONE, William

Striker Billy Livingstone, who played for Scotland's Youth team as a teenager, had a relatively brief career as a professional footballer.

Born in Coventry on 13 August 1964, he joined Wolves as an apprentice at the age of 16 (via a job opportunities scheme provided by the local Manpower Services Department) and was taken on the full-time staff in August 1982.

He remained at Molineux for the next two seasons before transferring to Derby County in July 1984. He quit top-class football at the end of that season.

Wolves' record: 22+ 3 sub apps. 4 goals.

LLOWARCH, Albert

Goalkeeper Albert Llowarch took over from Isaac Griffiths between the posts for Wolves during the 1887-88 season. Born in Nechells, Birmingham in 1865, he stood six feet tall, weighed 13 stones and played his early football for Ward End Swifts and Nechells Park. He spent twelve months with Wolves (from August 1887) before joining Willenhall, later assisting Saltley Works (Birmingham).

Wolves' record: 3 apps.

LLOYD, Arthur Amos

A useful left-half, strong and determined, Arthur Lloyd was recruited by Wolves from Halesowen Town in May 1905, having previously been with Smethwick St. Mary's and Oldbury Broadwell.

He left Molineux for Hednesford Town in August 1908 after giving Wolves three years excellent service. Born in Smethwick in 1881, Lloyd retired in 1912 and died in Birmingham in 1945.

Wolves' record: 80 apps. 3 goals.

LLOYD, Harold

Harry Lloyd (no relation to Arthur above) had just one season with Wolves (July 1913 to April 1914.).

Born on the outskirts of Cannock Chase in 1888 he played his early football with Cannock Town and after spells with Walsall and Rotherham County, he moved to Molineux.

On leaving Wolves he went to Hednesford Town and rounded off his career with a spell at Walsall Wood.

Wolves' record: 8 apps. one goal.

LOCKETT, William Curfield

Bill Lockett was born in Tipton on 23 April 1893 and died in Market Harborough, Leicestershire, on 25 September 1974.

A former pupil at Dudley Grammar School, he later attended Dudley Training College where he won an athletics runners-up medal in the 1912 championships as well as skippering the college cricket team and playing in a Birmingham Amateur Cup Final.

An inside-forward, who could also play as a wing-half, Lockett joined Wolves on amateur forms in August 1913. He became semi-professional the following month but remained at the club for just a season, leaving for Northampton Town in July 1914, later playing for Kidderminster Harriers.

A schoolmaster, he served in the South Staffordshire Regiment during the First World War. A fine all-round sportsman, Lockett represented Birmingham Amateurs in games against London and Lancashire and he also played for England versus Wales as a 15 year-old.

Wolves' record: 6 apps. 2 goals.

LOCKHART, Keith Samuel

During his nine months at Molineux (March-December 1986) the versatile Keith Lockhart appeared in a variety of positions, including those of left-back and midfield. Born at Wallsend-on-Tyne on 19 July 1964, he joined Cambridge United as an apprentice in June 1980 and turned professional at The Abbey Stadium in July 1982.

Two years later he moved to Wolves and from Molineux he went north to sign for Hartlepool United, later assisting Cambridge City. A fiery temper occasionally got the better of Lockhart who was sent-off three times in his career, once with Wolves.

Wolves' record: 29+1 sub apps. 5 goals.

LOMAX, Geoffrey William

Geoff Lomax was a capable full-back, who was taken on loan by Wolves boss Bill McGarry from Manchester City during October/November 1985.

Born in Droylsden, near Manchester on 6 July 1964, he joined the Maine Road club as a professional in July 1981 and after returning there following his sojourn at Molineux, Lomax signed for Carlisle United in December 1985 and later assisted Rochdale (from July 1987) before becoming Bolton Wanderers' Football in the Community Officer at The Reebok Stadium.

Wolves' record: 5 apps.

LOWDER, Arthur

Born in Wolverhampton on 11 February 1863, and a former pupil at St. Luke's School, Blakenhall, Arthur Lowder joined Wolves in September 1882 and retired through injury in October 1891.

In later years he went over to Europe where he coached in France, Germany and Norway, before returning to England in 1924 to become Chairman of the Brewood Parish Council, a position he held for 12 years. As a player he was an extremely hard but fair tackler, preferring the left-half berth although occasionally figuring in the forward-line.

He appeared in Wolves' first-ever FA Cup-tie in 1883 and then followed up by playing in the club's first Football League game v. Aston Villa five years later. He wasn't a tall man, standing 5ft. 5ins tall, yet he loved a challenge and never gave an inch. A grand competitor he was capped by England against Wales a month after playing for Wolves v. Preston in the 1889 FA Cup Final.

Lowder died in Taunton, Somerset, on 4 January 1926.

Wolves' record: 71 apps. 3 goals.

LOWTON, Wilfred George

Right-back Wilf Lowton was already an experienced defender in the Third Division when he joined Wolves

Wilf Lowton

from Exeter City, his hometown club, in 1929. Born in the Devon city on 3 October 1899, he joined the Grecians from local amateur club Heavitree United in 1924 and eventually won his place over the great Exeter full-back Bob Pollard in 1928. Lowton made 75 League appearances for the St. James' Park club before joining Wolves for £1,400.

He proved a great success in the 1930s, being a key figure in the 1931-32 Second Division promotion side when he was successful with 11 out of 12 penalties and also skippered the side, a job he did for four seasons. In May 1935, after Wolves had again struggling in their effort to raise themselves into the upper reaches of the First Division, he returned to Exeter.

Lowton made a further 18 League appearances for the Grecians before spending three months as their assistant trainer, eventually quitting football in 1939. Lowton - who was a keen model railway enthusiast - died in Exeter on 12 January 1963.

Wolves' record: 209 apps. 27 goals (20 penalties).

LUCAS, William Henry

Welsh international left-half or inside-forward Billy Lucas was released by Wolves in 1937...after failing to impress at Molineux. He joined Swindon Town where he stayed until 1947, guesting for Lovells Athletic in the war.

After that he spent six seasons with Swansea Town and between 1953 and 1958 starred for Newport County (as player-manager). He then became full-time boss at Somerton Park (March 1962-67) before taking over the reins at Swansea (1967-69) and again at Newport (1970-74). In total Lucas made almost 450 League appearances and won seven full and eight Wartime caps for his country. He was born in Newport on 15 January 1918, and educated at Corporation Road School from where he went to Molineux...certainly another player 'missed' by Wolves!

LUMBERG, Arthur Albert

One-time furniture remover Albert Lumberg was an efficient right-back, who was good enough to win four caps for Wales at full international level (one with Wolves). Born in Connah's Quay, Flintshire on 20 May 1901, he played for Connah's Quay & Shotton United, Mold Town (early 1924) and Wrexham (November 1924) before joining Wolves in May 1930. Acting as reserve to Wilf Lowton, he spent most of his three years at Molineux in the second team.

On leaving Wolves in June 1933, he signed for Brighton & Hove Albion for £250. In May 1934 he switched to Stockport County and the following January moved south to London to sign for Clapton Orient, diverting north again to Lytham FC in July 1935. Four months later he was recruited by New Brighton (in November 1935) and after a two-year spell with Winsford United (from July 1936) he became player-manager of Newry Town (June 1938).

After the war Lumberg remained in Ireland for a while, but returned to England to become Wrexham's 'A' team trainer in 1950. Thereafter he acted as coach at The Racecourse Ground and also assisted Wrexham Old Boys FC. He played in 169 League games for Wrexham with whom he won a Welsh Cup winners medal in 1925.

Lumberg died in Wrexham on 16 February 1986.

Wolves' record: 22 apps.

LUNN, Thomas Henry

Goalkeeper Tommy Lunn was signed by Wolves from Brownhills Albion in August 1904, having moved down to the area after being educated in County Durham.

A real tough nut, as brave as a lion and ever-reliable, he always wore a floppy peaked cap, but this never detracted from his performances between the posts. Born in Bishop Auckland on 9 July 1883, he helped Wolves win the FA Cup in 1908 and went on to play in the first XI until the end of the 1909-10 season when his place was taken by Frank Boxley. In April 1911 he was transferred to Tottenham Hotspur and for the Londoners he made 106 first team appearances before joining Stockport County in June 1913. Unfortunately after playing only twice for the Edgeley Park club he suffered a serious leg injury which forced him into an early retirement, allowing him to return to London.

Tommy Lunn

He died in the capital, in an Edmonton hospital on 29 March 1960.

NB - One interesting point is that Lunn appeared for Spurs v. Wolves in the first ever Football League game staged at White Hart Lane - on the 1 September 1908.

Wolves' record: 142 apps.

LUTTON, Robert John

Winger 'Bertie' Lutton was born in Banbridge, Northern Ireland on 13 July 1950.

He joined Wolves as a 15 year-old and turned professional at Molineux in September 1967. Basically a reserve, his first team outings were rather limited and after four years at the club he was transferred to Brighton & Hove Albion in September 1971, later assisting West Ham United from January to May 1973.

He won six caps for Northern Ireland, two of them whilst at Molineux, playing against England and Scotland in season 1969-70.

Wolves' record: 19+6 sub apps. one goal.

LYDEN, Joseph

Slimly built inside-forward, born in Walsall in February 1870, Joe Lyden played for Bloxwich St. Luke's and Walsall Pilgrims before having a shade over a season with Wolves (April 1896 to September 1897).

He then returned to non-League football with Darlaston.

Wolves' record: 8 apps. 3 goals.

McALLE, John Edward

John McAlle had a magnificent career with Wolverhampton Wanderers, making his debut for them as a teenager and going on to amass 406 League appearances (over 500 in all matches). He was born in Liverpool on 31 January 1950 and signed for Wolves as an apprentice in July 1965, turning professional in February 1967, although he did not become a first-team regular until 1970.

He made his debut in the defence against Chelsea in April 1968, helped Wolves win the Texaco Cup in 1971 and was ever present in 1971-72, the season Wolves lost to Tottenham Hotspur in the UEFA Cup Final. Club commitments denied him an England Under-23 cap, but he won a League Cup winners' trophy in 1974, when Manchester City were defeated at Wembley and was in the side that won the Second Division championship in 1976-77. He was rewarded with a richly deserved testimonial in 1978-79.

In February 1980 McAlle was introduced from the subs' bench during a FA Cup-tie against Watford at Molineux, but before he had touched the ball he fractured his leg in a tackle. He was never the same player again and in August 1981 was transferred to Sheffield United for £10,000, moving to Derby County in April 1983.

Alas, he was one of several players who fell out with the Rams management when Peter Taylor returned to the Baseball Ground and in 1984 he left Derby, who had just been relegated to the Third Division. McAlle went into non-League football at that point, joining a local Black Country team, Harrisons FC.

NB - In 1988 he was appointed head groundsman at the Merryhill shopping centre at Brierley Hill, and afterwards soon started his own landscape gardening business.

Wolves' record: 495+13 sub apps. 3 goals.

McALOON, Gerald Padva

Scotsman Gerry McAloon was born in the Gorbals district of Glasgow on 13 September 1916. He played junior football with St. Francis Juniors and joined Wolves from Brentford in March 1939.

But the Second World War severely disrupted his progress at Molineux and after the hostilities were over he returned to Griffin Park, later assisting Celtic (Glasgow) and Belfast Celtic. A well-built inside-forward, McAloon died in Bridgeton on 13 April 1987.

Wolves' record: 2 apps. one goal.

John McAlle

Jim McCalliog

McCALL, William

Outside-left Billy McCall joined Wolves in June 1922 from Blackburn Rovers. A sprightly footballer with good skills, he was born in Wallacetown, Scotland on 5 May 1898 and played initially for Queen of the South Wanderers and Dumfries before being engaged at Ewood Park in December 1920. He lined up in the first twelve League games of the 1922-23 season for Wolves before being replaced by Len Rhodes. The two men then contested the left-wing berth over the next few months.

But McCall, unable to hold down a regular place in the side, became disillusioned and was transferred to Southampton in January 1923.

Following a bright start he never quite fitted the bill at The Dell and after scoring twice in eight outings for the Saints (over a period of eighteen months) he was sold to Queen of the South in September 1925 for a reduced fee of £250.

Wolves' record: 16 apps. one goal.

McCALLIOG, James

Midfielder Jim McCalliog was born in Glasgow on 23 September 1946 and began his career as an amateur with Leeds United in 1962-63 before being released to join Chelsea as a full-time professional on his 17th birthday.

McCalliog could not establish himself in Chelsea's first team, making only 12 appearances (five in the League Cup) before they let him go to Sheffield Wednesday for £37,500 in July 1965, which made him Britain's costliest teenage footballer at the time. His mother and father, three brothers and a sister moved to Yorkshire with him, all living in the same house near Hillsborough. For the Owls, McCalliog made 150 League appearances, playing in the 1966 FA Cup Final against Everton, before Wolves signed him for £70,000 in October 1969.

The money was well spent and McCalliog remained at Molineux for almost five years, making 210 appearances and scoring 48 goals. He left in March 1974, when a £60,000 deal took him to Manchester United. He helped them regain their First Division place but was soon on the move again, this time to Southampton for £40,000.

McCalliog won a FA Cup winners' medal in 1976 (when Southampton beat his former club, Manchester United at Wembley) and he made 72 League appearances for the Saints before becoming player-manager of Lincoln City in September 1978, having appeared for Chicago Sting in the North American Soccer League. In March 1979 he was appointed player-manager of non-League Runcorn.

McCalliog eventually drifted out of football but in April 1990 he came back as manager of Fourth Division strugglers Halifax Town. It was a thankless task and in October 1991 he went the way of all the men who have tried their luck as boss at The Shay!

His personal honours from the game included five full Scottish caps (one gained with Wolves) as well as Under-23 and Schoolboy caps. McCalliog, a publican since 1982, was the licensee of the George & Dragon at Wetherby, North Yorkshire in 1997.

Wolves' record: 204+6 sub apps. 48 goals.

McDONALD, John Christopher

John McDonald was a useful utility forward, who played for Wolves during the last two seasons before World War Two. A Yorkshireman, born in Maltby on 27 August 1921, he moved to Molineux in August 1937, as cover for the main attackers.

Unfortunately his chances were restricted and in March 1939 he was one of the many ex-Wanderers' who went south to join Bournemouth. However, the fighting in Europe disrupted McDonald's career but in 1946 he re-entered League soccer with the Cherries and later played for Fulham (1948-52, making 75 League appearances), Southampton (for season 1952-53) and Southend United before dropping into non-League football with first Weymouth and then Poole Town.

McDonald made over 200 League appearances during his career (64 goals scored).

Wolves' record: 2 apps.

McDONALD, Robert Wood

Left-back Bobby McDonald had a fine career in League football, amassing well over 500 appearances for five different clubs. Born in Aberdeen on 13 April 1965, he was educated north of the border and won Scottish Schoolboy caps as a 15 year-old.

After playing for King Street Sports Club (Aberdeen) he joined Aston Villa as an apprentice in June 1971, turning professional in September 1972.

During the next four years he played for his country's Youth team, gained Junior Floodlit League Cup and FA Youth Cup winners medals in 1972, collected a League Cup winners tankard in 1975 and helped Villa win promotion from the Second Division. In August 1976 he was transferred to Coventry City for £40,000.

Four years later he moved to Manchester City, being one of John Bond's first signings in October 1980 and in February 1987 he was recruited by Leeds United for £25,000. McDonald was then on loan to Wolves during February and March 1988 (he was signed to fill in for the injured Andy Thompson). But soon after returning to Elland Road he quit the bigtime to sign for VS Rugby (July 1988) later assisting Burton Albion (1990), Redditch United (1991), Armitage (1991-92) and Burton Albion again (1992-93).

Wolves' record: 7 apps.

McDONALD, Thomas

Right-winger Tommy McDonald was born in Glasgow on 24 May 1930 and after service with the Edinburgh club, Hibernian, he moved to Wolves in April 1954 as cover for England international Johnny Hancocks.

McDonald found it difficult to get first team football at Molineux and in July 1956 was transferred to Leicester City for £6,000. He scored 27 goals in 113 League games for the Foxes before moving back to Scotland to sign for Dunfermline Athletic in July 1960.

He later assisted Raith Rovers (December 1962 to June 1963), Queen of the South (from August 1963) and finally Stirling Albion (December 1963-May 1964). He won a Scottish 'B' cap during his time at Easter Road.

Wolves' record: 6 apps. 2 goals.

MacDOUGALL, Alexander Lindsay

Born in Flemington near Motherwell in 1900, Alex McDougall was signed by Wolves boss Fred Scotchbrook from Wishaw Juniors in February 1925 as cover for Jack Mitton. A hard worker, determined in his approach, he had earlier had trials with Motherwell and had assisted Wishaw White Star and Carluke.

After leaving Molineux in August 1928 he had a spell with Derby County before returning to Scotland to sign for Barrhead (September 1929).

Wolves' record: 22 apps. one goal.

McGARRY, William Harry

Bill McGarry had two separate spells as team manager of Wolves - the first one lasted seven-and-a-half years from 25 November 1968 to 5 May 1976, the second just 61 days from 4 September to 4 November 1985.

Born in Stoke-on-Trent on 10 June 1927, McGarry played at first as an inside-right for Northwood Mission before becoming a professional with Port Vale in June 1945. At both of these clubs he played behind Ronnie Allen whom he succeeded as manager at Molineux in 1968.

After switching to right-half he spent six good years with the Valiants, up to March 1951. He was then transferred for £10,000 to Huddersfield Town where he remained until March 1961 when, for a fee of £2,000, he became

Bill McGarry

player-manager of Bournemouth.

A solid tackler who passed the ball well, McGarry made over 500 senior appearances for the Terriers, helping them into the First Division.

He also gained four full England caps and represented his country at 'B' team level (1954-56). From Dean Court he took charge of Watford (July 1963 to October 1964) and after serving in the same capacity at Ipswich Town, he arrived at Molineux, after being 'wanted' by the club's directorate for quite some time!

During his first spell with Wolves McGarry guided the team to the 1972 UEFA Cup Final and win the League Cup two years later. He rebuilt the whole team and signed some excellent players as well as baptising plenty more who went on to become superb footballers. Unfortunately things started to go wrong for McGarry - and the team - in season 1975-76 and after relegation had been suffered he departed company, handing over the reins to Sammy Chung, who had previously been trainer-coach and assistant-boss at the club. At this juncture McGarry went abroad to coach in Saudi Arabia and the United Arab Emirates (June 1976 to October 1977).

Between November 1977 and August 1980 he was manager of Newcastle United, and after scouting briefly for Brighton & Hove Albion during the first half of the 1980-81 season, he went off to coach in Zambia, at club level with Power Dynamo and the Zambian national team. He then turned down a lucrative job in South Africa, before returning to Molineux for a second term of office in September 1985, following Wolves' disastrous start to the season. Sadly he stayed for just two months after seeing his deflated players win only twice in 12 games.

McGarry was then out of football for quite awhile before taking a coaching job in Bophuthatswana in 1993, a position he held for a year.

McGarry was in charge for 410 games as Wolves manager: 158 ended in victories and 145 in defeats.

McGARVEY, Scott Thomas

Scott McGarvey was a useful inside-forward who spent more than 12 years in the Football League (1979-91). Born in Glasgow on 22 April 1963, he joined the groundstaff of Manchester United as a teenager and turned professional at Old Trafford in April 1980.

He assisted Wolves on loan from March to May 1984 and finally left United for Portsmouth in a £100,000 deal in July 1984. He later assisted Carlisle United (from January 1986), Grimsby Town (signed for £30,000 in March 1987), Oldham Athletic (May 1989), Wigan Athletic (on loan, September/October 1989), Mazda in Japan (June 1990), Aris Limasol (September 1992), Derry City (as player-coach), Witton Albion (February 1994), Barrow (March 1994) and latterly with Redbridge Forest.

Capped four times by Scotland at Under-21 level, McGarvey made over 300 appearances at senior club level. Wolves' record: 13 apps. 2 goals.

McGHEE, Mark Edward

Born in Glasgow on 25 May 1957, Mark McGhee was an excellent goalscorer who netted over 200 goals in more than 500 senior appearances at club and international level.

He played, in turn, for Bristol City (initially as an amateur); Greenock Morton (scoring 37 goals in 64 League games); Newcastle United (signed for £150,000 in December 1977); Aberdeen (bought for £80,000 in 1979, he went on to score 100 goals in 263 matches in all competition for the Dons); SV Hamburg (recruited for £285,000 in 1984 - he hit seven goals in 30 appearances in the German Bundesliga); Celtic (secured for £200,000 in 1985); Newcastle United (signed for a second time in 1989) and then Reading, acquired initially as player-manager in 1991.

He gained four full caps for Scotland and one with the Under-21 side. With Aberdeen and Celtic he won four Scottish League championships, five Scottish Cups (1982-89) and in 1983 helped the Dons lift the European Cup-winners Cup. After holding office at Elm Park for three years, during which time the Royals won the Second Division title (1994), he took over as manager of Leicester City, replacing ex-Wolves caretaker-boss Brian Little, who switched to Aston Villa. But then, just like Little had done before him,

Mark McGhee

McGhee walked out of Filbert Street to take over the reins at Molineux, moving into the Wolves' hot seat in December 1995.

Forty-eight hours after taking office McGhee admitted that the squad he had inherited was short on both physical and mental strength, certain players looked under-coached and had practically no desire to try and appreciate tactics. It took an awful lot of hard work to change that, and at the end of his first season in charge Wolves finished a poor 20th in the First Division. The following term they reached the Play-offs, only to miss out on a trip to Wembley after losing to Crystal Palace over two legs.

Unfortunately McGhee saw Wolves struggle in 1997-98 despite an appearance in the FA Cup semi-final when they were beaten by Arsenal. And after some more disappointing results during the first third of the following campaign when Wolves were dumped out of the Worthington League Cup by lowly Bournemouth, McGhee left the club by mutual consent (in November 1998).

He then spent some time out of the game, turned down a

few offers, missed out on others before being appointed manager of Millwall in September 2000, replacing the popular duo of Keith Stevens and Alan McLeary at The New Den. With Steve Gritt as his aide, he did tremendously well, leading the Lions to the Second Division championship in his first season in charge.

McGhee's record as Wolves' boss: 159 games played, 65 won, 55 lost and 39 drawn.

McILMOYLE, Hugh

Few players have moved around the Football League as much as all-action striker Hughie McIlmoyle. Born at Cambuslang, Scotland, on 29 January 1940, McIlmoyle was involved in ten separate transfer deals during a career which saw him play for Carlisle United in three different spells as well as Leicester City, Rotherham United, Wolves, Bristol City, Middlesbrough and Preston North End.

All this after he had started his career with Port Glasgow and played for Greenock Morton in the Scottish League. A good old-fashioned centre-forward he scored well over 170 goals in 450 senior games for eight clubs.

He began his English career as an apprentice with Leicester in August 1959, then, after playing in the 1961 FA Cup Final v. Tottenham with just seven first team outings under his belt, he moved to Rotherham. Joining Wolves for £30,000 in October 1964 after his first spell with Carlisle, McIlmoyle scored 45 goals in 105 games in his spell at Molineux before being transferred to Bristol City in March 1967.

He rejoined Carlisle in September 1967, then went to 'Boro (September 1969), Preston (July 1971) and back to Morton (in August 1973) before ending his career with yet another spell at Brunton Park, from July 1974 to May 1975. In his two and a half years at Molineux he developed a good understanding in attack with players like Ray Crawford, Jimmy Melia, Ernie Hunt, Terry Wharton, David Burnside and Dave Wagstaffe.

He scored his first goal for Wolves at home to Blackburn Rovers in January 1965 and netted one hat-trick, against Aston Villa in a FA Cup fifth round second replay at The Hawthorns in March of that year. Nine days later he scored twice against Manchester United in the quarter-final, but Wolves went down 5-3.

That season Wolves were relegated, but before leaving for Ashton Gate, McIlmoyle helped set them on the road back to the old First Division with 13 goals in 24 League games. Wolves' record: 104+1 sub apps. 45 goals.

McINTOSH, Alexander

Inside-right Alex McIntosh played competitive football before, during and after World War Two. Born in Dunfermline on 14 April 1916 and a junior with St. Mirren (as an amateur) and Hearts of Bleith FC, he was playing for Folkestone Town when Wolves spotted his undoubted talent and recruited him to Molineux in October 1937.

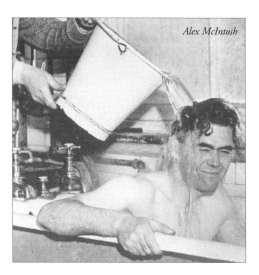

Alex McIntosh

He became a regular in the Wolves League side in 1938-39 and was in their line-up against Portsmouth in that season's FA Cup Final. He played for the Wanderers when he could during the hostilities and he also guested for Newport County and Watford. He made almost 40 appearances for Wolves in the war and gained a League Cup winners medal in 1942 (v. Sunderland) despite spending some time inside a Prisoner of War camp in Holland, having served with the Hearts Regiment.

But afterwards McIntosh found if difficult to get into the first team under manager Ted Vizard. In January 1947 he was transferred to Birmingham City and after helping Blues on their way to winning the Second Division championship, he left St. Andrew's for Coventry City in February 1948.

He ended his League career in 1950 when he moved to Kidderminster Harriers, later assisting Bilston Town and Hednesford Town before retiring in 1953.

Wolves' record: 50 apps. 9 goals.

McLEAN, Angus

Gus McLean was unusual in that he was born a Welshman of Scottish parents. He was born at Queensferry on 20 September 1925 and after appearing for Aberystwyth Town, was playing for Hilton Main when Wolves signed him during the early days of wartime football.

At first he appeared as a wing-half, but later played in both full-back

Gus McLean

134

positions, centre-half and even at centre-forward. McLean signed as a professional in November 1942 and after 125 appearances during the war, he quickly made his mark in the Football League and FA Cup competitions. Although he played in a Wolves side that was always challenging for First Division honours, McLean was denied a FA Cup winners' medal in 1949 when a cartilage injury kept him out of the Final against Leicester City. The nearest he came to an international honour was when he was selected as reserve for Wales against Scotland in 1947-48.

In May 1951, he left Wolves to become player-manager of Aberystwyth Town and then took over as first-team trainer at Bury in May 1953. He later worked for Crewe Alexandra and was manager of Hartlepools United from May 1967, when he took over from Brian Clough, to April 1970.

With Clough's team he won Hartlepools their first-ever promotion, from the Fourth Division, but they were relegated the following season and after having to seek re-election at the end of the next campaign, he was sacked.

A brief spell in charge of Bromsgrove Rovers followed before he announced his retirement from full-time involvement in football in May 1975, though he did continue to work as a scout for a number of Midlands-based clubs.

Wolves' record: 158 apps.

McLOUGHLIN, Paul Brendan

Midfielder Paul McLoughlin was born in Bristol on 23 December 1963 and played his early football in the South-west, having trials with Bristol City in 1979 and serving with Yeovil Town (1980).

Soon afterwards he went to New Zealand, collecting several medals in domestic competitions while playing for Gisborne FC before returning to Britain to sign full-time professional forms with Cardiff City in December 1984. He won Welsh international honours at Ninian Park where he played until 1986.

He then returned to Ashton Gate as a non-contract player, transferring to Hereford United in June 1987. From Edgar Street McLoughlin moved to Wolves for £45,000 in July 1989. He never really settled in at Molineux and after loan spells with Walsall (September 1991, when former Wolves favourite Kenny Hibbitt was in charge of the Saddlers) and York City, he joined Mansfield Town in a £35,000 in January 1992, staying at Field Mill until May 1994.

Wolves' record: 12+17 sub apps. 4 goals.

McMAHON, Douglas David Alexander

Inside-right Doug McMahon made his League debut for Wolves against Blackpool (away) in December 1938, having joined the club the previous month from Caledonian Juniors in his homeland in Winnepeg, Canada, where he was born in 1915.

He returned to Winnepeg in March 1939 joining the Union Weston Sencor club.

Wolves' record: one app.

McMAIN, Joseph

Joe McMain

Following the departure of Charlie Henderson from Molineux at the end of the 1895-96 season, Wolves quickly recruited Joe McMain from Kettering Town as his replacement. Born in Wolverhampton circa 1872, McMain, previously with Stafford Rangers, did a splendid job for the club and scored some cracking goals including six in five matches in December 1898.

In the summer of 1899, after suffering a couple of niggling injuries, he left Molineux for Notts County and later returned to Kettering Town.

Wolves' record: 51 apps. 19 goals.

McMILLAN, Stuart Thomas

Outside-right Stuart McMillan had one good season with Wolves, making 23 senior appearances in 1922-23 under manager George Jobey. But when Jobey left Molineux in May 1924, so did McMillan, who immediately joined Bradford City.

He spent three years at Valley Parade, making 73 appearances, before transferring to Nottingham Forest in June 1927. He left Forest in August 1928 after just 10 outings to sign for Clapton Orient, retiring in 1930. In 1942 he become football advisor with Derby County and managed the Rams from January 1946 to November 1953. He then turned his hand to scouting.

Born in Leicester on 17 August 1896, McMillan was educated in Rutland, yet played his early League football with Derby County (December 1914 to June 1919). He then had two years with Chelsea before moving to Gillingham in March 1921, from where he joined Wolves in June 1922.

McMillan died in Ashbourne, Derbyshire on 27 September 1963.

Wolves' record: 39 apps. 5 goals.

McNAB, Robert

In his prime Bob McNab was a fine full-back with good ball control and excellent vision. A Yorkshireman, born in Huddersfield on 20 July 1943, he played local junior football in his home town and for Rawthorpe CSM and Mold Green Civic Youth Club before joining Huddersfield Town as an amateur in June 1961, turning professional at Leeds Road in April 1962. After more than 70 games for the Terriers he was transferred to Arsenal for £40,000 in October 1966.

Over the next nine years McNab became a star performer with the Gunners, helping them win the Fairs Cup in 1970, complete the League and FA Cup double twelve months later and finish runners-up in the FA Cup in

Bob McNab

1972. He also collected two League Cup runners-up prizes in 1968 and 1969.

He made 365 appearances for Arsenal and was also capped four times by England as well as representing the Football League. He signed for Wolves in July 1975, but stayed only a season at Molineux before going over to America to play for San Antonio in Texas. Returning to this country in September 1977, McNab signed for non-League Barnet but he remained at Underhill for only a short time prior to becoming a publican in North London (Tottenham).

He later went abroad to coach in Vancouver where he now resides with his wife and family.

Wolves' record: 16 apps.

McPARLAND, Peter James

Peter McParland was a brilliant goalscoring outside-left, fast, direct, with a grand shot in either foot, who came to Wolves far too late in his career! Born in Newry, County Down, Northern Ireland on 25 April 1934, 'Packy' McParland joined Dundalk on leaving senior school in Newry.

In August 1952, while serving his apprenticeship as a coppersmith and having been watched over a period of time, George Martin, the Aston Villa manager, paid £3,880 for his services and over the next ten years he gave the Birmingham club supreme service, scoring 120 goals in 341 appearances.

He netted both goals when Villa beat double-chasing Manchester United 2-1 to win the 1957 FA Cup Final, he helped Villa take the Second Division championship in 1960 and then captured a League Cup winners tankard in 1961. In between times he represented the Football League XI and gained 33 caps for Northern Ireland (he added another to his collection when a Wolves player). He moved from Villa Park to Molineux in January 1962 but a year later switched due south to sign for Plymouth Argyle for £30,000. A spell in America with Atlanta Chiefs preceded a brief association with Peterborough United and after serving with Worcester City from 1966, he returned to Ireland where he became player-manager and then manager of Glentoran from 1968 to 1971.

Thereafter McParland coached in Kuwait, Lybia and Hong Kong and was also briefly in charge of No.1 Club of Kuwait before returning to England to take up residence in Bournemouth, where he ran a successful property business with his son.

Wolves' record: 21 apps. 10 goals.

McVEIGH, James

Jimmy McVeigh was a reserve defender at Molineux during a four-year period to 1970. Born in Hathersage on 2 July 1949, he joined the Wolves apprentice staff in 1966 and turned professional in May 1968, but just over two seasons later was released to join Gillingham in October 1970.

He remained at the Priestfield Stadium until May 1972, making 51 League appearances.

Wolves' record: 2 apps.

MacLAREN, David

Goalkeeper Dave MacLaren was born in Auchterarder, Scotland on 12 June 1934. He played for St. Johnstone Juniors before entering the RAF for his national service. In February 1956 he became a professional with Dundee, joining Leicester City in January 1957. He made almost 100 senior appearances during his three-and-a-half years at Filbert Street before transferring to Plymouth Argyle in June 1960.

At Home Park he became a firm favourite with the fans and had 131 League outings for the Pilgrims prior to his transfer to Wolves in January 1965. He did well at Molineux where he contested the No.1 position with Fred Davies. In September 1966, however, MacLaren was sold to Southampton after playing in the opening

Dave MacLaren

game of that season under Wolves boss Ronnie Allen.

From The Dell MacLaren switched back to the Midlands to play for Worcester City (July 1967), retiring two years later.

In 1954, when serving in the RAF he won both the 'Sportsman of the Year' award and unofficial representative honours for Malaysia and in 1970 he returned to that country as a coach, assuming the management of the Malaysian national team in 1972. He also coached the Australian club, Hakoah in 1973-74.

NB - His two brothers - Jimmy and Roy - both kept goal in League football.

Wolves' record: 47 apps.

MADDEN, Lawrence David

Lawrie Madden was already a studious, experienced defender when he joined Wolves on a free transfer from Sheffield Wednesday in August 1991.

Born in London on 28 September 1955, he commenced his career with Arsenal, but failed to make the breakthrough at Highbury and subsequently made his League debut for Mansfield Town as a non-contract player in March 1975.

He moved from Field Mill to Charlton Athletic and made over 120 appearances for the Addicks before drifting out of competitive football to assist Boston United. He returned to the fray with Millwall in March 1982 and in August 1983 teamed up with Sheffield Wednesday.

After playing in more than 250 games for the Owls he became surplus to requirements at Hillsborough and a loan spell with Leicester City (January 1991) preceded his move to Wolves. Madden, who helped Wednesday win the League Cup in 1991 (v. Manchester United) was given a free transfer from Molineux in May 1993 and four months later he signed for Darlington, later assisting Chesterfield (from October 1993).

Madden was 37 years, 222 days old when he last played for Wolves v. Derby County on 8 May 1993. He is a now a match summarizer on TV and radio.

Wolves' record: 71+5 apps. one goal.

MAGUIRE, James Edward

During the late 1930s Teddy Maguire was part of two excellent wing pairings - first on the right with big Tom Galley and then on the left with hard-shooting Dicky Dorsett. Maguire, in fact, could occupy either wing position and he was also a very useful inside-forward.

Keen and aggressive, he was born in Meadowfield on 23 July 1917 and joined Wolves from Willington FC early in the 1936-37 season, claiming a regular first team place by the November. During the war he guested for Hartleppols and remained at Molineux until May 1947 when he transferred to Swindon Town, later assisting Halifax Town (from October 1948 to May 1950) and retiring out of League football a year later after a brief spell with Spennymoor United.

Maguire played outside-left for Wolves in the 1939 FA Cup Final defeat by Portsmouth. In his League career he netted 19 times in 162 games.

Wolves' record: 85 apps. 9 goals.

MALPASS, William

Half-back Billy Malpass had a 'storming' game when Wolves won the 1893 FA Cup Final against Everton at Fallowfield, Manchester. And three years later, as skipper, he was again outstanding in the Final, although on this occasion Wolves went down 2-1 to Sheffield Wednesday at Crystal Palace.

Yet in that same 1895-96 season, Malpass, together with team-mates Tommy Dunn and Alf Griffin, had been suspended by the club for allegedly not trying on the pitch! It was a remarkable indictment, especially when made against Malpass, who had given Wolves such yeoman service since joining them from Wednesbury Old Athletic in August 1891. Born in Wednesbury on 5 March 1867, Malpass's Wolves career lasted almost eight years, until May 1899, when he was forced to retire because of a knee injury. Most of his games were at centre-half, although he also appeared at wing-half, doing so in the 1893 Final, when he skippered the side.

In November 1896 he played for the Football League

against the Irish League in Belfast, in a team which included nine Midlands-based players, three of them from Wolves, the others being Beats and Wood.

Billy Malpass died at Darlaston just before World War Two.

Wolves' record: 155 apps. 9 goals.

MANNION, Gerry Patrick

Right-winger Gerry Mannion had pace, good skills, an appetite for the game and he could score goals as well as make them. Unfortunately from Wolves' point of view he did far better after leaving Molineux than he did while he was there, although to be fair he did have some competition for the No.7 shirt during his time with the Wanderers.

Born in Rugby League territory at Burtonwood near Warrington on 21 December 1939, Mannion joined Wolves as a youngster and turned professional in November 1957.

After winning England Youth honours and two Under-23 caps, he was transferred to Norwich City in September 1961 for £13,000 and during the next six-and-a-half years he appeared in 119 senior games for the Canaries, scoring 21 goals.

From Carrow Road he switched to Chester (January 1968) and pulled out of League football five months later.

Wolves' record: 21 apps. 7 goals.

MARDENBOROUGH, Steven Alexander

Utility forward Steve Mardenborough had the pleasure of silencing the Anfield Kop when he scored a dramatic winning goal (his only one for Wolves) against Liverpool in a First Division match there in January 1984.

A native of Birmingham (born on 11 September 1964), he joined Coventry City as a professional in 1982 and after a brief spell with Birmingham City, he switched to Molineux, making his League debut in September 1983. After a loan period with Cambridge United (February 1984) Mardenborough signed for Swansea City (July 1984) and a year later went to neighbouring Newport County, transferring to his third Welsh club, Cardiff City, in March 1987.

He switched from Ninian Park to Hereford United and after assisting IFK Osterlund (Sweden) and Cheltenham Town he re-entered League football with Darlington (June 1990). In July 1993 he moved to Lincoln City for £10,000, switched to Scarborough in February 1995 and after a brief spell with Stafford Rangers he was recruited by Colchester United in August 1995.

Four months later he teamed up again with Swansea City and in 1996 signed for Merthyr Tydfil, later assisting Inter Cardiff (League of Wales).

Fast and direct, Mardenborough made well over 300 appearances during his professional career, including more than 80 as a substitute.

Wolves' record: 9+2 sub apps. one goal.

MARR, Andrew

A Wolves player during the last season prior to the suspension of the Football League competition in 1915, outside-right Andy Marr found it difficult to get first team football at Molineux and after the hostilities he did not re-sign for Wolves.

Born in Gateshead circa 1893, he played for Coventry City before moving to Molineux.

Wolves' record: 3 apps.

MARSDEN, Christopher

Yorkshireman Chris Marsden, an astute and highly competitive midfielder, was born in Sheffield on 3 January 1969. He joined his home-town club Sheffield United as an apprentice in June 1985 and turned professional at Bramall Lane in January 1987.

In July 1988 - after 18 first team games for the Blades - he was transferred to neighbouring Huddersfield Town. Over the next six years he amassed 155 League and Cup appearances for the Terriers before moving to Wolves for £250,000 in January 1994 after a loan spell with Coventry City (November 1993).

Unfortunately he failed to make an impact at Molineux although injuries (including a broken leg) didn't help matters and in November 1994 he went to Notts County, also for £250,000, switching to Stockport County for £70,000 in January 1996. He helped the Edgeley Park club gain promotion from the Second Division in 1997.

In October 1997, after 86 games, Marsden left Stockport to sign for Birmingham City for a fee of £500,000 and on his debut for Blues he scored the winner in a 1-0 Nationwide League win over his former club, Wolves.

In January 1999 Marsden left St. Andrew's and signed for Southampton in a £850,000 deal.

Wolves' record: 11 apps.

MARSDEN, Frederick

Fred Marsden was a steady, reliable half-back, standing well over six feet tall, who was reserve to George Laking during his time at Molineux.

A Lancastrian, born in Blackburn on 6 September 1911 and now deceased, he attended Blackburn Council School and played for Clitheroe, Manchester Central and Accrington Stanley before joining Wolves in January 1935 with Jack Aspin in a combined deal worth £750.

He left Molineux in May 1936 for Bournemouth and later assisted Weymouth (from June 1949) prior to retiring in 1952. Marsden died in Bournemouth in November 1989.

Wolves' record: one app.

MARSHALL, George Harold

Left-back George Marshall made his League debut for Wolves on the opening day of the 1920-21 season at Fulham. But by the end of that season, Marshall was turning out in a FA Cup Final at Stamford Bridge where Wolves lost to Tottenham Hotspur. He missed only four

George Marshall

games, all through injury, and went on to make well over 100 senior appearances for Wolves before being transferred to Walsall in February 1924, after the emergence of Harry Shaw.

Marshall was born at Walker-on-Tyne on 3 March 1896 and after beginning his career with the Newcastle club Shankhouse FC, he had trials for Portsmouth in 1913-14 before signing for Southend United in July 1914. Of course, war was declared before his career could get going but in August 1919, Wolves signed him and after a season in their reserve side he made his League debut in August 1920.

He was with Walsall for only a short time before being transferred to Reading, moving to Bournemouth in 1924-25 and then ending his career with Darlaston in 1925-26.

Wolves' record: 111 apps. one goal.

MARSHALL, John

Right-winger Johnny Marshall appeared in Wolves' first XI during the last pre-war season of 1938-39.

Born in Cambridgeshire circa 1917, and now deceased, he was recruited to the Molineux staff from Norwich City in June 1938, but owing to the hostilities his career was cut short and he never appeared in the League again.

Wolves' record: one app.

MARSHALL, William Harry

Wing-half or inside-forward Harry Marshall (no relation to George or John) was born in Hucknall, Notts on 16 February 1905.

He started out with his local club, Hucknall Primitives and after brief spells with Bromley Athletic and Bromley United he joined Nottingham Forest (February 1924), later playing for Southport (July 1926) before signing for Wolves in March 1928.

He was transferred from Molineux to Port Vale for a substantial fee in March 1930 and played over 50 games for the Valiants before switching to Tottenham Hotspur in March 1932.

Over the next few years he assisted Kiddermister Harriers (July 1933), Brierley Hill Alliance (1934), Rochdale (August 1935) and Linfield (June 1938), retiring during the 1939-40 campaign. Marshall died in Linby, Notts on 9 March 1959.

NB - Marshall's brother Bob played for Sunderland and Manchester City.

Wolves' record: 54 apps. 13 goals.

MARSON Frederick

Inside-left Fred Marson had a fair amount of ability, but failed to settle at Molineux following his transfer from Darlaston in July 1923.

Born in Moxley on 18 January 1900, he played for a number of local clubs early in his career and after leaving Wolves in 1925, he joined Sheffield Wednesday, later assisting Swansea Town (1928-29) before returning to play in the Black Country, first with Darlaston, then Wellington Town and back to Darlaston for a third time, finally retiring in 1938.

Wolves' record: 8 apps. 4 goals.

MARTIN, David Kirker

Irish centre-forward David 'Boy' Martin was born in Belfast on 1 February 1914 and played and scored for his home town club, Belfast Celtic, before joining Wolves in December 1934.

Formerly an orphanage lad, Martin came to the fore when leading the Royal Ulster Rifles and Army attacks while serving in the forces as a drummer (hence his nickname). He was engaged by Belfast Celtic in 1932 at a cost of just £5 and quickly set the footballing fraternity in Ireland alight with some superb displays. He went on to win nine full caps for his country (four against Scotland, three versus England and two v. Wales).

Unfortunately he never really settled down at Molineux despite scoring plenty of goals especially for the reserves, and he left Wolves in August 1936, transferring to Nottingham Forest for whom he accumulated a fine record - 48 goals in only 86 appearances.

He then had a season in the Third Division (South) with Notts County, hitting a record 26 goals in 26 League games in 1938-39, before returning to Ireland to play for

Glentoran. 'Boy' Martin, who was a prize boxer in his younger days, died on 9 January 1991.

Wolves' record: 27 apps. 18 goals.

MARTIN, James Colin

Inside-forward Jimmy Martin spent one season at Molineux (from September 1923 to July 1924), acting as reserve to strikers Stan Fazackerly and Tom Phillipson.

Born at Basford, North Staffs on 2 December 1898, he played for Stoke St. Peter's before joining Stoke for £750 in July 1916, and on leaving The Victoria Ground in June 1921 (after 16 games) Martin switched to Aberdare Athletic.

During a lengthy career (1914-38) he also assisted Reading (from July 1924), Aberdare again (June 1925), Bristol City (May 1926), Blackpool (February 1928), Southend United (February 1929), Halifax Town (July 1929) and Congleton Town (August 1930 to May 1931).

He died in Stoke on 27 June 1969.

Wolves' record: 11 apps. 6 goals.

MARTIN, Tudor James

Tudor Martin was another prolific goalscorer, capable of finding the net at any level, against the best defences in the game.

Born in Caerau, near Bridgend on 20 April 1904, he played for Careau Corinthians and Bridgend Town before joining West Bromwich Albion in October 1926 at a time when the Baggies were well blessed with forwards, all of them exceptional goalscorers. Consequently Martin never got a first team outing at The Hawthorns and he duly left for Newport County in July 1929, switching to Wolves in May 1930.

He scored a goal every two games during his stay at Molineux - and 74 for the reserves in League and Cup games - but in July 1932 he became surplus to requirements and boss Major Frank Buckley sold him to Swansea Town.

At the Vetch Field Martin did extremely well, netting 45 goals in 116 League games for the Swans, up to July 1936, when he moved to London to sign for West Ham United, later assisting Southend United (February 1937 to May 1939). He retired at the age of 35 and returned to South Wales where for many years he worked for a tube manufacturing company and regularly attended Newport County's home matches at Somerton Park.

A Welsh international, capped against Northern Ireland in 1930, Martin scored a club record 49 reserve team goals (in both League and Cup competitions) for Wolves in season 1931-32. He died in Newport on 6 September 1979.

Wolves' record: 15 apps. 9 goals.

MASON, Charles

Robust full-back Charlie Mason was born in Wolverhampton on 13 April 1863. Founder member of the club after leaving St Luke's School in 1877, he went on to enjoy 15 splendid years with Wolves, making almost 300 appearances, including over 100 in the League and FA Cup competitions before announcing his retirement during the summer of 1892.

When he was capped for England against Ireland in 1887, he became the first Wolves player to appear in an international match and he won further caps in 1888, against Wales, and in 1890, against Ireland again.

He was at left-back when Wolves played in their first FA Cup Final against double winners Preston in 1889, and he played in all but four games in their first season in the Football League (1888-89).

Indeed, he seems to have been in at the start of every facet of Wolves' history, appearing in the club's first-ever FA Cup-tie and their first Football League game.

In May 1888, Mason guested for West Bromwich Albion, the FA Cup holders, when they met Renton, winners of the Scottish Cup, in the so-called 'Championship of the World'.

Mason died in Wolverhampton on 3 February 1941.

Wolves' record: 108 apps. 2 goals.

MASON, James

A well built footballer of some merit, Jimmy Mason played as an inside-forward for Wednesfield Rangers prior to joining Wolves in August 1907.

He was given limited opportunities in the first team during his two years at Molineux and left Wolves for Bristol Rovers in July 1909. He later served with Wrexham (August 1910), Llandudno Town (1913) and Rhyl Athletic (1914-15).

Mason was born in Wolverhampton in 1885 and died in Llandudno in 1952.

Wolves' record: 8 apps. one goal.

MASON, Jeremiah

Hardy left-back, no relation to Charles or James (q.v), Jerry Mason was born in Wolverhampton in 1865 and played for Blakenhall St. Luke's before joining Wolves in July 1889.

He spent two years at Molineux, as a reserve to Charlie, before leaving for Willenhall Swifts in May 1891.

Wolves' record: 7 apps.

MASON, Robert Henry

Inside-right Bobby Mason won League championship medals with Wolverhampton Wanderers in consecutive seasons, 1957-58 and 1958-59, but missed the 1960 FA Cup Final after losing his place to Barry Stobart.

Mason, who was born in Tipton on 22 March 1936, spent two seasons as an amateur on the Molineux staff before becoming a full-time professional in May 1953. His League debut was hardly an auspicious occasion when in November 1955, Wolves were hammered 5-1 at Kenilworth Road, but he quickly put that defeat, and disappointment, behind him and did well after that, going

Bobby Mason

on to play in two championship-winning sides.

Mason opened Wolves' second championship season with a hat-trick in a 5-1 home win over Nottingham Forest and in his time at Molineux he was never out of place in a front-line that included the likes of wingers Norman Deeley, Mickey Lill and Jimmy Mullen, centre-forward Jimmy Murray and inside-men Peter Broadbent, Dennis Wilshaw and Colin Booth.

In May 1962, after a short period with Chelmsford City in the Southern League, Mason joined Leyton Orient for £10,000. He made 23 League appearances for the O's before retiring from first-class football in 1965, following a spell with non-League side Poole Town.

He returned to the Midlands to work, although in later years he moved to Christchurch in Dorset where he resides today.

Wolves' record: 173 apps. 54 goals.

MASTERS, Neil Bradley

An Irishman, born in Ballymena on 25 May 1972, full-back Neil Masters played over 50 games for AFC Bournemouth before joining Wolves for £300,000 three days prior to Christmas, 1993.

He started his career in his homeland and came over to England to sign for the Cherries in August 1990 after representing his country at Youth team level. Unfortunately niggling injuries disrupted his performances at Molineux and in March 1997 he joined Gillingham for £150,000.

Masters left the League scene in May 1998 with only 74 senior appearances under his belt.

Wolves' record: 10 apps. 2 goals

MATTHEWS, Michael

Born in Hull on 25 September 1960, Mick Matthews represented Yorkshire Boys as a teenager before joining Wolves as an apprentice in August 1976, turning professional at Molineux in October 1978.

A strong, hard working midfielder, he did well with the Wanderers before transferring to Scunthorpe United for £5,000 in February 1984. After a brief spell with Peterborough United (no first team outings), he assisted the Humberside club, North Ferriby Unted (August 1985) before joining Halifax Town in September 1986.

A little over two years later - in December 1988 - a fee of £25,000 took Matthews to Scarborough.

He switched his allegiance to Stockport County for £15,000 in February 1989, went back for a second spell with Scarborough (for £15,000) in December 1989 and after serving Peterborough United (again) from June 1990, he had a second stint with North Ferriby United.

Rejoining Hull City in August 1991, Matthews remained at Boothferry Park until May 1992. He then went back to play for Halifax Town, quitting the League scene in May 1993 with 434 appearances under his belt, having done extremely well in the lower Divisions. He was a member of the over '35s Wolves team during the period 1997-2000.

Wolves' record: 79+4 sub apps. 7 goals.

MATTHIAS, John Samuel

Before he was forced to retire through injury in June 1902 at the age of 24, Jack Matthias had performed superbly well as a full-back and central defender with Shrewsbury Town (August 1896), Wolves (May 1897) and Wrexham (from August 1901 to May 1902). Born in Broughton near Wrexham in June 1878, he came through his early footballing career with Brymbo Institute (from 1891) before joining Shrewsbury. A Welsh international, capped five times between 1896 and 1900 (once as a Wolves player) Matthias was as keen as mustard, always totally committed, but unfortunately his career ended after suffering a bad knee injury playing for Wales against Scotland when he collided with John Bell. Thereafter he struggled to regain full fitness. When he joined Shrewsbury he became one of the Shropshire club's first paid players.

A fine cricketer with Broughton CC, Matthias worked at Brymbo Steel Works for many years and played in the work's band. He was also a caretaker and Sunday School teacher at a local church, positions he held until his death in the village of Moss, near Wrexham, on 16 November 1938.

Wolves' record: 45 apps.

MAY, George James

George 'Kosher' May was a solidly built wing-half, bold and brave in the tackle who did far better in non-League circles than he did with Wolves.

Born in Aston, Birmingham in May 1891, he was educated in Bromsgrove and played for Redditch and Verity Athletic (Birmingham Works Association with Ted Collins) before signing professional forms at Molineux in July 1908.

He stayed with Wolves for two seasons before transferring to Nuneaton Town in May 1910, later assisting Atherstone (1912-14).

Wolves' record: 16 apps.

MAYSON, Thomas F

Adroit in footwork, Tom Mayson was a classy forward, a star on his own in some games, who was well into his thirties when he joined Wolves.

His age was certainly against him and he never really adapted to the system used at Molineux. Born in Whitehaven on 8 December 1886, he spent quite some time playing in the Northern Alliance with Walker Celtic before entering the Football League with Burnley in December 1907.

From Turf Moor he moved to Grimsby Town (£300 in October 1911) and after spells with Everton (July 1919) and Pontypridd (£350 in July 1920) he was recruited by Wolves in August 1921. Ten months later (in June 1922) he moved to Aberdare Athletic where he stayed until May 1926 and on retiring he became trainer at Queens Park Rangers (retaining this position until 1933). During the First World War Mayson guested for Leeds City and he gained a Welsh Cup winners medal with Pontypridd in 1921. Mayson, who broke a leg during the 1912-13 season, died in Cleveland in 1972.

Wolves' record: 2 apps.

MEEK, Harold Leonard

Harry Leek spent just five months at Molineux - from November 1925 until March 1926. An inside-left, born in Belfast in 1903, he played initially for Belfast Rangers and then Cliftonville and Glentoran before joining Wolves.

On leaving Molineux he returned to Ireland to sign for Shelbourne, later assisting Burradon FC.

Wolves' record: 8 apps. one goal.

MELIA, James John

Inside-forward Jimmy Melia was born in Liverpool on 1 November 1937, fifth in a family of eleven children. He played for Liverpool Boys and was on the groundstaff at Anfield in 1953, turning professional with Liverpool in November 1954.

A clever schemer, with good vision and passing technique, he spent the next ten years on Merseyside before transferring to Wolves for £55,000 in March 1964, after helping the Reds win promotion to Division One in 1962. He stayed with Wolves for seven months, failing to settle in the Midlands and consequently, in the November was sold to Southampton for £30,000. Four years later he went to Aldershot for £9,000 and was player-manager at The Recreation Ground from April 1969 to January 1972. Melia took up a similar position with Crewe Alexandra

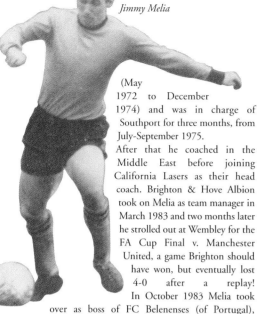

Jimmy Melia

(May 1972 to December 1974) and was in charge of Southport for three months, from July-September 1975.

After that he coached in the Middle East before joining California Lasers as their head coach. Brighton & Hove Albion took on Melia as team manager in March 1983 and two months later he strolled out at Wembley for the FA Cup Final v. Manchester United, a game Brighton should have won, but eventually lost 4-0 after a replay!

In October 1983 Melia took over as boss of FC Belenenses (of Portugal), remaining there for two years. From July to November 1986 he managed Stockport County and in 1992 went to coach in Texas. He remained in football for a short time after that, taking a variety of jobs before coaching in the Far East in 1993-94 and also back in Texas.

In his League career Melia, easily recognisable by his receding hairline, scored 105 goals in 571 League games (76 in 269 outings for Liverpool).

Capped twice by England at senior level, having earlier represented his country as a schoolboy and youth team player, he also turned out for the Football League XI.

NB - It is interesting to know that Melia helped Liverpool win the First Division title in 1963-64, was relegated with Wolves the following season and then gained promotion back to the top flight with Southampton in 1966-67.

Wolves' record: 24 apps. 4 goals.

MELROSE, James Millsopp

Ginger-haired Jim Melrose was a useful striker, born in Glasgow on 7 October 1958, who played for Eastercraigs FC before joining Partick Thistle in 1975.

After that he became something of a soccer nomad serving, in turn, with Leicester City (signed for £25,000 in July 1980), Coventry City (secured in a player-exchange deal involving Tommy English in September 1982), Celtic (captured for £100,000 in August 1987), Wolves (on loan, September-October 1984), Manchester City (bought for £40,000, November 1984), Charlton Athletic (acquired for £45,000, March 1986), Leeds United (a £50,000 buy, September 1987), Shrewsbury Town (on loan, February 1988, joining the Shrews for £50,000 the following month), Macclesfield Town (on a free transfer in July 1989) and finally Curzon Athletic (from October 1990 to May 1991).

He won eight Scottish Under-21 caps and twice represented for the Scottish League. With Celtic Melrose gained runners-up medals in both the Scottish Cup and League Cup competitions in 1984 and then played for Charlton in the Full Members Cup Final at Wembley in 1987.

A year later Melrose received a fractured cheek-bone during an incident involving Swindon's Chris Kamara. At Shrewsbury Magistrates Court Kamara was found guilty of assault, and fined £1,200 (plus costs). In his professional career north and south of the border, Melrose scored 131 goals in 486 appearances. He later worked as a 'rep' in the West Midlands.

Wolves' record: 8+1 sub apps. 4 goals.

METCALF, Thomas Clark

Wolves recruited half-back Tommy Metcalf from Salisbury City in July 1906 as cover for the Reverend Kenneth Hunt and Alf Bishop. He got few opportunities to show what he was made of and left Molineux in March 1909 for Bristol Rovers.

Born in Burton-on-Trent in 1879, Metcalf went abroad before the Great War.

Wolves' record: 9 apps.

MICKLEWRIGHT, William

Billy Micklewright was a stocky right-winger, reserve to Billy Harrison, who spent three years at Molineux: June 1909 to May 1912.

Born in Reading circa 1890, he moved to Molineux from Wellington Town and on leaving Wolves entered non-League football in Berkshire.

Wolves' record: 5 apps.

MIDDLETON, Henry

Centre-forward Harry Middleton was the first Wolves player to be capped by England at Youth international level.

Unfortunately he became the odd man out at Molineux simply because there were so many other useful strikers registered with the club at the same time. Consequently he missed out and was transferred to Scunthorpe United in September 1959.

Born in Birmingham on 18 March 1937, Middleton started off as an amateur at Molineux, turning professional in August 1954. Then, over the next five years, he made only one senior appearance - in a 2-1 defeat at Everton in April 1956 when he deputised on the right-wing for Johnny Hancocks.

From Scunthorpe, he switched to Portsmouth in June 1961 and eight months later he joined Shrewsbury Town. After netting 37 goals in 85 League games for the Shrews he was transferred to Mansfield Town in November 1964 and continued to score regularly for the Stags (24 goals in 46 League outings). In March 1966 he returned to the West Midlands to sign for Walsall and at Fellows Park he again did well, scoring 30 goals in 65 senior appearances for the Saddlers.

He left Walsall in May 1968 for Worcester City, retiring in 1970. In his League career Middleton scored 103 goals in

236 games - and his claim to fame with Wolves was his five goals in a 10-0 FA Youth Cup win over his future club Walsall in 1954-55.

Wolves' record: one app.

MILLER, David

David Miller was a tough-looking footballer, as hard as nails, muscular, weighty and versatile, able to occupy a number of positions, including those of left-half, inside-forward or winger.

Born in Middlesbrough on 21 January 1921, he played for South Bank FC before becoming a professional with Middlesbrough in 1938.

David Miller

Near the end of the war (when he served in the RAF) he moved from Ayresome Park to Molineux (August 1945) and spent two seasons with Wolves before transferring to Derby County in April 1947.

From the Baseball Ground he moved to Doncaster Rovers (January 1948) and after a short spell with Aldershot (March to May 1954) rounded off his career by assisting Boston United, retiring through injury in 1957.

In fact, during his time with Boston he returned to his old stamping ground at Derby and helped inflict upon the Rams a hefty 6-1 FA Cup hammering in 1955-56.

Miller appeared in more than 150 games during his six years with Doncaster whom he helped win the Third Division (North) championship in 1950.

Wolves' record: 2 apps.

MILLER, George

George Miller was a long-striding wing-half, who played in an international trial for Scotland, represented the Scottish League XI and starred in the 1962 Scottish Cup Final while with Dunfermline Athletic, the club he assisted for four years prior to joining Wolves for £26,000 in October 1964.

Born in Larkhall, Lanarkshire on 20 May 1939, his performances at Molineux were mixed and he left the club to sign to return to Scotland in May 1966, retiring in 1970.

Wolves' record: 45 apps. 3 goals.

MILLER, Kenneth

Scotland international Kenny Miller was born in Edinburgh on 23 December 1979 and played for Hibernian, Stenhousemuir (on loan) and Glasgow Rangers (signed for £2 million from Easter Road in the summer of 2000) before joining Wolves for an undisclosed fee in June 2001 (initially on a three-month contract). Unfortunately three months into his Molineux career he fractured his collarbone against Nottingham Forest and

returned to Ibrox Park for treatment.

A striker, with dash and commitment, he netted eight goals in 27 Scottish Premiership games during his only season at Ibrox Park.

Wolves' record: 4 apps.

MILLER, Thomas John

Physically strong, left-winger Jack Miller, with his well-manicured moustache, was a fine footballer.

Born in Hednesford early in 1875, he joined Wolves from

John Miller

Hednesford Town in September 1895, initially as cover for David Black and Alf Griffin.

After establishing himself in the side, he was virtually an ever-present from September 1896 to November 1904. Miller, who represented the Football League in 1899-1900, left Molinuex for Stoke for £400 in the summer of 1905 and after scoring five goals in 63 games for the Potters he moved, in April 1907, to Willenhall.

Miller retired in 1910 to become a publican.

Wolves' record: 249 apps. 49 goals.

MILLS, Rowan Lee

Tall, hardworking and very efficient goalscorer, born in Mexborough on 10 July 1970, Lee Mills played his early football with the Stocksbridge Park Steels Works team, joining Wolves as a full-time professional in December 1992.

He failed to establish himself in the side at Molineux and in February 1995 was transferred to Derby County for

£400,000, moving on to Port Vale in August 1995 in a £475,000 deal involving Robin Van der Laan (Mills being rated at £200,000).

He did very well at Vale Park (under manager John Rudge) but was perhaps surprisingly sold (certainly as far as the ardent Vale supporters were concerned) to Bradford City for £1 million in August 1998.

In season 1998-99 he top-scored for the Yorkshire club, helping them reach the Premiership as runners-up to Sunderland. In March 2000 Mills was loaned out to struggling Manchester City and when the season ended so did his career with the Bantams as Mills was transferred to Portsmouth, again for a fee of £1 million.

At Fratton Park he teamed up with another ex-Wolves striker Steve Claridge.

Wolves' record: 19+14 sub apps. 4 goals.

MITTON, John

Solid defender Jack Mitton was born at Todmorden on 7 November 1895 and played his early football for Brierfield FC and as an amateur for Burnley before guesting for Bury from 1916.

By the time World War One had ended Mitton was on Exeter City's books, but in October 1920 Sunderland, then a force in the First Division, thought enough of him to pay the Grecians £250 for his signature after he had made only 11 League appearances in Exeter's first season in the new Third Division.

In the Southern League he had been ever-present in 1919-20 and his brother James had also played in the same Exeter team.

For the Wearsiders, Mitton made 82 senior appearances, scoring seven goals before Wolves signed him for £500 in May 1924, just after they had won the Third Division (North) championship. As they re-established themselves in the Second, finishing sixth, Mitton made 36 League appearances and the Molineux fans loved his powerful performances in defence. He also skippered the side occasionally.

In May 1927, Wolves sold him to Southampton for £150, but he played only eight times for the Saints before being released in the 1928 close season. After a spell in the Hampshire County League he retired in 1930. Mitton died in Kings Lynn on 5 August 1983.

Wolves' record: 107 apps. 6 goals.

MORRIS, William Walker

Bill Morris was born a goal-kick away from West Bromwich Albion's ground at The Hawthorns, on 26 March 1913, and was educated at Handsworth New Road and Niniveh Road Schools.

He played his early football for Handsworth Old Boys and the Baggies' colts side and was also with Halesowen Town before Albion let him slip through their net - allowing him to sign for Wolves as a professional in May 1933.

Morris was the regular centre-half until the emergence of

Bill Morris

Stan Cullis, after which he switched to right-back and it was in that position that he won three full England caps in 1938-39, the same season he played in the FA Cup Final against Portsmouth at Wembley. Morris, who was famed for running backwards at speed, was only 24 when the Football League was suspended on the outbreak of war (in September 1939) and when competitive soccer resumed in August 1946 he was past his 30th birthday, having guested for Wrexham during the hostilities.

The following year (June 1947) he retired. Morris made only ten appearances for the club in that first post-war season when Wolves finished third in Division One, and altogether he totalled close on 200 senior appearances as well as starring in 68 wartime games. In fact, during one League Cup North game v. Birmingham in 1944-45 he scored a dramatic winning goal in the 153rd minute of a prolonged encounter!

After leaving Wolves he enjoyed two seasons with Dudley Town in the Birmingham Combination, playing at centre-forward. Indeed, it was as a forward that he joined Wolves in the first place.

Morris died in old people's home in Dudley in 1995.

Wolves' record: 197 apps. 3 goals.

MORRISSEY, John Joseph

Left-winger Johnny Morrissey followed his father into League football, Morrissey senior having played for Liverpool, Everton and Oldham Athletic between 1957 and 1973.

Morrissey junior was born in Liverpool on 8 March 1965 and signed as a junior for Everton in 1981, turning professional at Goodison Park in March 1983. After representing England at Youth team level and making just two appearances for the Merseysiders he was transferred to Wolves in August 1985.

Playing in a struggling team, he never really settled at Molineux and in October 1985 was sold to Tranmere Rovers for £8,000. Over the next 12 years he did very well at Prenton Park, scoring more than 60 goals in over 550 senior appearances.

Morrissey was awarded a testimonial for his service to Tranmere (a game against his former club Everton in July 1999).

Wolves' record: 6+5 sub apps. one goal.

MOSS, Craig Anthony

Born in Birmingham on 11 March 1961, left-winger Craig Moss, whose brother Paul was also on Wolves' books in the mid-1970s, had a relatively short career in League football. He joined the apprentice ranks at Molineux in June 1977 and turned professional in March 1979.

Unfortunately he became surplus to requirements and left the club in 1982, moving into non-League soccer, first with Worcester City, then Trowbridge Town and Worcester City again.

Wolves' record: 4 apps.

MOUNTFIELD, Derek Neal

Wolves signed experienced defender Derek Mountfield from Aston Villa for £150,000 in November 1991 and by the time new manager Graham Taylor released him in May 1994 Mountfield had made over 90 senior appearances for the club.

He was born in Liverpool on 2 November 1962 and began his professional career with Tranmere Rovers in November 1980 after two years as an apprentice at Prenton Park. He had made only 29 appearances for Tranmere when Everton paid £30,000 for his signature in June 1982.

It was a good move for Mountfield who went on to make 154 appearances for the Goodison club, scoring 25 goals and helping them to the Football League championship glory in 1985 and 1987, FA Cup success in 1984 and European Cup-winners' Cup joy in 1985. Villa paid £450,000 for Mountfield in June 1988 and he made 120 appearances for them before moving to Wolves.

From Molineux Mountfield went to Carlisle United on a free transfer in August 1994 and after a loan spell with Northampton Town (October 1995) he switched back to the Midlands to sign for Walsall (November 1995). In July 1997 he was appointed player-coach at The Bescot Stadium and whilst with the Saddlers took his senior appearance tally to past the 600 mark.

In September 1998 Mountfield joined Bromsgrove Rovers and in January 1999 he became caretaker-assistant manager of Scarborough. He represented England at both Under-21 and 'B' team levels.

Wolves' record: 87+4 sub apps. 5 goals.

MULHOLLAND, Thomas

Reserve inside-forward at Molineux, Tommy Mulholland (5ft 6ins tall, 10st 4lbs in weight) was born in Ireland in 1890 and played for Distillery, Leeds City (May 1909) and Distillery again before joining Wolves in November 1912.

He spent less than a season at Molineux, moving to Brewood and then onto Scunthorpe and Lindsey United. In 1913 he went 'back 'home' to sign for Belfast Celtic and played briefly for Hartlepool United before ending his career in Ireland with Cliftonville.

Wolves' record: 6 apps. one goal.

MULLEN, James

Speedy left winger Jimmy Mullen was another of the great names in a magnificent Wolves side of the post-war era, a player destined to be a star from his schooldays, he gave Wolves 23 years' splendid service.

With the club he gained three League championship medals, won an FA Cup winners' medal and collected 12 full England caps as well as appearing in three 'B' internationals and having outings for the Football League. He also helped Wolves win the Wartime League (North) Cup in 1942.

A guest for Leicester City, Newcastle United and

Jimmy Mullen

MUNRO, Francis Michael

Sturdy centre-half Frank Munro made almost 300 League appearances for Wolves. Born at Broughty Ferry, near Dundee, on 25 October 1947, he was released by Chelsea as a youngster having been on amateur forms at Stamford Bridge. On leaving London he signed for his home town club, Dundee United, with whom he won four Scottish youth caps and two amateur caps before becoming a professional in July 1963. In October 1966 he was transferred to Aberdeen and the following year played on the losing side in the Scottish Cup Final.

Wolves took a keen interest after he had scored a hat-trick (including two penalties) against them in a summer tournament in the USA in 1967 and he joined the Molineux ranks for £55,000 in January 1968. A tough-tackling defender he was banned for a month during the 1969-70 season, but came back with great tenacity.

For Wolves, he played in the 1972 UEFA Cup Final and gained a League Cup winners' prize in 1974.

He was also capped four times by Scotland at Under-23 level and appeared in nine senior internationals for his country whilst with Wolves, whom he helped win the Second Division title in 1976-77. However, in December 1977 they allowed him to move for Celtic for £20,000 after he had been on loan to the Parkhead club for two months.

Munro appeared for Celtic in the 1978 Scottish League Cup Final and then went into Australian football, playing for Hellas and later coaching Albion Rovers, Hamlyn Rangers and Keilor Austria. He returned to England but, alas, in 1993 he suffered the first of two strokes.

Wolves fans loved him and he scored some vital goals for the club as well as being a magnificent defender.

Wolves' record: 365+6 sub apps. 19 goals.

Frank Munro

Darlington during the war, Mullen also played for Northern Command against Western Command, scoring a hat-trick in the last ten minutes of this game to earn his side a 3-3 draw. One of his full caps came as a substitute for Stan Mortensen against Belgium in Brussels in 1950. It was the first time that England had used a sub and 15 minutes after coming on, Mullen scored. In all he appeared in more than 480 senior games for Wolves and scored well over 100 goals, and that was in addition to his 91 wartime appearances (27 goals), when he was also an Army Corporal.

Mullen, who was born at Newcastle-upon-Tyne on 6 January 1923, had a terrific shot and he was already an England schoolboy star when he joined the Molineux staff in July 1937, at the age of 14. He made a somewhat sensational League debut, when he played against Leeds in February 1939, when he was barely 16, and Major Frank Buckley signed him on professional forms as soon as he could, in January 1940.

With Mullen on the left flank and Hancocks on the right, the Wolves forward line of the 1940s and early '50s played some of the most attractive attacking football the game has ever seen. Indeed, they were regarded as the best pair of club wingers in the country (perhaps in Europe, even the world). Jimmy Mullen, who later ran his own sports shop in Wolverhampton, was only 64 when he died in Oct 1987.

Wolves' record: 486 apps. 112 goals.

MURRAY, James Robert

Jimmy Murray had a magnificent scoring record for Wolves, and all told in his professional career (when he also served with Manchester City and Walsall) he struck 211 goals in 404 League games.

With Wolves he gained two League championship winners' medals, an FA Cup winners' medal two England Under-23 caps and he represented the Football League. Born in Dover on 11 October 1935, Murray joined Wolves as a full-time professional in November 1953 after George Poyser, the man who also spotted Peter Broadbent, recommended him to championship-chasing Wanderers. In 1955, he was brought in to the side to replace the injured Roy Swinbourne and soon settled down, stayed there for the rest of the season, scoring 11 goals in 25 games as Wolves finished third.

In the first of two successive championship-winning seasons, 1957-58, he was leading scorer with 29 goals, and he top-scored with 21 when the title was retained the following season. In 1960 he played in the side which beat Blackburn Rovers in the FA Cup Final and the following year set a Wolves' record by scoring a double hat-trick (six goals) for the reserves v. Chesterfield in a Central League match.

Although he stood only 5ft 9in, Murray gave opposing defenders plenty to think about and after he moved to Manchester City for £27,000 in November 1963 he continued his rich vein of form at Maine Road. In his first six games for City he scored 12 goals including two hat-tricks as he formed a great striking partnership with former West Brom and England centre-forward Derek Kevan.

After 43 goals in 70 games for City, Murray was transferred to Walsall. He netted 15 goals in 64 League and Cup games for the Saddlers before dropping into non-League football with Telford United in August 1969, helping the Shropshire club to consecutive FA Trophy Finals at Wembley. He retired in 1971 and ran a very successful greengrocery business in Tamworth for 24 years until 1995.

Murray now lives in Lichfield and works for a contract car hire firm.

Wolves' record: 299 apps. 166 goals.

MUSCAT, Kevin Vincent

Despite being born in Crawley, Sussex on 7 August 1973, left-back Kevin Muscat was brought up in Australia.

Now an established Antipodean, he represented the Victoria State side, played in two Youth World Cup tournaments (1991 and 1993) and in the Olympic Games in Atlanta, and starred for South Melbourne before entering English League football by signing for Crystal Palace for £35,000 in August 1996.

An Aussie international (with at least 34 full caps in his locker, plus others at youth and Under-23 levels) he is a strong-tackling defender, who made over 60 appearances

Jimmy Murray

for the London club, helping them gain Premiership status before transferring to Wolves in October 1997.

The £1 million deal of which £200,000 was placed on Muscat's had, also saw striker Dougie Freedman move to Molineux from Selhurst Park, while Jamie Smith went in the opposite direction. Muscat, who made his debut for Wolves in the Nationwide home League game v. Tranmere Rovers 24 hours after joining the club, had his disciplinary problems at Molineux, picking up 10 yellow cards in 27 games in 1997-98 and another handful the following season when he was voted Wolves 'Player of the Year.'

In December 1998, he was hauled before the FA for an alleged 'over-the-top-tackle' on Norwich City Welsh international Craig Bellamy. He had also been involved in an incident with Charlton's Matty Holmes the previous season which resulted in the London-based player suffering a broken left leg which required lengthy surgery whereby a metal rod was inserted into his limb. Holmes has since quit competitive football on medical advice.

NB - Muscat, who has captained both Wolves and Australia, scored four goals for his country when they hammered hapless Tonga 22-0 in a qualifying game for the 2002 World Cup, and soon afterwards he led his country when they whipped American Samoa 31-0 in the same competition.

Wolves' record: 175+2 sub apps. 4 goals*

Kevin Muscat

MUTCH, Andrew Todd

Striker Andy Mutch, a former Liverpool and Everton apprentice who was born on Merseyside on 28 December 1963, was playing in non-League football with Southport when Wolves boss Sammy Chapman gave him another chance to make the grade! Wanderers signed him in February 1986

Andy Mutch

and after making his League debut the following month Mutch ended the season with seven goals in 15 games. Alas, he came too late to prevent Wolves dropping into the Fourth Division. The following season they lost out in the Play-off Final and then in consecutive seasons jumped from the Fourth Division to the Second with Mutch enjoying a lucrative goals partnership with Steve Bull.

In addition, Wolves won the Sherpa Van Trophy in 1988, Mutch scoring in the Final against Burnley. In that spectacularly successful season he and goalkeeper Mark Kendall were the only ever-presents in the Wolves team. In the summer of 1989 his marksmanship was rewarded with England 'B' honours, when he played against Switzerland, Norway and Iceland.

As Wolves consolidated themselves in the Second Division (which, of course, eventually became the First when the Premier League was formed), Mutch continued to find the net, although the goals were few and far between in the higher sphere and he missed much of the 1990-91 season.

In August 1993, Swindon Town, newly promoted to the Premiership, paid £250,000 for his signature but Mutch and the Robins found life desperately difficult in the top flight. It did not prove a happy move for Mutch who, after a loan spell with Wigan Athletic (August-September 1995), moved to Stockport County in April 1996, and he helped the Edgeley Park club win promotion to the First Division the following year. In July 1998 Mutch left Stockport to sign for the Conference side Barrow, later rejoining his old club Southport (January 1999) before linking up with Telford United early in 1999 as player/assistant-manager.

Wolves' record: 325+13 sub apps. 105 goals.

N

MYERS, James Henry

Outside-left Jim Myers played for Wolves in season 1938-39, acting as reserve to Teddy Maguire and Dicky Dorsett. A Yorkshireman, born in Barnsley on 5 March 1920, he was signed from Barnsley (where he hadn't made a first team appearance) in June 1938 and left Molineux for Cardiff City during the first part of the war. He did appear in League football when it recommenced in 1946.
Wolves' record: 3 apps.

MYNARD, Leslie Daniel

Left-winger Les Mynard was born in Bewdley on 19 December 1925. He played for his home-town club, Bewdley, before joining Wolves for season 1945-46.
Basically a reserve at Molineux, his first team appearances were restricted and in July 1949 he was transferred to Derby County, later assisting Scunthorpe United (August 1952 to May 1953) before reverting back to non-League soccer.
Wolves' record: 3 apps.

NAYLOR, Lee Martyn

Defender Lee Naylor made his Football League debut for Wolves in the televised local derby against Birmingham City at St. Andrew's in October 1997 (lost 1-0).
Born in Walsall on 19 March 1980 and educated at Sneyd Community School, Walsall, he joined Wolves in the summer of 1996, turning professional on his eighteenth birthday. He represented Wolverhampton Boys before embarking on his career at Molineux and has since played for England at Youth team level, representing his country in the 15th European Under-18 championships in Spain in April 1999 and also at Under-21 level.
Naylor, who prefers the left wing-back position, had an excellent 2000-01 season when as well as being voted 'Player of the Year' he also took his appearance-tally past the 135 mark as well as gaining more international honours at Under-21 level v. Mexico and Greece.
Wolves' record: 125+16 sub apps. 5 goals*

NDAH, George Ethialimolisa

Hard-shooting, strong-running striker George Ndah had the ill-luck to break a leg in the local derby against rivals West Bromwich Albion in October 1999 - only his third game for the club following his £1 million transfer from Swindon Town.
He battled hard and long to regain full fitness but the crack in the fibia took time to heal and it wasn't until April that he got back into match action. However, it was a different story in 2000-01 as Ndah came on strongly, scoring some smart goals and now he's hoping for better things as time progresses.
Born in Dulwich, London on 23 December 1974, he signed as a trainee for Crystal Palace in June 1991, and after representing England at youth team level, turned professional at Selhurst Park in August 1992.
He went on to score 11 goals in exactly 100 first-class games for the Eagles, and had loan spells with both AFC Bournemouth in 1993 & Gillingham in 1997, before transferring to Swindon Town for £500,000 in Nov 1997. He continued to find the net for the Robins, notching a further 115 goals in 74 League and Cup appearances prior to his big-money move to Molineux by Mark McGhee.
Wolves' record: 29+9 sub apps. 6 goals*

NEEDHAM, Archibald

Forceful inside-forward Archie Needham spent a season at Molineux when he played alongside his brother Jack (q.v). Born in Sheffield in August 1881, he represented Sheffield Schools before joining Sheffield United for the 1901-02 season. In the summer of 1905 he transferred to Crystal Palace for whom he scored 27 goals in 104 outings.
Afterwards he had a spell with Glossop North End (from June 1909) before signing for Wolves in August 1910. Leaving Molineux for Brighton & Hove Albion in July 1911, Needham did not play football after World War One and he died in Sussex in 1961.
Wolves' record: 35 apps. 7 goals.

NEEDHAM, John

Jack Needham (Archie's younger brother) was a goalscoring utility forward, who starred for Wolves between April 1910 and January 1920.
Needham was born at Newstead, Notts on 4 March 1887 and played for Mansfield Wesleyans and Mansfield Invicta before joining Mansfield in July 1907 (the present day Mansfield Town did not come into being until the summer of 1910). From there Needham - known as 'Mr Consistency' - switched to Birmingham and he scored five goals in 20 games for the Blues between June 1909 and April 1910 when he was transferred to Wolves.
He made his debut in the last game of that season, scoring in a 3-2 win over Manchester City at Molineux. The following season Needham was Wolves' top scorer with 13 goals. Before the war he formed an excellent left-wing partnership, first with Archie Walker, then Sammy Brooks and occasionally Tommy Yule.
Needham, who guested for Port Vale in 1916-17, was still in the Wanderers side when League football resumed in 1919-20. But towards the end of that season he was transferred to Hull City, who probably remembered the hat-trick he had scored against them in an 8-0 drubbing at Molineux back in November 1911.
By now, though, Needham's powers were waning and he managed only one goal in 18 games for the Tigers before drifting out of League football in 1922.
Wolves' record: 206 apps. 61 goals.

NEIL, Patrick Thomas

Born in Portsmouth on 24 October 1937, left winger Pat Neil won an amateur cap for England as a teenager with Portsmouth, whom he joined on leaving school in 1953. He never turned professional and after scoring three goals in nine League games for Pompey he was transferred to Wolves in August 1956.

Recruited by Stan Cullis, he was basically a reserve at Molineux and never really threatened the club's other main wingers, Harry Hooper, Jimmy Mullen and Norman Deeley (Johnny Hancocks was by now in the reserves and preparing to move on).

He left Wolves for Pegasus in the summer of 1957 and later returned for a second spell at Fratton Park (1962) before quitting League soccer the following year.

Wolves' record: 4 apps. one goal.

NELSON, John Henry

Jack Nelson was born in Chorley on 15 March 1906 and worked in a bleach factory in the Lancashire town whilst playing for the local club, Chorley All Saints and then Chorley Town.

He became a full-time professional with Preston North End in March 1926 and was transferred to Wolves in November 1932, after making 72 League appearances whilst at Deepdale.

Initially, he arrived as cover for the centre-half position in a Wolves team which had just returned to the First Division and was struggling in their first season back in the top flight, eventually finishing 20th. Nelson, a tough stopper, a 'policeman' type of defender standing 6ft 2ins tall, played an important part in their fight against instant relegation. He stayed with Wolves for another two seasons, in which they battled to improve on lowly positions, before moving to Luton Town in May 1935.

Nelson spent two seasons at Kenilworth Road, making 134 appearances and helping the Hatters win the Third Division (South) title in 1936-37. He later returned to Molineux as Wolves' trainer and prior to, during and immediately after the Second World War Nelson acted as trainer/coach at Walsall.

Also a very fine cricketer and tennis player, Nelson eventually retired to live in Wolverhampton where he remained until his death in May 1986.

Wolves' record: 75 apps. 4 goals.

NEWELL, Percy John

Full-back Percy Newell deputised for Dickie Baugh in Wolves' defence during his three seasons at Molineux. Born in Wolverhampton in 1901, he played for Stourbridge before joining Wolves in May 1920.

He returned to Stourbridge on leaving the club in August 1923 and later assisted Bloxwich Strollers.

Wolves' record: 10 apps.

NEWTON, Shaun O'Neill

Enterprising right wing-back or attacking midfielder Shaun Newton, who loves to go past defenders, joined Wolves from Charlton Athletic for £850,000 (with another £150,000 to follow after a set number of appearances) in August 2001.

Born in Camberwell, London on 20 August 1975, he signed as an apprentice with the Addicks in 1991, turning professional in July 1993. Capped three times by England at Under-21 level, he appeared in 285 senior games for Charlton (27 goals scored) and he helped them win the First Division championship and a place in the Premiership in 2000.

Wolves' record: 10 apps.*

NICHOLAS, Charles

Charlie Nicholas, who was to become a superstar with Celtic, Arsenal and Scotland, was having a trial with Wolves when one evening he was chased round the streets of Wolverhampton by a gang of Youths. He became homesick and returned to Glasgow!

NICHOLLS, Alfred

Smart, determined outside-right, Alf Nicholls was born in Birmingham circa 1875 and after attending Abbey Road School, he played, in turn, for Hockley Brook, Hockley Belmont, Walsall Primitives, Wednesbury Royal and Wednesbury Old Athletic before joining Wolves in August 1896.

He spent just a season at Molineux, moving to Walsall Alma in April 1897. He later assisted Alma Swifts and Bushbury Park, and scored six goals for the latter club against Featherstone in 1900.

Wolves' record: 3 apps. 2 goals.

NIELSEN, Allan

Born in Esbjerg, Denmark on 13 March 1971, attacking midfielder Allan Nielsen joined Tottenham Hotspur for £1.75 million from Brondby IF in September 1996, having previously served with FC Esbjerg, Bayern Munich, FC Sion (Switzerland), FC Odense and FC Copenhagen.

He spent almost five years at White Hart Lane during which time he scored 18 goals in 115 Premier League and Cup games and had a loan spell with Wolves (March-May 2000) before transferring to Watford for £2.25 in the summer of 2001. Capped 30 times by his country during his time at White Hart Lane (he is now chasing the 40 mark) Nielsen is a direct player, who loves to drive forward.

Wolves' record: 7 apps 2 goals.

NIESTROJ, Robert

Tall, hard-working midfielder, Robert Niestroj was signed from Fortuna Dusseldorf for £350,000 in October 1998. He had been associated with the Dusseldorf club since he was a fourteen year-old and had been a professional in the Bundesliga since 1993. He agreed a three-and-a-half year contract at Molineux.

Born in Germany on 2 December 1974, he made his Wolves debut, as a second-half substitute, in the local derby with neighbours West Bromwich Albion at the

Hawthorns in November 1998. Unfortunately he struggled to hold down a first team place and in July 2000 he left Molineux to sign for OF Iraklion in Greece.
Wolves' record: 3+3 sub apps.

NIGHTINGALE, John Gladstone
Wolves recruited left-winger Jack Nightingale from Kidderminster Harriers in December 1919.
Born in Oldbury in June 1899, and a player with Brandhall Rovers, he unfortunately failed to make the grade at Molineux and left for Shrewsbury Town in July 1920. He switched to Brighton & Hove Albion in 1921 for whom he made almost 200 senior appearances up to 1927, when he returned to Shrewsbury.
On retiring Nightingale moved down to Sussex, living in Hove until his death in December 1967.
Wolves' record: 3 apps.

NIXON, Eric Walter
A real soccer journeyman, goalkeeper Eric Nixon, tall, agile, with a safe pair of hands, confident with his kicking and courageous, has had a fine career in the Football League. Born in Manchester on 4 October 1962, he began his soccer life with Curzon Ashton and entered League action with Manchester City in 1983.

Eric Nixon

He remained registered at Maine Road until March 1988 when he was transferred to Tranmere Rovers for £60,000. During his five years with City, Nixon played on loan with Wolves (August-November 1986 - during which time he saved two penalties), Bradford City (November 1986) and Carlisle United (January-March 1987).
He went on to amass 431 senior appearances for Tranmere, up to May 1997 when he joined Stockport County for £100,000, having in between times served on loan with Reading (January 1996) and Blackpool (February 1996). In September 1998 Nixon joined Wigan Athletic (on loan from Edgeley Park), making the move a permanent one in March 1999.
Four months later he returned to his former club, Tranmere Rovers and when the 2000-01 season came to a close Nixon, who by now was employed as player-coach at Prenton Park, had taken his career appearance-tally (in major League and Cup competitions) to well past the 650 mark.
A great practical joker, he helped Tranmere win the Leyland DAF Trophy at Wembley in 1990.
NB - One interesting point is that Nixon played in every Division of the Football League over a period of six months from August 1986 to January 1987, lining up for Wolves (Div. 4), Bradford City (2), Southampton (1) and Carlisle United (3)....the quickest in League history.
Wolves' record: 16 apps.

NORTH, Stacey Stewart
Blond central defender Stacey North had an exceptionally long throw, once catapulting the ball almost 75 yards from the right-hand touchline when playing for Luton Town.
Born in Luton on 25 November 1964, North was on loan at Molineux from the Hatters during November and December 1985, having initially joined the staff at Kenilworth Road as a junior in 1980, turning professional in August 1982.
Capped by England at Youth team level, he went on to play in 25 League games for Luton before moving to The Hawthorns in December 1987.
He left Albion for Fulham in October 1990 for £135,000 after making more than 100 senior appearances for the Baggies. Unfortunately North was forced to quit football with serious knee and back injuries in January 1993.
Wolves' record: 3 apps.

NURSE, Daniel George
Right-half Dan Nurse was able to feed his forwards assiduously, a stern tackler, he was also strong-hearted in his overall play.
Born in Princes End, Tipton in June 1873, he attended Princes End School, played for Princes End FC and then Coseley before joining Wolves in June 1894. He spent seven excellent years at Molineux although he was only a regular in the first XI in 1895-96. In May 1901 he was transferred to West Bromwich Albion and at the end of his first season at The Hawthorns collected a Second Division championship medal as skipper of the Baggies.
In 1903 he represented the Football League and went on to play in 88 games for Albion before injury forced him into an early retirement in April 1905. Five years later he became a Director at The Hawthorns, a position he held until May 1927.
He was also elected as a Life Member of Albion in 1920 ...in recognition of his sterling effort in saving the club from going into liquidation in 1910.
Nurse died in West Bromwich in April 1959.
Wolves' record: 39 apps. one goal.

OAKES, Michael Christian
Born in Northfield, Birmingham on 30 October 1973, goalkeeper Michael Oakes joined Aston Villa as an apprentice in July 1989 and turned professional in July 1991.
Unable to gain a regular first team place, he went on loan to Scarborough (two games in September 1993), Bromsgrove Rovers and Gloucester City before transferring to Wolves for £400,000 in October 1999...after becoming third-choice goalkeeper at Villa

Park (behind David James and Peter Enckelman).

Oakes, in fact, had no hesitation in moving across the Midlands to Molineux when Wolves boss Colin Lee came in with a substantial bid. He had made 61 first-team appearances during his time at Villa Park and was also won six caps for England at Under-21 level.

An excellent shot-stopper Oakes was rated as one of the best goalkeepers in the First Division in the 2000-01 season.

NB - His father, Alan, appeared in 669 games for Manchester City and also played for Port Vale.

Wolves' record: 95 apps.

O'CONNOR, John Patrick

Small, frail-looking outside-right or inside-forward, Jack O'Connor was born in Wolverhampton circa 1901.

He played for Lea Hall Ramblers and Quarry Bank Rangers before joining Wolves in May 1923. He spent two years as a reserve at Molineux before transferring to Gillingham in August 1926.

He later assisted Tranmere Rovers, Darlington and Crewe Alexandra (all in season 1927-28), Flint Town (1928), Stafford Rangers (October 1929), Darlaston, Halesowen Town, Dudley Town, Netherton and Cradley Town, retiring in 1939-40 on the outbreak of World War Two.

Wolves' record: 11 apps. 2 goals.

O'GRADY, Michael

Despite his Irish-sounding name, Mike O'Grady was a Yorkshireman, born in Leeds on 11 October 1942. A smart utility forward, able to occupy both flanks as well as an inside berth, he joined Huddersfield Town on leaving school and turned professional with the Terriers in October 1959.

He did well at Huddersfield, scoring 26 goals in 160 League games, winning the first of his two full England caps and also lining up for his country in three Under-23 internationals. In October 1965 he was transferred to Leeds United for £30,000 and over the next four years became part of that fine Don Revie footballing-machine at Elland Road.

He netted 12 goals in 91 First Division appearances and helped United reach successive Fairs Cup Finals in 1967 and 1968 (gaining a winners medal in the latter) and carry off the League championship in 1969. He also added a second England cap to his collection, and represented the Football League on three occasions.

In September 1969, O'Grady joined Wolves for £80,000, remaining at Molineux for three years, although during this time he was plagued by injury and, indeed, he hardly got a first team outing after his initial campaign with the club.

After a loan spell with Birmingham City (February 1972 - being Blues' first loan player to make a League appearance) he was transferred to Rotherham United where he stayed until retiring through injury in May 1984.

Wolves' record: 35+6 sub apps. 6 goals.

O'HARA, Gerald John

Midfielder Gerry O'Hara was born in Wolverhampton on 3 December 1956. He joined Wolves on leaving school in the summer of 1972 and turned professional at Molineux in December 1974. He spent the next four years or so in the reserves, making only fleeting first team appearances before being released in May 1978.

Three months later (August 1978) he signed for Hereford United as a non-contract player, dropping out of League soccer in 1979 after only one game for the Bulls. O'Hara played for Bilston Town (two spells), Worcester City, Redditch (two spells), Willenhall, Dudley Town and Bridgnorth Town before retiring in 1995.

Wolves' record: 9+2 sub apps.

OLDERSHAW, Walter

Full-back Wally Ollershaw was first reserve to Charlie Mason during his one season with Wolves (1889-90). His only outing for the club was against Accrington on New Year's Day when Wolves lost 6-3!

Oldershaw was born in Walsall in 1867. He joined the club from Walsall Alma and left Molineux for Wednesbury Town.

Wolves' record: one app.

OLDFIELD, John Stephen

Goalkeeper John Oldfield was born in Lindrick on 19 August 1943. He joined Huddersfield Town on leaving school and turned professional at Leeds Road in August 1961. He made over 150 League appearances for the Terriers before transferring to Wolves in December 1969. A competent 'keeper, with good reflexes, he remained at Molineux for two years, acting in the main as reserve to Phil Parkes. A month before leaving Wolves he had a loan spell with Crewe Alexandra (November) and signed for Bradford City in December 1971, remaining at Valley Parade until May 1973, making 34 appearances for the Bantams.

Wolves' record: 19 apps.

OLDROYD, Darren Robert

It was anticipated that Darren Oldroyd would take over the right-back berth from Geoff Palmer at Molineux, but unfortunately he was dogged by injury and a promising League career ended abruptly in 1988.

Born in Ormskirk on 1 November 1966, Oldroyd joined Everton as an apprentice in 1982 and turned professional at Goodison Park in November 1984. He came to Molineux in August 1986, but was released in May 1987 when he joined Southport.

He later played occasional local non-League soccer until 1996.

Wolves' record: 13 apps.

P

ORDISH, Cyril Stanley

The versatile, red-faced Cyril Ordish was a neat and tidy footballer who played as a full-back, wing-half or outside-right who found it difficult to break into Wolves' first team. Born in Chesterfield, Derbyshire in 1910, he served with Blackwell FC before joining his home-town club Chesterfield in 1933, moving to Molineux in May 1936. He spent two seasons with Wolves and in May 1938 was transferred to Reading. He retired during the war.

Wolves' record: 2 apps.

OSBORN, Simon Edward

Midfielder Simon Osborn was born in Croydon on 19 January 1972 and was taken on as a trainee by Crystal Palace in June 1988, turning professional with the Eagles in January 1990. Over the next four years he did reasonably well at Selhurst Park, appearing in over 70 first team games before transferring to Reading for £90,000 in August 1994.

After just a season at Elm Park he switched back to London to sign for Queens Park Rangers for £1.1 million. He failed to settle down at Loftus Road and after only 11 outings was snapped up by his former manager at Reading, Mark McGhee, who bought him to Wolves for £1 million in December 1995.

A player with great stamina, he's always seeking the ball and loves to have a shot at goal, especially from long distances.

Osborn moved to Tranmere Rovers on a free transfer in March 2001 and four months later he was recruited by Port Vale.

Wolves' record: 126+4 sub apps. 13 goals.

OWEN, Brian Ernest

Brian Owen had a fine career as a energetic wing-half.

Born in Harefield on 2 November 1944, he joined Watford as an apprentice in June 1960, turned professional in July 1962 and went on to appear in 153 League games for the Hornets, lining up for them in the 1970 FA Cup semi-final versus Chelsea.

Two months after that game he went to Colchester United and switched to Wolves in January 1972, staying at Molineux until May 1973.

He later returned to the club as trainer-coach eventually became physiotherapist at Layer Road.

Wolves' record: 7 apps.

OWEN, Trevor

When Trevor Owen joined Wolves in September 1899, he was already the holder of two full Welsh caps, won whilst serving with Crewe Alexandra earlier that year. Owen was born at Llangollen in May 1873, the son of a local flannel factory owner, and played for Llangollen Rovers before joining Wrexham in 1892.

The Welsh club was in the Combination League and in 1892-93 Owen - regarded as a 'scientific forward' - was

their top scorer with nine goals in 19 League and Cup matches. A knee injury then interrupted his career, but he stayed with Wrexham until 1896, by which time he had helped them to consecutive Welsh League championships and two Welsh Cup Finals.

There followed a spell with rivals Druids, with whom he won a Welsh Cup winners' medal, and then with Crewe Alexandra in the Birmingham League. He played against Scotland and England in 1899 and Wolves gave him a chance of League football when he was 26. Owen soon acquitted himself well at Wolves, but just when it looked as though he would thrive at a higher level, he suffered ill health and after returning to Crewe, was forced to retire in 1901.

Owen later lived in Llangollen but spent the last few years of his life in the village of Acrefair where he died on 1 June 1930.

Wolves' record: 12 apps. 3 goals.

OWEN, William

Bill Owen was a key member of the Wolves first team during the middle to late 1890s when he had two separate spells with the club.

A strong tackling full-back or wing-half, he was born in Brierley Hill in 1869 and played for Dudley Road Excelsior and Loughborough before making his senior debut for Wolves against Bolton Wanderers at Molineux in a First Division match in September 1893 (replacing George Swift at left-back).

After appearing in 19 matches that term he returned to his former club Loughborough only to switch back to Wolves in the summer of 1895. He quickly became a permanent fixture in the left-half position and lined up against Sheffield Wednesday in the 1896 FA Cup Final.

He was an ever-present in the Wanderers' side for two successive seasons before transferring to Everton in July 1898, being replaced in the team by George Fleming, who he had played alongside the previous year when occupying the centre-half berth.

Owen died circa 1930.

Wolves' record: 117 apps. 8 goals.

PAATELAINEN, Mika Matti

Born in Helsinki, Finland on 3 February 1967, blond stocky striker Mixu Paatelainen joined Wolves from Bolton Wanderers for a £200,000 in August 1997 - having helped the Trotters win the First Division championship the previous season.

Nicknamed the 'Moose' he came over to Britain in October 1987 to sign for the Scottish club Dundee United from the Finnish side Valkeakosken and he became an instant hit north of the border, scoring 47 goals in more than 170 appearances.

Capped over 50 times by his country, Paatelainen moved from Dundee to Aberdeen in March 1992 and again he did the business in Scotland, netting 28 goals in less than

100 outings for the Dons. In July 1994, a fee of £300,000 took him from Pittodrie to Bolton Wanderers and in his first season at Burnden Park he linked up extremely well with John McGinlay to claim 15 goals in 56 games as the Trotters climbed into the Premiership.

Unfortunately in 1995-96, and again in 1996-97, he was plagued by injury and suffered a loss of form. Then, after amassing a record of 18 goals in 83 outings for Bolton, he switched to Molineux and scored a stunning goal on his debut in the Coca-Cola Cup clash against QPR in August 1997.

Paatelainen left Molineux for the Scottish club Hibernian in September 1998, helping the Easter Road club gain promotion (as First Division champions) back to the Scottish Premier League and then reach the Scottish Cup Final in 2001.

Wolves' record: 18+15 sub apps. 5 goals.

PALMER, Geoffrey

Uncompromising full-back Geoff Palmer had two separate spells with Wolves. All told his service with the club totalled 16 years and he certainly put in some sterling performances, helping the Wanderers win the Football League Cup in 1974 and 1980 and twice gain promotion from the old Second Division as his tally of appearances shot towards the 500 mark to make him one of the finest servants the club has ever known.

Palmer was born in Cannock on 11 July 1954 and became a Wolves apprentice in July 1970 before signing full-time professional forms on his 17th birthday.

The majority of his appearances came during his first period at Molineux when Wolves twice played at Wembley, with Palmer in the team on both occasions. They were also twice promoted from the Second Division, in 1976-77 as champions and in 1983 as runners-up. In that championship-winning season he was ever present and in the second promotion campaign of 1982-83, he missed only two League games.

An England Under-23 international, Palmer had made 388 League appearances and been awarded a testimonial game against Leicester City in 1983 when he was transferred to Burnley, who were then in the Third Division, in November 1984 for £5,000. The Clarets were relegated at the end of that season, although Palmer missed the closing weeks of the campaign, and in December 1985 he returned to Wolves.

He added a further 22 League appearances to his total before quitting professional football to join the West Midlands Police Force. He continued to play soccer for the Cannock Police team and also for the senior Birmingham Police side in the Midland Combination as well as acting as part-time coach under ex-Wolves man Steve Daley at Bromsgrove Rovers (1998-99).

Wolves' record: 489+7 sub apps. 15 goals.

PALMER, George

Wolves' physiotherapist George Palmer treated the injured players at Molineux for some 24 years, from 1946 to 1969 inclusive.

He had already completed a full career with the Royal Navy before coming to Wolves straight after the war and, in fact, the only time he had seen the team play was in that ill-fated 1939 FA Cup final when they lost 4-1 to Portsmouth. He was at the game with a contingent of Pompey supporters - for he was an avid Portsmouth fan at the time!

A Hampshire man, he had contemplated moving back home after completing his service in the Navy but successfully applied for the Wolves job and got it ahead of six other applicants.

Those 'Fabulous fifties' were just around the corner when Palmer arrived at Molineux and he was happy to keep the players in tip-top condition for all those exciting games in League and FA Cup and also against the crack European club sides.

His favourite player, however, was Jese Pye who never figured in the great mid-1950s era. And he told of the time when the England international centre-forward suffered a severe back injury on the eve of the 1949 FA Cup Final with Leicester City.

After intense treatment, sometimes up to six hours a day, Palmer got Pye fit for action although he had to wear a plaster cast right up until the Friday morning before the big game.

Palmer was highly regarded as one of the foremost men in his profession, but this was something the Navy discovered years previous when he was selected to serve as the medical officer (physio) on board His Majesty's Royal Yacht.

Wolves' manager Bill McGarry paid tribute to Palmer by saying: "We all got used to relying on George. The players had implicit faith in him and I knew that if he said a player will be fit in a certain time, then fit he would be."

PARFITT, George

Full-back George Parfitt was an efficient reserve at Molineux, acting as cover for Ted Collins and George Garratly.

Born in Longton, Stoke-on-Trent, circa 1890, and now deceased, he played for Newcastle St. George's (Staffs) before joining Wolves in May 1913. He left Molineux for Cocknage in September 1920.

Wolves' record: 4 apps.

PARKER, William David

Bill Parker spent just a season at Molineux (1938-39) when he deputised for full-back Bill Morris. He made his debut at Old Trafford in November 1938 in front of a near 33,000 crowd.

Born in Liverpool on 27 May 1915, Parker played for Marine and Hull City (making 30 League appearances for the Tigers in 1937-38) before linking up with Wolves in

Geoff Palmer

August 1938. Sadly he was killed whilst on active service during the war, having guested for Crewe Alexandra. He was aged 28.

Wolves' record: 3 apps.

PARKES, Philip Arthur

Goalkeeper Phil Parkes was born in West Bromwich on 14 July 1947, but it was Wolverhampton Wanderers who snapped him up (not Albion) when he left West Bromwich Grammar School in the summer of 1962. Parkes, 6ft 2ins tall, became a full-time professional at Molineux in September 1964, yet did not break into Wolves' first team until November 1966.

Standing in for Fred Davies, he marked his first appearance by saving a penalty against Preston at Molineux as Wolves won 3-2. He managed 14 games that

Phil Parkes

season, returning for the last 13 games of the campaign as Wolves won promotion to the First Division. Although he had a reputation for inconsistency, being brilliant one week and then making mistakes the next, Parkes battled hard to retain his place and eventually became a regular first choice, altogether making over 380 senior appearances for the Molineux club.

Only the great Bert Williams (420 appearances) had kept goal more times for Wolves, and Parkes also established a record of his own... between September 1970 and September 1973 he made 127 consecutive League appearances to beat the previous record set by fellow 'keeper Noel George. He actually made 171 first-class appearances on the trot during those three years.

Parkes helped Wolves finish fourth in Division One 1970-71, the same year they won the Texaco Cup. He gained a

UEFA Cup runners-up medal in 1972 but missed the 1974 League Cup Final win over Manchester City and did not play at all when Wolves won the Second Division title in 1976-77.

The following season he was awarded a testimonial and at the end of that campaign retired from League football. One of the tallest 'keepers ever to play for Wolves, Parkes assisted Vancouver Whitecaps in the North American Soccer League in 1976 and he returned there in 1979 to help them win the Soccer Bowl. He also played for Chicago Sting, Toronto Blizzard and San Jose Earthquakes in the NASL His rival for the goalkeeping spot that season was Bruce Grobbelaar.

After returning 'home' Parkes played in goal for Marstons FC and also for the Wolves Old Stars in charity matches, and managed several local clubs in the Wolverhampton area before taking over as coach at Telford United in 1997 (under ex-Wolves man Steve Daley).

Then when Daley became boss of Bromsgrove Rovers (1998-99) Parkes and another former Wolves star, Geoff Palmer went with him as part-time coaches. A keen cricketer, he turned out regularly for Fordhouses CC in the 1990s.

Wolves' record: 382 apps.

PARKIN, DEREK

Derek 'Squeak' Parkin was born in Newcastle-upon-Tyne on 2 January 1948, and made a record number of senior appearances for Wolves during his fourteen years at Molineux.

He helped the club twice win the League Cup (1974 and 1980) and also the Second Division championship in 1977, as well as gaining five caps for England at Under-23 level and representing the Football League. Never a reckless tackler, he was a steady rather than an enthusiastic defender, who had a wonderful left foot and always tried to use the ball rather than kick it long and aimlessly downfield. Parkin started his career with Huddersfield Town as a junior, turning professional at Leeds Road in May 1965.

He moved to Molineux on St. Valentine's Day 1968 for £80,000. After 14 years service and well over 600 appearances for Wolves (501 in the Football League) Parkin moved to Stoke City in March 1982, by Potters' manager Richie Barker who secured his services on a free transfer.

Parkin spent a season at The Victoria Ground, making a further 45 senior. He then retired to concentrate on his landscape gardening exploits near Bridgnorth.

A fine handicap golfer, Parkin now resides in the same locality as Bert Williams and Willie Carr, two former Wolves players.

Wolves' record: 607+2 sub apps. 10 goals.

Derek Parkin

PARSONAGE, Harold

A tall inside-forward, quick at times, Harry Parsonage was signed from Walsall by Wolves manager Jack Addenbrooke in July 1911.

Born in Aston, Birmingham in October 1889, he had been with the Saddlers since 1909 and spent two seasons with Wolves before leaving Molineux for Dudley Town in June 1913, later assisting Shrewsbury Town (1913-14).

He died in Birmingham in 1979.

Wolves' record 20 apps. 6 goals.

PARSONS, Dennis Ronald

Goalkeeper Dennis Parsons was reserve to England's Bert Williams at Molineux and then understudy to Welsh international Keith Jones at Aston Villa. Born in Birmingham on 29 May 1925, he was playing for BSA Cycles FC when Wolves spotted his talent and brought him to Molineux in February 1944.

Unfortunately the war was still on and the luckless Parsons had to wait three years before making his League debut, ironically against the team he was to join later in his career, Aston Villa.

In the summer of 1951 Parsons left Molineux to assist Hereford United (of the Southern League) and he rejoined the bigtime with Aston Villa in September 1952. Four years and 41 games later he moved to Kidderminster Harriers (September 1956) and was forced to retire through injury in May 1960.

Wolves' record: 27 apps.

PASKIN, John William

Centre-forward John Paskin was born in Capetown, South Africa on 1 February 1962. Tall, raven-haired, direct in his approach, he played for his school team in Capetown and then for Hellenic (from 1979) before joining Toronto Blizzard (Canada) in May 1983. The following year he assisted South China, then played for FC Seiko in Hong Kong (1985), KV Kortrikj of Belgium (1986) and Dundee United (on trial, August 1987) prior to signing for West Bromwich Albion in March 1988.

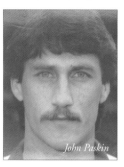
John Paskin

After almost 30 games for the Baggies Paskin moved to Wolves for £75,000 in June 1989 and in February 1992 was transferred to Wrexham, with Jimmy Kelly moving to Molineux in a player-exchange deal. During his stint with Wolves, Paskin, who failed to hold down a regular first team place, was loaned out to three clubs in 1991-92, namely Stockport County (September), Birmingham City (November) and Shrewsbury Town (February).

In July 1994 he signed for Bury on a free transfer and at the end of that season was in the Shakers' line-up which lost to Chesterfield in the Play-off final.

Paskin left Gigg Lane in the summer of 1996 after taking his League and Cup record in England to 183 appearances and 35 goals.

Wolves' record: 25+15 apps. 3 goals.

PATCHING, Martin

Utility forward Martin Patching won England schoolboy honours and followed up by representing his country at Youth team level. Rated a great prospect as a teenager, he did reasonably well with Wolves, but failed to build on his early success and after five years' at Molineux he joined Watford.

Born in Rotherham on 1 November 1958, Patching arrived at Wolves as an apprentice in June 1974 and turned professional in March 1976, playing in that year's FA Youth Cup Final defeat by West Bromwich Albion. He went to Vicarage Road in December 1979 and after a loan spell with Northampton Town (January-February 1983) he was forced to quit top-class football in the summer of 1984. He later became a publican in Berkhamstead near Watford.

Wolves' record: 86+15 sub apps. 11 goals.

PAYNE, Charles Edgar

Reserve outside right Charlie Payne played for Wolves between 1907 and 1910. Understudying Billy Harrison he was given very little opportunity in the first team and he left Molineux in June 1910 to sign for Blakenhall.

His only goal for Wolves, was the winner in a 3-2 away win at Bradford in his last but one outing for the club. Payne was born in Wednesfield circa 1888 and died in Wolverhampton in 1957.

Wolves' record: 12 apps. one goal.

PEACOCK, Darren

Born in Bristol on 3 February 1968, solid, experienced defender Darren Peacock - clad with ponytail - joined Wolves on loan from Blackburn Rovers in October 2000 (following an injury crisis). He appeared in five first-class games for the club before returning to Ewood Park.

Peacock, 6ft 2ins tall, began his career as an apprentice with Newport County, turning professional at Somerton Park in February 1986. After that he assisted Hereford United (from March 1989), Queen's Park Rangers (signed for £200,000 in December 1990), Newcastle United (transferred to St James' Park for £2.7 million in March 1994), Blackburn (arriving on a free transfer in July 1998) and West Ham United (on loan in September/October 1999).

A Welsh Cup winner with Newport in 1990, he had amassed close on 500 senior appearances at club level when the 2000-01 season drew to a close.

Wolves' record: 3+2 sub apps.

PEARCE, Dennis Anthony

Full-back or defensive midfielder Dennis Pearce spent four years with Aston Villa before joining Wolves on a free transfer in July 1995. Having signed for Villa as a junior, he turned professional in June 1993 but failed to make the first team at Villa Park.

He arrived at Molineux to bolster the club's reserve strength, but was released from his contract at the end of the 1996-97 season. He immediately joined Notts County and had the pleasure of helping the Magpies win the Third Division championship in his first season at Meadow Lane.

Pearce, who had trials with Wycombe Wanderers in 1997-98, was born in Wolverhampton on 10 September 1974.
Wolves' record: 9+2 sub apps.

PEARSON, Alfred

Hard-working wing-half Alf Pearson was one of Wolves' most consistent players in the mid 1880s. Born in Wolverhampton circa 1861, he played for St. Luke's before joining Wolves in August 1884.

He left the club for Stafford Road in September 1887.
Wolves' record: 12 apps.

PEDLEY, John

Jack Pedley, a former steel worker, was playing for Wednesbury Old Athletic when Wolves signed him in November 1905.

Alf Pearson

The Wanderers had been looking for a good outside-left ever since Jack Miller's departure and Pedley who was born in West Bromwich in February 1881, fitted the bill. Wolves had been particularly attracted by his ability to beat an opponent by sheer speed over 20 yards, but he also had overall class and was a clever 'one-touch' player.

In his first season at Molineux Pedley scored ten goals in 21 League games to finish second highest scorer and his goals included a hat-trick in a 6-1 win over Notts County in the penultimate game of the campaign. Wolves won their last game 7-0 against Derby County but it was not enough to prevent them from being relegated and consequently the following season Pedley found himself in Division Two.

In 1907-08 he helped Wolves, still a Second Division side, beat Newcastle United in the FA Cup Final and was a regular in the team until the end of the 1909-10 season. In May 1919, Pedley joined Wrexham but was forced to quit football through injury at the age of 30. He returned to the steel industry and later ran the Plumber's Arms in Tyndal Street, West Bromwich for a number of years.
Wolves' record: 168 apps. 28 goals.

PEERS, Edward John

Goalkeeper Teddy Peers started his football life as an outside-right and then switched to full-back before finding lasting success as a goalkeeper.

Teddy Peers

Born at Connah's Quay on 31 December 1886, he played as an amateur with Oswestry St Clare's and Chirk. After an unsuccessful trial with Shrewsbury Town, he played for three local clubs in Connah's Quay, gaining a Welsh Cup winners' medal with his home town club in 1911, having captured a Welsh Amateur Cup winners' medal with Connah's Quay Juniors before that. He first appeared for a Wolves team in April 1911 before being signed as a professional eight months later.

After taking over from Frank Boxley during the last few weeks of the 1911-12 season, he became a regular in the team and held his place until Noel George ousted him in 1921. Peers thus missed that season's FA Cup Final, although he had returned to first team duties in the weeks leading up to the Final.

Peers won eight full caps for Wales whilst with Wolves and also played in two Victory internationals in 1919, but after he had joined Port Vale in August 1921, he made only four more international appearances because Vale were reluctant to release him all that often!

Peers, who guested for Stoke and Walsall during the First World War, left Vale in May 1923 and ended his playing career with Hednesford Town. He later took over the New Inn public house in Bilston Road, Wolverhampton, then another in Bilston, and died in Wolverhampton on 20 September 1935.
Wolves' record: 198 apps.

PEMBLE, Arthur

Arthur Pemble played in goal for Wolves in season 1908-09, deputising for Tommy Lunn in two away games when he conceded a total of six goals.

Born in Bridgnorth circa 1885, he played for Beacon Rangers prior to joining Wolves and Willenhall Pickwick after leaving Molineux (July 1909). He later assisted Lowton Manor and Fordhouses FC.
Wolves' record: 2 apps.

PENDER, John Patrick

John Pender was a permanent fixture at the heart of the Wolves defence for three during the mid-19080s.

John Pender

He was born in Luton on 19 November 1963 but came to live in the West Midlands as a youngster and it was his performances as a goalscoring centre-forward with Lichfield Social in the Lichfield Sunday League that alerted Football League scouts. Pender had trials with several clubs (including Wolves) whilst he was still at school and then joined the Molineux staff as an apprentice in June 1979 before becoming a full-time professional in 1981.

He was now playing in defence as a healthy six-footer and developing well, winning Republic of Ireland caps at both Youth and Under-21 levels, having qualified for Eire through his parentage. In March 1982, with Wolves fighting a losing battle against relegation, he was given his League debut at centre-half, replacing Joe Gallagher at home to Swansea. The following season he missed only three games as Wolves went back into Division One as runners-up.

Twelve months later, alas, they were down again, Pender playing 34 times in the relegation team. This time there was no quick way back - just the opposite in fact - and in July 1985, with Wolves facing Third Division football, Pender was transferred to Charlton Athletic for £35,000. He made 41 appearances for the Addicks before moving to Bristol City in October 1987. He then helped the Ashton Gate club to promotion to the old Second Division.

In October 1990, after a month's loan at Turf Moor, he signed for Burnley for £70,000 and was in the Claret's side that won the old Fourth Division championship in 1992. He skippered Burnley and in 1994 was in their line-up that beat Stockport County in a stormy Second Division Play-off Final at Wembley. In August 1995, the hard-tackling Pender switched his allegiance to Wigan Athletic and two years later he joined Third Division Rochdale.

In 1998-99 he passed the career milestone of 600 League and Cup games at club level.

Wolves' record: 127+2 sub apps. 4 goals.

PENDREY, Garry James Sidney

Although he never played for Wolves, Garry Pendrey gave the club excellent service as a coach, having two separate spells in that capacity during the late 1980s/early 90s.

He did, however, give Birmingham City terrific service as a defender - amassing 360 appearances and scoring five goals.

A West Bromwich Albion supporter as a lad, he joined the apprentice ranks at St Andrew's in July 1965 after doing well with Stanley Star and Harborne Lynwood in local junior football. He became a professional in October 1966 and at the end of that season played in the FA Youth Cup Final defeat by Sunderland. In 1972, having established himself in defence, he helped Blues win promotion from the Second Division.

He remained at St Andrew's until the summer of 1979 when, after his testimonial match against neighbours West Brom, he moved to The Hawthorns to strengthen the Baggies defensive squad. During the early 1980s Pendrey assisted Torquay United and Bristol Rovers and in July 1982 was named player-coach of Walsall, later acting as assistant-manager to former Blues striker Alan Buckley (1983-86).

His next appointment took him to Molineux as coach in November 1986. He then had an eventful two-year spell as manager of Blues from June 1987 to April 1989 before returning to Molineux to take up his coaching duties for a second time. Pendrey later became coach under Gordon Strachan at Coventry City and he went with Strachan as his assistant at Southampton in October 2001.

Born in Lozells, Birmingham on 9 February 1949, Pendrey was Blues' youngest captain when in 1969 he skippered the side at the age of 20 years, six months.

PERRETT, William Walter

Bill Perrett served Wolves for three years, from 1909 to 1912, during which time he was initially first reserve to centre-half Billy Wooldridge.

Well built, with a fair kick, he was born in Willenhall in 1888 and played for Wood Cross Links FC, Fazeley Rovers and Bilston United before moving to Molineux.

On leaving Wolves, Perrett went briefly to Dudley and later assisted Halesowen before a broken leg ended his playing career in 1913.

Wolves' record: 4 apps.

PERRY, Walter

A naturally gifted footballer, able to play as a forward or wing-half, Walter Perry came from a sporting family, two of his brothers, Tom and Charlie, both played for West Bromwich Albion and also represented England.

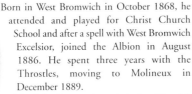

Walter Perry

Born in West Bromwich in October 1868, he attended and played for Christ Church School and after a spell with West Bromwich Excelsior, joined the Albion in August 1886. He spent three years with the Throstles, moving to Molineux in December 1889.

The following year he switched to Warwick County and thereafter served with Burton Swifts, Albion again (from October 1894 when he played with his two brothers) and Burton Swifts for a second time, retiring in June 1900.

He was later appointed manager of Albion's reserve team (1906-07) and also qualified as a Football League linesman (1909). Perry died in West Bromwich in September 1928.

Wolves' record: 8 apps. 3 goals.

PHEASANT, Edward

Ted 'Cock' Pheasant packed a great deal into his 33 years. Born in the back streets of Wednesbury on 15 February 1877, he was a bustling forward with the Joseph Edward Cox School team and with Wednesbury Excelsior and Wednesbury Old Athletic.

Wolves signed him as an 18-year-old in the summer of 1895 and he made his debut in the forward-line in September 1896, in a 4-3 defeat at Derby. He missed the following season because of injury, but returned at centre-half in 1898-99 and it was in that position where he settled down, going on to make well over 160 appearances for Wolves.

He was, by all accounts, a fearsome character who would shave his head almost bald and roll his sleeves up and his socks down to appear as fearsome as possible to opposing forwards. He was physically dominating anyway, standing 6ft 2in tall and weighing 15st, and he skippered the Wolves side many times.

He was a fierce hitter of a dead ball, took free-kicks and penalties, and in March 1902 scored a hat-trick against Newcastle United at Molineux, one of the goals coming from a 35-yard free-kick. To mark the feat, the Wolves chairman Mr AH Stanley presented Pheasant with a specially inscribed gold watch. He was reportedly the highest paid Wolves player of his day earning £3 10s (£3.50) per week during the season and £3 in the summer. On one occasion he was selected to represent the Football League, but preferred to play for Wolves instead - such was his dedication.

In November 1904 Pheasant moved to West Bromwich Albion and made over 150 appearances for the Baggies, scoring 22 goals, before Leicester Fosse signed him in July 1910. Alas, he was never able to play for Leicester because two weeks after leaving The Hawthorns he was admitted to a Birmingham hospital with peritonitis and died on 17 July that year.

NB - Pheasant's hobbies included bee-keeping and gardening (he loved his roses).

Wolves' record: 168 apps. 19 goals.

PHILLIPS, Cuthbert

Cuthbert Phillips, who was always known as Charlie, was born in Victoria, Monmouthshire, on 23 June 1910 and won Welsh Schoolboy honours while working as a boilerman and playing Welsh League football for Ebbw Vale in 1925.

Several clubs wanted to sign him and he had offers from Plymouth Argyle, Torquay United and Cardiff City before signing professional forms for Wolves in August 1929. He was a speedy forward, mostly at home on the right wing, and that is where he played the majority of his 200 plus senior games for Wolves.

Capped ten times by Wales while at Molineux, he helped Wolves win the Second Division championship in 1931-32, scoring 18 goals.

Phillips netted on his international debut v. Northern Ireland at Wrexham in 1931 and captained his country on six occasions. At Christmas 1935 he was sent-off whilst skippering Wolves against Bolton and a month later, in January 1936, he was transferred to Aston Villa for £9,000.

He was capped three more times as a Villa player, but made only 25 appearances for the Birmingham club and although he scored on his debut (in a 3-1 win at Derby) he could not save them from relegation. When they returned as Second Division champions in 1937-38 he managed only a handful of games before moving across the city to play for Birmingham in March 1938.

In 1939 Phillips went into non-League football with Chelmsford City; he then guested for several clubs until retiring at the end of the war. Phillips was a fine all-round sportsman who also excelled at cricket, golf, tennis, rugby union and various athletics events. He was later a licensee in Bushbury and Lichfield, dying in the latter city on 21 October 1969.

Wolves' record: 202 apps. 65 goals.

PHILLIPSON, William Thomas

Broad-shouldered, compact, hard-shooting and fast, Tom Phillipson has been one of the best strikers ever to play for Wolves.

Born at Ryton-on-Tyne on 31 October 1898, he once scored 14 out of his school side's 15 goals in one Saturday morning match and then netted ten in the next game.

In December 1919 - after serving as a sergeant in the West Regiment in Russia - he joined Newcastle United from Scotswood FC for whom he had played since 1914 and had gained two England schoolboy caps (1913). He made

Tom Phillipson

senior level and left the club for Bolton Wanderers, later playing for Derby County reserves, Gillingham (1928-29), Wellington Town and Crewe Alexandra before retiring in 1934.

Born in Wellington in 1900, Picken, who joined Wolves from Audley F.C, later became a bricklayer.

Wolves' record: 12 apps.

PICKERELL, Jack

Inside-forward Jack Pickerell was born in Bilston circa 1875, and was given a month's trial by Wolves in March 1890 after having starred for Dudley Road Swifts.

He failed to catch the eye and left Molineux for Dudley Town, later assisting Netherton St. Luke's (1900-02).

Wolves' record: one app.

PIERCE, Gary

Goalkeeper Gary Pierce was born in Bury on 2 March 1951. After playing local junior football at weekends he signed for Mossley in 1969 before Huddersfield Town took him on as a full-time professional in February 1971.

He appeared in 23 games for the Terriers before Wolves signed him in June 1973, as cover for Phil Parkes.

Gary Pierce

Pierce went on to play in well over 100 senior games for the Wanderers. Having initially gained a first team place in September 1973, he went on to have 19 further outings that term, the highlight coming in March when he made his first League Cup appearance for the club in that terrific 2-1 Wembley Final victory over Manchester City, Pierce was superb as he celebrated his 23rd birthday in style.

For two seasons he and Parkes shared the goalkeeping position and in 1976-77, with Wolves back in Division Two, Pierce was ever-present as Wanderers won the title.

His joy was short-lived, however, and after Paul Bradshaw had been signed from Blackburn, he did not play at all in 1977-78 and managed only three games in 1978-79. In July 1979, his future at Molineux bleak, Pierce was allowed to join Barnsley. He made 81 appearances in four years at Oakwell and then had 27 games for Blackpool before his contract was cancelled in May 1984.

He later managed Accrington Stanley, Netherfield, Radcliffe Borough (1991-92) and Ainsworth FC (Bolton Combination).

Wolves' record: 111 apps.

only 15 League and FA Cup appearances for the Magpies, scoring five goals, before they let him go to Swindon Town in May 1921 for £500.

Wolves, then in the Third Division (North), paid £1,000 for his signature in December 1923 and made a great start to his Molineux career with a hat-trick in only his fourth game against Ashington.

At the end of the season he had 14 goals to his credit and Wolves were Northern Section champions. In the next four seasons, Phillipson scored another 97 goals, including a club record 37 in League and Cup games in 1925-26 with another 33 coming the following season.

In April 1926 he scored four goals past Barnsley and on Christmas Day that same year he netted a fivetimer in a game against Bradford City.

Having captained the side, he surprisingly moved to Sheffield United in March 1928, but spent only a short time at Bramall Lane before returning to the West Midlands to play for Bilston United, later having a season with Walsall (1931-32).

On retiring Phillipson concentrated on his business interests in Wolverhampton and went into local politics. In the spring of 1938 he was elected Lord Mayor of Wolverhampton and in 1947 watched Dennis Westcott beat his scoring record for the club.

Tom Phillipson died in Wolverhampton on 19 November 1965, aged 77.

Wolves' record: 159 apps. 111 goals.

PICKEN, Albert Henry

Albert Picken played for Wolves between 1921 and 1925. A reserve outside-left, he was given very little scope at

PILSBURY, Charles

Charlie Pilsbury was a reserve centre-forward at Molineux in season 1903-04 - scoring in his only senior outing for the club in a 6-1 home defeat by Manchester City when he came in for the injured Billy Wooldridge.

Born in Bilston in 1881, Pilsbury played his early football with Queen Street Methodists and Dudley Central. On leaving Molineux he signed for Bilston Swifts and later served with Tipton Victoria.

He died in June 1964.

Wolves' record: one app. one goal.

PINCOTT, Frederick Charles

Fred Pincott played for Wolves' first team in season 1932-33 when he deputised for George Bellis at centre-half in two games - against Arsenal and Manchester City - when Wolves were defeated 7-1 at home and 4-1 away respectively!

A strong player, born in Bristol on 19 March 1913, and now deceased, Pincott represented Bristol Royal Victoria before moving to Molineux in the summer of 1931. A six-footer, weighing almost 11st. 5lbs, he did far better at reserve team level and on leaving Wolves in 1934 he joined forces with a number of former Wanderers' players at Bournemouth before drifting into non-League soccer just before the war, first with Dartford and then with Gravesend.

During the hostilities he guested for Bristol City, Chester and Northampton Town. In season 1947-48, Pincott made 14 League outings for Newport County before rounding off his career with Bideford Town, retiring in 1951.

Wolves' record: 2 apps.

PLATT, Frederick Douglas

Reserve outside-right Fred Platt spent three seasons with Wolves from 1897 to 1900, during which he was reserve to Jack Tonks.

Born in Wolverhampton in 1869 he played for Lanesford Boys before joining Wolves and after leaving Molineux he played in turn for Oxley, Castle Hill Rovers and St. Augustine's.

Platt died circa 1940.

Wolves' record: 6 apps.

POLLET, Ludovic

Born in Vieux-Conde near Valenciennes, France on 18 June 1970, tall, rugged defender Ludo Pollet, formerly of Cannes, initially joined Wolves as a trialist from Le Havre in September 1999.

However, quick-thinking Molineux boss Colin Lee had second thoughts and the following month he snapped up the experienced player on a three-year contract for £350,000 - fearing that another club would come in a steal him from under the club's nose!

During the first two seasons of his Molineux career he

produced some outstanding performances, taking the 'Player off the Year' trophy in 2000.

Wolves' record: 71+1 sub apps 7 goals*

POPE, Frank Worrall

Frank Pope was a strapping 12 stone inside-right, who found it hard to get first team football at Molineux, especially during his first spell with the club.

Born in Brierley Hill circa 1880, he played initially for Pensnett Albion and then Cradley Heath before linking up with Wolves for the first time in August 1903. He left Molineux for Stourbridge in July 1904, only to return to the Wanderers' camp in May 1905. After another year, spent mainly in the reserves, he was sold to Notts County (August 1906) and followed up by assisting Walsall (June 1907) and Netherton (1909-11).

Wolves' record: 8 apps.

POPE, Harvey Frank

Frank Pope was a reserve centre-forward, no relation to Frank (q.v) who spent two years with Wolves: 1900-02.

Frank Pope

Well built, he was signed as cover for Billy Beats and George Harper, but got very little opportunity, although he did score in a 3-1 home win over Notts County in October 1901.

Born in Wolverhampton in 1879, Pope had played for Compton Rovers immediately before joining Wolves and on leaving Molineux he signed for Darlaston, but was injured after two games.

Wolves' record: 5 apps. one goal.

POPPITT, James

Right-winger Jim Poppitt spent two seasons at Molineux round the turn of the century, appearing in over 20 first team games.

Fast and clever, and perhaps a shade too eager and over-elaborate at times, he was born in Shropshire circa 1879 and joined Wolves in 1900 from Wellington. Poppitt left Molineux for Swindon Town (in May 1902), and then played in turn for Reading (1903-04), Swindon again, Notts County (1905-07) and Lincoln City. In 1908 he moved back to the Midlands and signed for Walsall Wood, later assisting Gnosall Olympic. He died in 1940.

Wolves' record: 21 apps. 3 goals.

POTTS, Arthur Arnold

Inside-left Arthur Potts was born in Cannock on 26 May 1888 and was on Wolves' books for two full seasons: 1920-22. He attended Cannock Council School and played for Willenhall Swifts before turning professional with Manchester City, He failed to make the grade at

Maine Road and joined up with arch rivals Manchester United for whom he made 27 League appearances either side of the Great War.

Having guested for Birmingham during the hostilities, he switched to Molineux in May 1920 and left Wolves for Walsall, playing one game for the Saddlers prior to serving Bloxwich Strollers.

After quitting football in 1925 Potts became licensee of the Blue Ball pub in Pipers Row, Wolverhampton. He died in Walsall in 1981...after a long innings.

Wolves' record: 42 apps. 10 goals.

POWELL, Barry Ivor

Barry Powell started out in football in June 1970 when he joined Wolves as an apprentice. He was born at Kenilworth on 29 January 1954 and played for Warwickshire Schools before signing for the Wanderers. Powell became a full-time professional in January 1972

Barry Powell

and made his League debut in midfield in season 1972-73, appearing ten times as Wolves finished fifth in Division One. A very useful player, always concentrating on the game and never giving less than 110 per-cent out on the park, he came on as substitute in Wolves' 1974 League Cup Final win over Manchester City at Wembley.

He began his footballing travels in September 1975 moving from Molineux to Coventry City. Thereafter he served with Portland Timbers (he had two spells in the NASL), Derby County, Burnley, Swansea City and two three-month periods in Hong Kong with the Bulova and South China clubs before returning to Wolves as player-coach in November 1986.

He was basically a reserve second time round at Molineux, but managed to get into the side which lost the Fourth Division Play-off Final second leg (and consequently the tie on aggregate) against Aldershot in May 1987.

Although he made one FA Cup appearance in 1987-88, as a substitute in the first round against Cheltenham Town, he did not play in the side at all when the Fourth Division championship trophy was won that season.

That Cup outing turned out to be his last in senior football and afterwards Powell was employed as reserve-team and Youth-team manager at Molineux before becoming Coventry City's assistant Youth Development Officer in 1991.

He also played, ironically, for Cheltenham Town, under Ally Robertson's management, and for Moor Green, and returned to Highfield Road as Football in the Community Officer in 1993.

Powell made 392 senior appearances for his five League clubs and scored 45 goals. He also won four England under-23 caps with Wolves.

Wolves' record: 83+13 sub apps. 8 goals.

POYSER, George Henry

George Poyser was born in Mansfield on 6 February 1910 and after playing for Nottingham Schools and Tieversal Colliery, he enlisted as a full-back with Wolves in July 1927.

He failed to make the grade at Molineux and moved to Stourbridge in October 1928, from where he switched back into the Football League with Mansfield Town (late 1928-29). From Field Mill he went to Port Vale (1931), then Brentford (1934) and onto Plymouth Argyle (1945) before becoming player-manager of Dover Town in 1947. He returned to Molineux as Wolves' chief scout in 1950, staying with Wolves for three years before becoming manager of Notts County in October 1953, a position he held until January 1957, when he took over as assistant-boss of Manchester City.

From May 1963 to April 1965 he was in charge of team affairs at Maine Road, but then resigned with City in mid-table and rivals Manchester United on course for the First Division title. He was replaced in the 'hot seat' at Maine Road by the former Arsenal and England international wing-half Joe Mercer.

Poyser died on 30 January 1995, aged 84.

PREECE, John Causer

Full-back John Preece was signed by Wolves from Sunbeam Motors FC in March 1934. He played twice in the Wanderers' League side (in place of the injured Wilf Lowton) but didn't quite fit the bill.

Born in Wolverhampton on 30 April 1914, and now deceased, he earned a living in a local car factory and played for its football team before going to Molineux. Preece joined Bristol Rovers in 1935 and made 79 League appearances for the Pirates before joining Bradford City in 1938.

After the war he assisted Southport and Swindon Town and ended his career by having two seasons with Chippenham United.

Wolves' record: 2 apps.

PRESTON, Henry

Useful inside or centre-forward Harry Preston was on Wolves' books for four seasons: from August 1901 to May 1905.

Born in Shropshire circa 1880, he joined Wolves from Ironbridge and acted as reserve to Billy Beats, Adam Haywood and Billy Wooldridge. He made his Wolves debut in a 2-0 home win over Grimsby in November 1901 and his only goal came in a 3-1 home defeat of Liverpool in March 1902.

On leaving Molineux Preston joined Kidderminster Harriers and in 1907 he switched to Hatherley FC.

Wolves' record: 26 apps. one goal.

PRICE, Arthur Bertrand Richard

Arthur Price was a tall inside-right, born in Birmingham circa 1883, who was given a trial by Wolves in April-May 1907, but failed to make an impact.

He played his early football with Sheldon Heath and Moor Green and after his brief association with Wolves, joined Acocks Green.

Wolves' record: one app.

PRICE, Frederick

Right-half or right-winger Fred Price was born at Brierley Hill in 1888 and played for Aston FC, Wellington Street Citadels and Dudley Town, winning Junior international honours for England, before signing for Wolves in June 1912.

He got his chance in the first XI in February 1913, playing in the last 15 games of the season after Albert Groves had been moved into the forward line. In fact he missed only three out of 91 games played by Wolves up to World War One.

During the hostilities Price served in the Army, guested for Port Vale and Sunbeam Motors FC and then made a two appearances for Wolves in the Midland Victory League prior to the resumption of the Football League. In that first post-war season of 1919-20 he played 28 times before losing his battle against a knee injury.

Val Gregory took over his position. Price was then transferred to Port Vale in May 1920 and he served Newport County from July 1921 to May 1922 before retiring at the age of 34. He later became licensee of the King's Head, Mill Street, Brierley Hill.

Wolves' record: 124 apps.

PRICE, Frederick Thomas

Fast and clever outside-left Fred Price spent two seasons with Wolves - from July 1925 to May 1927.

Born in Ibstock on 24 October 1901, he played for Whitwick Imperial before becoming a professional with Leicester City in May 1921.

From Filbert Street he moved to Southampton (May 1924) and from The Dell he joined Wolves. On leaving Molineux, after failing to establish himself in the senior side, he signed for Chesterfield (season 1927-28) and later assisted Burton Town, Nuneaton Borough and Midland Price died in Leicester in November 1985.

NB - Fred Price's brother Jack played for Bristol Rovers,

Leicester City reserves, Swindon Town and Torquay United, while his uncle Cliff also assisted Halifax Town, Leicester City, Nottingham Forest and Southampton. Wolves' record: 41 apps. 8 goals.

PRICE, John Arthur

Outside-right or centre-forward Jack Price was a competent reserve at Molineux during the early 1920s.

A Lancastrian born in Blackburn circa 1900, he joined the staff at Molineux in July 1920 (from Barnoldswick Town) and left Wolves for Heanor Town in May 1922, later playing for Buxton and Clithroe.

His only goal for Wolves proved to be the winner in a 2-1 success at South Shields in December 1920.

Wolves' record: 13 apps. one goal.

PRITCHARD, Roy Thomas

Former Bevin Boy Roy Pritchard joined Wolves as a full-time professional in August 1945 after being associated with the club since 1941 when he left Dawley Council School.

Born in Dawley on 9 May 1925, he was a tough tackling full-back who guested for Mansfield Town, Notts County, Swindon Town and Walsall during the War. He made his Football League debut in the first post-war season, playing four times in the Wolves team that eventually finished third in Division One.

Pritchard established himself in the team the following season when he played 20 times and in 1948-49 he appeared in 30 League games and played his first games in the FA Cup. By the end of that season he had collected a winners' medal after Wolves had beaten Leicester City 3-1 in the Final at Wembley.

When Wolves won the League championship in 1953-54, Pritchard played in 27 matches and by the time he was transferred to Aston Villa in February 1956, he had made over 200 appearances for the club. He had the misfortune to mark his first League outing in a claret and blue shirt by breaking his jaw against Arsenal. That proved to be his only appearance of the season and

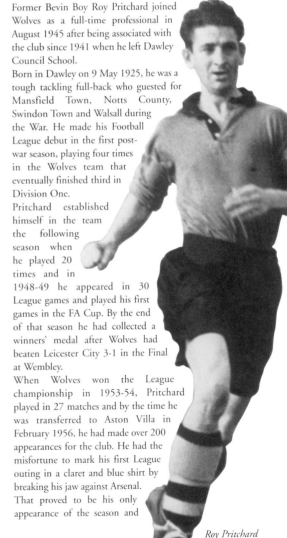

Roy Pritchard

he played once more in 1956-57 and in one game the following term before joining Notts County in November 1957. Eighteen League games for County were followed by a move to Port Vale in September 1958, where he made 24 appearances before ending his career with Wellington Town (August 1960 - June 1964).

Pritchard continued to appear in charity games right up until 1990. He died at Willenhall in January 1993.

NB - In the 1990s Wolves introduced the Roy Pritchard trophy for their 'Young Player of the Year'.

Wolves' record: 223 apps.

PRITCHARD, Thomas Francis

Wolves signed 6ft 1in centre-half Tom Pritchard from Newport County for £1,000 in September 1927, following injuries to Sammy Charnley and Jack Williams and he spent two seasons at Molineux.

Pritchard was born at Wellington, Shropshire on 18 June 1904 and began his career with the Great Western Railway works side whilst working as a boiler-maker.

He had trials with Wolves as a youngster but was working in a cycle factory and playing for Sunbeam FC before signing amateur forms for Stockport County in June 1925. Newport signed him in the summer of 1926 and he became a Wolves player just over a year later. Pritchard, a tall, commanding defender, made 35 League appearances in 1927-28 and 21 in 1928-29 as Wolves hovered around the lower half of Division Two.

In May 1929, he was transferred to Charlton Athletic and made 43 appearances for the Addicks, his run being interrupted after he broke a leg when Charlton visited Molineux on Boxing Day 1929.

In November 1931, he signed for Thames FC, the club with a fleeting League presence, and played 27 times in the Third Division (South) before spending a year in the French League with Olympique Marseille.

He returned to England to play for Preston North End, then spent a season with Lancaster Town before becoming Mansfield Town's trainer in June 1935, playing in one League game for the Stags in August of that year. Pritchard made over 150 League appearances in his career.

Wolves' record: 58 apps. 3 goals.

PROUDLOCK, Adam David

Born in Telford on 9 May 1981, striker Adam Proudlock joined the apprentice ranks at Molineux in June 1997 and turned professional two years later.

An England Youth international, he entered competitive League football during the 1999-2000 season and he also assisted the Scottish club, Clyde on (loan) in August/September 2000.

He has already impressed all and sundry with his style and attitude and scored his first League hat-trick in a 3-0 victory away to Bradford City in October 2001.

Wolves' record: 43+9 sub apps. 15 goals*

PURDIE. Jonathan

Jon Purdie will be remembered for scoring a spectacular winning goal for non-League Kidderminster Harriers against Birmingham City in the FA Cup in January 1994,

Jon Purdie

but earlier in his career he had given Wolves useful service on the left wing.

Purdie, who was born in Corby on 22 February 1967, started his career with Arsenal, joining the Gunners as an apprentice in 1983 and signing full-time professional forms in January 1985. An England Schoolboy international, he failed to break into the first team at Highbury and joined Wolves in July 1985.

Wolves were relegated to Division Four in his first season, when he missed only five games, but he helped them to the Play-off Final the following year. By the time they were Fourth Division champions a year later, however, Purdie managed only nine appearances (two as substitute) and was loan to Cambridge United in October that season.

In July 1988, Purdie moved to Oxford United and later played for Brentford and Shrewsbury Town before entering non-League soccer with Worcester City.

He played for Cheltenham Town before joining Kidderminster Harriers in January 1993 and after helping the Harriers win the GM Vauxhall Conference in 1994 he was transferred to Telford United, having earlier been on

R

tour with the famous Middlesex Wanderers side. In August 1997 Purdie was appointed assistant-manager to Steve Daley (ex-Wolves) at Bucks Head.

But in 1998 he moved to Bromsgrove Rovers, only to return to his former club Kidderminster Harriers in January 1999, soon after Graham Allner had quit as manager. Then in February 1999, Purdie switched his allegiance back to Worcester City.

Wolves' record: 94+9 sub apps. 13 goals.

PYE, Jesse

Jesse Pye, who was born in the village of Treeton near Rotherham on 22 December 1919, had plenty of experience of life by the time he became a professional footballer.

An apprentice joiner, he played for his village team and for Catliffe FC in the Rotherham Intermediate League and was an amateur trialist with Sheffield United before World War Two broke out in 1939.

He served with the Royal Engineers in several theatres

Jesse Pye

during the conflict as well as playing alongside some fine players in services football and listed his most memorable performance as scoring seven goals (three penalties) for 556 Coy RE in the Tripoli Army League.

In August 1945, Pye signed for Notts County, but after less than 12 months at Meadow Lane, during which time he played in a Victory international for England, the goalscoring inside-forward was transferred to Wolves, who paid out a club record fee of £12,000 in May 1946. Pye, who had been the target of several leading clubs, immediately won over the Molineux fans with a hat-trick on his debut, in a 6-1 win over Arsenal.

He scored 20 League goals in that first season with Wolves, then netted 16 the following campaign and was leading scorer in 1948-49 with 21 in League and FA Cup, when Wolves won the Cup by beating Leicester City 3-1 at Wembley, Pye scoring twice.

He continued to score regularly for Wolves until leaving for Luton Town in July 1952. Pye had also appeared for the Football League, won three England 'B' caps and played once for the full international team, against the Republic of Ireland in September 1949. From Luton, where he scored 31 goals in 60 League games, Pye joined struggling Derby County in October 1954 but was unable to halt their slide into the Third Division (North). He was on the fringes of the team when the Rams won the Northern Section title in 1956-57, and in July 1957 he signed for Wisbech Town, taking over as player-manager from March 1960 to 1966.

Pye died in Blackpool on 20 February 1984.

Wolves' record: 209 apps. 95 goals.

* See also under Poyser, George

RADFORD, Walter Ivor Robert

Goalscoring inside-forward Wally Radford had two spells with Wolves but his second was much more productive in terms of goals scored and, indeed, it ended successfully with an FA Cup winners' medal in his pocket.

Radford was born in Wolverhampton in July 1886 and first joined the Molineux staff in August 1905.

That season he played only twice for Wolves and in 1906-07 was on the books of Southampton, for whom he scored twice in nine Southern League matches, both goals coming against Northampton Town in April 1907.

Radford then rejoined Wolves, having failed to make an impression at The Dell, but in 1907-08 he hit nine goals in 26 Second Division games and was at inside-left in the team that beat Newcastle in the FA. Cup Final.

In 1908-09 he top-scored with 24 goals and then hit 11 the following season before joining Southport Central in the summer of 1910. When Radford retired in 1913 he took up refereeing and later officiated in the Football League.

Wally Radford

Wolves' record: 94 apps. 48 goals.

RAE, Alexander Scott

Alex Rae was born in Glasgow on 30 September 1969 and played initially for Bishopbriggs before signing professional forms for Falkirk in June 1987. He went on to score 21 goals in 91 outings for the Scottish club who then sold him to Millwall for £100,000 in August 1990. Capped by his country's 'B' team four times he has also appeared in eight Under-21 internationals, and he netted 71 goals in 256 games for the Lions, up to June 1996 when he was transferred to Sunderland for £750,000. On Wearside he continued to produce the goods as an attacking midfielder (even emergency striker) and in 1999 he helped Sunderland win the First Division title and with it a place in the Premiership. He was recruited to Molineux by manager Dave Jones in September 2001 for a fee of £1.2 million.

Wolves' record: 12 apps.*

RAFFERTY, William Henry

Tall, rather leggy but dangerous Glaswegian centre-forward Billy Rafferty (born on 30 December 1950) had a pretty useful career as marksman which spanned almost 20 years.

After starting his goalscoring exploits with Port Glasgow Rovers in Scotland in 1967 he entered League soccer with Coventry City, signing for the Sky Blues as a full-time professional in July 1968.

Thereafter he travelled around the country playing, in turn, for Blackpool (signed for £40,000 in October 1972), Plymouth Argyle (bought for £25,000 in March 1974), Carlisle United (secured for £20,000 in May 1976), Wolves (a £125,000 capture in March 1978), Newcastle United (acquired for another £125,000 fee in October 1979), Portsmouth (transferred for £80,000 in December 1980) and finally AFC Bournemouth (recruited for £4,000 in February 1984). He later played Second Division football in Portugal until retiring in 1988.

Rafferty appeared in more than 500 senior games and scored in excess of 150 goals, including 40 in 102 League outings for Pompey and 35 in 90 matches for Plymouth. He gained a Third Division championship medal in 1983 with Portsmouth having earlier helped Plymouth gain promotion to the Second Division in 1975.

Rafferty now runs two health, fitness and beauty salons with his wife in Carlisle and nearby Cockermouth.

NB - His brother, Stewart, played in the Scottish League for a number of years.

Wolves' record: 47+3 apps. 8 goals.

RAMSCAR, Frederick Thomas

As a 20 year-old, Fred Ramscar was whisked away to fight in World War Two and during the hostilities, while serving in France and Germany, he gained valuable experience on the soccer pitch which put in good stead when peacetime football returned in 1945.

Born in Salford on 24 January 1919, he had represented Salford Boys and played as an Amateur for both Manchester City and Stockport County prior to entering the forces.

In August 1945 he was recruited by Wolves and remained at Molineux until October 1947 when he switched to Queens Park Rangers.

A useful, ball-playing inside forward with good strong right-foot shot, Ramscar then switched to Preston North End in November 1949 where he teamed up with Tom

Finney. From Deepdale he moved to Northampton Town (July 1951) and after spells with Millwall (from September 1954) and Peterborough United, he returned to Northampton to coach the club's youngsters.

He later served with Wellingborough and retired out of football in 1960. Ramscar scored 56 goals in 159 games for Northampton and on the day he joined Stockport he was offered a contract by Manchester United, but decided to stay with the Edgeley Park club.

Wolves' record: 17 apps. one goal.

RANKINE, Simon Mark

The versatile Mark Rankine was born in Doncaster on 30 September 1969 and after representing his school team and Doncaster Boys, he went on to play in almost 200 games for his home town club Doncaster Rovers before joining Wolves for £70,000 in January 1992.

A strong, forceful player, who prefers the right-back or right-half berths, he did well at Molineux before losing his

Mark Rankine

place to Jamie Smith, hence his transfer to Preston North End in September 1996 for £100,000.

He was in North End's Second Division promotion-winning team in 1998-99 and was a key member of the Lillywhites' line-up as they reached the 2001 First Division Play-off final where they lost to their Lancashire neighbours Bolton Wanderers.

Wolves' record: 142+25 apps. one goal.

RATCLIFFE, Patrick Christopher

Irishman Paddy Ratcliffe was born in Dublin on 31 December 1919. He played Gaelic football at school and in 1935 joined Bohemians.

As an Air Gunner during the Second World War, his plane was shot down in Essen, Germany. Fortunately he parachuted to safety, but was captured and forced to spend two years in a POW camp with shrapnel still embedded in his left leg, a legacy from that horrific incident. After being liberated Ratcliffe returned to Ireland and continued his association with Bohemians.

In 1945 he was transferred to Notts County, but failed to impress at Meadow Lane and in June 1946 was signed by Wolves boss Ted Vizard. A useful full back, he found it difficult to get first team football at Molineux and in June 1947 moved to Plymouth Argyle. He gave the Pilgrims sterling service, appearing in almost 250 games up to May 1956 when he pulled out of League football.

He and his family later emigrated to America.

Wolves' record: 2 apps.

RAYBOULD, Thomas

Tom Raybould spent two seasons at Molineux (1905 to 1907) during which time he acted, in the main, as a versatile reserve half back who deputised for the likes of Bishop, Corfield, Lloyd, Ward, Whitehouse and Williams. Born in Wilden (near Stourport) in July 1884, he joined the Molineux staff from Kidderminster Harriers and left in the summer of 1907 for Grimsby Town. He failed to make the first team at Blundell Park and in 1908 switched to Worksop, later returning to the Midlands to play for Brierley Hill (1909) and Stourbridge (1910). Raybould died in Birmingham in 1944.

Wolves' record: 15 apps. 1 goal.

RAYNES, William

Yorkshireman Billy Raynes was a steady, unspectacular but hard-working midfielder. A Yorkshireman born in Sheffield on 30 October 1964, he represented Sheffield & District Schools and played for Heanor Town (from 1981) before joining Rotherham United as a professional in September 1983. A loan spell with Stockport County (January 1985) preceded his transfer to Wolves in December 1985.

Unfortunately he failed to fit in at Molineux and quit English football for the NASL in May 1986.

Wolves' record: 7+1 sub apps. no goals.

REDFEARN, Leslie F

This player's name has been seen spelt two ways - Redfern and Redfearn.

An inside-forward, born in Burton-on-Trent on 6 December 1911, and now deceased, he played for Stafford Rangers (with whom he won a Staffordshire Senior Cup medal) before joining Wolves in April 1931.

After two full seasons at Molineux he moved to Southend United and later played for Crewe Alexandra and Folkestone. He was reserve to Walter Bottrill and Jimmy Deacon at Molineux. In March 1933 he rejoined Stafford Rangers and during the war guested for several non-League clubs.

Wolves' record: 6 apps. one goal.

REED, Johnson

Well-built inside-right, born in Bruselton in 1908 and now deceased, John Reed played for Bruselton FC and Spennymoor United before spending six weeks at Molineux (February-April 1931).

He never really fitted the bill and after his release from Wolves he went on to have an excellent spell with Walsall, making over 120 appearances for the Saddlers before retiring through injury in the summer of 1938 at the age of 30.

Wolves' record: one app.

REGIS, Cyrille

One of the great goalscorers of the late 1970s and '80s, 'Smokin' Joe' Regis made a rapid rise from non-League football with Hayes to reach the FA Cup semi-final with West Bromwich Albion in the space of eight months! Born in Maripiasoula, French Guyana on 9 February 1958, he cost Albion a mere £5,000 in May 1977 having been

spotted by former Wolves boss and Baggies centre-forward Ronnie Allen.

He scored on his Central League, Football League, FA Cup and League Cup debuts for Albion and went on to claim a total of 140 goals in 370 outings for the Baggies' first XI, including a record of 112 strikes in 302 competitive appearances. He played in three major Cup semi-finals and in a UEFA Cup quarter-final encounter.

Capped four times by England at senior level whilst at The Hawthorns, he also appeared in three 'B' internationals and lined up for the Under-

Cyrille Regis

21s on six occasions. In October 1984, he left Albion for Coventry City in a £250,000 deal and three years later helped the Sky Blues win the FA Cup - and he added another full cap to his collection in the process.

After 282 outings for Coventry (62 goals scored) the 'big fella' moved to Aston Villa in July 1991. He then switched to Wolves on a free transfer in August 1993 (joining mainly as a squad player) and left Molineux for Wycombe Wanderers, also on a 'free' in August 1994, ending his senior career with a brief spell at Chester City.

Regis, who in May 1996 became the oldest player ever to star for Wycombe in a senior game (aged 37 years, 86 days v. Leyton Orient) retired through injury in the summer of 1996. He netted over 200 goals in more than 700 League and Cup games for his six major clubs. In fact, Regis became the first player to be registered as a professional, and to play at senior level, for the following four West Midlands clubs - Albion, Coventry, Villa and Wolves. He returned to his first club, West Brom, as reserve team coach in the summer of 1997 under Ray Harford's management, but left following the arrival of new chief Gary Megson.

A very popular player and true gentleman, Regis now a football agent based in the West Midlands.

Wolves' record: 10+13 sub apps. 2 goals.

REYNOLDS, Charles Jasper

Outside-right Charlie Reynolds played for Wolves' first team during season 1894-95. He was born locally in

Charlie Reynolds

Wolverhampton circa 1873 and starred for the Church Taverners before joining the staff at Molineux in the summer of 1893. It was introduced to League action following an injury to David Wykes in September 1894 and made a reasonable contribution before losing his form and his place at the turn of the year.

He left Molineux in June 1895 and signed for Berwick Rangers (Worcester), quickly switching to Banbury before retiring through injury in 1902.

Wolves' record: 14 apps. 5 goals.

RHODES, Leonard

No relation to Dicky (q.v) Len Rhodes was a left-winger, who played for Wolves during the early twenties, having one good season with the club (1922-23).

Born in Darlaston circa 1900, he played initially for Willenhall and moved to Wolves in May 1920. On leaving Molineux in May 1922 he signed for Shrewsbury Town.

Wolves' record: 19 apps. one goal.

RHODES, Richard Alma

Dicky Rhodes was one of the most skilful half backs in the

Football League in the early 1930s and a big influence when Wolves returned to the First Division in season 1931-32.

Born in Wolverhampton on 22 June 1908, Rhodes joined Wolves from Redditch United in July 1926. In those days he was a centre forward, a position he had occupied as a schoolboy when playing for Wolverhampton Town Boys in 1922-23 and winning England Junior honours against Scotland two seasons later.

Major Frank Buckley switched him to right-half and Rhodes went on to make well over 150 appearances, winning a Second Division championship medal in 1931-32 when he missed only two games. He was transferred to Sheffield United in October 1935 and later played for Swansea Town and Rochdale before hanging up his boots in 1939.

After the war, Rhodes returned to Wolverhampton and became landlord of the Old Still pub in the town and later of the Posada in Lichfield Street. He was also a champion canary breeder and won the national title in 1973 when he beat off the challenges of 1,500 competitors.

He had his aviary at Wednesbury and was also a keen pigeon fancier as well as a member of the Lower Gornal Homing Society.

He died in Wolverhampton in January 1993.

Wolves' record: 159 apps. 7 goals.

RICHARDS, David

Born in Wolverhampton on 1 October 1897, Dave Richards was a reserve at Molineux who failed to make the breakthrough with Wolves and left to join Port Vale in 1922. Thereafter his footballing career took off.

He played only once for the Vale, but after a useful spell as captain of the Scottish club Dundee United (1923-25) he appeared in more than 150 League and Cup games as skipper of Luton Town, spending six-and-a-half seasons up to 1931 with the Hatters. He then starred in almost 40 matches for Watford (1931 to May 1933).

Richards retired to become trainer of Queens Park Rangers, a position he held for two years. Another player 'missed' by Wolves!

RICHARDS, David Thomas

'Dai' Richards was born in Abercanaid near Merthyr on 31 October 1906 and his early clubs were River Field, Bedlingog and Merthyr Town, who were then a Third Division (South) side, before he signed for Wolverhampton Wanderers in August 1927, for £300. Originally a full-back, Richards was converted to a scheming wing-half and occasionally inside-forward by Major Frank Buckley.

He remained at Molineux for nine seasons, helping Wolves win the Second Division championship in 1931-32. He forged a good understanding with fellow countryman Charlie Phillips and won 11 of his 21 full Welsh caps as a Wolves player.

Dai Richards

before transferring to Wolves.

Capped four times by England at Under-21 level, he had an excellent first full season at Molineux, but in 1996-97 and again the following term he was dogged by injury, one after being involved in a car crash (on an icy road) which badly damaged his knee. Nevertheless, when fit and chosen, Richards was solid in defence, strong in the tackle, dominant in the air and consistent in his outfield play.

He was named Wolves skipper in 1996, but two years later, after some injury and contractual problems he was placed on the transfer list by Wolves (December 1998).

Richards, determined to play at a higher level, moved to Southampton on a free transfer in July 1999, and over the next two seasons gave Saints excellent service, appearing in almost 80 first-class matches, scoring some important goals.

In September 2001, after a lot of pre-transfer debate, he left Southampton to join Tottenham Hotspur for a cool £8.1 million, filling the hole left by Sol Campbell.

Richards then went out and scored on his home debut in a pulsating eight-goal thriller against the champions Manchester United at White Hart Lane, a game which Spurs lost 5-3.

Wolves' record: 128+6 sub apps. 6 goals.

In November 1935 he was transferred to Brentford for £3,500. The Bees were in their first-ever season in Division One but although Richards earned some excellent reports, he did not settle in London and in March 1937, he moved to Birmingham in the most extraordinary circumstances. Richards woke up one Saturday morning expecting to play for Brentford against Birmingham but was transferred just before the start of the game and when kick-off time came around he was on the pitch ready to face his former colleagues.

In July 1939, Birmingham allowed him to join Walsall on a free transfer, but the new season was only three games old when war was declared. He played a few times in the early wartime seasons, but by 1945 he was registered with Sedgley, at the age of 39. His trade was a builder and contractor and he was also a good cricketer and keen motorist. His younger brother, Billy, made 31 senior appearances for Wolves from 1927 to 1929.

Richards died at Yardley, Birmingham on 1 October 1969. Wolves' record: 229 apps. 5 goals.

RICHARDS, Dean Ivor

Described as a 'classy central defender' when he joined Wolves on loan from Bradford City in March 1995, Dean Richards made such an impact at Molineux that he was signed on a full contract for an agreed club record fee of £1.8 million as soon as the season was over. Wolves, in fact, paid £1,300,000 down and added the final payment of £500,000 in November 1998.

Born in Bradford on 9 June 1974, Richards was a trainee at Valley Parade before turning 'pro' with City in July 1992. He played over 100 times for the Yorkshire club

Dean Richards

RICHARDS, John Peter

Studious centre-forward John Richards was the most prolific scorer in Wolves' history until his record was beaten by Steve Bull.

He had two rewarding partnerships at Wolves, the first with Derek Dougan, the second with Scotsman Andy Gray. He was exceptionally fast, had acute positional sense and was, indeed, a very fine marksman. An intelligent footballer, Richards undoubtedly leaned a lot from Dougan in the art of holding an attack together with constructive passes.

Born deep in the heart of Rugby League territory in Warrington on 9 November 1950, Richards joined Wolves after leaving school in July 1967 and turned full-time professional two years later. He made his debut at The Hawthorns in February 1970 and claimed his first senior goal away to Fiorentina in May of that year, in the Anglo-Italian Cup.

Thereafter Richards scored in every season for Wolves up to and including the 1981-82 campaign.

He netted almost 200 goals - and his tally included 144 in the Football League and 24 in the FA Cup, three of the latter being netted against Charlton Athletic in 1976 after he had come onto the field as a substitute. He also secured 18 goals in the Football League Cup and four in European competitions. And he holds the distinction of scoring one of the fastest-ever goals for Wolves from the start of a game... finding the back of the net after just 12 seconds play against Burnley at Turf Moor in November 1975 (Division One).

Richards appeared in the 1974 and 1980 League Cup Finals, scoring the winner against Manchester City in the first game, and he won a Second Division championship medal in 1976-77 and a UEFA Cup runners-up prize in 1971-72.

The following season Richards was the country's leading scorer with 33 goals, but he won only one full England cap for his efforts, in 1973 against Northern Ireland at Wembley.

John Richards

He had been capped at Schoolboy, Under-21 and Under-23 level prior to that and his scant reward at full level was certainly a surprise considering his goalscoring record with Wolves.

Richards is the only Wolves player to receive two benefits: in 1982 and 1986. But he left the club in unhappy circumstances, moving to the Portuguese side Maritimo Funchal of Madeira in August 1983, after a short loan spell with Second Division strugglers Derby County. He was in Wolves reserves when he offered his experience to the Rams in what turned out to be a successful battle against relegation that season. He scored twice in ten games for Derby.

Whilst working for Wolverhampton Leisure Services Department he was made a Director of the club (appointed in 1995) and in October 1997 Wolves' owner Sir Jack Hayward appointed Richards as the club's Managing Director on a salary of £150,000 a year.

Richards left Molineux, however, in the summer of 2000, following the arrival of Chief Executive Jez Moxey from Stoke City.

Wolves' record: 461+25 sub apps. 194 goals.

RICHARDS, Richard William

Dick Richards played for Wolves from 1913 to 1922, World War One excepted of course.

He was born in Chirk, a one-time hotbed of Welsh football, on 14 February 1890, and first played serious soccer for Bronygarth FC in 1907. He then served Chirk and Oswestry United before joining Wolves in July 1913, after trials with both Wrexham and Everton. He managed only 13 games in the last two pre-war seasons but in 1919-20 was top scorer with ten goals.

He played in only half the games in 1920-21, missing the FA Cup Final against Spurs, and managed 27 League outings the following season before transferring to West Ham United in June 1922. He scored six goals in 53 games for the Hammers and played in the first-ever Wembley FA Cup Final in 1923 v. Bolton Wanderers.

His career then took him to Fulham (1924-25), Mold Town (1925-27) and Colwyn Bay United (1927-28) before he was forced to retire because of a serious back injury sustained when unloading electric light pylons. He had returned to North Wales for domestic reasons and had taken a job with an electricity company. The injury eventually led to his death in a Salford hospital on 27 January 1934, aged 43.

Dick Richards

John Richards and Geoff Palmer celebrate winning the League Cup of 1974 at Wembley Stadium

Richards, who won five Welsh caps as a Wolves player, subsequently added three more to his tally whilst with West Ham and another with Mold - the only time a player from this small club has ever achieved full international honours, although at the time they were pioneers of big spending in the Welsh National League.

In his early international career Richards played with Wolves goalkeeper Teddy Peers and Ted Vizard, who was to be his boss at Upton Park and who later managed Wolves.

Wolves' record: 94 apps. 26 goals.

RICHARDS, William Edward

Brother of David Thomas Richards (q.v), Billy Richards was born in Abercanaid in August 1905 and worked down the pit, while also playing junior football with Troedyrhiw Carlton and then mid Rhondda (July 1923).

More than useful at outside-right, fast raiding, he joined Wolves in July 1927 and was a member of the first team squad for two seasons before moving to Coventry City in March 1929.

Richards scored 12 goals in 80 appearances during a two-and-a-half -year spell at Highfield Road and then, in the summer of 1931, he moved south to Fulham, helping the Cottagers win the Third Division (South) championship in 1931-32. Later he assisted Brighton & Hove Albion, Bristol Rovers and Folkestone Town.

Winner of one Welsh cap v. Northern Ireland in 1933 whilst with Fulham, he was in fact, the first player from the London club to win full international honours.

Richards, who was also a competent cricketer and good golfer, died in Wolverhampton on 30 September 1956.

Wolves' record: 31 apps. 2 goals.

RICHARDSON, Jonathon T

Hard tackling defender, good in the air, but a shade slow on the ground, Jon Richardson was born in Durham circa 1905.

He joined Wolves from Spennymoor Black & Whites in June 1928 and stayed two years at Molineux before transferring to Southend United in June 1930. He later played for Waterford Celtic in Ireland (August 1931-32).

Wolves' record: 3 apps.

RILEY, Alfred

Half-back Alf Riley played for Wolves before and after World War One. He began as a centre-half, being relatively small for that position - he stood only 5ft 7in - but in those days that mattered little because the position was not purely a defensive one.

He was born in Stafford on 7 December 1889 and played his early football for Stafford Excelsior (1905), Bostocks FC (in two spells), Stafford Rangers reserves, Siemens Institute and Wellington Town, whom he joined in 1910. In August 1911 he went back to Stafford Rangers and two years later he signed for Wolves.

It was the start of useful association with the club and Riley made his League debut against Huddersfield Town in April 1914. He appeared ten times in 1914-15 and during the hostilities guested for Wellington for three years from 1915 to 1918. When League football resumed after World War One, he became a regular in the left-half position at Molineux, gaining a FA Cup runners-up medal in 1921.

Alfred Riley

Riley made his last appearance in November 1922 (at Meadow Lane) and at the end of that season he was forced to retire through injury. His only goal for Wolves came in a 3-0 home win over Leicester City in April 1921. Alf Riley died circa 1958.

Wolves' record: 130 apps. one goal.

ROBERTS, Brian Leslie Ford

'Harry' Roberts could play in either full back position or as a central defender.

A cheerful, likeable chap with a great sense of humour, he

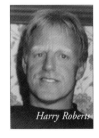
Harry Roberts

was strong in every department of defensive play and made well over 500 appearances during a fine career. Born in Manchester on 6 November 1955, he joined Coventry City as an apprentice in June 1972 and turned professional in May 1974. The following year (February) he gained experience as a loan player with Hereford United and afterwards went on to star in almost 250 games for the Sky Blues before transferring to Birmingham City for £10,000 in March 1984.

After overcoming the boo-boys at St. Andrew's, Roberts amassed 213 outings for the 'second city' club up to June 1990 when Wolves recruited him on a free transfer. Ever-reliable and a sound competitor, he was released in May 1992 and immediately rejoined his former club Coventry as a scout and was later appointed reserve team coach. Now a sports teacher, he also penned a witty column in a local sports-paper and wrote an excellent book!

Wolves' record: 20+4 apps.

ROBERTS, Darren Anthony

Striker Darren Roberts made a terrific start to his Football League career - scoring a hat-trick on his debut for Wolves against Birmingham City in the televised Sunday game on

27 September 1992 in front of 14,391 fans at St Andrew's. Born in Birmingham on 12 October 1969, the six-foot Roberts joined Wolves in March 1992 from Burton Albion for £20,000 and he quickly helped the reserves win promotion from the Pontins League Division Two before making a name for himself in League action.

Unfortunately he failed to carry on the good work and after a loan spell with Hereford United (March 1994) he left Molineux four months later for Doncaster Rovers but quickly switched his allegiance to Chesterfield within 12 days.

After two loan spells with Telford United (December 1993 and December 1994) he moved to Darlington in July 1996.

Another loan period followed, this time with Peterborough United in February 1998, before Roberts joined Scarborough in February 1999, switching his allegiance to Exeter City in July 2000 before playing for non-Leaguers Barrow (in 2001).

Wolves' record: 13+11 sub apps. 5 goals.

ROBERTS, Iwan Wyn

Welsh international striker at four levels (full, 'B', Youth and Schoolboy) Iwan Roberts (6ft 3ins. tall and weighing more than 14 stones) joined Wolves for £1 million from Leicester City in July 1996.

Born in Bangor on 26 June 1968, he initially signed apprentice forms for Watford in 1985 and turned professional at Vicarage Road in July 1988. He scored 12 goals in 83 games for the Hornets before transferring to Huddersfield Town for £275,000 in August 1990.

After almost three-and-a-half seasons at Leeds Road, during which time he netted 68 times in 182 appearances, he switched his allegiance to Leicester City, signing for the Foxes in November 1993 for £100,000. He continued to hit the target during his time at Filbert Street and when he moved to Wolves had claimed 45 goals in 111 outings for the East Midland club.

Roberts did well at Molineux, especially when teaming up with co-strikers Steve Bull and Don Goodman. And there is no doubt that the highlight of his stay with Wolves came early in the 1996-97 season when he cracked in a terrific hat-trick in a 4-2 League win at rivals West Bromwich Albion, thus becoming the first Wanderers player ever to score a treble against the Baggies at The Hawthorns.

He was perhaps surprisingly sold by manager Mark McGhee to Norwich City for £1 million in June 1997, being replaced at Molineux by the Finnish international Mixu Paatelainen (signed from Bolton Wanderers). Since then the toothless Roberts has carried on finding the net while also adding to his tally of senior caps.

Wolves' record: 28+10 sub apps. 12 goals.

ROBERTS, Jack

Left-winger Jack Roberts was a member of Wolves' first team squad during the 1894-95 season when he challenged for a place in the side along with Messrs. Fleming, Griffin and Brocksopp.

Born in Wednesbury circa 1873 he had played for Swan Athletic (West Bromwich) and Tipton Excelsior before teaming up with Wolves. After leaving Molineux he returned to non-League soccer with Ewells FC (Wednesbury).

Wolves' record: one app.

ROBERTS, Jason Andre Davis

Signed by Wolves in September 1997 from Hayes for £250,000 - the biggest fee paid out by the club for a non-League player - Jason Roberts is a striker, whose uncle is Cyrille Regis (ex Wolves of course who also served with Hayes).

Born in Park Royal, London on 25 January 1978, Roberts never really made his mark at Molineux and after loan spells with Torquay United (December 1997 and January 1998) and Bristol City (March 1998) he left Wolves in August 1998, transferring to Bristol Rovers for £250,000. Capped by Grenada on three occasions in the Shell Cup in April and May 1998, he scored a hat-trick in a 17-1 win in one game when his uncle Otis also scored. Roberts did well at The Memorial Ground and scored some fine goals for the Pirates.

He grabbed a total of 48 in 93 first-team appearances before transferring to West Bromwich Albion for a club record fee of £2.3 million in July 2001. In his first season at The Hawthorns he teamed up superbly well with fellow striker Lee Hughes and helped the Baggies reach the Play-offs.

Unfortunately a broken foot disrupted the start of the 2001-02 season for Roberts.

ROBERTS, John

Utility forward Jack Roberts, 5ft 9ins tall and 11st 6lbs in weight, had one excellent season with Wolves (1906-07) when he formed a fine left-wing partnership with winger Jack Pedley.

Born in Walsall circa 1885, he was signed from Darlaston and left the club for Bristol Rovers for whom he appeared in 85 League games, scoring 28 goals.

He returned to the Midlands in 1911 to play for Stourbridge and then Walsall Phoenix and in 1914-15 went off to war. He seems that he quit playing football after the hostilities.

Wolves' record: 25 apps. 14 goals.

ROBERTSON, Alistair Peter

Ally Robertson had already enjoyed an excellent career with Black Country rivals West Bromwich Albion before he joined Wolves in September 1986.

The tough-tackling, resilient Scottish defender, who was born at Philipstoun, Lothian, on 9 September 1952, first played for Linlithgow Academy and Uphill Saints before spending 18 years at The Hawthorns.

Ally Robertson

ROBINSON, Carl Phillip

Midfielder Carl Robinson was born in Llandrindod Wells on 13 October 1976 and went to Shrewsbury Town as a 16 year-old trialist, but was released and ended up at Molineux as a trainee, turning professional with Wolves in July 1995.

Capped by Wales at Youth, 'B', Under-21 and senior levels, his first full cap was obtained against Ukraine at the Millennium Stadium in March 2001 when he received the 'Man of the Match' award. Robinson was a vital member of the Wolves' first team squad during seasons 1996-2001 and in the latter campaign took his appearance tally for the club past the 150 mark.

He actually went back to his old hunting ground, Gay Meadow, as a loan player in March 1996 and gained an Auto-Windscreen Shield runners-up medal with the Shrews. Robinson actually played at Wembley before he made his senior debut for Wolves!

Wolves' record: 139+28 sub apps. 21 goals*

ROBINSON, Philip John

Equally adept in defence or midfield, the red-headed Phil Robinson always gave a good account of himself out on the park.

Born in Stafford on 6 January 1967, and educated at the town's Rising Brook High School where he gained eight 'O' levels, he represented Stafford & District Schools before joining the groundstaff of Aston Villa at the age of 14.

He then became an apprentice (June 1983) and signed professional forms at Villa Park in January 1985. Wolves paid £5,000 for his services in June 1987 and he went on to help the Wanderers win both the Fourth and Third Division championships as well as the Sherpa Van Trophy before transferring to Notts County for £67,500 in August 1989.

He was a key member of County's Third Division promotion winning side in 1990 and whilst on loan from Meadow Lane, he helped Birmingham City lift the Leyland DAF Cup at Wembley in 1991. In September 1992, he was sold by County to Huddersfield Town and after a two-month loan period with Northampton Town (September-October 1994) he joined Chesterfield in December 1994.

Robinson had a second loan spell with Notts County (August 1996) and during the 1997-98 season he passed the personal milestone of 300 senior appearances at club level. In July 1998 he became one of Brian Little's first signings for Stoke City.

Robinson quit the Football League scene at the end of the 1999-2000 season when he joined Hereford United, taking over as team manager at Edgar Street (from ex-Wolves boss Graham Turner) in the summer of 2001....preferring to stay in football rather than pursue a career in physiotherapy after qualifying with flying colours two years earlier.

Wolves' record: 80+10 sub apps. 9 goals.

Joining the Baggies as an apprentice in July 1968, Robertson made his League debut as a 17-year-old against Manchester United (facing Charlton, Best and Co.) in October 1969. He then overcame a broken leg, suffered in a League Cup-tie v. Charlton in 1970 and went on to total over 620 first-team appearances, although he never won a major honour with Albion and even his international appearances were limited to Schoolboy and Youth caps.

He was in the Albion sides that lost three major semi-finals (one in 1978 and two in 1982) and also featured in the 1969 FA Youth Cup Final defeat v. Sunderland. Considering the number of games he played for West Brom, his lack of personal silverware was remarkable enough.

Yet, after moving to Wolves and playing in more than 100 League games, he managed two championship medals - from success in each of the old Fourth and Third Divisions - and he also gained a Sherpa Van Trophy winners' medal at Wembley, besides helping Wolves reach the Fourth Division Play-off Final v. Aldershot at the end of his first season at Molineux.

Robertson was released in June 1990 and became player-manager of Worcester City and then manager of Cheltenham Town, before leaving football altogether in 1992 to become a car salesman in Dudley.

Wolves' record: 136 apps.

ROBSON, David

Dave Robson was a well built, stocky defender who spent two seasons with Wolves, making his debut on the last day of the 1893-94 campaign at Burnley when he replaced George Swift at left-back.

Born in Scotland circa 1869, he played for Ayr United and Ardwick before joining Wolves in August 1893. He left Molineux in May 1895, returning to Ardwick who by now had become Manchester City.

He played 57 League games for City before moving to London to play for Millwall (1896-98). He then returned to Scotland, retiring in 1900.

Wolves' record: 5 apps.

RODGER, Graham

Graham Rodger was a competent Scottish centre-half, who became one of a fine plethora of excellent defenders at Grimsby Town during the 1990s.

Graham Rodger

Born in Glasgow on 1 April 1967, Rodger joined Wolves as an apprentice in 1983, but before he had the chance to turn professional at Molineux, he was whisked away by Coventry City (February 1985). A little over two years later, after signing full-time for the Sky Blues, he stepped out at Wembley and helped City win the FA Cup Final (v. Spurs).

He made over 40 appearances during his stay at Highfield Road that ended in August 1989 when he was transferred to Luton Town for £150,000.

From Kenilworth Road he switched to Blundell Park for a then record fee for the Mariners of £135,000 (January 1992) and over the next five years was a regular member of Grimsby's senior squad, amassing more than 165 appearances

In the summer of 1997 he joined the coaching staff at Blundell Park while still a player but in July 1998 Rodger left the Cleethorpes-based club to sign as a player-coach for Hull City.

Wolves' record: one app.

ROMANO, Serge

French full-back - born in Metz on 25 May 1964 - Serge Romano joined Wolves on a free transfer from FC. Martigues in August 1996, having previously played for his home town club Metz and Toulouse.

Unfortunately he never adapted to the pace of the English game, looking far too fragile. He was released in May 1997 when his contract expired and returned home to France.

Wolves' record: 2+3 sub apps.

ROONEY, John

John Rooney was born in Newcastle-upon-Tyne in 1919. A useful centre-half, signed from Romsley, he broke into the first team at Molineux in season 1938-39, but the following year, like so many other footballers, he went into the forces to serve his country.

He was sadly killed in Italy in 1943, aged just 24.

Wolves' record: 2 apps.

ROPER, Francis L

Frank Roper stepped out for his one and only appearance for Wolves in a 3-0 home defeat by Blackpool in a Second Division match in March 1920 when he replaced Jack Sambrook in the attack.

Born in Walsall in 1899, he joined Wolves from Pleck in July 1919 (when the club was engaging several relatively unknown players after the war) and left Molineux for Wolverhampton Rangers in May 1920.

Wolves' record: one app.

ROSARIO, Robert Michael

Tall, raven-haired striker, Robert Rosario won England Youth honours as a teenager. Born in Hammersmith, London, on 4 March 1966, he joined Norwich City from non-League Hillingdon Borough in December 1983 and during his time at Carrow Road he added four England Under-21 caps to his collection.

He made only 20 League appearances for the Canaries in his first three years with the club and in January 1986 was loaned to Wolves. After returning to Norwich the following month, he quickly established himself in the first team and went from strength to strength, netting 29 goals in 158 games up to March 1991 when he moved to Coventry City for £600,000.

In March 1993 - after netting ten goals in 67 games for the Sky Blues - he went to Nottingham Forest for £400,000, staying at The City Ground until May 1996.

Wolves' record: 4 apps. one goal.

ROSE, William Crispin

Goalkeeper Billy Rose, was born in St Pancras, London on 3 April 1861 and was one of the leading 'keepers of the 1890s.

He began his career with Small Heath (later Birmingham City) before making his name with the Swifts club of London. He played for Wiltshire, Staffordshire and London in county matches and also appeared for Preston North End (in 1885-86) and Stoke (whom he joined in August 1886) before signing for Wolves in January 1889. Rose enjoyed a fine career with the club, appearing in more than 150 senior games overall and gaining an FA Cup winners' medal in 1893, although he missed another Final three years later because of injury. He was capped four times by England before joining Wolves and won another cap as a Wolves player.

In his five internationals he conceded only four goals. In July 1894 his Molineux career was interrupted when he was 'sacked' and he had a brief spell with Loughborough Town.

The Loughborough club was elected to the Second Division in the summer of 1895, but by then Rose was back with Wolves, whom he finally left 12 months later. In 1893 he had circulated a letter in which he stated that he was 'instrumental' in forming a Players' Union. It was that which apparently upset Wolves.

After he finished playing, Rose ran a pub in Birmingham, then another in Wolverhampton, and also had a shop in Bordesley Green, near St Andrew's.

He died in Bordesley Green on 4 February 1937.

Wolves' record: 155 apps.

ROSS, Ian

Early in 1982 player-coach Ian Ross, ex-Aston Villa and Liverpool and former manager of FC Valur, took over as caretaker-manager of Wolves. He held the team together for four games from the 16 January 1982 to 2 February 1982 inclusive prior to the arrival at Molineux of Ian Greaves.

Born in Glasgow on 26 January 1947, Ross joined the playing staff at Anfield as a 16 year-old, turned professional in August 1965 and played in 58 League games before transferring to Aston Villa in February 1972. Nicknamed 'Roscoe' he helped Villa win the Third Division championship and League Cup during his four years with the club during which time he accumulated 204 senior appearances, several as captain.

In December 1976 - after loan spells with Notts County and Northampton Town - Ross moved to Peterborough United. He played in almost 140 games for Posh before joining Wolves in August 1979 (as player/coach).

He rounded off his playing days in England with Hereford United (October 1982-May 1983). He then took a coaching position in Oman, returned briefly to England where he acted as reserve team coach at Birmingham City and then became manager/coach of the Icelandic club, FC Valur (August 1984-June 1988).

After that Ross coached in South Africa and Australia (1988-91) and was in charge of Huddersfield Town for a short while (from March 1992-93). On leaving the football scene he entered the licensing trade, taking over the Gardeners' Arms in Timperley near Altrincham. He now resides in Wolverhampton.

ROSS, Stewart

Stewart Ross was a blond full-back or midfielder, who made his League debut for Wolves in front of almost 54,000 fans at Old Trafford in December 1967.

Born in Woking on 11 September 1945, and a former Wolverhampton Grammar School pupil, Ross joined Wolves on schoolboy forms, became an amateur in June 1965 and signed as a part-time professional at Molineux five months later, staying there until May 1971, basically as a reserve. He then qualified as a Chartered Accountant (the profession he's in today) and between 1977 and 1980 he assisted Old Wulfrunians.

Wolves' record: 1+2 sub apps.

ROSTANCE, James Colin

Jim Rostance was one of a number of goalkeepers registered with Wolves for the first season after the Great War (1919-20). Born the son of a local foundry worker in Penkridge, Staffs in May 1898, he joined the Molineux staff in April 1913 from Siemen's FC, having earlier played for Cannock Town and Featherstone Boys Club.

He was unlucky to be between the posts when Wolves crashed to a 10-3 defeat at Hull City in December 1919 and seven months later was transferred to Hednesford Town, later assisting Rugeley Swifts and Cannock Welfarers.

Wolves' record: 9 apps.

ROTTON, William Harry

Amateur inside-forward Billy Rotton was born in Wednesbury circa 1909. He played local intermediate football in the West Bromwich and Walsall areas before joining Wolves as a reserve in August 1927.

After spending only one season at Molineux, he began his tour of the Midlands, playing, in turn, for Shrewsbury Town (from August 1928), West Bromwich Albion (for a year from May 1929), Brierley Hill Alliance (signed in May 1930), Cradley Heath (from March 1931), Walsall (for two seasons from August 1931), Hereford United (briefly in 1933), Worcester City (for a short spell in 1934) and finally Dudley Town (from October 1935 until May 1936).

He won a Junior International cap for England whilst with Wolves (1928).

Wolves' record: 4 apps. one goal.

ROUSE, Valentine Alfred

Although born at Hoddesdon, near Harlow, on 14 February 1898 (St. Valentine's Day - hence his Christian name) left-half Val Rouse started his playing career in South Wales with Pontypridd, where, in 1921, he was discovered by a keen Wolves scout. He made only a handful of senior appearances during his brief stay a Molineux before transferring to Stoke for £1,000 in 1922. A gentleman both on and off the field, Rouse scored twice in 94 outings for the Potters, up to May 1925, when he returned to South Wales to sign for Swansea Town. He returned to the Potteries in June 1926 and joined Port Vale for whom he made 103 appearances in three seasons.

He next assisted Crewe Alexandra and later played for Connah's Quay and Shotton FC before retiring in 1933.

Wolves' record: 5 apps.

ROUSSEL Cedric

Born in Mons, Belgium on 6 January 1978 and capped by his country at Under-21 level, 6ft 3in striker Cedric Roussel played for La Louviere and KAA Ghewnt (in his homeland) before joining Coventry City for £1.5 million in October 1999. He had a fine first season in the Premiership, but then, following the arrival at Highfield Road of Robbie Keane (from Wolves) he found it hard to recreate the form he had shown previously. As a result he was transferred to Molineux for £1.53 million in February 2001, having scored 11 goals 43 first-class games for the Sky Blues. He was manager Dave Jones' second signing for the club.

Wolves' record: 3+8 apps*

ROWBOTHAM, Harold

Wolves signed Harry Rowbotham as a reserve half-back in June 1900. He remained at Molineux for three seasons, making only seven first team appearances, while occupying all three middle-line positions as well as that of inside-right.

Born in Bilston circa 1879, he played for Bilston Town prior to joining Wolves and on his departure from Molineux Rowbotham signed for Fulham, later moving back to the Black Country to play for Stourbridge, Netherton and Oldbury St. Michael's. He died in Birmingham in 1969.

Wolves' record: 7 apps. one goal.

ROWLEY BROTHERS (Arthur and Jack)

Arthur Rowley (born in Wolverhampton on 21 April 1926) played for Blakenhall St. Luke's as a 14 year-old and was a junior and then reserve with Wolves during World War Two, netting three goals in nine games.

After serving in Germany and Palestine, and guesting for Crystal Palace (as a left-back), Manchester United, Middlesbrough, Brighton & Hove Albion and Lincoln City during the hostilities, he went on to score a record 434 Football League goals while serving with West Bromwich Albion (1946-48), Fulham (1948-50), Leicester City (1950-58) and Shrewsbury Town (1958-68).

He helped both West Brom and Fulham gain promotion to the First Division in season 1948-49 and after retiring managed Sheffield United (1968-69), Southend United (1970-76) and Oswestry Town (1979-80).

Capped by England 'B' he also represented the Football League and won three Second Division championship medals (1949, 1954 and 1957) and a Division Four runners-up prize (1972), also helping Shrewsbury gain promotion in 1959.

Rowley was only 15 years of age when he made his 'debut' for Manchester United (as a guest) in a wartime fixture in 1941, lining up alongside his brother Jack. He left Molineux for The Hawthorns initially in March 1944, turning professional two months later.

Jack Rowley guested for Distillery, Spurs, Walsall and Wolves during the 1939-45 hostilities and scored all eight goals in a Regional League game for the Wanderers versus Derby County in November 1942.

Born in Wolverhampton on 7 October 1920, Rowley senior joined Wolves in November 1935 from Dudley Old Boys and after a loan spells with Cradley Heath and Bournemouth, he moved to Manchester United in October 1937 for £3,500. He went on to score 208 goals in 422 games for United before becoming Plymouth Argyle's player-manager in February 1955.

He remained at Home Park until March 1960, having retired as a player in 1957.

From July 1960 to May 1963, Rowley managed Oldham Athletic; from August 1963 to July 1964 he was coach at Ajax and on returning to Great Britain, managed Wrexham (January 1966-April 1967), Bradford Park Avenue (March 1967 to October 1968) and Oldham, again (from October 1968 to December 1969) before pulling out of bigtime soccer.

Capped six times by England at senior level and once during the war, Rowley also played in a 'B' international and represented the Football League. He won FA Cup and First Division championship winners medals with Manchester United in 1948 and 1952 respectively, helped Argyle to promotion in 1959 and the took Oldham to the Fourth Division title in 1963. He also won a League War Cup winners' medal with United in 1942.

NB - On 22 October 1955, both Arthur and Jack scored the 200th League goal of their respective careers - Arthur for Leicester City at Fulham and Jack for Plymouth Argyle against Barnsley, both in the Second Division. Arthur was first to reach the milestone by just 12 minutes.

ROWLEY, Kenneth Frank

Utility forward Ken Rowley joined Wolves as a professional in October 1947, a few weeks before entering the Army.

Born in Pelsall, Walsall on 29 August 1926, he originally came to the club as an amateur from Elkington's FC in June 1946, and after completing his national service, returned to play for Wolves, staying until January 1951 at which time he moved to Birmingham City, later assisting Coventry City (November 1954 to May 1955) and Bromsgrove Rovers.

Wolves' record: 3 apps.

RUDGE, Dale Anthony

Dale Rudge did a reasonable job in the midfield engine room for Wolves during his short time at Molineux. Born in Wolverhampton on 9 September 1963, he represented Staffordshire Boys before joining Wolves as an apprentice in July 1979, turning professional in August 1981.

In July 1984 he moved to Preston North End and after a three-year spell in Norway with FC Djvre 1919 (January 1987 to June 1990) he rounded off his career with Hednesford Town (to 1992).

He then became a market trader in Kingswinford, and later worked for Dudley Council Adult Education (catering for special needs) while also running a junior football team, Ashwood Boys in Wordsley near Stourbridge.

Wolves' record: 25+4 apps.

S

RUSSELL, Edward Thomas

Wing-half Eddie Russell was signed by Wolves from St. Chad's College during the 1945-46 season. He turned professional immediately and went on to play 30 League games during his time at Molineux which lasted until December 1951 when he switched north to join Middlesbrough.

From Ayresome Park he moved to Leicester City (October 1953) and after 101 appearances for the Foxes, he rounded off his senior career with Notts County (August 1958 to May 1959).

Russell was born in Cranwell on 15 July 1928.

Wolves' record: 33 apps.

RUSSELL, Peter William

Born in Gornal, near Dudley on 16 January 1935, half-back Peter Russell (no relation to Eddie, q.v) joined Wolves as a junior in 1950 and turned professional at Molineux in October 1952.

With so many excellent footballers occupying the same position around that time, Russell's first team outings were limited and in March 1956 he was transferred to Notts County for whom he played more than 100 League games before quitting the big time in May 1959.

Wolves' record: 4 apps.

RUTTER, Hubert

Full-back Hubert Rutter acted as cover for Dickie Baugh during his short spell at Molineux. Born in Walsall circa 1869, he played initially for Bradley Swifts and was recruited by Wolves in March 1891.

He stayed with the club for barely three months before moving to Ashwood Villa, later assisting Tutbury Town and Dresden Celtic.

Wolves' record: 2 apps.

RYAN, Derek Anthony

A reserve inside-forward or winger at Molineux, Derek Ryan joined Wolves as an apprentice in June 1982.

He signed professional forms in October 1984 and had three fairly good years at the club before being released in May 1987 by manger Graham Turner. Born in Dublin on 2 January 1967, he returned to Ireland after leaving the Midlands.

Wolves' record: 29+11 sub apps. 5 goals.

SAMBROOK, John Henry

Jack Sambrook was a good-class centre-forward who joined Wolves towards the end of the First World War and was a valuable member of the first team squad for two seasons: 1919-21.

Born in Wednesfield on 10 March 1899, he played initially for Willenhall Town and after leaving Molineux he signed for Liverpool in 1922 (appearing in two League games) and thereafter assisted Stockport County, Willenhall Swifts and C & L Hills FC, retiring in 1937.

Sambrook died in Heathtown, Wolverhampton on 30 December 1973.

Wolves' record: 21 apps. 7 goals.

SAMWAYS, Vincent

Midfielder Vinny Samways was on loan to Wolves from Everton in December 1995. Born in Bethnal Green, London on 27 October 1968, he joined Tottenham Hotspur on leaving school and turned professional at White Hart Lane in November 1985.

A determined player, he went on to score 17 goals in almost 250 appearances for Spurs, helping them win the FA Cup in 1991. He was transferred to Everton for £2.2 million in August 1994 but never really settled on Merseyside and, indeed, after his loan spell at Molineux he had a similar one at Birmingham City (February 1996).

Samways, who won five England Under-21 caps while with Spurs and also represented his country at Youth team level, joined the Spanish club Las Palmas in September 1996. He was dubbed something of a 'villain' in Spanish footballing circles after a series of extravagant clashes with opponents, resulting in a handful of reprimands and suspensions!

Wolves' record: 3 apps.

SANJUAN Jesus Garcia

Spanish midfielder Jesus Sanjuan - known as the 'Bulldozer' - was signed by Wolves' boss Mark McGhee on a three-month loan deal from Real Zaragoza in September 1997. He scored on his debut in a 1-0 Coca-Cola Cup win at Fulham but unfortunately after a bright start he never really fitted into the manager's plans and he returned home before his 12 weeks were up!

Born in Zaragoza on 22 August 1971, Sanjuan represented his country at Under-21 and Under-23 honours and gained a European Cup Winners Cup-winners' medal in 1995 as substitute v. Arsenal.

Wolves' record: 6+1 sub apps. one goal.

SCOTCHBROOK, Frederick

Fred Scotchbrook was Wolves' manager from March 1926 to June 1927.

He was born in Horwich, near Bolton in 1886 and on leaving school, played for two local clubs, Gymnasium FC and Horwich. In 1914 he joined Bolton Wanderers as a professional, but failed to make the grade at Burnden Park and retired during the war to become Wanderers' coach, later taking over as assistant-secretary at the Lancashire club.

He left Bolton in 1924 to become manager of Stockport County, moving to Molineux two years later to succeed Albert Hoskins. Wolves finished 4th in the Second Division at the end of the 1925-26 season, but the following year they slipped to 15th.

Then, shortly after the club's AGM in June 1927, Scotchbrook had a heated argument with two Directors and was subsequently relieved of his duties, allowing Major Frank Buckley to take over the reins. He quit football at this juncture.

Wolves' record as manager: played 56, won 24, drawn 9, lost 23.

SCOTT, Henry T

Inside-right Harry Scott was a tall, well built six-footer, weighing over 12 stones, who made opponents realize his presence in no uncertain terms!

Born in Newburn, Northumberland on 4 August 1897, Scott played for Newburn Grange before teaming up with Sunderland in 1922. After three years at Roker Park he was transferred to Wolves (July 1925).

He stayed at Molineux until November 1926 when he signed for Hull City, later assisting Bradford Park Avenue (from June 1928), Swansea Town (July 1932), Watford (1933-34) and Nuneaton Borough (July 1934).

On his retirement in 1936, Scott chose to live in Warwickshire.

Wolves' record: 37 apps. 6 goals.

SCOTT, Robert Alexander

Alex Scott, an eminently safe goalkeeper, cost Wolves just £1,250 when signed from Burnley in February 1936.

Bringing a secure style of goalkeeping to Molineux which was to be of inestimable value over the next ten years, Scott went on to play in almost 130 League and FA Cup

Alex Scott

games for the Wanderers, plus 68 in wartime. He collected two League Division One runners-up medals in his first two seasons at Molineux, when he missed only four matches out of 84.

Scott, who also finished on the losing side in the 1939 FA Cup Final, was originally a centre-half.

Born in Liverpool on 29 October 1913, he won England Schoolboy honours and was also a fine baseball pitcher for Oakmere in the Zingari League while playing soccer for Forest Dynamos. Standing 6ft. 4ins tall, he joined Liverpool in 1930, but at that time there was another goalkeeper called Scott in charge at Anfield - Elisha (no relation) - along with a big South African, Arthur Riley, and consequently after failing to break through into the first team, Scott was transferred to Burnley in May 1933. He made 60 appearances for the Turf Moor club, helping them reach the FA Cup semi-finals in 1935, before switching to Wolves. Scott, a big man with the ability to kick the ball huge distances downfield, was sent-off twice playing for Wolves in December 1936 against Huddersfield and Leeds, although the latter game was abandoned late on.

For his misdemeanour against Huddersfield, the FA suspended Scott for seven days and fined him £8 (a week's wages) and at the time of his dismissal his manager Major Buckley no doubt had something to say as Wolves lost 4-0. Scott, who had played for England at baseball, represented the Football League and played for an All British XI in the first wartime season of 1939-40 and he also guested for Aston Villa and Southport during the hostilities.

With Bert Williams installed at Molineux after the war, Scott left for Crewe Alexandra in August 1947 and made 44 League appearances for the Railwaymen before quitting the bigtime in 1949. He later ran a general stores in Dunstall Road, Whitmore Reans, Wolverhampton and became a detective in the Wolverhampton Borough Police Force.

Wolves' record: 129 apps.

SEAL, James

Striker Jimmy Seal was born in Pontefract on 9 December 1950 and joined Wolves on leaving school in 1966, turning professional at Molineux in March 1968. Unfortunately he had far too many established forwards to battle with for a place in the first XI at Molineux and consequently, in May 1971, he was transferred to Barnsley having had a lengthy loan spell with Walsall the previous year.

From Oakwell he switched to York City (July 1972) and at Bootham Crescent he did extremely well, scoring 43 goals in 161 League outings before joining Darlington in November 1976. Again he did the business at Feethams, claiming 19 goals in his 122 League outings up to November 1979 when he left the Quakers for Rochdale.

After a fine career Seal eventually pulled out of bigtime football in 1981 with a record of 92 goals in 420 League matches.

Wolves' record: 1 app.

SEDGLEY, Stephen Philip

Born in Enfield, Middlesex on 26 May 1968, Steve Sedgley joined Wolves in June 1997 from Ipswich Town in a £650,000 deal which took fellow defender Mark Venus (rated at £150,000) from Molineux to Portman Road. He made his debut against Norwich City on the opening day of that 1997-98 season, starring in a 2-0 win.

A stern tackler, keen and competitive, Sedgley began his career as an apprentice with Coventry City, signing professional forms at Highfield Road in June 1986. He remained with the Sky Blues until July 1989, when a fee of £750,000 took him to Tottenham Hotspur. Two years later Sedgley helped Spurs win the FA Cup.

Capped 11 times by England at Under-21 level, he made over 220 appearances during his five-year spell at White Hart Lane, before leaving the London club for Ipswich Town in a £1 million deal in June 1994.

During the 1997-98 season Sedgley passed the milestone of 450 senior appearances in his career. Unfortunately injury forced him to retire from competitive football in December 2000, at which point he joined the Conference side, Kingstonian as player-coach.

Wolves' record: 70+5 sub apps. 3 goals.

SEGERS, Johannes

Six weeks after being found not guilty in the footballers' bribe case (with Bruce Grobbelaar, John Fashanu and a Malaysian businessman) Dutch goalkeeper Hans Segers signed a one-year contract with Wolves in September 1997 after being at Molineux as a non-contract player the previous season.

Born in Eindhoven, Holland on 30 October 1961, Segers came over to England from his hometown club, PSV Eindhoven (whom he joined as a 16 year-old in 1977) to sign for Nottingham Forest for £50,000 in August 1984.

He made almost 70 appearances for Forest and during his time at The City Ground he was loaned out to Stoke City. He also assisted both Sheffield United (November/December 1987) and Dunfermline Athletic (March 1988) before transferring to Wimbledon for £180,000 in September 1988, replacing Dave Beasant.

Segers remained with the 'Dons' until the summer of 1996 when he moved to Molineux (as cover for Mike Stowell) having made more than 320 appearances for the London club.

In July 1998, Segers left Wolves to become goalkeeping coach at Tottenham, who also registered him as a player, making him deputy to Ian Walker. This was cancelled in 2000 following the arrival of the Scottish international Neil Sullivan from Wimbledon, although he still remained at the club as a goalkeeping coach..

Wolves' record: 13 apps.

SHAW, Bernard

Full-back Bernard Shaw was born in Sheffield on 14 March 1945.

Bernard Shaw

He joined Sheffield United as a junior, turned professional in October 1962 and made 134 League appearances for the Blades up to July 1969 when he was transferred to Wolves ...after United had been relegated to the Second Division!

Shaw was a steady defender who won England Youth and Under-23 caps and he played for Wolves in the 1972 UEFA Cup Final against Tottenham Hotspur. He partnered Derek Parkin in a number of games before transferring back to Sheffield - this time to play for Wednesday in May 1976.

He had served in a period of relative success under Bill McGarry and afterwards made 113 senior appearances for the Owls before being released in May 1976 after Wednesday had dropped to the bottom of the Third Division.

His brother Graham was also a Sheffield United full-back, who later played for Bristol Rovers.

Wolves' record: 152+4 sub apps. 2 goals.

SHAW, Bertram

A Black Country man, born in Lower Gornal in 1863, Bert Shaw was a utility forward who played for Gornal Wood before joining Wolves in July 1887.

He remained with the club for two seasons, leaving for Willenhall in September 1889.

Wolves' record: 3 apps. one goal.

SHAW, Cecil Ernest

Full-back Cecil Shaw was born at Mansfield on 22 June 1911 and played for Mansfield Boys, Mansfield Invicta, Blidworth Juniors, Rainworth Church and Rufford Colliery before Wolves recruited him in February 1930. He signed the appropriate forms outside a cinema. Shaw had spent some of his early career playing as a centre-forward, but at Wolves he was used exclusively as a full-back after making his League debut in a 2-0 defeat against Hull City at Anlaby Road on the last day of the 1929-30 season.

He did not come back into the side until the final nine games of the following season and managed only ten games in 1931-32 when Wolves won the Second Division championship.

He was more regular in 1932-33 and then, as Wolves began to settle down in the First Division, he became virtually a permanent fixture in the side until his departure to West Bromwich Albion in December 1936.

A left-back with a fiercesome challenge, Shaw made over 180 appearances for Wolves, all but 20 of them in the First Division. From 4 November 1933 (at Ewood Park) to 19 September 1936 (at home to Arsenal) he made 121 consecutive League appearances. Shaw had been a penalty expert with Wolves and had never missed from the spot, but he fluffed the first one he took for the Baggies, in an FA Cup tie against Coventry City. With Albion he made 127 senior appearances and after guesting for Blackpool and Nottingham Forest during World War Two, he joined Southern League Hereford United in June 1947. He retired three years later and took up refereeing in the Oldbury & District League, where he remained for ten years. He then spent three seasons scouting for his former club West Brom. Shaw, who was a very capable cricketer, died in Handsworth on 20 January 1977.

Wolves' record: 183 apps. 8 goals.

SHAW, Harold

Harry Shaw was another splendid left-back, who served Wolves exceedingly well during the 1920s. Born at Hednesford on 5 February 1906, he was only 15 when he made Hednesford Town's first team while working as an engineer's fitter! Wolves' boss George Jobey signed him at the end of the 1922-23 season and, still in his early 20s, Shaw was the 'baby' of the side that won the Third Division (North) championship in 1923-24.

He missed only five League games that season and was a regular for the rest of that decade, making almost 250 senior appearances altogether.

A natural footballer - described as a stylist of the first water - he formed a good partnership with Ted Watson and later with Len Williams followed by Wilf Lowton, and Wolves fans were surprised when Major Frank Buckley sold Shaw to Sunderland for just over £7,000 in February 1930. He was with the Roker Park club when they won the League championship in 1935-36, but played only once that season in what turned out to be the last League game of his career.

Shaw retired in May 1938, after making 217 appearances for Sunderland. He had been an ever-present for them in 1931-32 and claimed the first goal of his career that season against Everton at Goodison Park in January 1932. Always a keen golfer, he was a member of the South Staffs and Penn club. He also worked as an engineer's fitter at Cannock Colliery. Shaw died in 1960.

Wolves' record: 249 apps.

Harry Shaw

SHEARGOLD, Arthur L

Born in Princes End, Tipton in April 1888, Arthur Sheargold was a competent goalkeeper, who played three seasons with Great Bridge Unity before joining Connah's Quay, moving to Wolves in the summer of 1910.

He remained at Molineux for two years, acting as reserve to Frank Boxley and Teddy Peers. In May 1912 he signed for Dudley Town and later played for Netherton and Gornal Town.

Wolves' record: 4 apps.

SHELLITO, Kenneth John

Coach at Molineux for some three months (January-March 1985) Ken Shilleto was born in East Ham, London on 18 April 1940 and was a full-back with Chelsea whom he served as a professional for nine years (1957-66) making well over 120 senior appearances. He gained one full and one Under-23 cap for England.

SHELTON, John

Right-half or inside-forward Jack Shelton was born in Wolverhampton in June 1884 and played for Willenhall Pickwick and Compton Rovers before signing for Wolves in March 1907.

He had to wait until the following season before making his League debut, lining up at right-half against Derby County at Molineux in October, but he soon moved into the forward-line with great effect. He scored a hat-trick against Grimsby in only his fifth game up front - and by the end of the season had collected an FA Cup winners' medal.

John Shelton

Shelton was an all-action player whose overall career at Molineux saw him as a provider for others rather than as an out-an-out scorer himself. By the time he left for Port Vale in August 1911 (along with Harry Jones and Alf Walker) he had made almost 100 appearances for Wolves.

Shelton, who helped Vale win the Staffordshire Cup, Birmingham Cup and North Staffordshire Infirmary Cup, also played briefly for Stourbridge and Dudley Town and his son, also Jack, played for Walsall either side of World War Two.

Jack Shelton was sadly killed in action in September 1918 and soon afterwards his widow married Jack Needham, the former Wolves player of the 1910-20 era.

NB -Shelton's elder brother George Henry also played football for Port Vale and Wellington Town.

Wolves' record: 94 apps. 17 goals.

SHINTON, Bertram

Bert Shinton was a reserve inside-forward, born in Wednesbury in November 1885 who joined Wolves from Ettingshall Church in July 1909.

He spent just the one season at Molineux, scoring the winning goal on his home debut against Stockport County (won 2-1). He moved to Halesowen on leaving Wolves and died in Wolverhampton circa 1959.

NB - Shinton's brother Fred played for West Bromwich Albion, Bolton Wanderers and Leicester Fosse.

Wolves' record: 1 app. 1 goal.

SHIRTLIFF, Peter Andrew

Sturdy central defender Peter Shirtliff was born in Hoyland on 6 April 1961.

He played over 200 games for Sheffield Wednesday between October 1978 and August 1986 before transferring to Charlton Athletic for £125,000. He added a further 125 appearances to his tally with the Addicks and then returned to Hillsborough for a second spell in July 1989 for £500,000.

Again he served the Owls well, having another 135 outings for the Yorkshire club before signing for Wolves for £250,000 in August 1993.

He stayed at Molineux for two seasons, leaving the club to join Barnsley for £125,000 in August 1995. Two years later he celebrated as the Tykes gained a place in the Premiership. Shirtliff, who reached the milestone of 600 senior appearances in 1996, was appointed player-coach at Oakwell in June 1997.

Peter Shirtliff

Wolves' record: 83+2 sub apps.

SHORT, John

Yorkshireman Jack Short was born in Barnsley on 18 February 1928. He played for Wath Wanderers (a Molineux nursery side) during the latter stages of the war before joining Wolves as a professional in May 1948. A competent full-back, he waited patiently in the wings behind a possee of good defenders before breaking into the first team in 1950.

Short made well over 100 appearances for the club, helping them win their first League title, but with so much talent at Molineux, he was allowed to leave for Stoke City in June 1954, Potters manager Frank Taylor (a former Wolves full-back) acquiring him to 'bolster up his defence'. Short played 55 times for the Potters before returning 'home' to sign for Barnsley in a £3,000 deal in October 1956. He made 109 League appearances for the Tykes, up to 1960 when he announced his retirement. Wolves' record: 107 apps. 2 goals.

SHORTHOUSE, William Henry

Defender Bill Shorthouse, nicknamed 'The Baron' by his Wolves team-mates, was born at Bilston on 27 May 1922 and joined the Molineux club as an amateur in June 1941. By the time he turned professional in April 1945, Shorthouse had guested for Burnley, served in the Army and had been wounded on a Normandy beach on D-Day. He learned his football at St Martin's School, Bilston, and with St Mirren Old Boys in the Wolverhampton & District League. His early days with Wolves were spent with the club's Wath Wanderers nursery side. For practically a decade from 1947-48, Shorthouse was a

Bill Shorthouse in action against Charlton in 1953-54

Bill Shorthouse

regular member of the Wolves first team, winning an FA Cup winners' medal in 1949 and a League championship medal in 1954.

He played in all the Cup rounds in 1948-49 and when the League title went to Molineux for the first time, in 1953-54, he missed only two games all season. He was only ever out of the side through injury, never dropped, and played in almost 380 senior matches. The majority of his career was spent a centre-half but in 1954 he switched to full-back when Billy Wright took over the number five shirt. After retiring during 1956-57 - some 44,000 saw his last game, against Birmingham City at Molineux in September that season - Shorthouse worked as a coach.

He gained a fine reputation working with young players and was coach briefly to the England Youth team in 1970-71 and also served in that capacity with Birmingham City and Aston Villa, guiding Villa to an FA Youth Cup Final victory in 1980.

At the height of his playing career, one writer described him as 'resolute, determined, strong-tackling and a dedicated club man....one of the game's most conscientious players'. He now resides in the Wolverhampton area.

Wolves' record: 376 apps. one goal.

SHOWELL, George William

George Showell was another Bilston-born defender who served Wolves well, although it took him some considerable time to become established. Born on 9 February 1934, Showell played for South-east Staffordshire Boys before joining Wolves straight from school in July 1949. He became a full-time professional two years later, but the club had such a strong squad that he had to wait until March 1955 before making his first-team debut, at home to Preston North End.

By the end of the 1958-59 season he had managed less than 40 League appearances, despite having been with the club for almost a decade. However, during the next six campaigns Showell's fortunes changed dramatically and by the time he moved to Bristol City in May 1965, his total number of senior appearances had shot past the 200 mark (he also had 196 outings for Wolves' second XI in League and Cup competitions).

Showell missed out on medals in successive League championship triumphs - simply because he never made enough appearances to qualify - but he did gain an FA Cup winners' medal in 1960 and always proved a versatile performer, playing at full-back, centre-half and even as a centre-forward for Wolves.

He spent only a short time at Ashton Gate before being transferred to Wrexham in November 1966, and in May 1968 he quit playing to concentrate on coaching.

In a long association with Wrexham, Showell saw the club rise from the Fourth Division to the Second and back again and qualify many times for European competition as winners of the Welsh Cup.

Wolves' record: 218 apps. 3 goals.

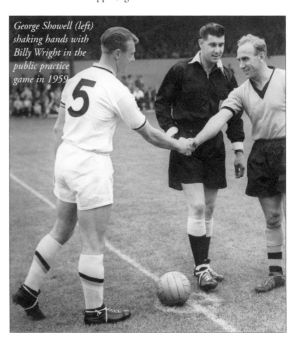

George Showell (left) shaking hands with Billy Wright in the public practice game in 1959

SIDEBOTTOM, Geoffrey

Goalkeeper Geoff Sidebottom was born in Mapplewell, Yorkshire on 29 December 1936. He played his early football with Mapplewell Village Youths and then Wath Wanderers before joining Wolves in January 1954, turning professional at Molineux the following September.

Despite being told by his doctor not to play football because of a chest complaint, Sidebottom developed quickly as understudy to the great Bert Williams.

His debut at West Bromwich in November 1958 wasn't brilliant (lost 2-1) but he came through that experience and did well afterwards before leaving Wolves to join Aston Villa in February 1961, where he was reserve to another ex-Molineux man, Nigel Sims. He went on to make 88 appearances for Villa, up to January 1965 when he transferred to Scunthorpe United, later assisting New York Royal Generals (1968-69) when he also coached the Columbia University side in the States and Brighton & Hove Albion (from January 1969).

He retired in May 1971 after recovering from serious head injuries suffered in a reserve game in October 1970. He gained a League Cup winners' tankard with Villa in 1961 (playing in the first-ever Final v. Rotherham United) and was awarded a testimonial by Brighton some ten years later.

Wolves' record: 35 apps.

SIDLOW, Cyril

Although goalkeeper Cyril Sidlow played in only a handful of peacetime League games for Wolves, he helped the club win the Wartime League (North) Cup in 1942, starring in the 6-3 two-legged Final victory over Sunderland.

He later enjoyed a very successful career in the First Division, was capped by Wales and might have done much more with Wolves, the club he re-joined in later years, but for the intervention of World War Two.

Sidlow, who guested for Wrexham during the hostilities, was born at Colwyn Bay on 26 November 1915. He played for Colwyn Bay United (in two spells), Abergele, Flint Town and Llandudno Town before signing for Wolves in July 1937.

He made his League debut in a 3-2 home win over Birmingham in April 1938 and played in the next two matches, the last a 10-1 home victory against Leicester City, and made one appearance the following year. War ended League football for seven years and by the time peace was restored, Bert Williams was the first-choice and in February 1946, Wolves felt they could afford to let Sidlow go to Liverpool for £4,000.

Ironically, he had a fine game in the last match of the 1946-47 season when Liverpool clinched the League championship at Molineux. During the war Sidlow had guested for Notts County, Wrexham, Darlington and Hartlepools United as well as representing the Army Northern Command. He also appeared in 11 wartime

internationals for Wales before making his full international debut in 1947. In all, he won seven full caps.

After 146 League appearances for Liverpool and an appearance in the 1950 FA Cup Final, he moved to New Brighton in August 1952 and returned to Molineux as emergency cover for Williams in 1953. Sidlow did not appear in the first team again, though, and after coaching the youngsters he retired

Cyril Sidlow

in 1955 and returned to his former trade as a carpenter. Possibly the oldest former Wolves player, he now lives in Codsall, near Wolverhampton.

Wolves' record: 4 apps. (plus 92 apps. in wartime).

SIMKIN, Darren Spencer

Left-back or central defender Darren Simkin was born in Walsall on 24 March 1970. He joined Wolves from non-League Blakenhall Town for £10,000 in November 1991 and made his debut in a 1-1 draw at Luton in April 1993. He failed to establish himself in the first XI at Molineux, despite some excellent performances in the reserves, and subsequently left Wolves for Shrewsbury Town in a £35,000 deal in December 1994. He spent three years at Gay Meadow during which time he also had a loan spell with Telford United (1996-97).

Wolves' record: 15+1 apps.

SIMPSON, Alexander

Wing-half Alex Simpson was born in Glasgow on 24 November 1924 and played for the local Scottish junior team, Benburb before moving south to sign professional forms for Wolves in January 1947.

He stayed at Molineux until October 1949 during which time he found it difficult to get first team football due the abundance of talent at the club and moved on to Notts County. After 80 appearances for the Magpies he was transferred to Southampton (November 1952) and after three years and 68 League outings for the Saints, he signed for Shrewsbury Town in June 1955. He eventually pulled out of competitive football in May 1959 after more than 100 games for the Gay Meadow club.

Wolves' record: 2 apps.

SIMPSON, Paul David

Left-winger with pace, good ability and strong shot, Paul Simpson joined Wolves from Derby County for a fee of £75,000 in October 1997, making his debut in a 1-0 League defeat away to Birmingham City.

Born in Carlisle on 26 July 1966, Simpson joined Manchester City as a junior in the summer of 1982 and turned professional at Maine Road in August 1983. He went on to score 24 goals in 155 outings for City, gaining

England Youth and Under-21 honours in the process before transferring to Oxford United for a record fee for the 'Us' of £200,000 in October 1988. At The Manor Ground he improved his scoring record considerably, netting exactly 50 times in 168 appearances, up to February 1992 when he moved to Derby County for £500,000.

Again he did well at The Baseball Ground and in the next four years was a regular in the Rams' first XI. He went on loan to Sheffield United in December 1996 and by the time he arrived at Molineux, his record for County was a useful one: 57 goals in a little over 225 senior outings. He never really established himself in the first XI at Wolves and during the 1998-99 season he had two separate loan spells with neighbours Walsall (he appeared in a total of 10 League games and helped the Saddlers win promotion to the First Division).

He was given a free transfer from Molineux at the end of the 1999-2000 campaign and immediately joined Blackpool. He was an outstanding pivotal figure for the Seasiders as they stormed through to win promotion from the Third Division in his first season at Bloomfield Road, Simpson scoring in the 4-2 Play-off Final win over Leyton Orient. In fact, he was voted the Seasiders' Player of the Year' and was also included in the 2000-01 PFA side for Division Three.

Wolves' record: 34+6 sub apps. 6 goals.

SIMS, Nigel David

For his size and build Nigel Sims was a tremendously agile goalkeeper.

Born in Coton-in-the-Elms near Burton-on-Trent on 9 August 1931, he played for Coton Swifts and Stapenhill FC before joining Wolves in August 1948, turning professional the following month.

With Bert Williams bedded in as first-choice 'keeper at Molineux, Sims bided his time in the reserves, having only a few senior outings, although he did gain an England 'B' cap in 1954 before being transferred to nearby Aston Villa in March 1956. He performed superbly well over the next eight years at Villa Park, amassing 309 senior appearances, collecting an FA Cup winners medal (1957), a Second Division championship medal (1960) and a League Cup winners' tankard (1961).

He was also voted Villa's 'Terrace Trophy' winner in 1958, represented Young England against the Football League and in May 1959 he even guested for Arsenal. Sims left Villa for Peterborough United in September 1984 and the following year went over to play for Toronto City in Canada and then Toronto Italia (1966).

On his return to England he worked for an Insurance Company in Wolverhampton. Sims is now living in Swansea.

Wolves' record: 39 apps.

SINCLAIR, Nicholas John Thomas

Defender, born in Manchester on 3 January 1960, Nicky Sinclair preferred the full-back position and did well with Oldham Athletic, making 75 League appearances for the Latics between June 1978 and September 1984.

He then had a month on loan with Wolves (September 1984) and on leaving Molineux was transferred from Boundary Park to Tranmere Rovers where he ended his senior career in 1986.

Wolves' record: one app.

SINTON, Andrew

Able to perform in a variety of positions from left-wing back to wide midfielder to direct winger, operating down both flanks, Andy Sinton started his career as an apprentice with Cambridge United in June 1981, signing as a professional in April 1983.

He made over 100 appearances (15 goals scored) over the next two-and-a-half seasons before transferring to Brentford for £25,000 in December 1985. He continued to do well at Griffin Park, netting 34 times in 182 outings for the Bees who sold him to QPR for £350,000 in March 1989. Still he clocked up the appearances - 190 for the Loftus Road club (25 more goals) before he was off again, this time to Sheffield Wednesday for £2.75 million in August 1993.

He had 78 outings for the Owls (three goals) up to January 1996 when a fee of £1.5 million enticed him to White Hart Lane where he became a firm favourite with the Spurs fans while having exactly 100 first-class games and netting seven goals. In July 1999, a Bosman 'free' transfer saw Sinton move out of the Premiership to join First Division Wolves. He began by having two very good seasons at Molineux, but his experience and presence failed to ignite the team into promotion contenders.

Born in Cramlington on 19 March 1966, Sinton was a League Cup winner with Spurs in 1999 and earlier in his career had won 12 full England caps while also representing his country at both Schoolboy and 'B' team levels.

Wolves' record: 67+7 sub apps. 2 goals*

SLATER, Robert David

Wolves' manager Mark McGhee, desperate to bolster up his midfield, signed Australian international Robbie Slater from Southampton for £75,000 in March 1998. But the 33 year-old never really settled in at Molineux and cited family reasons for wanting to leave Wolves. He returned to his home in France (Lens) with just seven first team outings to his name after his contract was cancelled on 7 July 1998.

Capped 39 times by Australia, Slater had unsuccessful trials with Nottingham Forest (1981) prior to spending some time in Australia playing for St George's (1982-83). He then served with RSC Anderlecht (Belgium) and the French club Lens before helping Blackburn Rovers win the

Premiership title in 1994-95. In August 1995 he was transferred to West Ham United for £600,000 and switched from Upton Park to The Dell for £250,000 in September 1996 with only 50 League appearances under his belt in English soccer. In September 1998 Slater signed for Northern Spirit of Sydney in the newly-formed Australian pro-League.

He was born in Ormskirk on 22 November 1964, he played for Australia in the 1988 Souel Olympic Games and skippered the national side under Terry Venables.

He made 90 League appearances for his English clubs. Wolves' record: 4+3 apps.

SLATER, William John OBE, CBE, BSc

Bill Slater was an amateur when he appeared in the 1951 FA Cup Final for Blackpool against Newcastle United at Wembley. He finished on the losing side that day, but nine years later, by now a semi-professional with Wolverhampton Wanderers, he at last collected an FA Cup winners' medal as captain of the side that defeated Blackburn Rovers at Wembley.

Born at Clitheroe, Lancashire, on 29 April 1927, Slater played in the Lancashire & District Youth League before joining Blackpool in 1944. At the same time he was also turning out for Yorkshire Amateurs and Leeds University.

After scoring nine goals in 30 League games for the Seasiders he was transferred to Brentford in December 1951.

He played only seven times in the Bees' League team before Wolves signed him in August 1952, still as an amateur. Slater made his League debut for the club as an inside-forward that season, but was at wing-half when Wolves won the League championship the following campaign, when he missed only three games.

In February 1954 he became a part-time professional and went on to win two more League championship medals and that Cup medal. He had been capped 21 times at amateur level before playing 12 times for the full England team.

In 1960 Slater gained a Bachelor of Science degree at University and was voted 'Footballer of the Year', although he had started the Cup winning season out of the first team. In the summer of 1963 he returned to Brentford, having played for Wolves in all three half-back positions.

After a season at Griffin Park he played for Northern Nomads before retiring late in 1964. Slater became deputy director of the Crystal Palace Sports Centre and later worked as director of PE at both Liverpool and Birmingham Universities. In 1982 he was awarded the OBE for his services to sport and in 1998 received the

Bill Slater (left) and Ronnie Clayton of Blackburn Rovers toss-up before the 1960 FA Cup Final

Bill Slater raises the FA Cup in 1960

CBE. From 1984 to 1989, Slater was director of National Services and in July 1989 was elected president of the British Gymnastics Association. Slater is now a member of the National Olympic Committee and also sits on the Panel of the National lottery.

Slater now lives in London and his daughter Barbara, a former national champion gymnast, represented Britain in the 1976 Olympic Games and later worked for Central TV.

NB - On 2 May 1956, an aeroplane was chartered to fly Slater, who at the time was working at Birmingham University, for evening League game away at Sheffield United. The Auster pilot was unable to locate the landing strip and when the aircraft finally came down, unheralded at the RAF aerodrome at Worksop, it was immediately surrounded by fire-tenders, ambulances and angry security officers. When Wolves kicked off against the Blades, Slater was still hitch-hiking a lift to Bramall Lane, having been replaced in the team by George Showell!

Wolves' record: 339 apps. 25 goals.

SMALL, Michael Anthony

Born in Birmingham on 2 March 1963, six-foot striker Mike Small played for Bromsgrove Rovers before entering the Football League with Luton Town in October 1979. From Kenilworth Road he moved to Peterborough United (on loan October 1982), then served with FC Twente Enschede (Netherlands), Standard Liege (Belgium), Go Ahead Eagles (Netherlands), PAOK of Salonika (in Greece) and Brighton & Hove Albion (August 1990) before joining West Ham United in the summer of 1991 for £400,000.

He top-scored with 13 goals in 40 League games in his first season at Upton Park, but then lost his place in the side, leaving him unsettled at Upton Park.

In September 1993 he was loaned out to Wolves for a month and then assisted Charlton Athletic in the same capacity in March 1994 before being released by the Hammers at the end of that 1993-94 season.

Wolves' record: 3+1 apps. one goal.

SMALLEY, Thomas

Wing-half Tom Smalley joined Wolves from South Kirkby Colliery, Yorkshire in May 1931. Born at Kingsley, near Barnsley, on 13 January 1912, he remained at Molineux until August 1938, when he was transferred to Norwich City.

Capped once for England, against Wales at Molineux in October 1936, all but two of his League outings for Wolves came in the First Division.

After appearing in 43 League games for the Canaries, Smalley joined Northampton Town in October 1941 and by the time he left League football ten years later he had amassed over 400 senior appearances for the Cobblers, half of them in wartime football when he also guested for West Bromwich Albion.

Tom Smalley

Smalley later spent two years as player-coach with Lower Gornal (1952-53). A good club cricketer, he resided in Wolverhampton until his death on 1 April 1984.

Wolves' record: 196 apps. 12 goals.

SMART, Frederick Laurence B

Fred Smart was the cousin of the Aston Villa and England full-back Tommy Smart and brother of Herbert Smart, a Wolves reserve who was with Fred at Molineux.

Born in Birmingham in 1899 inside-forward Fred Smart was given little opportunity with Wolves, whom he joined in September 1919 from Redditch having earlier assisted Cotteridge FC. He left Molineux for Aston Villa in November 1921 and later served with Kings Norton (January 1922 to May 1924).

Wolves' record: 7 apps. 2 goals.

SMART, Herbert Horace

Bert Smart was a well built reserve full-back, who served Wolves for two seasons from August 1912 to May 1914.

Born in Smethwick in April 1892 and a junior with Bilston United, he joined the playing staff at Molineux from Aston Villa for whom he made one League appearance. He left Molineux for Willenhall and later played for Dudley Town and Bloxwich Strollers.

Wolves' record: 3 apps.

SMITH, Alun Arnold

Amateur left-half who was recommended to Wolves by his Welsh colleague and friend, Dai Richards, Alun Smith was born in Aberaman in 1906 and played initially for Merthyr Town, joining Wolves in August 1930.

He spent just the one season at Molineux, deputising for Richards in the side before leaving for Caerphilly in May 1931. He later assisting Pontypridd.

Wolves' record: 4 apps.

SMITH, Arthur John

Jack Smith was a good quality full-back, not the flashy type, but a player who enjoyed a bold confrontation.

Born in Merthyr on 27 October 1911, he had trials with West Bromwich Albion in 1928 when playing for Aberaman, and before joining Wolves as a professional in September 1929 he assisted Aberdare Athletic.

After five years at Molineux he moved to Bristol Rovers, and then served with Swindon Town before assisting Chelsea (from 1937). During the war he guested for Cardiff, West Bromwich Albion and Wolves, also starring for a Welsh International XI v. Birmingham in November 1941.

Smith's playing career came to an end in late 1943 when he slipped on a Wolverhampton kerbstone whilst out walking and a bus (driven by a Wolves supporter) ran over his foot!

He returned to Molineux as coach in 1946 but two years later, in June 1948, he was appointed manager at The Hawthorns. He held office for four years (until April 1952) and steered the Baggies to promotion to the First Division in 1949.

From 1952 to 1954 Smith was in charge of Reading and later became a hotelier in Dorset. He died in hospital in Weymouth on 7 June 1975.

Wolves' record: 27 apps.

SMITH, Edwin Eric

An all-purpose defender who could play as a full-back or left-half, Eric Smith was born in Wednesbury circa 1880 and served with Key Hill FC, Wednesbury Old Athletic (1899), Walsall Unity (1900) and Bilston United before joining Wolves in August 1903. He remained at Molineux until May 1906 when he transferred to Darlaston, later assisting Dudley Town. He died circa 1955.

Wolves' record: 15 apps.

SMITH, Gordon Melville

Winner of ten Youth and four Under-23 caps for Scotland, full-back Gordon Smith played in well over 150 League games in England following his transfer from St. Johnstone to Aston Villa for £80,000 in August 1976.

Born in Glasgow on 3 July 1954 he was educated in Perth and was watched by a number of leading clubs before he chose to join Villa. He replaced Charlie Aitken at Villa Park and won a League Cup winners' medal in 1977.

A stern tackler, Smith moved to Tottenham Hotspur in February 1979 for £150,000, but sadly missed out on two FA Cup Final appearances with Spurs before switching to Molineux in August 1982.

With Wolves he took over the number 4 shirt and played only occasionally at full-back and then surprisingly quit

British football to play in South African (June 1984). Seven months later (January 1985) he switched to the USA where he spent four years playing indoor soccer for Pittsburgh Spirit before injury forced him into an early retirement at the end of the 1989 season. Smith now works for an advertising company based in Glasgow.

Wolves' record: 39+3 sub apps. 3 goals.

SMITH, James Jade Anthony

Right-back Jamie Smith was born in Birmingham on 17 September 1974. He joined Wolves as a trainee at the age of 16 and turned professional at Molineux in June 1993. He made rapid progress and after establishing himself in the first team at Molineux he gained representative

Jamie Smith

honours when coming on as substitute for the Football League Under-21 side against Italy's Serie 'B' XI.

Excellent at over-lapping, Smith was able to release some fine crosses and his speed in recovery helped him out of many difficult situations. He was transferred from Molineux to Crystal Palace in October 1997 in a £1 million deal that saw two Palace players - Kevin Muscat and Dougie Freedman - move to Molineux.

Later that season - March 1999 - Smith moved from Selhurst Park to neighbours Fulham and duly helped the Cottagers clinch the Second Division championship, scoring once in nine League games.

Wolves' record: 97+7 sub apps. one goal.

SMITH, John

Jack Smith joined Wolves in July 1902. Born at Wednesfield in April 1882, he first played for Cannock and then Stafford Road FC before signing moving to Molineux. A short, stocky forward, he soon established himself in the team, scoring nine goals in 25 games in his first season.

Standing only 5ft 3ins tall, he formed a very useful left-wing partnership with Jack Miller, but following Wolves' relegation to Division Two in 1906, he surprisingly left the club for Birmingham. He made only six appearances for the Blues before switching to Bristol Rovers.

For the Pirates he hit ten goals in 31 games and then netted 24 in 41 outings for Norwich City (whom he joined in May 1909). Smith then assisted Luton Town (July 1909), Millwall (March 1911) and Coventry City (May 1912) before retiring in 1915.

Wolves' record: 114 apps. 43 goals.

SMITH, John James

Born in Penn in 1875, inside-right Jack Smith played for Springfield Royal Star before joining Wolves in December 1897. He failed to impress at Molineux and was released in August 1898 when he signed for Dudley Town.

For his only outing for Wolves, he replaced England international Harry Wood against Bolton at Molineux in April 1898 (won 2-0).

Wolves' record: 1 app.

SMITH, Leslie Joseph

Les Smith was a fast, clever and direct winger, who was seen by Wolves as an eventual successor to either Johnny Hancocks or Jimmy Mullen, having joined the club as an amateur in June 1945.

Born at Halesowen on Christmas Eve 1927, Smith became a full-time professional in April 1946 and made his League debut the following season, at Stoke in the April. He played only four times in the 1953-54 League championship season and it was not until 1954-55 that he really broke through, starring in 34 games as Wolves finished runners-up in the table behind Chelsea.

In February 1956, with Hancocks and Mullen still the regular wingers and Norman Deeley in reserve and ready to step forward, Smith, who scored 78 goals in 214 reserve team appearances for Wolves, moved to Aston Villa for £25,000. At Villa Park he found less competition and went on to make 130 appearances, scoring 25 goals and collecting an FA Cup winners' medal against Manchester United at the end of his first season in the claret and blue strip. An Achilles tendon injury forced Smith into an early retirement in 1960.

Wolves' record: 94 apps. 24 goals.

SMITH, Reginald George Charles W

Born Westbury in 1916, and now deceased, Reg Smith replaced Welsh international Bryn Jones at inside-left for two League games for Wolves in December 1937.

A compact footballer he spent just a season as a reserve at Molineux before leaving to join Tranmere Rovers, failing to re-appear after the war. Prior to moving to Wolves Smith played for Westbury Town (his first club), Trowbridge Town and Bristol City (from 1935).

Wolves' record: 2 apps.

SMITH, William Courtney

Billy Smith was a useful centre-half, who was born in Hednesford in September 1912. Now deceased, he learnt his football with Denaby United, moving to Molineux in the summer of 1932 as cover for Bellis and Nelson.

He was called upon only occasionally and left Wolves to join Southend United in late 1933. He remained with the Shrimpers until 1936, helping them win the prestigious Hospital Cup.

Wolves' record: 5 apps.

SMITH, William R

Billy Smith was an excellent goalscorer for Wolves whom he served from July 1896 until November 1898 when he joined Portsmouth.

He remained at Fratton Park until May 1908, amassing a record of 74 goals in 231 League appearances. He then had a brief spell with Gosport United before retiring in 1911.

Born in Bilston circa 1872 he played for Willenhall prior to his move to Molineux where he partnered Jack Miller on the left-wing.

Wolves' record: 62 apps. 19 goals.

SMYTH, Samuel

For five years, from 1942, inside-forward Sammy Smyth had played only amateur football in his native Northern

Sammy Smyth

Ireland, serving with Distillery and Linfield, and a handful of junior clubs.

In the summer of 1947, after agreeing to sign professional forms for Dundella, which allowed him to be transferred for a fee, he moved to England to join Wolves for £1,100. A schoolboy international trialist, he had gained several amateur caps for Ireland (with Distillery) and also represented the Irish League, and once at Molineux he quickly made an impact, netting eight goals in 30 games in his first season there.

He was immediately upgraded to senior international football (he won a total of nine full caps) and at the same time continued to impress at Wolves, collecting an FA Cup winners' medal in 1949 when he scored a superb goal in the 3-1 Final victory over plucky Leicester City at Wembley.

He left Wolves for Stoke City for £25,000 in September 1951 and netted 19 times in 44 games for the Potters before switching to Liverpool for £12,000 in January 1954.

He spent only five months at Anfield, quitting competitive League football at the age of 29 to return home to Belfast where he got married and took a full-time job, later working for a bookmaker prior to running his own sports shop. He is now an agent for the sportswear company of Halbro and Falcon. Smyth is also an enthusiastic golfer and is both captain and president of the Clandeboye 36-hole complex in Ireland.

Born in Belfast on 25 February 1915, Smyth hit 72 goals in 187 League games in English football. He still resides in Northern Ireland.

Wolves' record: 116 apps. 43 goals.

SPIERS, Cyril Henry

Goalkeeper Cyril Spiers was born in Witton, Birmingham on 4 April 1902 and played his early football with Witton Star, Birchfield Boys Brigade, The Swifts (Perry Barr), Brookvale United, Soho Rovers and Handsworth Central, and after a useful spell with Halesowen he was signed by Aston Villa in December 1920.

Standing bolt upright at 6ft. 1in. tall and weighing over 12 stones, Spiers had all the necessary attributes for a 'keeper. He was both agile and alert and during his first two years at Villa Park he understudied Tommy Jackson, finally establishing himself in the League side in 1922, only to lose it (to Jackson) and then reclaim it again in 1924.

He stayed with Villa until August 1927, amassing 112 appearances before transferring to Tottenham Hotspur where he spent another six years, accumulating a further 186 senior appearances.

In September 1933 he was recruited by Wolves boss, Major Frank Buckley, as reserve to Alex Scott and proceeded to have just eight games between the posts before quitting the club in 1935.

He later became a successful manager with Cardiff City (1939-46), Norwich City (1947) and Crystal Palace

(1954-58) and General Manager of Exeter City (1962-63). He then served as Leicester City's chief Scout (February 1963). Spiers died on 21 May 1967.

Wolves' record: 8 apps.

SPRINGTHORPE, Terence Alfred

If World War Two hadn't intervened full-back Terry Springthorpe may well have developed into an England international...that was the firm belief of Wolves manager Major Frank Buckley. Born in Draycott, Shropshire on 4 December 1923, Springthorpe joined Wolves as a 15 year-old in the summer of 1939 and virtually throughout the war was a part-time professional, guesting for Leicester City and Wrexham before finally signing as a full-time 'pro' in 1947.

Terry Springthorpe

With so many quality defenders on the books at Molineux, he found it hard to hold down a first team position, but there is no doubt he was certainly a fine player, and in 1949 he helped Wolves win the FA Cup, replacing the injured Lawrie Kelly against Leicester City in the Final. In December 1950, after more than 11 years' service with Wolves, Springthorpe was transferred to Coventry City, where he stayed for a year, making just 12 League appearances for the Highfield Road club.

He went over to South Africa soon afterwards and then moved to America where he played for New York Americans, who, in 1956, became known as the Amerts after amalgamating with Hakoah. Springthorpe lived 200 miles from the New York ground and chose to fly to home games. These days he lives in Devon.

Wolves' record: 38 apps.

STANCLIFFE, Paul Ian

Born in Sheffield on 5 May 1958, central defender Paul Stancliffe had almost 20 years in League football. He signed for his first club, Rotherham United, as a junior in June 1974 and turned professional at Millmoor in March 1976.

During the next seven years he appeared in well over 300 games for the Millers before transferring to Sheffield United in August 1983. At Bramall Lane he continued to do well at senior level and added a further 337 League and Cup appearances to his tally before returning to Rotherham United for a loan spell followed by a similar venture with Wolves (from November 1990).

He then transferred to York City from Bramall Lane in July 1991 and skippered the Minstermen to promotion from Division Three in 1993. He became assistant-manager/coach at Bootham Crescent on his retirement as a player in 1996 and later (in 1998) was appointed the Minstermen's Youth team manager.

Wolves' record: 20 apps.

STANFORD, Sidney

Wolves signed inside-forward Sid Stanford from Mossley White Star in August 1884. He spent two seasons with the club, playing in several friendly matches as well as two FA Cup games against Derby St. Luke's in November 1884. Born in Wolverhampton circa 1860, he was not retained for the following season.

Wolves' record: 2 apps.

STANLEY, John

Durable full-back Jack Stanley had Dick Betteley barring his way to the first team at Molineux, but he still managed to play in half of the games during his only season with the club.

Born in Cheshire circa 1880, he served with Crewe Alexandra before joining Wolves in August 1905 and from April 1906 to October 1909 he was with Bolton Wanderers for whom he made over 70 senior appearances. Thereafter he played for Burton United, retiring in 1912.

Wolves' record: 22 apps.

STEELE, Timothy Wesley

Tim Steele - born in Coventry on 1 December 1967 - played over 60 games as a wide midfielder for Shrewsbury Town (from December 1985) before transferring to Wolves in February 1989 for a fee of £80,000.

He had a couple of good seasons at Molineux, but after a loan spell with Stoke City in February/March 1992, he was allowed to leave Molineux for Bradford City on a free transfer in July 1993. Steele later assisted Hereford United (from January 1994) although injuries (which required surgery) disrupted his performances at Edgar Street.

In 1996 Steele joined Exeter City and a year later signed for Tamworth.

Wolves' record: 85 apps. 10 goals.

STEEN, Alan William

On 2 October 1943, Alan Steen who had made his senior debut as a 16 year-old for Wolves during the 1938-39 season was reported missing after a bombing raid over Germany.

He was captured by the enemy and spent the remainder of the war as a POW in Stalag IV 3. On returning to

Tim Steele

England, he went on to play on the wing for Luton Town (May 1946), Aldershot (June 1949), Rochdale (June 1950) and Carlisle United (December 1951), moving into non-League soccer in May 1952 after more than 80 League appearances in total.

Born in Crewe on 26 June 1922, Steen joined Wolves from local junior football and turned professional at Molineux in the summer of 1939. He guested for New Brighton during the first part of the war.

Wolves' record: one app. one goal.

STEVENSON, Ernest

Utility forward Ernie Stevenson was a very competitive footballer, a strong dribbler, hard to dispossess who enjoyed a challenge.

A Yorkshireman, born in Rotherham on 28 December 1923, he played for Wolves' junior team, Wath Wanderers during the early part of the Second World War, signing on a full-time basis at Molineux in 1943.

He made over 30 appearances during the hostilities - when he also guested for Blackpool and Tranmere Rovers - but only a handful afterwards before transferring to Cardiff City in November 1948.

In March 1950 he surprisingly left Ninian Park for Southampton but failed to settle down as he had hoped at The Dell and after just 23 games for Saints (8 goals scored) he went to Leeds United in February 1951. He later switched to Wisbech Town (July 1952) where he ended his career. Stevenson died in St. Helens on 15 October 1970.

Wolves' record: 9 apps.

STEWART, Paul Andrew

Utility forward Paul Stewart spent a month on loan at Molineux soon after the start of the 1994-95 season (September/October).

Born in Manchester on 7 October 1964, he signed for Blackpool as a junior in June 1980 and turned professional at Bloomfield Road in October 1981. Capped by England at Youth team level he went on to score 62 goals in 225 games for the Seasiders before transferring to Manchester City for £200,000 in March 1987. He did well at Maine Road, adding 30 goals in 63 starts to his record up to June 1988 when he moved to London to sign for Tottenham Hotspur for £1.7 million.

He stayed at White Hart Lane for four seasons during which time he netted 37 more goals in 172 outings for Spurs, helping them win both the F.A Cup and Charity Shield in 1991. In July 1992 Stewart went north to Liverpool, who paid £2.3 million for his services, hoping he would fit in alongside Ian Rush. Unfortunately he never really settled down at Anfield and during the next four years managed only 42 outings (three goals scored) for the Reds, while also having loan spells with Crystal Palace (January 1994), Wolves, Burnley (February 1995) and Sunderland (August 1995).

In March 1996 Stewart signed permanently for the Roker

Park club (on a free) and quickly helped them clinch the First Division championship, having achieved a similar feat with Palace two years earlier. He moved from Sunderland to Stoke City again on a free transfer in July 1997.

Capped three times by his country at senior level, on five occasions by the 'B' team and once by the Under-21s, Stewart is perhaps only one of a handful of footballers who has played in four major local derbies - the North east, Black Country, Merseyside and North London. He left League football to sign for Workington in September 1998. Wolves' record: 7+3 sub apps. 2 goals.

STOBART, Barry Henry

After making only five first team appearances, inside-forward Barry Stobart was called into Wolves' 1960 FA Cup Final team against Blackburn Rovers as a late replacement for Bobby Mason, manager Stan Cullis having no second thoughts about playing the 21year-old

Barry Stobart

in front of 100,000 fans at Wembley. Stobart did a good job and celebrated by collecting a winners' medal after helping his team-mates beat Rovers 3-0.

Born in the village of Dodsworth, near Doncaster on 6 June 1938, Stobart attended the local school and played for Wath Wanderers before joining Wolves as an amateur in 1953, turning professional in December 1955.

He found it hard to get a game in the first XI at Molineux with so many talented goalscorers in the squad, but he stuck in there and went on to create a record of scoring 110 goals in the Central League for Wolves in 197 appearances. He remained at Molineux until August 1964 when a £20,000 fee took him to Manchester City. Unfortunately Stobart failed to settle at Maine Road and

he quickly switched to Aston Villa (for £22,000) in the November.

He hit 20 goals in 53 games for the Villa who then released him to Shrewsbury Town for £10,000 in October 1967. Three years later Stobart left the League scene to join Willenhall Town. He later ran a successful grocer's shop and was team manager of Willenhall for two seasons (1979-81) and then held a similar position with Dudley Town (from 1984 to 1990).

Wolves' record: 54 apps. 22 goals.

STOCKIN, Ronald

Inside-forward Ronnie Stockin was born in Birmingham on 27 June 1931.

He played junior football before the Second World War and local services soccer during the hostilities. In 1950 he became an amateur with West Bromwich Albion and the following year teamed up at the same level with Walsall, turning professional at Fellows Park in January 1952. The following month Wolves manager Stan Cullis recruited Stockin for £10,000 (as cover for his main goalscorers).

He remained at Molineux for two-and-a-half years before switching to Cardiff City for £12,000 in June 1954, having had six League games during Wolves' First Division championship winning campaign. He stayed at Ninian Park for three years before moving to Grimsby Town in June 1957 for £5,000.

He dropped out of bigtime football in July 1960 when he signed for Nuneaton Borough. It was Stockin who scored Cardiff's goal when they lost 9-1 to Wolves in a League game in 1955..

Wolves' record: 21 apps. 7 goals.

STOKES, DAVID

When he turned out in his last Football League game for Wolves against Sheffield Wednesday at Hillsborough in April 1921, David Stokes was over 41 years of age - the second oldest player ever to line-up for the club at senior level (behind Archie Goodall).

A utility forward, born in Ketley, Staffordshire in March 1880, he played for Kingswinford Albion, Wordsley Olympic, Halesowen, Brierley Hill Alliance and Aston Villa reserves in the Birmingham & District League) before joining Bolton Wanderers in December 1901, the Lancashire club having to pay Villa 10 guineas for his signature!

A right-winger, he scored 46 goals in 420 senior games for Bolton, helping them win promotion three times (in 1904-05, 1908-09 and 1910-11), collecting a Second Division championship medal in the 1908-09 campaign when he played in 34 of his team's 38 League games.

He also appeared in the 1904 FA Cup Final and represented the Football League v. the Irish League in Belfast.

Having worked in a munitions factory during the Great War, he left Burnden Park inn the summer of 1920, rejoining his old club Brierley Hill. But in an injury crisis

he was signed by Wolves during their Second Division campaign of 1920-21 and deputised for both Tancy Lea and Harry Lees in the first XI. He was released from Molineux in May 1921.
Wolves' record: 7 apps.

STOUTT, Stephen Paul
Steve Stoutt was a good, solid performer able to occupy a number of defensive berths and a player who was always confident in his own ability. Born in Halifax on 5 April 1964, he was one of manager Tommy Docherty's last signings for Wolves when the team was heading towards the Third Division.
He had done very well in Yorkshire junior football before joining Huddersfield Town on non-contract terms in January 1984. He switched to Molineux in April 1985 and spent three years with Wolves before moving to Grimsby Town in August 1988. Later he assisted Lincoln City from December 1989.
Wolves' record: 114+3 apps. 5 goals.

STOWELL, Michael
Born in Preston on 19 April 1965, goalkeeper Mike Stowell played initially for Leyland Motors FC before joining Preston North End as a professional in February 1985. From Deepdale he switched to Goodison Park on a free transfer in December 1985 (signed as cover for Neville Southall) and over the next five years - before signing for Wolves on a permanent basis for £250,000 in June 1990 - he made only one senior appearance for Everton, but played in 54 games while serving on loan with Chester City (September 1987), York City (December 1987), Manchester City (February 1988), Port Vale (October 1988), Wolves (March 1989) and his earlier club, Preston North End (February 1990).
Over the last eleven years he gave Wolves excellent service. Standing 6ft. 2in, he possesses fine reflexes, good positional sense and is a fine shot-stopper.
In November 1998, Stowell kept his 100th clean sheet for Wolves in the away game at Norwich City, and soon afterwards, when he turned out against neighbours West Bromwich Albion in a Nationwide League Division One game on 29 April 1999, he set a club record for most senior appearances for the club by a goalkeeper, surpassing Bert Williams' tally of 420.
After Michael Oakes had established himself between the posts, Stowell received a 'Bosman' free transfer from Wolves in May 2001 - a month later he joined Bristol City.
NB - In November 1990 Stowell hired a tractor to beat severe snow drifts in the West Midlands in order to report for international duty with the England 'B' team in Algeria.
Wolves' record: 448 apps.

STREETE, Floyd Anthony
Tough-tackling central defender Floyd Streete was born in Jamaica in the West Indies on 5 May 1959 and after plying

Mike Stowell

Floyd Streete

his trade in the sun with Rivet Sports FC he entered English football with Cambridge United in July 1976.

He played in 125 League games for United over the next seven years before signing for the Dutch club, Utrecht, later assisting SC Cambuur.

He returned to the Football League with Derby County for the 1984-85 season and was transferred to Wolves in October 1985 at a time when Molineux was a rather depressing place to be (gates were down to around the 4,000 mark).

He came through well with Wolves and went on to give the club excellent service, helping them twice win promotion (from the Fourth and Third Divisions) and also carry off the Sherpa Van Trophy at Wembley.

In May 1990 after being released by Wolves, Streete joined Reading, staying with the Royals for two seasons. He is now a PT instructor at a senior boys' school in Berkshire.

Wolves' record: 192+2 sub apps. 6 goals.

STREETS, John William

Born in Nottingham in November 1893, inside-forward Jack Streets played for Long Eaton Rangers before joining Wolves in August 1913.

He stayed at Molineux for just one season, transferring to Notts County in the summer of 1914 and later assisting Mansfield Invicta. He did not re-appear in the Football League after the Great War.

Wolves' record: 2 apps.

STRINGER, James

Jimmy Stringer was a sound, vigilant goalkeeper whose height (6ft 1in) and weight (13 stones) enabled him to dominate his area for high crosses.

Born at Netherton, Dudley in May 1878, he represented Netherton & Dudley Schools and played for Netherton Rovers before joining Wolves as a professional in August 1900.

Doing well in the reserves at Molineux, he found it hard to gain a regular place in the first XI.

Consequently in April 1905 he was transferred to near neighbours West Bromwich Albion whom he served until October 1910, making a total of 172 senior appearances. Stringer wound down a useful career with Dudley Town (1910-12) before becoming trainer of Port Talbot. He retired out of football in 1915 and died back home in Dudley in December 1933.

Wolves' record: 16 apps.

STUART, Edward Albert

South African full-back Eddie Stuart was a fine footballer. As hard as they come, he was quick, competitive and a battler to the end. He tackled hard and fair, and always gave 100 per-cent out on the park. Born in Middleburg, Cape Town on 12 May 1931, he played intermediate football in his homeland for Rangers FC before joining Wolves as a professional in January 1951.

He went on to appear in over 300 games for Wolves after surprisingly making his League debut as a centre-forward v. West Bromwich Albion in April 1952, scoring a goal to celebrate the occasion. Stuart helped Wolves win the First Division championship in 1954, 1958 and 1959 and then he added an FA Cup winners' medal to his tally in 1960.

In July 1962 after 11 years excellent service, he was transferred to Stoke City for £8,000, and in his first season at The Victoria Ground skippered the Potters to the Second Division title. He netted twice in 71 games for Stoke up to August 1964 when he moved across country to Tranmere Rovers for £4,000.

In July 1966 he signed for Stockport County and helped them win the Fourth Division crown in 1967. Retiring from competitive football in 1968 with 510 League appearances under his belt, Stuart then had an excellent two-year spell with Worcester City, making 110 appearances.

Thereafter he managed the non-League club and in the late '70s/early '80s, while living in Tettenhall, he played in several charity matches in the Midlands as well as running a successful hairdressing business with shops in Wolverhampton, Codsall and Newcastle under Lyme.

NB - In 1952, Stuart had to return to South

Eddie Stuart

Africa after being infected by a 'mystery illness'. Thankfully he responded to treatment and came back to England to continue his career.

Wolves' record: 322 apps. one goal.

STURRIDGE, Dean Constantine

Striker Dean Sturridge was signed on loan in late November 2001 by from Leicester City - after Wolves had failed to bring Ade Akinbiyi back to Molineux. Vastly experienced, Sturridge then made a scoring debut against Wimbledon just 24 hours after signing for the club, earning Wolves a 1-0 victory.

Born in Birmingham on 27 July 1973, he signed as an apprentice for Derby County in July 1997 and turned professional at The Baseball Ground in July 1991. He went on to score 59 goals in 214 senior appearances for the Rams before transferring to Leicester City for £350,000 in January 2001, having been on loan to Torquay United during the 1994-95 season when he was struggling with his form.

He arrived at Filbert Street when the Foxes were doing well (7th in the Premiership and still in the FA Cup) and went on to score four goals in 15 senior games despite a chest injury keeping him out for a short time.

* Sturridge's brothers Michael & Simon were professionals, the former with Birmingham City & Wrexham, the latter also with Blues, Stoke City, Blackpool, Northampton Town & Shrewsbury Town.

SUNDERLAND, Alan

During his time at Molineux, the versatile Alan Sunderland donned nine different shirts for Wolves - numbers 2, 3, 4, 7, 8, 9, 10, 11 and 12. Originally billed as an out-and-out striker, he did play in a variety of positions including those of right-back, defender, midfielder (all under manager Bill McGarry), winger and target man - and he did a good job wherever he appeared.

Born in Mexborough on 1 July 1953, he signed as an apprentice for Wolves in July 1969 and turned professional in June 1971.

He made intermittent first team appearances during seasons 1971-72 and 1972-73 before establishing himself in the side in 1973-74 that culminated with League Cup glory at Wembley.

Six months after helping Wolves regain their First Division status - and having recovered from a double fracture of the leg suffered in a training session - Sunderland was transferred to Arsenal for £240,000 in November 1977 and with the Gunners he did even better than he'd done at Molineux!

An instinctive player, Sunderland knew precisely where to get most out of an attacking situation and playing alongside Frank Stapleton and Malcolm Macdonald at Arsenal certainly did him a power of good.

He appeared in 321 senior games for the Londoners and scored 101 goals, including a last-ditch winner against

Manchester United in the 1979 FA Cup Final. Sunderland left Highbury for Ipswich Town in February 1984 where he added a further 12 goals in 50 outings to his tally before going over to Ireland to serve with Derry City (1986-87). Capped by England at senior and Under-21 levels, he accumulated a fine set of statistics in an excellent League career: 422 appearances and 96 goals.

Wolves' record: 176+22 apps. 34 goals.

SWALLOW, John Eli

Jack Swallow played as a reserve with Wolves in season 1895-96. A useful goalkeeper in his own right, he understudied Joe Hassall and then Billy Rose and had very few first team opportunities.

Born in Wednesbury in February 1873, he was six feet tall and weighed 12 stones, and his two appearances were four weeks apart. In June 1896 following the arrival of Billy Tennant, Swallow was transferred to Darlaston. He later served with Walsall Town, Dudley Phoenix and Hill Top Victoria, retiring in 1912. He died in 1944, aged 71.

Wolves' record: 2 apps.

SWIFT, George Harold

George Swift was a marvellous all-purpose full-back, strong in the tackle, with a good left foot and fine positional sense.

Born in St. George's, Wellington on 3 February 1870, he was educated at St. George's Church of England School (Oakengates) and played for Wellington Street Swifts, Wellington Town 1885), Stoke (trialist 1886), Wellington St George's and Crewe Alexandra (from 1888) before joining Wolves in August 1891.

Two years later he gained an FA Cup winners medal, but in August 1894, after three excellent seasons at Molineux, he was transferred to Loughborough. In August 1896 he switched to Leicester Fosse, later assisting Notts County (from June 1902) before retiring in June 1904 to become trainer of Leeds City. (He was called out of retirement to play in one League game in March 1906).

In August 1907 Swift was appointed secretary-manager of Chesterfield; between April 1911 and April 1912 he worked in the same capacity with Southampton (he was, in fact, Saints' first official team manager) and thereafter lived on the Isle of Wight until his death during World War Two. Swift won Football League representative honours.

Wolves' record: 66 apps. one goal.

SWIFT, Walter George

Born in Coseley in 1874, inside-forward Walter Swift made a scoring debut for Wolves v. Grimsby Town in November 1901 - his only outing for the first team.

Recruited as cover for the main three central strikers, he arrived at Molineux in the summer of 1894 and was released in May 1902 when he joined Bilston United.

He made a record 84 consecutive Birmingham & District

League appearances for Wolves' second XI between January 1895 and December 1899. Prior to his arrival at Wolves, he had played for Tipton St. Phillip's and Coseley Town.

Wolves' record: one app. one goal.

SWINBOURNE, Royston Harry

Roy Swinbourne was a fine goalscoring centre-forward whose career came to an abrupt end in 1957 after a serious knee injury. A Yorkshireman, born in Denaby Main on 25 August 1929, the son of a former Aston Villa reserve defender, he joined Wolves' nursery side, Wath Wanderers as a 15 year-old in 1944 and turned professional on his 17th birthday in 1948.

He made his League debut in December 1949 and scored the first of his 114 goals for Wolves in the local derby v. Aston Villa that same month.

He established himself in the first XI in 1950-51, netting 22 goals in 48 first team games, and although injuries disrupted his progress the following season, he bounced back with 21 more goals in 1952-53. The following season - leading a terrific forward-line - he helped bring the League championship to Molineux in 1953-54 by netting 24 goals in 40 First Division outings.

Swinbourne weighed in with another 18 goals in 1954-55 and had already cracked in 17 in the opening 12 League games of the 1955-56 campaign before badly injuring himself when he tried to avoid a group of cameramen, who were crouched near the bye-line during Wolves' away game at Luton.

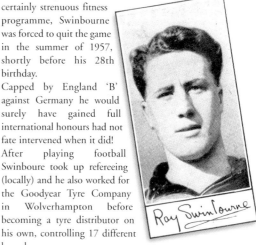

He came back to play in just two more matches, but never looked right and despite going through a sometimes painful and certainly strenuous fitness programme, Swinbourne was forced to quit the game in the summer of 1957, shortly before his 28th birthday.

Capped by England 'B' against Germany he would surely have gained full international honours had not fate intervened when it did!

After playing football Swinboure took up refereeing (locally) and he also worked for the Goodyear Tyre Company in Wolverhampton before becoming a tyre distributor on his own, controlling 17 different branches.

Swinbourne is now living in the village of Kinver, near Kidderminster.

Wolves' record: 230 apps. 114 goals.

Roy Swinbourne scoring with a back-heeler against Cardiff City in a 9-1 win at Ninian Park in 1955

TAGG, Ernest

Reserve outside-right Ernie Tagg made his debut for Wolves in April 1939, in front of 51,000 fans at Molineux when Aston Villa were beaten 2-1. That was his only game for the club. Born in Crewe on 15 September 1917, he had scored seven goals in 19 games for Crewe Alexandra before moving to Wolves in the summer of 1938.

In May 1939, he transferred to Bournemouth and having guested for his former club Crewe during the hostilities, after the war he went on to make 80 League appearances for the Cherries before moving to Carlisle United in November 1948.

Tagg retired from first-class soccer the following May and was appointed trainer of Crewe Alexandra, later taking over as manager at Gresty Road (November 1964-1971). He then held the post of club secretary (1972) before becoming caretaker-boss of the Railwaymen (December 1974-January 1975). Tagg later served on the board of directors at Gresty Road for seven years (1976-83).

Wolves' record: one app.

TATEM, Frank Arthur

Born in West Bromwich in 1888, goalkeeper Arthur Tatem was a loser in each of his first team outings for Wolves v. Chesterfield and Leeds City in 1907-08. He joined Wolves in July 1907 from Willenhall Pickwick and left Molineux for Brierley Hill in June 1909. He later played for Stourbridge and Netherton.

Wolves' record: 2 apps.

TAYLOR, Colin David

Colin Taylor was a useful goalscoring inside or centre-forward, who did very well at youth and reserve team level for Wolves, but failed to establish himself in the first XI, owing mainly to the fact that he had Messrs. Bull and Mutch to contend with.

Born in Liverpool on Christmas Day 1971, he came to Molineux on the YTS in the summer of 1987 and turned professional with Wolves in March 1990.

Capped by England at Under-18 level, he went on loan to Preston North End (October 1992), Wigan Athletic (January 1992) and Doncaster Rovers (February 1993) and was released by Wolves in June 1993, joining non-League Telford United, later assisting Runcorn (1995-96).

Wolves' record: 10+14 sub apps. 3 goals.

Colin Taylor

TAYLOR, Douglas

Centre-forward Doug Taylor was an amateur with West Bromwich Albion before turning professional with Wolves in October 1949.

Born in West Bromwich on 20 April 1931, he was understudy to the likes of Jesse Pye, Roy Swinbourne, Dennis Wilshaw and Ken Whitfield (among others) during his six years at Molineux, getting very few first team opportunities. Then, in November 1955, he was transferred to Walsall for whom he scored eight goals in 38 Third Division (South) games before entering non-League football in 1957.

Wolves' record: 3 apps.

TAYLOR, Frank W

Full-back Frank Taylor was born in Hemsworth, Yorkshire on 30 April 1916. Educated at Barnsley Grammar School, he joined Wolves in July 1936 and spent eight years at Molineux before being forced to retire through injury in August 1944. He made over 100 appearances for Wolves (all games including wartime fixtures), his best moment coming in the 1939 FA Cup Final when he partnered England international Bill Morris.

During the hostilities Taylor also won an England cap, playing against Scotland at Hampden Park in April 1944 in front of 133,000 fans, and he guested for Aldershot, Darlington, Millwall and St Mirren. On his retirement he was taken on the training/coaching staff at Molineux before taking over as manager of Scarborough in June 1948.

From there he became Major Frank Buckley's managerial-assistant at Hull City (briefly in mid 1950) and did a similar job at Leeds United (for two years) prior to becoming team manager of Stoke City in June 1952, a position he held for eight years until June 1960.

Taylor was a track-suit manager who loved to be out on the field training with the players and he was so keen that he placed a sign in the dressing room at Stoke which read 'Are you 90 minutes fit? It's the last 20 minutes that count - train for it!' Taylor's brother, Jack, played with him at Molineux. Taylor died at Chapeltown, Sheffield on 10 January 1970.

Wolves' record: 57 apps.

TAYLOR, Gerald William

Gerry Taylor was a neat and tidy defender, able to play at full back (his best position) or as a centre-half. He had a good spell at Molineux where, for the first eight years of

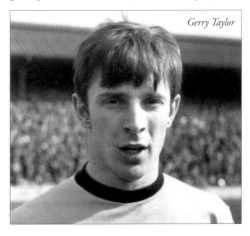

Gerry Taylor

his professional career, he acted, in the main, as reserve to first Joe Wilson and Bobby Thomson and then Derek Parkin and Bernard Shaw before finally gaining a regular place in the League side in 1972.

A dedicated club man, Taylor, who made 210 reserve team appearances for Wolves, helped the senior side gain promotion to the First Division in 1967, win the Texaco Cup in 1971, reach the UEFA Cup Final twelve months later and was reserve for the 1974 League Cup Final at Wembley.

Following a loan spell with Swindon Town (October 1975) he retired from the professional game in 1976 and joined the Staffordshire Constabulary, playing for the Cannock Police team. He progressed to the rank of sergeant and was later based at Wombourne and Kinver.

Wolves' record: 187+5 apps. one goal.

TAYLOR, Graham

Graham Taylor was team manager at Molineux from 29 March 1994 until 12 November 1995, during which time he took Wolves into the First Division promotion Play-offs where they lost to Bolton Wanderers.

As a defender, full-back Taylor served as a professional with Grimsby Town from July 1962 until July 1968 when he moved to Lincoln City. He stayed at Sincil Bank until the summer of 1972 when he retired to become Imps' team manager a position he held for five years, leading the team to the Fourth Division championship in 1976.

He appeared in 189 League games for the Mariners and 152 for Lincoln.

From Sincil Bank he switched to Vicarage Road, becoming team boss of Watford under the club's owner Elton John, having rejected an offer from West Bromwich Albion.

Whilst at Vicarage Road he did a superb job, guiding the Hornets into Europe and to the 1984 FA Cup Final (where they lost to Everton). Earlier he had seen the team rise from the Fourth to the First Division in double-quick time, taking the Fourth Division title in 1979 and finishing runners-up Football League in 1983.

After leaving Watford in 1987 Taylor took charge of Aston Villa, but failed to bring success to the Birmingham-based club after winning promotion back to the top flight. However, in 1990 Taylor was given the highest honour in English football - that of team manager of the national team - and although he strove manfully to get things going he didn't quite fit the bill and after World Cup failure he lost his job.

After a short spell out of the game he was brought back into League football by Wolves, who appointed him as team manager in late March 1994. Taylor unfortunately failed to bring eagerly awaited Premiership football to Molineux and was subsequently dismissed after less than eighteen months in office. Soon afterwards he returned to his former club Watford, as General Manager and guided them to promotion from Division Two.

In November 1998 Taylor was rushed to hospital with a throat infection. He made a full recovery as - against all the odds - guided the Hornets into the Premier League of English football after a 2-0 victory over Bolton Wanderers in the First Division Play-off Final at Wembley in front of almost 71,000 spectators on Bank Holiday 31 May 1999. A year after Watford had lost their Premiership status Taylor quit the Vicarage Road club and returned as a non-Executive Director at Villa Park (May 2001).

Wolves won 38 and drew 28 of the 92 competitive games played during Taylor's reign at Molineux.

TAYLOR, John

Born in Barnsley on 15 February 1914 and brother of Frank (q.v) Jack Taylor was an efficient, no-nonsense defender who played the game hard but fair. After leaving Barnsley Grammar School he played briefly for Worsborough Bridge FC (Barnsley) and joined the groundstaff at Molineux in June 1931, turning professional in January 1934.

He played alongside his brother in five League games during the 1936-37 campaign and the following season was a key member of the team before being sold to Norwich City for £4,500 in June 1938. During the war Taylor guested for Barnsley and Watford and after the hostilities went to Hull City (1947), helping the Tigers win the Third Division (North) title in 1949.

In May 1950 he was appointed player-manager of the Southern League side Weymouth, later taking over as team boss of Queens Park Rangers (from June 1952) before moving in as team manager of Leeds United (from May 1959 to March 1961).

Taylor, who was fine tennis player, died in Barnsley on 22 February 1978.

Wolves' record: 89 apps.

TAYLOR, John Emphraim

Centre-forward Jack Taylor started his career with Stockton before entering League football as a professional with Luton Town in February 1949.

He netted 29 goals in 85 League games for the Hatters, gained an England 'B' cap and left Kenilworth Road for Wolves in May 1952.

He remained at Molineux until February 1954, deputising in the main for Dennis Wilshaw. Taylor, big and strong, wanted regular first team football though, and he subsequently left for Notts County, for whom he struck 19 goals in 53 League outings before rounding off his senior career with Bradford Park Avenue (July 1957 to May 1958).

Wolves' record: 10 apps. one goal.

TAYLOR, Robert Anthony

Born in Norwich on 30 April 1971, and formerly with Norwich City (professional, March 1990 after two years as a trainee at Carrow Road), Leyton Orient (on loan, March

1991), Birmingham City (signed in August 1991), Brentford (a £100,000 buy in March 1994), Gillingham (secured for £500,000 in August 1998) and Manchester City (recruited for £1.5 million in November 1999) striker Robert Taylor joined Wolves in mid-August 2000. Standing an inch over six feet tall, he scored three goals in 12 games during his first season at Molineux.

Prior to that he had netted a total of 139 in almost 400 appearances. Taylor joined Gillingham on loan in 2001.

Wolves' record: 8+4 sub apps. 3 goals.

TAYLOR, Scott Dean

Scott Taylor was given a 'Bosman' free transfer by Wolves manager David Jones in May 2001 after serving the club for almost two full seasons.

Born in Portsmouth on 28 November 1970, he joined Reading as a trainee in 1987 and turned professional in June 1989. He went on to appear in almost 250 first-class games for the Royals (29 goals) and helped them win the Second Division title before transferring to Leicester City for £250,000 in July 1995 - following his Elm Park boss Mark McGhee to Filbert Street.

He added a League Cup winners medal to his collection with the Foxes while also netting a further six goals in 70 outings before his free transfer to Wolves in September 1999 - signed again by McGhee. In fact, Taylor had been invited to take part on Wolves' pre-season tour to Sweden before he actually put pen to paper and signed a fully agreed contract with the club. He had only just recovered from a serious knee injury before switching to Molineux. In November 2001 Taylor had trials with Cambridge Utd.

Wolves' record: 21+11 sub apps, 3 goals.

TEASDALE, John

A Scotsman, born in Glasgow on 15 October 1962, left-winger John Teasdale joined Wolves from Nairn County in December 1980, as understudy to mainly Mel Eves and a few others. He didn't get too many opportunities in the first team at Molineux and in March 1982 was transferred to Walsall, where he stayed for ten months before joining forces with Hereford United as a non-contract player in January 1983.

Later he assisted Blackpool in the same capacity during November/December 1984.

Wolves' record: 6+2 sub apps.

TENNANT, William

Goalkeeper Billy Tennant was a hefty fellow, weighing over 14 stones, who cost Wolves a mere £30 when signed from Hartshill Unity in January 1896.

With a heavy moustache and often seen wearing a neck-tie, he replaced Billy Rose between the posts at Molineux and did an excellent job before surprisingly leaving the club for Walsall for £75 in the summer of 1897, a year after playing in the FA Cup Final v. Sheffield Wednesday. Born in Wolverhampton in July 1865, Tennant played

initially for Willenhall Pickwick (1881-85) having earlier tried his luck at rugby with Moseley where it is reported that he was on the verge of representative honours!

After his playing days with Walsall he switched to Grimsby Town (May 1901), but made only 13 appearances for the Mariners before retiring to become second team manager at Blundell Park (appointed September 1903), occasionally taking over the first XI.

He quit football soon after the war and went into the fish business in Hull. He died in that city on 6 December 1927, aged 62.

Wolves' record: 45 apps.

TETHER, Colin

Full-back Colin Tether never got a chance at Molineux owing to depth of talent at the club during his brief spell there. Born in Halesowen on 11 August 1938, he joined the Wolves groundstaff in 1954 and turned professional in August 1955. Five years later, after having represented England at youth team level, and seemingly confined to reserve team football at Molineux, he was transferred to Oxford United where he stayed until May 1962, making 32 appearances in the Southern League.

Wolves' record: one app.

THETIS, Jean-Manuel

Giant French defender Manu Thetis (6ft 3ins tall and almost 15 stones in weight) joined Wolves on loan from Ipswich Town in August 2000. He appeared in just three League games for the club before returning to Portman Road. In March 2001 he signed permanently for Sheffield United.

Born in Dijon on 5 November 1971, he played for Seville in Spain before transferring to Ipswich for £50,000 in September 1998. He appeared in almost 60 games for the Portman Road club.

Wolves' record: 3 apps.

THOMAS, Archibald Albert

An early 1920s player with Wolves, Archie Thomas was born in Birmingham circa 1900. He was a reserve at Molineux from July 1920 to May 1922, making almost a dozen senior appearances. He played for Hall Green before joining Wolves and on leaving the club he assisted Stourbridge and later Cradley St. Luke's.

Wolves' record: 11 apps.

THOMAS, David

An England international left-winger who won eight full and 11 Under-23 caps, as well as representing his country at youth team level, Dave Thomas had a fine career, which spanned fifteen years. Born in Kirkby-in-Ashfield on 5 October 1950, he joined Burnley as a junior in 1966 and turned professional at Turf Moor in October 1967.

He went on to score 19 goals in 157 League games for the Clarets before transferring to Queens Park Rangers in

October 1972 for a record fee of £165,000. After notching a further 29 goals in 182 First and Second Division games for the London club, he switched to Everton in August 1977 and was given over 75 first team outings by the Merseysiders before moving to Wolves in October 1979.

He never really adapted to life or the surroundings at Molineux and after less than eight month he went over to play for Vancouver Whitecaps in the NASL.

In March 1982 he returned to England to sign for Middlesbrough and eventually rounded off his senior career with a spell at Portsmouth (July 1982 to May 1985).

Wolves' record: 16 apps.

THOMAS, Geoffrey Robert

Geoff Thomas was born in Manchester on 5 August 1964, and played his early football with Littleborough FC before entering the League scene with Rochdale in August 1982. A strong, powerful midfielder, standing over six feet tall and weighing more than 13 stones, Thomas loved to drive forward. He moved from Spotland to Crewe Alexandra in March 1984, and it was here, at Gresty Road, under the shrewd guidance of manager Dario Gradi, where his career took off!

He played in almost 140 games for the 'Alex' who then sold him to Crystal Palace for a bargain fee of £50,000 in June 1987.

Over the next few years Thomas developed into an international class footballer, winning nine full and three 'B' caps for England, as well as appearing in some 250 matches for the Eagles. He helped them win the Full Members Cup in 1991 and reach the 1990 FA Cup Final (versus Manchester United).

Wolves, requiring a 'grafter' in the centre of the park, secured his services for £800,000 in June 1993 and he had an excellent first season at Molineux.

But thereafter he struggled desperately with injury and made only two substitute appearances in 1995-96 before undergoing surgery on his right knee that eventually resulted in him having his cruciate ligament removed completely.

He came back briefly in 1996-97 but at the end of that campaign went on a free transfer to Nottingham Forest. Sadly, after one reasonable campaign at The City Ground when Forest won promotion, injuries again ruined Thomas's game as Forest battled to stay in the Premiership! After two years with Barnsley (from July 1999) Thomas joined forces with Notts County in March 2001, and five months later he completed almost a full circle by returning to Gresty Road for a second spell.

Thomas has now made almost 600 senior appearances at club and international level.

Wolves' record: 44+9 sub apps. 8 goals.

THOMPSON, Andrew Richard

Andy Thompson was born at Featherstone, near Cannock,

Andy Thompson

Staffs on 9 November 1967. And after playing junior football for Featherstone Primary School, Wednesfield Social Under-16s, Featherstone Boys (under his mentor George Hewitt) and Cresswell Wanderers, he became an apprentice with West Bromwich Albion (after being recommended to the club by scout Sid Day), turning professional at The Hawthorns in November 1985.

A midfielder, with grim determination despite being rather on the small side at 5ft 4ins 'Thommo' was given limited first team football by Albion and in November 1986, along with Steve Bull, was transferred to Wolves, his fee going down as £35,000.

Over the next eleven years Thompson became Wolves' penalty expert (he equalled the club record of nine successes from the spot in 1994-95) and he was one of the most versatile players at Molineux, starring in five different positions for the Wanderers, giving nothing less than 100 per-cent every time he took the field.

He produced some outstanding performances when helping Wolves climb majestically from the Fourth to the First Division in rapid time and he also gained a Sherpa Van Trophy winners' medal at Wembley in 1988. After a well deserved Testimonial (v. Chelsea in July 1996) he was released by manager Mark McGhee twelve months later and joined forces with First Division Tranmere Rovers where he played as an orthodox left-back. He switched from Prenton Park to Cardiff City in August 2000 and helped the Welsh club gain promotion to the Second Division before being placed on the transfer list in June 2001.

NB - During his time with Wolves 'Thommo' wore every outfield jersey at first team level and he even went in goal during a friendly match against the Worcestershire Cricket Club soccer XI at Molineux!

Wolves' record: 431+20 apps. 43 goals.

THOMPSON, David Stanley

Born near the racecourse at Catterick camp on 12 March 1945, Dave Thompson was a useful outside-right, fast and alert, who signed for Wolves as a junior before turning professional at Molineux in April 1962.

His first team outings were restricted and in August 1966 he was transferred to Southampton where he remained for more than four years prior to joining Mansfield Town in October 1970.

He did exceedingly well with the Stags and scored 24 goals in 131 League games whilst at Field Mill, moving to Chesterfield in December 1973. He dropped out of League soccer in the summer of 1974.

Wolves' record: 10 apps. one goal.

THOMPSON, Harold

Inside-left Harry Thompson was a Wolves player from May 1935 to November 1938 when he moved to Sunderland. Born in Mansfield on 29 April 1915, he played for Mansfield Invicta and Mansfield Town reserves

before switching to Molineux.

A brief spell with York City (1939) followed his time at Roker Park and between 1946 to 1949 he made 38 League appearances for Northampton Town before joining Headington United (now Oxford United) as their player-manager, some thirteen years before the 'U's' entered the Football League.

Wolves' record: 73 apps. 17 goals.

THOMSON, Robert Anthony

Born in Smethwick on 5 December 1943, Bobby Thomson emerged as a classy right-back, who went on to play for his country at both Under-23 and senior levels (winning eight full caps). He joined Wolves as a youngster in June 1959 on leaving Lyndon High School and turned professional at Molineux in July 1961.

He made his first team debut in an F.A. Cup-tie against West Bromwich Albion the following January and thereafter gave the Wanderers excellent service, right up until March 1969 when he moved to Birmingham City for £40,000.

In July 1972, he switched to Luton Town, played next for Hartford US Bi-Centennials in the NASL (April 1976); assisted Port Vale (from October 1976 to April 1977) and then, after another spell in America as player-coach of the Connecticut Bi-Centennials (formerly Hartford) he returned to England to play for Worcester City, soon becoming player-manager of Stafford Rangers (August 1979-1981).

After that he served with Memphis Rogues (NASL), Brewood, Solihull Borough and Tipton Town, and for some years ran a sports shop in Sedgley, near Wolverhampton. During the 1980s Thomson played in several Charity matches around the Midlands. He now resides in the Wolverhampton area and makes regular visits to Molineux.

Wolves' record: 299+1 sub 3 goals.

THOMSON, Robert Gillies Mackenzie

Scottish inside-forward Bobby Thomson had a splendid career after leaving Molineux in June 1959. Born in Dundee on 21 May 1937, he represented Dundee and Dunblane Schools and was an amateur with Albion Rovers and Airdrieonians (August 1952) before joining Wolves as a junior in 1953, turning professional in August 1954. Unable to gain first team football he left the Wanderers for Aston Villa five years later in an £8,000 deal and here his career took off.

He went on to score 70 goals in 171 appearances in four seasons with Villa, helping them win the Second Division championship (1960) and the League Cup (1961) as well as gaining a runners-up medal in the latter competition against his future club, Birmingham City in the Final of 1963.

As hard as they come, the chunky, wavy-haired Thomson then left the Claret and Blues to sign for their arch rivals at St Andrew's in September 1963.

He stayed with Blues for a further four years (the last few under his former Molineux boss Stan Cullis). He netted 25 goals in 129 games before rounding off his League duties by having six months with Stockport County (December 1967 to May 1968). He then had a brief spell with Bromsgrove Rovers (to 1970) and thereafter kept himself supremely fit by playing squash and tennis on a regular basis.
Wolves' record: one app. one goal.

THOMSON, Samuel
Wolves recruited Scotsman Sammy Thomson from Preston North End in the summer of 1890 after he had scored 14 goals in 34 League games for the Deepdale club, whom he helped complete the double in 1888-89, playing against Wolves in that season's FA Cup Final!
A dashing, all-purpose forward, able to adapt, he was born in Lugar on 14 February 1862, and joined Preston from Glasgow Rangers in the summer of 1888. From Wolves he moved to Everton and from Goodison Park he went to Accrington, retiring to live and work in Preston, the town where he died on 23 December 1943, aged 81.
Wolves' record: 24 apps. 9 goals.

THORPE, Albert Edwad
Albert Thorpe played for Wolves in season 1928-29, replacing Bill Brown in the away game at Nottingham Forest in December - his only first team outing for the club. Born in Pilsley on 14 July 1910, Thorpe played for Shirebrook FC and represented East Derbyshire Schools in 1924 before joining the Molineux camp in May 1928. On leaving Wolves in the summer of 1929 he signed for Mansfield Town, later serving with Notts County, Norwich City (for whom he made 61 League appearances between 1932-35, helping the Canaries win promotion from Division Three (South) in 1933-34), Crystal Palace, Scunthorpe United and Hereford United, retiring in 1939. Thorpe died in Langwith on 3 January 1971.
Wolves' record: One app.

TIMMINS, Beniah
Ben Timmins was an early 1920s star with Walsall for whom he played over 100 League games before being transferred to Wolves (with Bowen) in March 1924 for a combined fee of £130.

A fiercesome tackler with a prodigious kick, Timmins could occupy either full-back berth and was always willing to occupy a more central position if required.
Born in Great Barr, Birmingham in August 1898, he attended Christ Church School and played for Beeches Road Methodists and Dartmouth Victoria before signing for Walsall in 1920. He was

Ben Timmins

unfortunately badly injured in 1926 and as a result decided to retire to go and work in a factory. Timmins died in Birmingham on 13 August 1965.
Wolves' record: 11 apps.

TODD, Kenneth
Born in Butterknowle on 24 August 1957, busy midfielder Kenny Todd joined Wolves as a junior in 1974 and turned professional in August 1975. Given very little opportunity at Molineux, he was eventually bought by Port Vale in August 1978 for a record fee of £37,000.

Kenny Todd

After 45 League and Cup games (9 goals) for the Valiants, he rounded off his League career with a spell at Portsmouth, moving south for £20,000 in October 1979. He stayed at Fratton Park until to May 1980, when he switched to Fareham Town. He later assisted Waterlooville prior to making a return to Pompey as Youth team manager in 1985.
Wolves' record: 4+1 sub app. one goal.

TODD, Mark Kenneth
Born Belfast 4 December 1967, midfielder Mark Todd was an apprentice with Manchester United before turning professional at Old Trafford in August 1985.
He moved to Sheffield United in June 1987 and had a loan spell with Wolves in February 1991.
He then served on loan with Rotherham United before joining the Millmoor club for £135,000 in November 1991. Transferred to Scarborough in August 1995 Todd later served with Mansfield Town from February to May 1996.
Wolves' record: 6+1 sub apps.

TOMKYES, Thomas
Tommy Tomkyes was a member of Wolves' first team squad for two seasons, from August 1887 to May 1889. He made only one League appearance v. Notts County (away) in January 1889, replacing Jack Brodie at centre-forward.
Born in Heathtown Wolverhampton circa 1867, he joined Wolves from Stafford Road, returning there after leaving the Wanderers.
Wolves' record: one app.

TONKS, John
Dashing outside-right Jack Tonks (sometimes referred to as Joe) was a useful goalscorer in his time. As keen as mustard, tricky with a good shot, he played for Walsall Unity before joining Wolves in July 1894 and left Molineux for Walsall in June 1900.
Born in Wednesfield in 1872, Tonks went into the building trade after retiring in 1904. He was given a benefit match by Wolves in 1899. He died in 1948.
Wolves' record 119 apps. 23 goals.

TOOTILL, Alfred

Towards the end of the 1928-29 season Wolves introduced a promising new goalkeeper by the name of Alf Tootill, who made his senior debut against Notts County at Molineux on 2 April, helping his side win 3-1. That was the start of a fine career for Tootill, who was born in Ramsbottom, Yorkshire on 12 November 1908.

Nicknamed the 'Bird-catcher', he was small, acrobatic with great ability and a safe pair of hands, who in later years was described as 'brainy with a fine eye.' He starred for Ramsbottom United in the Bury & District Amateur League for two years before signing as a full-time professional for Accrington Stanley in September 1927.

After playing in the Third Division (North) for 18 months he was transferred to Wolves for £400 in March 1929 and quickly made an impression at Molineux.

He was first choice 'keeper from 1929 to November 1932, helping Wolves win the Second Division title in 1932. Then, after conceding seven goals against Arsenal, he was sold to Fulham by Major Frank Buckley for £1,000, Tootill actually signing the appropriate forms after being called out of a cinema!

He did as well at Craven Cottage as he'd done at Molineux, and after 214 appearances for Fulham he moved to Crystal Palace in May 1938, staying at Selhurst Park until after the war. In his professional career Tootill appeared in well over 400 senior games, 372 in the Football League and during the war he turned out for Palace more than 150 times in regional competitions.

Outside football Tootill enjoyed a game of cricket, turning out regularly for Ramsbottom in the Lancashire League. He died in London on 31 August 1975, aged 66.

Wolves' record: 143 apps.

Alf Tootill

TOPHAM, Richard T

Utility forward Dick Topham was born in Ellesmere Port on 3 November 1867 and remained an amateur throughout his career. A speedy player, difficult to contain, he played his early football at Oswestry School and whilst attending Keble College at Oxford, he assisted Oxford University and Oswestry FC, being selected by Wales against Scotland in 1885, but declined his first cap. Afterwards he starred for the Casuals (London), Chiswick Park FC and the Corinthians (1894-98), being registered to play for Wolves between 1891 and 1896.

A schoolmaster at Brighton College from 1892 to 1905, Topham gained an FA Cup winners medal in 1893, having earlier collected a Welsh Cup runners-up prize with Oswestry in 1885.

He later received a second runners-up medal with the Casuals in the 1894 FA. Amateur Cup Final.

Topham appeared in several amateur internationals for England and won two full caps v. Ireland in February 1893 and Wales in March 1894.

His best season at Molineux was in 1891-92 when he netted 12 goals in 13 games. After retiring from football and in his spare time, Topham became a highly respected hop grower in Kent. He died on 31 August 1951.

Wolves' record: 32 apps. 19 goals.

TOWNER, Anthony James

Wide-midfielder Tony Towner was born in Brighton on 2 May 1955. Between January 1973 and October 1978 he played 162 League games for his home town club, Brighton & Hove Albion, before transferring to Millwall. In August 1980 (after 68 outings for the Lions) he moved to Rotherham United for whom he starred in more than 100 senior matches. A loan spell with Sheffield United (March 1983) preceded his departure from Millmoor to Molineux in August 1983.

With Wolves he did reasonably well but with a struggling side he never really enjoyed his football and in September 1984 was sold to Charlton Athletic, later assisting both Rochdale (November 1985) and Cambridge United (March to May 1986) as a non-contract player. Towner then quit League football that summer, having amassed in useful record in the competition of 419 appearances and 54 goals.

In September 1986 Towner signed for Gravesend and later played for Fisher Athletic (1987), Crawley Town (1989) and Worthing (July 1990-91).

Wolves' record: 29+6 sub apps. 2 goals.

TRAVERS, James Edward

Wolves released 'George' Travers from Molineux at the age of 19 in 1907. He went on to appear in more than 150 League games over the next 15 years, serving, in turn, with Birmingham, Aston Villa, Queens Park Rangers, Leicester City, Barnsley, Manchester United, Swindon Town, Millwall, Norwich City and Gillingham.

Born in Newtown, Birmingham on 5 November 1888, he died in Smethwick on 31 August 1948....and was certainly another player missed by Wolves!

TROUGHTON, Samuel Edward
Inside-forward Sammy Troughton was born in Lisburn, Northern Ireland on 27 March 1964 and joined Wolves from Glentoran in December 1983.

Capped by his country at both schoolboy and youth team levels, he stayed at Molineux until May 1984 when he returned to his homeland because Wolves refused to pay £5,000 to his former club Glentoran after Troughton had made a certain number of appearances (20). In December 1984 he had a spell with Portadown.

Wolves' record: 20 apps. 2 goals.

TUDOR, Shane Anthony
A right-sided midfielder, born in Wolverhampton on 10 February 1982, Shane Tudor joined Wolves as an apprentice in July 1998 and turned professional in September 1999. He made his senior debut as a substitute against Sheffield Wednesday shortly before Christmas, 2000, replacing the injured Darren Bazeley.

One for the future, Tudor was part of Wolves' treble-winning youth team (in League and Cup) in 1998-99.

Tudor joined Cambridge Utd on loan in October 2001.

Wolves' record: 0+1 app.*

TUFT, Walter Eli
Wally Tuft was a sold player, reserve to full-back George Eccles. Born in Wolverhampton in 1875, he played for Tettenhall St Peter's before having half a season at Molineux (September 1897 to January 1898).

He then joined Darlaston and was signed by Bristol City in 1900 but never played a game for the Robins. He later assisted Castle Hill Rovers (Dudley).

Wolves' record: 8 apps.

TURNER, Andrew Peter
Andy Turner joined Wolves from Portsmouth in March 1999. A left-winger, born in Woolwich on 23 March 1975, he started his career with Tottenham Hotspur, signing professional forms at White Hart in April 1992 after two years' apprenticeship. He made 23 appearances for Spurs and had loan spells with Wycombe Wanderers, Doncaster Rovers, Huddersfield Town and Southend United before transferring to Fratton Park for £250,000 in September 1996. From Fratton Park he switched to Crystal Palace (October 1998) and joined Wolves in March 1999. Unfortunately he failed to get a first team outing at Molineux and left the club for Rotherham United four months after his arrival. A loan spell with Rochdale preceded a move to Yeovil Town in June 2001.

Capped by England at schoolboy and youth team levels, Turner also gained seven Under-21 caps for the Republic of Ireland. He made over 140 appearances in senior League and Cup football.

TURNER, Graham John
Graham Turner was Wolves' manager from October 1986 to mid November 1995, having collected his last 'Manager of the Month' award in September 1994. During his nine-year spell in the Molineux 'hot seat' Turner, no doubt, did a terrific job in guiding the club up from the depths of the Fourth Division and taking them to Wembley, as well as making some excellent signings, among them a certain Steve Bull!

Born in Ellesmere Port, Cheshire on 5 October 1947, Turner was a defender who played as a professional for Wrexham from July 1965 to January 1968, winning an England Youth cap during his time at the Racecourse Ground. He went on to appear in more than 250 games for Chester before transferring to Shrewsbury Town in January 1973. He then remained at Gay Meadow for thirteen years, until July 1984, when he became manager of Aston Villa.

Graham Turner

During his last season with the 'Shrews' he acted as player-manager and all told chalked up in excess of 400 first team appearances for the Shropshire club (355 in the Football League). He struggled to come to terms with the situation at Villa Park and left to take charge of Wolves just three months into the 1986-87 season.

He quickly snapped up Messrs. Bull and Thompson from neighbouring West Bromwich Albion and slowly built a squad which proved good enough to win promotion from the Fourth and then Third Divisions in successive seasons, as well as capturing the Sherpa Van Trophy at Wembley.

Once into the reconstructed First Division, however, frustration started to creep in. The fans weren't too happy either (especially with home performances) as Wolves struggled to put in a strong enough challenge to win a place in the top flight and eventually this sort of form inevitably led to Turner being axed in November 1995.

Into his place stepped another Graham - Taylor - the former England, Watford and Aston Villa boss.

Turner, himself, remained out of football for quite awhile. He returned in the summer of 1996 when he took over the reins at Hereford United, who, sadly under his control, lost their Football League status in May 1997 after failing to win their last game of the season at home to Brighton and Hove Albion. Two years later Turner was appointed Chairman and Director of Football at Edgar Street and one of his first signings was Steve Bull (as player-coach). During the 2000-01season Turner stepped down as team manager, allowing the former Wolves player Phil Robinson to step into the hot seat as the Bulls' new boss.

Turner's record as Wolves manager was played 412, won 179, drawn 109, lost 124. Goal scored 634, conceded 476.

TURNER, Graham Mark

Manager Graham Turner's son, Mark Turner was with Wolves for three seasons during which time he made only one senior appearance.

Born in Bebbington on 4 October 1972, he was signed as a wide midfielder by his father from Paget Rangers in July 1991 and was released in June 1994 when he signed for Northampton Town. He failed to make an impact with the Cobblers, who allowed him to leave for Telford United in December 1995.

After a trial with Leeds United (February 1997) his father then re-signed him again the following month, this time for Hereford United. And in the summer he switched back to Telford United.

Wolves' record: one app.

TURNER, John Alan

Wolves signed 6ft 3in goalkeeper Jack Turner from Stockport County in August 1928 as cover for Lewis Botto and Alf Canavon. Born in Swallownest, Sheffield in 1906, he had previously had a trial at Molineux (in 1924 from Silverwood Colliery FC.) but was rejected and went to Edgeley Park, appearing in 38 games for County before switching his allegiance to Molineux.

He conceded 14 goals in his seven outings for the club, including four v. Hull and five at Preston, before leaving in November 1927 to sign for Watford, later playing for Rotherham United.

Wolves' record: 7 apps.

TYLER, Sidney

Described as a 'polished full-back' Sid Tyler spent three years at Molineux where he acted as reserve to Ted Watson. Born in Wolverhampton on 7 December 1904, he played for Stourbridge from May 1921 before joining Manchester United in May 1922 (making one senior appearance).

In May 1924 he was recruited by Wolves and left Molineux for Gillingham in August 1927. He later assisted Norwich City (on trial) and Millwall (from April 1929), before rounding off his career with Colwyn Bay United (June 1931 to May 1933) and then Chamberlain & Hickham FC (Birmingham) as a re-instated amateur from September 1933 to his retirement in 1935. Tyler died in Walsall on 25 January 1971.

Wolves' record: 18 apps.

UTTERSON, James

Giant goalkeeper, upright, smart, Jimmy Utterson was at Molineux during the mid 1930s. Born in Gateshead on 26 November 1914, he played as a junior with South Shields and for Glenavon (Ireland) before moving to Molineux for £300 in the summer of 1934 as cover for Alex Scott.

He represented the Irish League v. The Football League whilst with Glenavon. Sadly Utterson died shortly before Christmas in December 1935, when only 21 years of age. He had suffered a serious head injury in a 4-2 defeat at Ayresome Park v. Middlesbrough in September 1935 and died in hospital of brain damage.

Wolves' record: 14 apps.

VAN DER LAAN, Robertus Petrus

Hardworking, hard running Dutch midfielder who played a handful of games for Wolves whilst on loan from Derby County in season 1996-97. Born in Schiedam in the Netherlands on 5 September 1968, Van der Laan played for SVV Schiedam and FC Wageningen in his homeland before joining Port Vale for £80,000 in February 1991.

He went on to appear in well over 200 first-class games for the Valiants, helping them win promotion to the First Division in 1994, a year after lifting the Autoglass Trophy at Wembley.

He left Vale Park for Derby County in a £475,000 deal (involving Lee Mills) in July 1995, a month after being hit in the face by a Stoke City supporter, Derek Massey, who was later fined £100 for assault.

He was a key figure in the Rams midfield when they stormed into the Premiership in 1996, but in July 1998 Van der Laan moved again, this time to Barnsley for

£500,000 (as a replacement for Neil Redfearn). He sadly announced his retirement from competitive football with a knee injury in March 2001.

Wolves' record: 7 apps. no goals.

VAUGHAN, Nigel Mark

Welsh international midfielder Nigel Vaughan was a hardworking player, a waif like figure who had a will o' the wisp tendency to ghost in and make the most of the half chances. He gave Wolves excellent service for three years, putting in some sterling performances.

Born in Caerleon, near Newport, Wales on 20 May 1959, Vaughan joined Newport County straight from school (June 1975) having played for The Lodge and the Cwmbran representative side. He turned professional at Somerton Park in May 1977. After 224 League games for County (34 goals scored) he was transferred to Cardiff City in September 1983 and in his four years at Ninian Park Vaughan netted a further 42 goals in 149 League outings.

After a loan spell with Reading (February-March 1987) he moved to Molineux for £12,000 in August 1987 and remained with Wolves until July 1990 when he switched to Hereford United, staying at Edgar Street for two seasons. During his time with Wolves Vaughan gained Fourth and then Third Division championship medals and a Sherpa Van Trophy winners medal at Wembley. And he scored in six successive League matches between 17 October and 24 November 1987 - quite a feat for a midfield player. He represented Wales at Youth and Under-21 levels before gaining 10 full caps (1983-85). Unfortunately he broke his leg while playing with Hereford and was out of the game for quite awhile. In 1996-97 Vaughan became caretaker-manager of Newport AFC (Wales) after spells with Worcester City, Stourbridge and Pershore. A fully qualified FA Coach, he was appointed manager of the Bridgnorth-based club Brandon (Banks Premier League) in 1999.

Wolves' record: 110+10 sub apps. 13 goals.

Nigel Vaughan

VENUS, Mark

Born in Hartlepool on 6 April 1967, Mark Venus occupied a number of positions during his time at Molineux, lining up as a full-back, central defender, sweeper, left-sided midfielder and an occasionally as an emergency attacker! And he always gave a good account of himself, especially in defence where he was confident, using his excellent left foot to good effect. Venus started his career with his home-town club, Hartlepool United whom he joined initially as a junior, turning professional in March 1985.

In September of that same year he was transferred to Leicester City and went on to make almost 70 appearances for the Foxes before moving to Wolves for £40,000 in March 1988.

He was placed in the League side immediately and at the end of his first season at Molineux collected a Third Division championship medal. During his nine-year stay he became a valuable member of the senior squad and passed the milestone of 300 competitive appearances for Wolves before his transfer to Ipswich Town (in a deal involving Steve Sedgley) in June 1997.

Venus then gave great service to the Portman Road club, missing out in two successive the First Division play-off semi-finals (1988 & 1999) before finally entering the Premiership at third attempt. He then proceeded to have an excellent campaign as the Suffolk Punchers clinched a place in the UEFA Cup for the 2001-02 campaign.

Wolves' record: 319+18 sub apps. 10 goals.

VEYSEY, Arthur John

Reserve outside-right Arthur Veysey drew up a useful record, albeit relatively small, during the 1904-05 season - scoring on each of his two League outings for Wolves against Middlesbrough at home (won 5-3) and Stoke away (lost 2-1).

Born in Willenhall circa 1884, he played initially for Featherstone Boys and on leaving Molineux in May 1905 he joined Oxley, later playing for Brewood.

Wolves' record: 2 apps. 2 goals.

VILLAZAN, Raphael Diego

Born in Uruguay on 19 September 1957, Raphael Villazan was a strong, hard-tackling midfielder who was recruited to Molineux from Huelva Sporting club in May 1980 by manager John Barnwell.

Unfortunately he never really fitted the bill although injuries didn't help his cause and after less than 30 first team outings he was released in May 1982, returning to his native Uruguay where he joined Nacional. Villazan won 11 full international caps for his country.

Wolves' record: 24+3 sub apps.

Raphael Villazan

W

Mark Venus

VIZARD, Edward

Ted Vizard was Wolves' manager for four years - from April 1944 to May 1948.

Born in Cogan, Wales, 7 June 1889, he attended St David's County School and played soccer for Cogan Old Boys and rugby for Penarth before establishing himself as an outside-left with Barry Town in 1909. He joined Bolton Wanderers in December 1910 and remained as a player at Burnden Park until May 1931, having guested for Chelsea during World War One. After hanging up his boots Vizard was appointed Bolton's scout and he also coached the 'A' team to April 1933.

In that same month he became manager of Swindon Town, a position he held for five years before taking over at Queen's Park Rangers (May 1939 to April 1944). From Loftus Road he switched to Wolves (April 1944) and nine months after leaving Molineux he was given the manager's job at non-League Cradley Heath (February 1949).

He quit football in May 1950 and was later licensee of the Tettenhall Hotel, Wolverhampton (1950-53).

A very accomplished footballer, he was nicknamed 'Vizard the Wizard' and was rated as clever a winger as ever stepped onto a football pitch (certainly in the 1920s). He formed a great left-wing partnership with Joe Smith at Bolton and was the Welsh idol in many an international match. He also represented his country as a rugby three-quarter. He had natural speed to go with dazzling skill.

Vizard was capped 22 times by Wales at soccer. He gained two FA Cup winners medals with Bolton (1923 and 1926) and also made 467 League appearances for the Lancashire club (64 goals scored - making perhaps another 100 or so more with his decisive wing play).

He scored 70 times in 512 outings in all competitions for Bolton and was the oldest player ever to appear for the Lancashire club, aged 41 years, 287 days versus Sunderland in March 1931. He died in Wolverhampton on Christmas Day 1973.

Wolves' playing record (League and Cup) under Vizard was a good one - played 94, won 48, drawn 18 and lost 28.

WAGSTAFFE, David

Outside-left Dave Wagstaffe is listed as one of the all-time greats of Wolverhampton Wanderers. A terrific crosser of the ball, he had both pace and skill and was a big favourite with the supporters.

There was no finer sight in the eyes of the Molineux faithful than to see the flying 'Waggy' racing down the touchline and swinging over a pin-point cross aimed for his goal-seeking strikers. 'Waggy' did this frequently during his eleven years with Wolves and there is no doubt whatsoever that he was one of the most accurate crossers of a ball in the game during the late 1960s and early '70s.

Born in Manchester on 5 April 1943, Wagstaffe joined Manchester City as a junior on leaving school, turning professional at Maine Road in May 1960. He went on to make 161 appearances for City (eight goals scored) before transferring to Wolves for what was to prove a bargain fee of £30,000 on Boxing Day 1964.

He soon started to produce the goods at Molineux, but sadly Wolves were relegated at the end of his first season with the club. However, his form never waned and he was instrumental in helping the team regain their First Division status in 1967 when he was an ever-present in the side. He played in two major Cup Finals for Wolves, collecting a winners medal when his former club Manchester City were defeated 2-1 in the 1974 League Cup Final at Wembley and a loser's prize after Spurs had beaten Wolves on aggregate in the UEFA Cup Final two years earlier.

In January 1976, after more than 400 appearances for the club, 'Waggy' was sold to Blackburn Rovers. He later switched his allegiance to neighbouring Blackpool (March 1979) and decided to retire from competitive football in May of that same year with a League record of 564 appearances and 42 goals scored safely under his belt.

Not for the want of trying, 'Waggy' received very few representative honours, playing for England at both schoolboy and youth team levels and getting one outing with the Football League XI.

In later years he returned to Molineux to run 'Waggy's' bar and later acted as steward of the Old Wulfrunians Club, Castlecroft, a position he filled until January 1993. He now lives and works in Staffordshire.

NB - One record 'Waggy' isn't proud of is that he was the first League footballer to be shown the 'red card' when playing for Blackburn Rovers at Bolton in a Second Division match on 2 October 1976.

Wolves' record: 404 apps. 32 goals.

WAKE, Benjamin

Centre or inside-forward Ben Wake was registered with Wolves for two seasons, initially signing for the club in July 1907. He deputised for Jack Shelton or George Hedley on four occasions, scoring once, in a 2-1 defeat at Fulham.

Born in Wolverhampton in 1888, he joined Wolves from St Augustine's FC, and left the club for Bloxwich in the summer of 1909. He later worked on the railway while also assosting several minor teams in the area.

Wolves' record: 4 apps. one goal.

WALDRON, John Joseph

Outside-right Jack Waldron was a Wolves player for one season, 1883-84, making his only senior appearance for the club in an FA Cup-tie against Wednesbury Old Athletic halfway through that campaign.

He was born in Wolverhampton in 1861 and prior to signing for Wolves had assisted St Paul's FC and Springfield Rovers. On his departure he signed for Whitmore Reans and later assisted Wednesfield and Wolverhampton Nomads. Waldron died circa 1935.

Wolves' record: one app.

Dave Wagstaffe

WALKER, Alfred J Samuel

A Londoner, born in the capital circa 1887, left-winger Alf Walker played for Northampton Town and Brentford before joining Wolves for the 1909-10 season. He spent two years at Molineux, the first in the reserves, but then he had some useful outings as partner to Jack Needham, having replaced Jack Pedley.

In July 1911 Walker was sold to Port Vale and he went on to play in over 90 first team games for the Potteries club before moving to Dunfermline Athletic in the summer of 1914. He later returned to the Stoke-on-Trent area where he became an ardent Vale supporter, while also coaching young footballers in the Potteries. Walker died in Newcastle-under-Lyme on 14 September 1961.

Wolves' record: 35 apps. 2 goals.

WALKER, David

Utility forward David Walker played for Wolves during the 1904-05 season, replacing Jack Smith and Bill Wooldridge in games against Preston and Stoke towards the end of the campaign.

Born in Oakdene, Walsall in July 1884, he played for Pleck Road School (Walsall), Walsall White Star and Birchfield Villa prior to his association with Wolves and after leaving Molineux he served in turn, with Bristol Rovers (signed in August 1905), West Bromwich Albion (April 1907, scoring 15 goals in 39 games), Leicester Fosse (May 1908), Bristol Rovers (again, from August 1911), Willenhall Swifts (1912) and finally Walsall (1913), his last club before retiring in 1920.

Walker died in October 1935, aged 51.

Wolves' record: 2 apps.

WALKER, George William

George Walker was a sturdy full-back with a solid frame who enjoyed a challenge. Perhaps a shade slow at times, he was nonetheless a capable player who was never 'roasted' by a winger.

Born in West Bromwich circa 1878, he played for several local teams in the town before joining Willenhall Pickwick in 1899, transferring to Wolves in August 1900. Over the next four years he gave Wolves excellent service before moving to Crystal Palace in August 1904. He had over 50 outings for the Londoners prior to his retirement from the senior game in 1906.

Walker, who died in 1945 aged 67, had three brothers. One of them, Billy, was the father of Billy Walker, a quality goalscorer with Aston Villa and England in the 1920s, who later managed both Sheffield Wednesday (1935) and Nottingham Forest (1959) to FA Cup Final triumphs.

Wolves' record: 132 apps. 2 goals.

WALKER, John

The tall, blond, red-faced and tough-tackling Jack Walker was a reserve left-half at Molineux in season 1903-04 and replaced the injured Billy Annis in the away game against Aston Villa and versus Stoke at home.

Born in Gornal in 1882, he played for Toll End and Tipton Excelsior before signing for the Wanderers from Coseley FC in August 1903. He joined Dudley Old Edwardians when he was released from Molineux.

Wolves' record: 2 apps.

WALKER, John Young Hilley

Inside-forward Johnnie Walker was born in Glasgow on 7 December 1928. He started his career north of the border with Campsie Black Watch FC in 1944-45 and in July 1947 became a professional with Wolves.

He did not establish himself in the Wanderers' first XI until 1949-50, but once in, he became a firm favourite with the fans.

Unfortunately with so much forward talent available for manager Stan Cullis to choose from Walker became surplus to requirements and in October 1952 he was transferred to Southampton for £12,000.

At The Dell his form was most impressive and he went on to net 48 times in 172 games for the Saints before moving to Reading in December 1957 for £2,500. He continued to do well for the Royals and claimed another 26 goals in just over 300 senior games in his seven years at Elm Park before retiring from competitive football in 1964.

Walker later returned to Elm Park as Reading's reserve team coach, a position he held until 1979 when he left the club to work for the Royal Mail, Reading branch.

He still follows the fortunes of the Royals and indeed the Wolves from his Berkshire home in Theale.

Wolves' record: 44 apps. 26 goals.

WALKER, Paul Graham

Paul Walker was an efficient midfielder, who played over half his games for Wolves as a substitute. A Yorkshireman, born in Bradford on 3 April 1949, he played initially as an amateur for his home-town club, Bradford Park Avenue, before becoming a professional with Wolves in October 1966.

Over the next seven years he flirted with first-team football and after loan spells with Watford (December 1971) and Swindon Town (March 1973) he was transferred to Peterborough United (July 1973), and later served with Barnsley (July 1975), Ottowa Tigers (Canada) and Huddersfield Town (November 1976 to April 1977).

He then drifted into non-League football in Yorkshire. Walker played in more than 80 matches for Posh and made over 125 League appearances all told.

Wolves' record: 21+11 sub apps.

WALKER, William George

Goalkeeper Billy Walker played in only one League game for Wolves and it wasn't the greatest of debuts.....he fractured his leg during the first-half of a 7-3 defeat by West Bromwich Albion at The Hawthorns on 28 December 1929.

Born in the heart of the Black Country at Netherton circa 1907, Walker played his early football in Dudley and joined Wolves in 1928. He never really recovered full fitness after his mishap against Albion and left Molineux in 1930, later assisting Bridgnorth, Stourbridge and then Halesowen.
Wolves' record: one app.

WALLACE, Ian Robert

Ian Wallace was born in Hedley, Northumberland, on 12 September 1948 and joined Wolves as a teenager in 1964, turning professional at Molineux in September 1966. A wing-half, he made his debut - and indeed his only senior appearance for Wolves - in that same month as a 'sub' against Blackburn Rovers at Molineux (won 4-0).

After that injuries seriously disrupted his progress and he left the club in 1967, choosing to play non-League football in the North of England.
Wolves' record: 0+1 sub app.

WALTERS, Mark Everton

Wing-forward Mark Walters can occupy either flank. A tricky player with pace and telling shot, he crosses a ball with great precision (on the run or otherwise) and has one marvellous feature whereby he drags his foot over the ball before gliding past a defender.

Born in Birmingham on 2 June 1964, he joined Aston Villa as a teenager (from the Holte Grammar School in Lozells) and remained with the Midlands club until moving to Scotland to sign for Glasgow Rangers for £500,000 in December 1987.

From Ibrox Park he moved to Liverpool for £1.25 million in August 1981 and after loan spells with Stoke City (March/April 1994 and Wolves (September/October 1994) he moved to Southampton (January 1996) on a free transfer, later switching to Swindon Town, also on a 'free' in July 1996. Thereafter he moved from The County Ground to Bristol Rovers in November 1999 and when the 2000-01 season ended he had taken his career record of 711 League and Cup appearances and a total of 165 goals. Winner of one full, one 'B', nine Under-21 and both Schoolboy and Youth caps for England, Walters gained a European Super Cup winners medal with Aston Villa in 1982. He then captured three Scottish Premier Division and two Skol League Cup winners medals while at Ibrox as well as an FA Cup winners medal with Liverpool in 1992.
Wolves' record: 11 apps. 3 goals.

WARD, Samuel

Rather on the small side for a defender, Sammy Ward was nevertheless a useful performer who did well in the Wolves side before losing out to Ted Collins.

Born in Wolverhampton circa 1880, he joined the Molineux staff from Springfield FC in April 1906 and spent over four years with Wolves before transferring to Dudley Town in July 1910, later assisting Brierley Hill Alliance (1912-13). His only League goal for Wolves was a real gem, scored against Burton United (away) in March

1907, sadly to no avail as his side lost 4-1.
Wolves' record: 47 apps. one goal.

WARING, Thomas

Tall, long striding, six feet of sinew, muscle and bone, Tom 'Pongo' Waring was a free-scoring centre-forward, supremely confident in his own ability.

A colourful character, the stories about him apocryphal or otherwise, are legion.

Over 23,000 fans witnessed his scoring debut for Aston Villa in a reserve team fixture against Birmingham in February 1928, shortly after he had netted a double hat-trick (six goals) for Tranmere Rovers in an 11-0 win over Durham City in a Third Division (North) game. The 'Mersey Wit' Waring used to taunt defenders as he stood by them at dead-ball situations. But it wasn't his tongue that did the damage....it was he feet (and head).

He put emphasis on power, and could shoot with either foot and old-timers say that they had rarely seen a player with such a long stride that used to eat up the ground with defenders left tackling his shadow!

Born in Birkenhead on 12 October 1906, Waring attended school in his native town and was a chocolate seller at Prenton Park while playing at weekends for Tranmere Celtic. He then joined Tranmere Rovers as a professional in February 1926, succeeding the great Dixie Dean in their attack, and two years later moved to Aston Villa for £4,700.

In his ten years at Villa Park, he netted 167 goals in 226 first team appearances. An England international (five caps won in 1931 and 1932) Waring claimed a record 49 League goals for Villa in 1930-31 when he was dubbed the 'Gay Cavalier' as he streaked past defenders time and again to smash the ball into the net!

Indeed, every kid around Villa Park wanted to be 'Pongo' Waring - for he was more popular than the Prime Minister. He was sensationally sent-off while playing against Spurs in January 1934, and as he walked, head bowed, from the field he received a bigger cheer than the whole team would have got if they'd won the FA Cup!

In July 1936, Waring moved to Molineux but he failed to settle down to Wolves' style of play and after barely three months with the club he returned to Tranmere (October 1936), later playing for Accrington Stanley (November 1938 to July 1939). He served with Bath City up to the outbreak of the war and after the hostilities he assisted Ellesmere Port, Graysons FC, Birkenhead Dockers and Harrowby whilst working in the Merseyside dockyards. He also guested for New Brighton in 1939-40.

In a sparkling career, Waring, who was also referred to as the 'Birkenhead Bombadier' and the 'Claret and Blue Torpedo', scored 245 goals in 362 League games. He won one medal at club level - helping Tranmere take the Third Division (North) championship in 1937-38.
He died on 20 December 1980, aged 74.
Wolves' record: 10 apps. 3 goals.

WASSALL, Kim

Strong-running forward, who preferred the left-wing position, Kim Wassall was on West Bromwich Albion's books, initially as a junior, before turning professional in June 1975. He failed to make the grade at The Hawthorns and left the Baggies for Northampton Town in September 1977.

Born in Wolverhampton on 9 June 1957, he made 20 League appearances for the Cobblers (one goal scored) before trying his luck in Australia where he played for a number of years. He returned to the U.K in the early '80s and served, as a non-contract player, with Hull City (August 1983), Swansea City (September 1984) and finally Wolves (from October to December 1983). A sojourn in Finland followed his brief stay at Molineux before he rounded off his League career with a short spell at Shrewsbury Town (November 1989-January 1990). He played non-League soccer for various clubs after that - mainly in the South of England.

Wassall now resides in Hertfordshire.

Wolves' record: 2 apps.

WATKISS, Stuart Paul

Stuart Watkiss was a tall, brave defender, who enjoyed a challenge.

Born in Wolverhampton on 8 May 1966, he was taken on at Molineux as an apprentice in 1982 and signed professional forms for Wolves in July 1984.

Unfortunately he failed to make an impression in the old gold and black strip and in February 1986 was transferred to Crewe Alexandra.

He then dropped out of League football for a while and played for Rushall Olympic before re-entering the bigtime with Walsall in August 1993. He went on to play in more than 75 games for the Saddlers, who then released him on a 'free' to Hereford United in February 1996. He was coach with Mansfield Town in 2001.

Wolves' record: 2 apps.

WATSON, Edward George

A strong-bodied defender, as solid as a rock, Ted Watson was a fearsome tackler who kicked long and true and never shirked a tackle. Born in Felling-on-Tyne in 1898, he moved down to South Wales as a youngster and played for Pontypridd before joining Wolves in May 1921.

He spent eight years at Molineux, establishing himself in the first team in 1923-24

Edward Watson

when he replaced Val Gregory in the Third Division (North) Championship winning side.

On leaving Wolves in March 1929 he signed for Coventry City and made over 100 appearances for the Highfield Road club before choosing to round off his career with Oakengates Town (1933-35).

Wolves' record: 206 apps. 4 goals.

WEARE, John Arthur

Goalkeeper Jack Weare, like his predecessor Frank Wildman, conceded five goals on his League debut for Wolves - against Newcastle United (away) in a First Division game in April 1934. As it happened he was given ample time to get over that debacle because his second outing for the club was not until the following February and then, by coincidence, Weare conceded another five goals, this time away at West Bromwich Albion.

Born in Newport, South Wales on 21 September 1912, Weare stood six feet tall and weighed a fraction over 12 stones. He joined Wolves from Lovells Athletic in March 1934 and made over 40 appearances during his time at Molineux, which ended in August 1936 when he agreed to sign for St. Mirren.

Unfortunately he never confirmed the move to Paisley and quickly went south to join West Ham United. During the war, having made 60 first-class appearances for the Hammers, he guested for Bristol Rovers, and after the hostilities he went on to appear in more than 150 League and Cup games for the Eastville Stadium club before announcing his retirement in 1950.

NB - Weare's son, Len (born in 1934) played in 526 League games for Newport County between 1955 and 1969.

Wolves' record: 42 apps.

WEAVER, Reginald

Reg Weaver and his brother Walter (q.v) were playing colleagues with Wolves in season 1927-28. And it was Reg who became the more prominent player of the two and in all he served with five different clubs in an excellent career.

Born in Clutton on 14 September 1905, he first played for Llanhilleth United and then Newport County, joining the latter club in 1926. He transferred to Wolves in November 1927 and did very well in the gold and black strip, top-scoring for the Wanderers in 1928-29 with 18 goals before switching his allegiance to Chelsea in March 1929.

After leaving Stamford Bridge he spent a season with Bradford City (June 1932 to March 1933) and following a brief spell with Chesterfield, he returned to Newport in 1934.

A fast-raiding winger, who preferred the left flank, Weaver won the Welsh Powderhall Sprint title at Caerphilly in July 1931.

Weaver died at Gloucester on 16 July 1970.

Wolves' record: 51 apps. 29 goals.

WEAVER, William Walter

Walter Weaver, brother of Reg (q.v) was born in Birkenhead on 9 November 1898. He played initially for Royal Ivanhoe FC and then South Liverpool before joining Burnley as a professional in 1921.

He then had a spell with Everton before returning to Turf Moor in 1924, transferring to Wolves in October 1926. He remained with Wolves until December 1927 when he left to sign for Accrington Stanley.

He retired through injury in 1930, and then chose to live and work in the Lancashire town. Basically a left-winger, Weaver could also occupy the inside-left position as well as the left-half berth.

Strong and determined, he did well during his fifteen-month stay at Molineux. Weaver died in Accrington on 8 June 1965.

Wolves' record: 47 apps. 13 goals.

WESTCOTT, Dennis

Dennis Westcott was a supreme goalscorer with dynamite in his boots!

Born in Wallasey on 2 July 1917, he played for England at schoolboy level and after unsuccessful trials with West Ham United, he joined New Brighton as a junior for the 1932-33 season.

Dennis Westcott

After turning professional he moved to Molineux in February 1937 while still a teenager and over the next ten years became one of the finest marksmen in the game. He played his first match for the Wanderers on the right-wing in an FA Cup replay against Grimsby Town, starring in a 6-2 win.

His first League goal arrived soon afterwards v. Stoke City - the first of 128 for Wolves at this level. Thereafter he established himself in the centre-forward position, remaining there for ten years, until his transfer to Blackburn Rovers in April 1948.

He was Wolves' leading scorer in 1937-38, 1938-39, 1939-40, 1941-42, 1942-43 and 1946-47. His tally of 43 goals in the 1938-39 season, which included a fourtimer against Grimsby Town in the FA Cup semi-final at Old Trafford, remained a club record until beaten by Steve Bull in 1987-88 with 52.

Westcott played for Wolves in their 1939 FA Cup Final defeat by Portsmouth and was a winner when Sunderland were beaten over two legs in the 1942 Wartime League (North) Cup Final. He was desperately unlucky not to have won a full England cap, but he did represent his country in four Victory internationals (1945-46) and starred for the Football League XI against the Scottish League in 1947.

For Blackburn, he scored 37 goals in just 63 League outings and after leaving Ewood Park he added 37 more goals to his tally in 72 starts for Manchester City whom he served from February 1950 to June 1952. He wound down his senior career by netting 21 goals in 40 League matches for Chesterfield before retiring from first-class soccer in 1953.

He then spent a short time with Stafford Rangers, finally hanging up his shooting boots in May 1956, aged 39.

Westcott died suddenly on 13 July 1960 in Stafford.

Wolves' record: 144 apps. 124 goals (Westcott also made 76 wartime apps. 91 goals).

WESTLEY, Shane Lee Mark

Shane Westley was a sound defender, able to play in a variety of positions, but it was as a centre-back where he produced his best displays.

Born in Canterbury on 16 June 1965, he attended Windcheap Primary and Frank Hooker Secondary Schools in London, and was a junior with Tottenham Hotspur before signing for Charlton Athletic as an apprentice in 1981, turning professional with the Addicks in June 1983.

Two years later, after a loan spell at Roots Hall, he was transferred to Southend United for £15,000, and made over 150 appearances for the Shrimpers' before switching to Wolves for £150,000 in June 1989. He had two good seasons at Molineux, but following a drop in form and a few injury problems he departed company, moving to Brentford for £100,000 in October 1992. After a loan spell with his former club Southend (February/March 1995) he went to Cambridge United on a free transfer in August 1995 and a little over two years later he switched to Lincoln City for £7,500.

After deciding to retire in 1997, Westley - who by now had become a qualified FA Coach - was appointed assistant-manager at Sincil Bank to John Beck, and when

Beck was dismissed in March 1998, he took over as caretaker-boss of the Imps. In season 2000-01 Westley was assistant-manager at Cambridge United.
Wolves' record: 55+2 sub apps. 3 goals.

WESTWOOD, Christopher John
Born in Dudley on 13 February 1977, utility defender Chris Westwood made his first full appearance for Wolves in a 1-0 Coca-Cola Cup win at Fulham in September 1997, along with the Spaniard, Jesus Sanjuan.
He did reasonably well for the remainder of that season but was perhaps surprisingly released in May 1998 when he joined Telford United.
He returned to League action with Hartlepool United in March 1999.
Wolves' record: 5+2 sub apps. one goal.

WHARTON, Guy
Wing-half Guy Wharton was an FA Cup winner at Wembley with Portsmouth in April 1939 (against Wolves) having left Molineux for Fratton Park a few weeks before the last pre-war Final.
Born in Broomfield, Kent, on 5 December 1916, he played initially for Broomfield Rangers and started his League career with Chester in 1935, joining Wolves in readiness for the 1936-37 season. He stayed with the club until his departure to Fratton Park in March 1939.
He stayed with Pompey until July 1948 when he transferred to Darlington, having guested for a number of clubs during the hostilities, also assisting Portsmouth when available.
Wolves' record: 35 apps. 2 goals.

WHARTON, Terence John
Terry Wharton was a fine goalscoring outside-right, who was first choice at Molineux for six years: 1962-67 inclusive.
He and his fellow winger Dave Wagstaffe were, in fact, two of the finest wing-forwards in League football during the mid-sixties with Wharton adding goalscoring prowess to his ability.
A wartime baby, born in Bolton on 1 July 1942, he joined Wolves on his 15th birthday in 1957 and became a full-time professional at Molineux in October 1959, making his League debut v. Ipswich Town in November 1961 when he scored in a 2-0 win.
Wharton went on to keep that No.7 short for the next five-and-a-half seasons, during which time he appeared in more than 240 first-class games, helping the club regain their First Division status in 1966-67.
In November 1967 he was transferred to his home town club, Bolton Wanderers for £60,000 and after more than 100 games for the Trotters he went south to sign for Crystal Palace (January 1971).
From Selhurst Park he switched to South Africa, having a brief spell with Durban City before returning to England

Terry Wharton

in November 1973 to assist Walsall. He retired from competitive football in 1974 with almost 100 goals to his credit in close on 350 League appearances.
Son of Johnny Wharton, the former Preston North End, Manchester City, Blackburn Rovers and Newport County outside-right, Terry was a fine penalty-taker, netting over 20 times from the spot during his career. He now lives on the outskirts of Wolverhampton.
Wolves' record: 241+1 sub apps. 79 goals.

WHATMORE, Ernest
Ernie Whatmore was a reserve centre-forward at Molineux during the early 1920s.
Born in Kidderminster on 25 April 1900, he joined Wolves' playing staff from Stourbridge in July 1922 and was released in January 1923, resulting in him signing for the then non-League side Shrewsbury Town.
He later returned to League football with Bristol Rovers (August 1923) and made over 140 appearances for the Pirates before adding a further 80 to his tally with Queen's Park Rangers. Whatmore rounded off his career with Shepherds Bush FC.
He died in Kidderminster on 31 July 1991, aged 91.
Wolves' record: 2 apps.

WHITE, Edward
Capable inside-left Ted White was born in Wolverhampton in 1900 and died in Shrewsbury in 1970. Brother of Jack (q.v) he played one season with Wolves (May 1922-July 1923) having been signed from

Wellington Town. He returned to his former club on leaving Molineux and later played for Welshpool.
Wolves' record: 11 apps. 3 goals.

WHITE, Jack

Born in Wolverhampton in 1903, inside-right Jack White's only senior outing for Wolves was against South Shields (away) in January 1923.

Like his brother Ted (q.v) he, too, played for Wellington before and after leaving Wolves. He died in Shropshire circa 1974.
Wolves' record: one app.

WHITE, Robert Nelson

Right-winger Bob White had a useful career in the game, serving with a number of clubs, starting off with Prudhoe Castle FC in 1919 before joining Huddersfield Town, from where he switched to Stoke in May 1924.

He transferred to Tranmere Rovers in March 1925; had a brief spell with Yeovil & Petters circa 1928 and was then associated with Wolves in season 1929-30.

Later he assisted Watford, Portsmouth and Carlisle United before retiring in 1939.

White was born in Newburn-on-Tyne in 1903.
Wolves' record: 3 apps. 2 goals.

WHITE, Walter

Walter White scored twice for Wolves in their first-ever Football League victory, a 4-1 versus Burnley in September 1888.

Born in Halesowen in 1864, he played for Coombs Wood before joining Wolves in readiness for that initial League campaign of 1888-89. Unfortunately he failed to establish himself in the first XI and was released by the club in April 1890, when he teamed up with Cradley St Luke's.
Wolves' record: 4 apps. 2 goals.

WHITEHEAD, Clive Robert

Two-footed and versatile, Clive Whitehead had a fine career, serving with Bristol City, West Bromwich Albion, Portsmouth, Wolves and Exeter at League level.

Able to play as a full-back, in midfield or left-winger, he was born on 24 November 1955 in Birmingham and played for Northfield Juniors before turning professional with Bristol City in August 1973.

After winning England Youth international honours he went on to play in more than 250 games for the Ashton Gate club before transferring to West Brom in November 1981. During his six years at The Hawthorns, Whitehead skippered the Baggies and made almost 200 League and Cup appearances for the club prior to his transfer to Portsmouth in June 1987, having been on loan to Wolves in January 1986.

After leaving Fratton Park he assisted Exeter City, first as a player then as player-manager before being sacked in April 1991 after just six months in charge.

He served with Yeovil Town next and in 1996 returned to his first club, Bristol City, as youth team coach in 1997.
NB -Whitehead's wife gave birth to twins whilst he was at The Hawthorns.
Wolves' record: 4 apps.

WHITEHOUSE, Jack

A very stylish, yet competitive half-back, the fair-haired Jack Whitehouse was a regular in Wolves' League side for five years from 1901, always giving 100 per-cent effort on the field of play (he was sent-off at least once during his time with Wolves).

Born in Swan Village, West Bromwich in August 1878, Whitehouse, who had four brothers, two of them footballers, played for Great Bridge Council School and Wednesbury Town before moving to Molineux in July 1900.

Acting initially as reserve to Ted Pheasant, he finally claimed his place in the first XI the following year, but after a misdemeanour within the club (he was involved in a flare-up with two colleagues) Whitehouse was banished to Stourbridge for two months to 'cool down.'

He came back and gave Wolves more sterling service before leaving to sign for Stoke in October 1906. He played in two League games for the Potters the following month and was released early in 1907.

He then went on to play for a number of Black Country sides, including Bloxwich Strollers, Darlaston, Dudley and Gornal Wood. He retired in 1915.
Wolves' record: 155 apps. 1 goal.

WHITFIELD, Kenneth

Ken Whitfield had a difficult time at Molineux, not in terms of playing football, simply because there were so many other quality wing-halves at the club around the same time. He began his career as an amateur with Shildon Colliery in County Durham, arriving at Molineux in December 1947.

He spent the next six years with Wolves playing mainly in the reserves and youth teams. Thus, with the likes of Ron Flowers, Eddie Clamp, Bill Slater and Billy Wright, permanently occupying the three half-back berths between them, Whitfield was allowed to leave for Manchester City in March 1953.

He stayed just over a season at Maine Road before moving south to play for Brighton & Hove Albion for whom he made almost 200 senior appearances. He rounded off his major career by having a season with Queens Park Rangers (1959-60).
Wolves' record: 10 apps. 4 goals.

WHITTAKER, Percy

Goalkeeper Percy Whittaker was a Yorkshireman, born in Swinton on 19 November 1905. He played his early football with Grantham and joined Wath Wanderers (Wolves' nursery club) in 1929 before being upgraded to full-time professionalism at Molineux in August 1930.

Acting as reserve to Alf Tootill and Jack Ellis, injuries unfortunately interrupted his progress and he found it difficult to get regular first-team football. With less than a dozen senior appearances under his belt, plus a Central League Championship medal (won in 1931) he left Wolves for Reading in June 1933.

Whittaker, 5ft 8ins tall, fearless, with a safe pair of hands, did exceedingly well at Elm Park and amassed well over 200 outings for the Royals prior to the outbreak of the Second World War. He gained a League Division South Cup winners' medal in 1938...his only tangible reward for some superb displays between the posts.

He played occasionally during the hostilities (for various local clubs in the Reading area) and was later employed by the Reading Greyhound Stadium, Oxford Road.

Whittaker married the stepdaughter of the Reading manager, Joe Smith.

Wolves' record: 11 apps.

WHITTAM, Ernest Alfred

Inside-forward Ernie Whittam was blind in one eye, but still managed to have a useful footballing career.

Born in Wealdstone on 7 January 1911, he played, in turn, for the Deighton Council School, Huddersfield Town (as an amateur from December 1926, turning professional in November 1928), Chester (signed for £500 in May 1933), Mansfield Town (May 1935), Wolves (February 1936), Bournemouth (September 1936), Reading (1937) and Rotherham United (1945).

His outings were restricted at Molineux due to the presence of so many utility forwards. He retired in 1947.

Wolves' record: one app.

WHITTINGHAM, Guy

Guy Whittingham was a goalscoring centre-forward in the Army when he decided to buy himself out of the forces and become a professional footballer with Portsmouth in June 1989, having assisted Yeovil Town for a season prior to that.

Born in Evesham on 10 November 1964, Whittingham did supremely well at Fratton Park, scoring 104 goals in 188 first-class matches before transferring to Aston Villa for £1.2 million in August 1993. Unfortunately he failed to match those goalscoring exploits with Villa and after a loan spell with Wolves (February/March 1994) he was sold to Sheffield Wednesday for £700,000 four days before Christmas, 1994.

At Hillsborough Whittingham was eventually asked to play as a midfielder where he did well, contributing much to the Owls' excellent 1996-97 season, laying on five goals in a 7-1 Coca-Cola Cup win over Grimsby Town. He reached the milestone of 100 senior appearances for Wednesday early in the 1997-98 campaign.

In November 1998 he had a second loan spell at Molineux. Two months later he had a similar spell with Portsmouth and followed up by spending a month with Watford.

In July 1999 Whittingham returned to Fratton Park on a free transfer. A year later he was transferred to Peterborough United, played briefly for Oxford United (on loan in September 2000) before going back to Pompey as player-coach and assistant-manager the very next month. Whittingham ended the 2000-01 season with Wycombe Wanderers for whom he played in the FA Cup semi-final against Liverpool at Villa Park - one of his old hunting grounds.

Wolves' record: 24 apps. 9 goals.

WIGNALL, Frank

Goalscorer Frank Wignall had a fine career in League football that began in 1959 and ended in 1973.

Born in Blackrod near Chorley, Lancashire on 21 August 1939, he played for Horwich RMI before becoming a professional with Everton in May 1958.

He made his League debut for the Merseysiders the following year and in June 1963, after scoring 15 goals in 33 First Division games, was transferred to Nottingham Forest. At The City Ground he did extremely well and netted 47 times in 156 League outings before moving to Molineux in March 1968. He remained with Wolves for just under a year, leaving for Derby County in February 1969.

After claiming another 15 League goals for the Rams (in 45 matches) he switched to his last senior club, Mansfield Town, in November 1971. He stayed at Field Mill until the end of the 1972-73 season by which time he had taken his record in League football to 107 goals in 322 appearances.

After leaving the Stags Wignall went on to play for a number of minor clubs including Kings Lynn and Burton Albion.

Capped twice by England v. Belgium and Holland in 1964, Wignall also represented the Football League.

Wolves' record: 35+1 sub apps. 16 goals.

WILDMAN, Frank

Goalkeeper Frank Wildman, born in South Kirkby in August 1910, joined Wolves from South Kirkby Colliery FC in November 1932, shortly after Alf Tootill had left Molineux for Fulham.

Unfortunately he made a disastrous entry into League football, conceding five goals on his debut at Craven Cottage on Christmas Eve, 1932. Poor old Wildman, in fact, let in 22 goals in his first eight outings for the club before losing his place in the side to Jack Ellis. In 1933-34 he bounced back and played in 34 games that season before being replaced between the posts early in the 1934-35 campaign by Cyril Spiers. With Arthur Weare also pushing for a first team place, Wildman was then sold to Reading in February 1935. He later assisted Swindon Town (94 League games) and thereafter played for a number of non-League clubs until retiring in 1945.

Wildman was also a very useful cricketer (with both bat and ball) and once scored a century in a Bank Holiday fixture as well as taking 5-35 with his slow left-arm all-sorts. He was a competent tennis player as well.

Wolves' record: 56 apps.

WILDSMITH, Thomas

Acting as a reserve to Jack Nelson, right-half Tom Wildsmith played once in Wolves' League side, at Sheffield United in February 1933.

He was signed from Hadfield FC in November 1932 and left Molineux for Bristol Rovers in August 1933, later assisting Doncaster Rovers (1935-36). Born in Sheffield in 1909, Wildsmith became an efficient, reliable and steady player after leaving Molineux.

Wolves' record: one app.

WILKES, Gilbert Harry

Born in West Bromwich in 1882, Harry Wilkes was related to the famous Wilkes family of photographers. He was a reserve inside-left and played his only League game for Wolves against Derby County (away) in December 1905.

He was a pupil at Beeches Road School, played for St. Phillips Church team, West Bromwich Standard and West Bromwich Albion (as an amateur) before being recruited by Wolves in September 1905. He left Molineux for Dudley Town in May 1906.

Wilkes died in Walsall in 1942.

Wolves' record: one app.

WILLIAMS, Adrian

The versatile Adrian Williams who has played in defence, midfield and as a striker, was one of a cluster of promising young players to emerge from Reading's junior and intermediate ranks.

Adrian Williams

He was born in the Berkshire town on 16 August 1971 and joined the Elm Park apprentice staff in June 1987, turning professional in March 1989. He made the first of what was to be almost 300 appearances for the Royals in October 1988 against Notts County.

In July 1996 Williams was signed by Wolves manager Mark McGhee (who had been his mentor previously) for £750,000, but unfortunately the Welsh international (who now has 12 full caps to his name) struggled with injuries during his three years at Molineux, making less than 40 appearances in that time. He was loaned back to Reading

twice before the end of the 1999-2000 season before rejoining the Royals on a permanent basis in August 2000...sold by his former Elm Park coach Colin Lee who by now had taken over the reins from McGhee.

Williams helped the Royals reach the 2001 Second Division Play-off Final where they lost 3-2 to Walsall at Cardiff's Millennium Stadium...his second such defeat, having scored in Reading's 4-3 defeat at the hands of Bolton Wanderers in the 1995 First Division Play-off Final at Wembley.

Wolves' record: 33+3 apps. one goal.

WILLIAMS, Bert Frederick

There is no doubt that Bert Williams was a great goalkeeper. He was Wolves' number one for a total of 12 seasons, from September 1945 until April 1957, and during that time starred in well over 400 senior matches, including 381 in the First Division of the Football League. Quite brilliant at times, he was agile, alert, fearless and utterly reliable. Known as 'The Cat' he won 24 England caps between 1949 and 1955 and played in the 1950 World Cup Finals in Brazil. In fact, he was between the

Bert Williams

Bert Williams towers above all the surrounding players to claim the ball during a League game against Birmingham City.

posts when the USA inflicted a 1-0 defeat on England in Belo Horizonte. His team-mates Billy Wright and Jimmy Mullen also played in that debacle.

Born in Bilston on 31 January 1920, Bert played for Thompson's FC on leaving school and after a brief spell on the Fellows Park groundstaff, turned professional with Walsall in April 1937. During the Second World War, Williams served in the RAF and when the hostilities were over he left the Saddlers to join Wolves for a bargain fee of £3,500 in September 1945.

In 1949 he helped Wolves win the FA Cup and five years later gained a League Division championship medal. He retired from first-class football at the end of the 1956-57 season, handing over his goalkeeping duties at Molineux to Malcolm Finlayson.

For a number of years afterwards Bert ran a highly successful sports-outfitters shop in Bilston, as well as organising a goalkeeping school for youngsters in the area. Today he lives near Shifnal.

Wolves' record: 420 apps. (606 goals conceded).

WILLIAMS, Evan Samuel

Despite his Welsh-sounding surname, goalkeeper Evan Williams was born in Dumbarton, Scotland on 15 July 1943. He was a capable 'keeper with good technique who acted as first reserve to both Phil Parkes and Fred Davies at Molineux.

He began his playing career with Third Lanark who signed him straight from school in 1958, making him a professional on his 17th birthday. He had 26 games for the now defunct Scottish League club before joining Wolves for £5,000 in March 1966.

Williams was loaned out to Aston Villa in August/September 1969 (following an injury to John Dunn) and after returning to Molineux he finally quit Wolves in March 1970, going back to his homeland to sign for Celtic.

He retired from first-class football in 1972.

Wolves' record: 15 apps.

WILLIAMS, George Harvey

Wing-half George Williams spent two seasons at Molineux (August 1904 to October 1906), playing reserve team football in his initial campaign.

Born in Wolverhampton in 1882, he was signed from Blakenhall and joined Tettenhall Rangers on leaving the club. He died in Bilston in 1939.

Wolves' record: 24 apps.

WILLIAMS, Leonard Henry

An efficient footballer, good on the ball and always totally committed, full-back Len Williams took over from Ted Watson in the Wolves team and did a good job until the arrival of Wilf Lowton.

Born in Rotherham in 1902, he graduated with Wath Athletic in 1922 before signing as a professional with

Sheffield Wednesday in July 1923. From Hillsborough he switched to Stockport County (May 1926) and arrived at Molineux in June 1927. On leaving Wolves he was recruited by Swansea Town (September 1930) and retired four years later.

Wolves' record: 50 apps.

WILLIAMS, Mark Frank

South African striker (born in Johannesburg on 11 August 1966), Mark Williams was a £300,000 signing by Wolves from the Belgian club RWD Molenbeek in September 1995. Capped several times by his country prior to his arrival at Molineux, he scored two early goals for Wolves, but failed to earn a work permit by not appearing in 75 per-cent of the games he was available for... and consequently he was released at the end of that season.

Wolves' record: 8+8 apps. 2 goals.

WILLIAMS, Nigel John

Nigel Williams was a steady defender, relaxed in his style whose first team outings were limited owing to the form of full-backs Geoff Palmer, Derek Parkin, Bernard Shaw and Gerry Taylor.

Born in Canterbury on 29 July 1954, he joined Wolves as an apprentice in July 1970 and turned professional in August 1972. Four years later he was transferred to Gillingham (July 1976) and stayed with the Kent club for two years (making over 50 appearances) before dropping into non-League football in Maidstone.

Wolves' record: 11 apps.

WILLIAMS, Walter

Wally Williams was born in Stafford in August 1883. Able to occupy either wing position, he was fast and direct, with smart footwork and was recruited from Ettingshall in the summer of 1905, initially as cover for outside-left Jack Hopkins.

But when Jack Pedley arrived to challenge for the left-wing berth Williams switched to the opposite flank and here he played extremely well...until being replaced by Billy Harrison. After this Williams found it hard to get into the side and in June 1908 he left Molineux for Darlaston, later assisting Walsall Swifts.

Wolves' record: 34 apps. 4 goals.

WILLIAMS, Walter John

Six-footer Jack Williams was Wolves' reserve centre-half from August 1925 to June 1928, and only managed three senior appearances, all at the start of the 1927-28 season when he deputised for the injured Sammy Charnley.

Born on 18 July 1906 in Wolverhampton he was recruited to Molineux from Wednesfield Rovers and left Wolves for Gillingham, later assisting Brighton & Hove Albion for whom he made over 40 first-class appearances.

Williams died in a Brighton hospital on 26 July 1982.

Wolves' record: 3 apps.

WILSHAW, Dennis James

Dennis Wilshaw was a natural goalscorer - a player who, in today's game, would have fitted into any forward-line superbly well. He was strong and determined, two-footed, and could unleash a powerful shot - and wasn't too bad with his head either!

Born in Stoke-on-Trent on 11 March 1926, Wilshaw was a pupil at Hanley High School and played junior football for the Packmoor Boys Club. From here he signed for Wolves in 1943, and when the hostilities began to die down (1945) he was loaned out to nearby Walsall - he also

DENNIS WILSHAW PUT WOLVES AHEAD WHEN HE FOUND A BALL FROM BILLY WRIGHT WITH AN "INVITATION" ON IT

guested for Port Vale v. Stoke in May 1946, when the Vale were beaten 6-0. Wilshaw returned to Molineux in 1949 to score a hat-trick on his League debut against Newcastle United, lining up in the No.11 shirt.

Indeed, during his long association with Wolves he played in four front-line positions, outside-right being the odd one out. Wilshaw established himself in the Wolves' first team in 1952 and two years later was a key member of the team which landed the First Division championship. He also won two 'B' and 12 full caps for England, netting four goals in that emphatic 7-2 win over Scotland at Wembley in April 1955.

He moved from Molineux to Stoke City in December 1957, and was a vital cog in the Potters' forward-line for four years before breaking a leg against Newcastle United in an FA Cup-tie in 1961. It was ironic that he should play

his first and last senior games of his career against the 'Geordies' ....as he was forced to retire after that second injury.

Wilshaw scored exactly 50 goals in over 100 games for the Potters, and on leaving The Victoria Ground, concentrated on his profession as a Schoolmaster, rising to the Head of Service and Community Studies at Crewe and Alsager College. He also scouted for Stoke for a short while. He now resides in Alsager.

Wolves' record: 232 apps. 117 goals.

WILSON, Joseph

Joe Wilson was a strong, forceful right-back, as hard as nails and a tireless competitor, who made over 500 appearances during his professional career which spanned 17 years.

Joe Wilson

Born in Workington on 6 July 1937, Wilson played as a junior for Workington (from May 1955) before turning professional in January 1956. In March 1962 he was transferred to Nottingham Forest, switching to Wolves in March 1965.

Two years later (May 1967) he was sold to Newport County and then returned to his former club, Workington as player-coach in September 1978. He retired from football in 1983.

Wolves' record: 63 apps.

WILSON, Joseph Frank

Outside-left Frank Wilson played in two League games for Wolves in season 1892-93, replacing Will Devey each time.

Born in Hockley, Birmingham in 1871 and the younger brother of the Albion player of the same name (Joe) he spent just the one season at Molineux before leaving for Castle Blues FC (Shrewsbury). He returned to the West Midlands in 1896 to sign for Walsall Wood and ended his career with Dudley Town. Earlier in his career (1890-92) Wilson had assisted Smethwick Swifts and Elwells. He died in Handsworth, Birmingham in 1949.

Wolves' record: 2 apps.

WILSON, Leslie John

Nicknamed 'The Reverend' Les Wilson had the honour of being the first substitute to score for Wolves when he was called off the bench during a League game with Everton at Goodison Park in September 1967.

A fully committed player, who could occupy a full-back or midfield position, he was born in Manchester on 10 July 1947 and signed apprentice forms with Wolves in 1963, turning professional in September 1964. He established himself in the first team at Molineux in the late 1960s, but was then sold to Bristol City in March 1971.

In September 1973 he moved to Norwich City but at the end of that season (May 1974) he decided to try his luck in the NASL by joining Vancouver Whitecaps as player-coach. He held a coaching position with the Whitecaps until 1983 when he was appointed manager/administrator of the Canadian national team, becoming a very important figure in North American and Canadian soccer in later years.

Wolves' record: 103+13 sub apps. 8 goals.

WINTERSGILL, David

Dave Wintersgill was a reserve defender with Wolves, making only a handful of first team appearances.

A Yorkshireman, born in Northallerton on 19 September 1985, he was a junior at Molineux from June 1981 before turning professional in June 1983. After a loan spell with Chester City (March/April 1984) he had a brief spell with Wimbledon and played in Finland for two years before returning to this country to sign for Darlington in November 1986. He dropped out of League football the following year.

Wolves' record: 3+1 sub apps.

WITHE, Peter

Peter Withe was a goalscoring nomad who had a splendid playing career in the game that spanned almost 20 years.

He netted over 200 goals in more than 600 appearances, while serving with Southport (1970), Preston North End (1971), Barrow (also in 1971), Wolves (November 1973 to August 1975), Birmingham City, Nottingham Forest (1976), Newcastle United (August 1978), Aston Villa (signed for £500,000 in 1980), Sheffield United (1985), Birmingham City (again, on loan) and Huddersfield Town (player-coach in season 1988-89).

He also went abroad to play in South Africa with Port Elizabeth and Arcadia Shepherds in 1972-73 and in 1987 he assisted Portland Timbers in the NASL, having started off right at the beginning with Smith Coggins FC and the amateur side Skelmersdale. He won League and Cup medals with Nottingham Forest and Villa, scoring the winning goal in the 1981 European Cup Final for the latter club. He was also capped 11 times by England and was a big favourite with the fans standing at the Holte End of Villa Park.

After leaving Huddersfield he returned to Villa Park as assistant to manager Josef Venglos and later had a spell as team manager of Wimbledon before embarking on a position as Football in the Community Officer with Port Vale. He later worked as a football summariser on local radio before being appointed manager/coach of the Thai national team (2000).

Wolves' record: 12+5 sub apps. 3 goals.

WOOD, George

Outside-left George Wood spent two seasons with Wolves: 1885-87, during which time he partnered his namesake, Harry Wood, in the forward-line.

Born locally in Wolverhampton circa 1862, he played for Goldthorn Villa and Wolverhampton Druids before joining Wolves and after leaving the club he served with Wednesbury Town and Walsall Pickwick, retiring in the summer of 1891 after breaking his right leg.

Wolves' record: 5 apps.

WOOD, Harry

England international utility forward Harry Wood was born in Walsall on 2 August 1868 and died in Portsmouth on 5 July 1951.

A real gentleman, he was a model professional who played the game with great skill and enthusiasm.

A pen-picture printed in 1889 described him as being

Harry Wood

"clever in ball manipulation and staidly exact in distribution." He certainly gave the fans something to cheer about during his two spells with the Wanderers.

On leaving school Wood played briefly for Walsall Town Swifts and Kidderminster Harriers, joining Wolves in the summer of 1885 and making his senior debut for the Wanderers in an FA Cup-tie v. Derby St Luke's on 31 October of that year. His first spell with Wolves lasted six years, until July 1891 when he re-signed for Walsall.

But he was persuaded to return to Molineux five months later and remained at the club for a further six years before transferring to Southampton in June 1898. In his first spell Wood scored 46 goals in 87 League and Cup matches for the Wanderers; in his second he netted another 80 goals in 202 appearances, finishing up with an impressive record of more than 125 goals in just under 300 first team games.

He won three full England caps (1890-96) and also represented the Football League. He starred in three FA Cup Finals with Wolves, those of 1889, 1893 and 1896, collecting a winners' medal in his second against Everton when he had an exceptionally fine match. He went on to skipper Southampton for seven years (up to 1905) when he retired at the age of 37. He scored 62 goals in 158 games for Saints; played for them in two losing FA Cup finals (1900 and 1902) and also gained four Southern League championship medals (1899, 1901, 1903 and 1904).

After hanging up his boots Wood - nicknamed 'Wolf' - was appointed trainer of Portsmouth, a position he held until 1912 when he became landlord of the Milton Arms public house, situated 200 yards from Fratton Park. Wood spent the rest of his life in Portsmouth, passing away at the age of 83.

NB - His son, Arthur Wood, also played for Southampton and Clapton Orient.

Wolves' record: 289 apps. 126 goals.

WOODFIELD, David

Dark, curly-haired Dave Woodfield was a dogged centre-half, honest and competitive, who could also play as a full-back or wing-half and even centre-forward if required. He gave Wolves excellent service during the 1960s, amassing well over 270 senior appearances.

Born in Leamington Spa on 11 October 1943, he joined Wolves as an amateur in January 1959 and turned 'pro' on his 17th birthday. He broke into the first team towards the end of the 1961-62 campaign and made the No.5 shirt his own early in the following season. A fine stalwart, Woodfield helped Wolves gain promotion from Division Two before leaving Molineux for Watford in a £30,000 deal in September 1971.

He retired out of first-class soccer in 1974 after returning to Molineux to celebrate a deserved Testimonial.

Wolves' record: 273+3 sub apps. 15 goals.

WOODHALL, George

George 'Spry' Woodhall made his name as a goalscoring inside-forward with West Bromwich Albion, helping the Throstles win the FA Cup in 1888 when he hit one of the goals which beat Preston North End 2-1 at Kennington Oval. Born in West Bromwich on 5 September 1863, he attended Hateley Heath School and played for West Bromwich All Saints and Churchfield Foresters before signing for Albion in May 1883, turning professional two years later. He went on to score 20 goals in 74 senior games for Albion, winning two England caps against Wales and Scotland in 1888 and also lining up in two

more FA Cup Finals (1886 and 1887).

He was almost 30 when he joined Wolves in July 1892 and did well during his brief spell at Molineux. He left the club in April 1894, signing for Berwick Rangers (a Birmingham League side). He later played for Oldbury Town (October 1894 to May 1898) before announcing his retirement.

Woodhall died in West Bromwich on 16 September 1924.

Wolves' record: 18 apps. one goal.

WOODRUFF, Robert William

Bobby Woodruff had a tremendous throw in, sometimes hurling the ball a distance of 50 yards from the touchline to the far post and beyond. A wing-half or inside-forward, he made more than 570 League appearances during his career which spanned 19 years.

Bobby Woodruff

Born in Highworth, Wiltshire on 9 November 1940, he was a junior with Swindon Town (September 1956) before turning professional at The County Ground in May 1958. He cost Wolves £40,000 when he transferred to Molineux in March 1964 and spent just over two years with the Wanderers before switching his allegiance to Crystal Palace in a £35,000 deal in June 1966.

In November 1969, Cardiff City recruited his services for a fee of £25,000 and in August 1974 he moved to Newport County for £5,000. Woodruff remained at Somerton Park until May 1976 when he quit major competitive soccer, winding down his career by playing at non-League level in South Wales.

He helped Swindon gain promotion from Division Three in 1963 and then helped Palace win a place in the First Division in 1969.

NB - Woodruff's son, Bobby junior, played for Swindon Town and Newport County.

Wolves' record: 72 apps. 21 goals.

WOODWARD, Maurice

Tall, elegant, strong and confident, centre-half or right-back Maurice Woodward was a professional footballer for 12 years during which time he appeared for Leicester Fosse (from August 1912), Southend United (June 1914), Wolves (from May 1919) and Bristol Rovers (June 1922 to May 1924).

Born at Enderby, Leicestershire on 23 February 1892, Woodward started out with Enderby Town and played for Wolves in the 1921 FA Cup Final v. Tottenham Hotspur. In the mid-1920s he was licensee of the Royal Oak, Compton Road, Wolverhampton.

He died in 1968, aged 76.

Wolves' record: 37 apps. one goal.

WOOLDRIDGE, William Thomas

Billy Wooldridge was a supreme goalscorer as well as a determined, no-nonsense defender. As hard as nails at both ends of the pitch, he appeared in more than 350 games for Wolves and hardly ever let the side down.

A down to earth Black Country yokel, he was born in Netherton, Dudley on 19 August 1878 and played his early football with Netherton St Mary's, Dudley Road and Cradley St Luke's before joining Wolves in July 1899.

Over the next 12 years, he gave the Molineux club excellent service, first as an attacker - he scored two cracking hat-tricks, one against New Brighton in an FA Cup-tie in 1901 and another versus Derby County in a League match in April 1906 - and then as a centre-half.

He scored a fourtimer in England's 10-0 unofficial international match victory over Germany in September 1901 and he also starred for the Football League against the Irish League in that same season when he netted another treble.

An FA Cup winner with Wolves in 1908 (when he skippered the side against Newcastle) Wooldridge retired as a player at the end of the 1910-11 season. He then worked and lived in the area for a number of years before his death in Dudley in April 1945, at the age of 66.

Wolves' record: 356 apps. 90 goals.

WORRALL, Arthur George

Arthur Worrall was a utility forward who spent two seasons with Wolves, 1889 to 1891, his best campaign being his first (1889-90) when he made 25 senior appearances on the right wing or as an inside-forward.

Born in Wolverhampton July 1869, he joined the club from Fallings Heath Rangers and left Molineux for Burton Swifts, later playing for Leicester Fosse, W. Arsenal, Stockport and Barnsley. Worrall died in 1935.

Wolves' record: 37 apps. 13 goals.

WORRELL, George

George Worrell was one of the club's early players who acted as team manager/secretary/committee member during an eight-year period from 1877-1885. In fact, his position at the club was secretary rather than manager.

Born locally, Worrell was a Wolves man through and through, and after giving up his job at the club, he remained a true supporter, cheering the team on from the terraces, first at the old Dudley Road ground and then at Molineux.

WORTON, Thomas

Tom Worton was a sharp-shooting, all-purpose inside-left - a creator, driver and instigator from centre-field.

Born in Heathtown, Wolverhampton on 5 February 1878, he played for Heathtown FC and Cannock Road Council school before joining Wolves as a junior in 1895, turning professional in March 1896.

He was transferred to West Bromwich Albion in May 1901 and helped the Throstles win the Second Division title before retiring through injury in June 1905. Worton died on 20 July 1940.

Wolves' record: 59 apps. 12 goals.

WRIGGLESWORTH, William Herbert

Billy Wrigglesworth, an extremely small and lightweight left-winger, was a veritable 'box of tricks'. He was at his best when working his way through a tightly packed defence with close, clever dribbling and the use of a pretty effective body swerve. For such a light man he possessed a strong shot and his goalscoring ratio was excellent for a wide player.

Born in South Elmshall on 12 November 1912, he played for Frickley Colliery before joining Chesterfield in May 1932. From Saltergate he switched to Wolves in December 1934 and spent just over two years at Molineux before moving to Manchester United in January 1937.

He scored 10 goals in 37 appearances for the Reds and after guesting for Arsenal, Brentford, Chelsea, Cardiff City, Queen's Park Rangers, Walsall and York City during the Second World War, he left Old Trafford for Bolton Wanderers in January 1947. Ten months later he switched to Southampton and after a spell with Reading became player-manager of non-League Burton Albion (July 1949). From December 1949 to April 1950 he played for Scarborough. He followed up by coaching at a Hampshire State School and from July 1952 until 1955 was trainer of Accrington Stanley. Wrigglesworth died on 11 August 1980.

Wolves' record: 58 apps. 22 goals.

WRIGHT, Darren James

Darren Wright looked a good prospect as a youngster, but sadly he never reached the heights his coaches had anticipated.

Born in West Bromwich on 14 March 1968, he joined the Molineux staff on the YTS in June 1983 and turned professional in July 1985. He was released in May 1986 and two months later signed for Wrexham where he stayed until May 1990, making well over 120 first-class appearances for the Welsh club before drifting into non-League soccer.

Wolves' record: one app.

WRIGHT, Harry Fereday

Harry Wright was an energetic forward who could occupy any position in the front-line, usually preferring the inside-right berth.

A gritty performer, he was born in West Bromwich on 12 October 1888 and represented both Beeches Road and St Phillips' Schools (West Bromwich) before plying his trade with West Bromwich St Mark's and West Bromwich Wednesbury Athletic. In November 1906 he was taken on as a full-time professional by West Bromwich Albion but after three years at The Hawthorns he was transferred to Stourbridge, returning to the Baggies for a second spell in June 1910.

He helped Albion win the Second Division title and reach the FA Cup Final in successive years (1911 and 1912) before moving to Molineux for £500 in November 1919. In September 1920, he switched to Newport County, moved north to Chesterfield in August 1921 and announced his retirement in May 1922.

Wright, who guested for Oldbury Town and Bilston during World War One, died in West Bromwich on 17 September 1950.

Wolves' record: 21 apps. 4 goals.

WRIGHT, Horace Raymond

Yorkshireman Horace Wright was born in Pontefract on 6 September 1918 and played his early football with Woodbourne Athletic before joining Wolves in September 1937.

A useful inside-forward, he remained at Molineux until July 1946 when he transferred to Exeter City, later playing for Yeovil Town (1948-49).

He scored 11 goals in his 55 League games for Exeter and during the War when playing in Regional games for Wolves, he was sometimes mistaken for Billy Wright! Horace Wright died in 1987.

Wolves' record: 8 apps. one goal.

WRIGHT, Jermaine Malaki

Born in Greenwich, London, on 21 October 1975, Jermaine Wright joined Millwall as a trainee in 1991 and turned professional at The Den in November 1992. An England Youth international, he failed to make the Lions' first team and in December 1994 was transferred to Wolves for £60,000.

An exciting winger, with pace and good skills, he found it hard to settle into a rhythm at Molineux and indeed, get a regular run out in the first XI. Consequently, after a loan spell with Doncaster Rovers (March/April 1996), Wolves boss Mark McGhee sold him to Crewe Alexandra for £25,000 in February 1998.

In July 1999 Wright was transferred to Ipswich Town for £500,000 - and how well he played for the Portman Road club over the next two seasons. He starred when George Burley's team gained promotion to the Premiership and then perhaps did even better as Ipswich took everyone by surprise by claiming a UEFA Cup place for the 2001-02 season.

Wolves' record: 5+20 sub. apps. one goal.

WRIGHT, Stephen

A Scotsman, born in Belshill on 27 August 1971, versatile defender Steve Wright played for Eastercraigs FC before turning professional with Aberdeen in November 1987.

He made 177 appearances for the Dons, up to July 1995 when he was transferred to Glasgow Rangers for £50,000. Unable to gain a regular place in the first XI at Ibrox Park, Wright was taken on loan by Wolves in March 1998 and made his Football League debut in a 3-0 defeat at Ipswich within hours of signing for the Molineux club.

In July 1998 Wright was secured by Bradford City on a free transfer and although mainly a reserve at the Pulse Stadium, he helped the Bantams gain a place in the Premiership. Capped by Scotland at senior, 'B' and Under-21 levels, Wright has suffered his fair share of knee and ankle injuries over the past three seasons.

Wolves' record: 3 apps.

WRIGHT, William Ambrose, CBE

Born in Ironbridge, Shropshire on 6 February 1924, former Madeley Schoolboy Billy Wright was actually turned away from Molineux in 1938 by the then manager Major Frank Buckley when he went along as a frail-looking 14 year-old asking for a trial. "You're too small - come back when you've put on some weight" said the Major. Wright did just that - and he turned out to become one of the greatest players ever to serve the club and, indeed, ever to play for England, gaining a then record 105 caps and captaining his country on 70 occasions.

Billy Wright

Billy Wright in his role as England captain against Switzerland at Highbury in 1950

After that initial meeting with Buckley at Molineux, Wright went off to build himself up and develop his game with Cradley Heath and he duly returned to sign for Wolves (in exchange for three bars of chocolate) on 2 June 1938, earning £2-a-week as a playing-member of the groundstaff. He was an inside-forward in those days, but after the war (during which time he guested for Leicester City along with his team-mate Jimmy Mullen) Wright was converted into a cool, footballing half-back by new manager Ted Vizard.

He had served in the RAF during the hostilities and made over 100 appearances for Wolves before peacetime football resumed in earnest in 1946-47.

By this time Wright had become a fully-fledged professional at Molineux and in 1949 - under Stan Cullis' leadership - he skippered Wolves to victory in the FA Cup Final at Wembley.

Five years later - and now an established member of the England side - he gleefully held aloft the League Division One championship trophy and followed up with two more League titles in 1958 and 1959 before announcing his retirement as a player at the end of the latter campaign. He had accumulated a total of 490 League appearances for Wolves and had played in over 650 first-team games all told.

In June 1959, he was awarded the CBE for services to football and then in a blaze of publicity, in October 1960, he was appointed manager of the England Youth team, later taking charge of the Under-23 side. In May 1962, with the press and media again taking full advantage of the story, Wright became manager of Arsenal, a position he held until June 1966. Thereafter he was associated with Sports Coverage on ATV, being totally in control until his retirement in 1989.

He was made a honorary member of the FA and also became a member of the Pilkington Commission on Television Broadcasting, before joining the Board of Directors at Molineux in May 1990 - a position he held until his death in 1996. Wright, who was married to one of the Beverley sisters, Joy, was living in Whetstone, North London, at the time of his death.

A stand at Molineux his named after him and there is a sculpture standing proudly outside the main entrance to the Wolves stadium in recognition of the service Billy Wright gave to the club over many years as a player and director.

Wolves' record: 541 apps. 16 goals.

WYKES, David

David Wykes was a useful, goal-hungry inside-forward, who sadly died in a Wolverhampton hospital of typhoid fever and pneumonia at the age of 28 just 24 hours after playing for Wolves against Stoke in a First Division fixture on 5 October 1895.

Born in Walsall on 15 September 1867, he played initially for Bloxwich Strollers, then Wednesbury Town and his

home club Walsall before signing for Wolves in August 1888. Lithe and subtle, his mobility and enthusiasm was sorely missed by Wolves.

Wolves' record: 179 apps. 69 goals.

YOUNG, Eric

Welsh international centre-back Eric Young, easily recognisible by a cavalier headband (worn just above his eyes to prevent scars re-opening!) was born in Singapore on 25 March 1960.

He played his early football in this country with Staines and then Slough Town before becoming a full-time professional with Brighton & Hove Albion in November 1982. He went on to appear in almost 150 games for the Seagulls before transferring to Wimbledon for £70,000 in July 1987. Twelve months later he starred in the Dons' defence as they lifted the FA Cup at Wembley.

Young played 125 times for Wimbledon, up to August 1990, when he moved to Crystal Palace for £850,000. He served the Eagles exceedingly well over the next five years, amassing a further 204 first-class appearances, helping the London club win the Full Members Cup in 1991 and gain promotion to the First Division in 1994.

He also took his total number of international caps won at senior level with Wales to 21 - Palace's most capped player! Wolves acquired Young's services in September 1995, signing him on a free transfer from Selhurst Park and he did a good job initially at Molineux before his release in the summer of 1997. Later he joined Egham Town of the Ryman League.

Wolves' record: 40 apps. 2 goals.

YOUNG, Robert Thomson

Craggy Scot Bob Young was born in Stonehouse, Lanarkshire in September 1886. He had a useful career as a solid, uncompromising defender, playing in his home country, in London, the Midlands, the North of England and on Merseyside.

Well built, physically strong and muscular, he signed for Paisley St Mirren at the age of 15 and in July 1907 switched due south to join West Ham United.

He stayed with the Hammers for one season, transferring his allegiance to Middlesbrough in October 1908. In January 1910 he was on the move again, this time across country to Everton. Wolves eventually caught up with him in August 1911 and

Eric Young

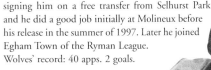

Z

he stayed at Molineux until May 1914 when, aged only 27, he announced his retirement owing to injury and ill-health.

Young later returned home to Scotland where he died in 1955.

Wolves' record: 73 apps. 11 goals.

YULE, Thomas

Wolves signed Tommy Yule from Lincoln City in the summer of 1911 to replace Alf Walker (sold to Port Vale). A sprightly winger with good pace, he scored six goals in 25 League games in his first season at Molineux, but was injured at Bury in October 1912 and thereafter struggled to get back into the first team.

Like Walker, he moved to Port Vale in 1913, staying with the Potteries club until January 1915 when he went to war. There is no record of Yule playing football after the hostilities.

Born at Douglas Water on 4 February 1888, he played for Portbello FC before joining Lincoln in 1909. He scored seven League goals in 63 games for the Imps.

Wolves' record: 33 apps. 7 goals.

ZELEM, Peter Richard

Born in Manchester on 13 February 1962, steady defender Peter Zelem played well over 130 senior games for Chester before joining Wolves (then under manager Tommy Docherty) in January 1985.

Just over two years later, on the transfer deadline of March 1987, Zelem was transferred to Preston North End; five months after that he switched to nearby Burnley and in May 1998 he quit the bigtime after amassing a total of 209 Football League appearances and scoring 19 goals.

Wolves' record: 54 apps. one goal.

Wolverhampton Wanderers F.C. 1905-06

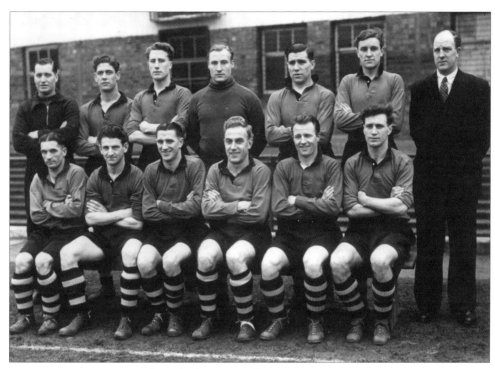

Wolverhampton Wanderers F.C. 1950-51

Wolverhampton Wanderers F.C. 1973-74

The Football Collection

Below is the range of publications available now from Britespot Publishing - one of the fastest growing sports publishers in the UK.

The Official Encyclopaedia of Tottenham Hotspur F.C.
250,000 words of facts & figures/stats. A virtual complete Who's Who (850 players), this will be one of the most comprehensive books ever published on the famous London club.
ISBN: 0-9539288-1-0   RRP: £19.95   Size: 210 x 297mm   256 pages

Duncan Edwards The Full Report
The story of the Black Country legend is familiar to most throughout the footballing world, but this new unique publication tells the story of Duncan Edwards on a match by match basis through the games in which he played.
ISBN: 0-9539288-5-3   RRP: £9.99   Size: 215 x 270mm   128pages

The West Bromwich Albion Memorabilia Pack
The first-ever West Bromwich Albion memorabilia pack contains some rare items, many of which are on view in the club's museum.
ISBN: 0-9539288-9-6   RRP: £9.99   Size: 210 x 297mm   22 items

The Complete Encyclopaedia of Aston Villa FC
This Official Encyclopaedia of Aston Villa Football Club - 275,000 words of facts & figures/stats. One of the most comprehensive books ever published on the famous Midland Premier club.
ISBN: 0-9539288-3-7   RRP: £19.95   Size: 210 x 297mm   320pages

The Encyclopaedia of Birmingham City FC - 1875-2000
Officially endorsed by the club. Over 200,000 words of facts & figures/stats. The biggest book ever published on the famous Midland club.
ISBN: 0-9539288-0-2   RRP: £16.95   Size: 210 x 297mm   256pages

The Road to Rotterdam - Aston Villa FC Champions of Europe 1982
This unique insight into the most successful event in Aston Villa's recent history which celebrates the 20th Anniversary in 2002. This round by round story highlights the most memorable events through the eyes of each of the participating Villa players.
ISBN: 0-9539288-7-X   RRP: £12.99   Size: 215 x 270mm   112 pages

The Baggies Strip
A colourful cartoon history of the famous Midland club from their formation through to present day by the well known football caricaturist Bob Bond.
ISBN: 1-904103-00-6   RRP: £6.99   Size: 170 x 248mm   28 pages

The Official West Bromwich Albion Picture Gallery 1960's-1990's
This officially endorsed publication compiled by the club historian highlights West Bromwich Albion through the 60's to the 90's including many unseen photographs from players and fans
personal collections.
ISBN: 0-9539288-4-5   RRP: £9.99   Size: 210 x 297mm   152 pages

The Wolves Who's Who
125 years of detailed biographies of almost 1,000 players who have served the great old Black County club. There are also write-ups of all the managers, certain trainers/coaches, directors, chairmen...etc.
ISBN: 1-9041030-1-4   RRP: £12.99   Size: 170 x 245mm   232 pages

Coming Soon
This book is the first in a series of Who's Who publications from Britespot. Those to follow include Aston Villa, Birmingham City, Stoke City and West Bromwich Albion.

Other publications to follow include:-
The Complete Encyclopaedia of Manchester United FC, The Complete Encyclopaedia of Manchester City FC, My Memories of Wolves by Steve Bull, The Complete Encyclopaedia of Devon Football (including Exeter City, Plymouth Argyle and Torquay United). The Official Encyclopaedia of Bolton Wanderers FC.

For ordering details or for further information on all the above titles contact:
Britespot Publishing Solutions Limited, Chester Road, Cradley Heath, West Midlands B64 6AB.
Tel: +44 (0) 1384 414170   Fax: +44 (0) 1384 414141   Email: info@britespot.co.uk   www.britespot.co.uk